D0503091

Bob Boyd

# Presidents *and* PROPHETS

THE STORY OF AMERICA'S PRESIDENTS AND THE LDS CHURCH

# OTHER BOOKS WRITTEN BY MICHAEL K. WINDER

*John R. Winder:*
*Member of the First Presidency, Pioneer, Temple Builder, Dairyman*
1999

*The Christmas Animals*
(A children's book illustrated by Lindsay E. Ayres)
2002

---

# COMPILED BY MICHAEL K. WINDER

*Counselors to the Prophets*
2001

*Presiding Bishops*
2003

*Utah 2050:*
*Glimpses of Our Future*
2003

# Presidents

# PROPHETS

*and*

## THE STORY OF AMERICA'S PRESIDENTS AND THE LDS CHURCH

### Michael K. Winder

Covenant Communications, Inc.

Cover images:
White House by Joe Sohm/Visions of America © 2007 Digital Vision/Getty Images
President Ford looking at Book of Mormon with Spencer W. Kimball, Courtesy of LDS Church Archives, Salt Lake City, Utah
President Reagan and Gordon B. Hinckley at Cannery, Courtesy of LDS Church Archives, Salt Lake City, Utah
Gordon B. Hinckley receives Medal of Freedom, by Susan Walsh Associated Press. Used by permission
Eisenhower, et. al., Courtesy of LDS Church Archives, Salt Lake City, Utah
Bush and Hinckley at SUU. By Jeffrey D. Allread. Courtesy of Deseret News
Truman at BYU, Courtesy of LDS Church Archives, Salt Lake City, Utah

Published by Covenant Communications, Inc.
American Fork, Utah

Copyright © 2007 by Michael K. Winder
Cover design by Jessica A. Warner © 2007 by Covenant Communications, Inc.

All rights reserved. No part of this work may be reproduced by any means without the express written permission of Covenant Communications, Inc., P.O. Box 416, American Fork, UT 84003. This work is not an official publication of The Church of Jesus Christ of Latter-day Saints. The views expressed within this work are the sole responsibility of the authors and do not necessarily reflect the position of The Church of Jesus Christ of Latter-day Saints, Covenant Communications, Inc., or any other entity.

Printed in Canada
First Printing: September 2007

14 13 12 11 10 09 08 07    10 9 8 7 6 5 4 3 2 1

ISBN 978-1-59811-452-2

# CONTENTS

# ACKNOWLEDGMENTS

There have been countless supporters throughout this project, but some of the friends who have been there from the beginning include Bret Eborn, who lent me books and pointed me in good directions; Bill Slaughter, who discussed publishing strategies and was a tremendous assistant in procuring historical photos; and Jeff Hawker, who is always a wise sounding board and listening ear on life's many projects.

I appreciate advice given to me by Pulitzer Prize–winning historian David McCullough (*Truman*, *John Adams*), who in an August 2006 telephone interview encouraged me to "first, make sure you take the time to do your book right. These things are in print for a long time, you know. And second, make sure and enjoy the journey. History is the best field around and writing a book is a grand adventure." Other encouragement from Senator Bob Bennett, Congressman Chris Cannon, and Mike Mower in various conversations is also appreciated.

Special thanks goes to my brother, Nate Winder, who as a University of Utah student borrowed books for me, assisted in library research, and assisted with historic photographs. Thanks also to Bruce Pearson of the Church Audiovisual Department, April Williamsen and other staff members of the LDS Church Historical Archives, Utah's state historian Allan Kent Powell, Doug Misner of the Utah History Research Center, and Lorraine Crouse and Krissy Giacoletto at the Special Collections of the University of Utah's Marriott Library. Assistance was also provided by Spencer Howard of the Hoover Presidential Library; David Clark of the Truman Library; Dwight Strandberg and Kathy Struss of the Eisenhower Library; Yael Wilkofsky of the Kennedy Library; Philip Scott and Barbara Constable of the Lyndon B. Johnson Library; Bridget Crowley, archives specialist of the National Archives' Nixon Presidential Materials Staff; Joshua Cochran of the Ford Presidential Library; James Herring of the Carter Library; Mary Finch and Debbie Carter of the George Bush Presidential Library; and John Keller and Kelly Hendren of the Clinton Presidential Library. A special thanks to Jeffrey Flannery in the Manuscripts Division of the Library of Congress, who worked hard before I arrived and while I was there to help me make the most of my time.

Award-winning author Greg Prince was especially magnanimous in sharing his pages of research on David O. McKay's interaction with various U.S. presidents. Thanks go to Derek

Brown, Lew Cramer, and Dave Hansen for putting me in touch with several of my key interviewees. And a particular thanks to those who were interviewed, for sharing their time, their anecdotes, and their viewpoints with me: Bay Buchanan, Tim Flanigan, former Senator Jake Garn, Senator Orrin Hatch, Ralph Hardy, Jim Jardine, Clyde Larsen, Secretary Mike Leavitt, Lachlan McKay, Richard Richards, Barbara Winder, and Elder Richard B. Wirthlin.

A special thanks goes to the talented team at Covenant Communications for turning some rough words on paper into a beautiful book on which I am honored to have my name. Editors Kathy Jenkins and Kirk Shaw lent their wisdom and skill in tightening up the manuscript, ironing out the wrinkles, and holding my hand through the process. Since books are inevitably judged by their cover, the superb work inside and out by designers Jessica Warner and Christina Ashby is invaluable. Thanks also to art director Margaret Weber. And, a book that nobody reads isn't worth much, so I am extremely grateful for Robby Nichols, Ron Brough, Melissa Dalton, and Rachel Langlois—some of the best book marketers in the business, who have worked hard to bring these important stories to a wide audience.

My parents, Kent and Sherri Winder, and in-laws, Rob and Lynda Hermansen, have shown great interest in and support of this project since its beginning; and their influence and examples have always been appreciated. Dad was an especially good sport to travel with me to Plains, Georgia, to visit former President Carter (see afterword). I also appreciate the patience and inspiration of each of my children—Jessica, Michael, and John.

Most significantly, my wife, Karyn, has been the paramount reason I am able to do what I do. Her support through my late nights and long hours working on this manuscript was essential; and her superb talents as a mother, wife, and homemaker have allowed me to balance work, government service, and writing. It is to her, the First Lady of my life, that I dedicate this book.

*We believe in being subject to*

*kings, presidents, rulers, and magistrates,*

*in obeying, honoring, and sustaining the law.*

—The Twelfth Article of Faith—
written by the Prophet Joseph Smith
during John Tyler's presidency

# PREFACE

As President Gordon B. Hinckley emerged from the White House on his 94th birthday with a freshly bestowed Presidential Medal of Freedom, he contrasted the way he was treated with the way his predecessor Joseph Smith was treated when he had come to the White House: "They came here to plead the case for our people who had been despoiled and persecuted and driven, and were turned down by President Van Buren—who said, 'If I help you, I will lose the state of Missouri,' and rebuffed him. And he went home without anything for which he had come." President Hinckley continued, "Now to have this invitation from the President of the nation is a very signal and significant honor." Indeed, during the preceding East Room ceremony, President George W. Bush declared of the prophet that "today this wise and patriotic man receives his country's highest civil honor."

As President Hinckley pointed out, there has been a continually improving relationship between the Latter-day Saints and the American President. Predecessor Wilford Woodruff enjoyed angelic visitations from Washington,

*23 June 2004: President George W. Bush presents President Gordon B. Hinckley with the Presidential Medal of Freedom. President Bush remarked at the time, "Today this wise and patriotic man receives his country's highest civil honor." No better moment could have symbolized how far the Church has come since Joseph Smith was rejected by Martin Van Buren.*

Adams, and Jefferson. Early antagonists in Mormon history, such as Martin Van Buren and James Buchanan, were succeeded by friendlier Presidents Grover Cleveland and Teddy Roosevelt. More recently, Presidents such as Dwight D. Eisenhower, Richard Nixon, and Ronald Reagan have relied on LDS statesmen as key advisors or cabinet members. The Oval Office perspective on the Church has been a journey of persecution, toleration, acceptance, and finally admiration—reflecting the pattern outlined by Mahatma Gandhi: "First they ignore you, then they laugh at you, then they fight you, then you win."

The idea to tell this story first germinated in 1999, when I was at the LDS Church Historical Archives researching my biography on John R. Winder. As a lifelong student of the American presidency I was deeply intrigued with an exhibit I saw in a display case on the second floor, which showcased a dozen or so images of various U.S. Presidents during their visits to Utah. One article I came across at the time, William W. Slaughter's "Teddy in the Tabernacle,"[1] further piqued my interest in the relationship between America's Presidents and the LDS Church. My curiosity about the stories behind these visits, and the collective mosaic such stories would form, eventually grew into this research project. The idea is not entirely new. An article-length treatment entitled "The American Presidency and the Mormons," by James B. Allen, appeared in the October 1972 *Ensign*; and United States Senator Bob Bennett presented a broad historical overview on the relationship between the Church and the capital at an annual conference of the Mormon History Association when the group met in Washington D.C. in 1998. However, this is the first book-length survey.

After years of research, my adventure in exploring the relationship between the Presidents and the Church led me to the Library of Congress, where I trolled through presidential diaries and papers for gems to enhance this project. I was in the capital anyway for my first National League of Cities and Towns Conference since being elected to the city council in West Valley City, Utah, and a full day at the library was a productive way to spend the day before the conference began that evening. However, while I thought that the Saturday spent among the manuscripts at the Library of Congress would be the apex of my journey, the next day would prove me wrong. Please forgive my personal indulgence as I share my journal entry from a memorable Sunday morning in the nation's capital. I hope you will agree it is a fitting anecdote with which to begin this particular book:

*12 March 2006, Washington D.C.*

> *As a history buff, it was an easy decision to decide to go to church at St. John's Episcopal Church on Lafayette Square instead of the LDS ward that was too far from my hotel. St. John's is nicknamed the "Church of the Presidents" since every President since James Madison has worshipped there. It is the little church across the square from the White House that always has the prayer service with the First Family on Inauguration Days, and that they are known to drop into now and then. Maybe we would be lucky, at the least it would be an interesting experience.*

*My fellow council member Steve Vincent and I were on our way there this morning when we were stopped by two police officers who told us we had to go around the block. On our way we were stopped by two more officers who asked us our destination. When we replied, "St. John's Episcopal Church for the 7:45 service," they replied, "You said the right password, go on in." At this point we realized that the First Family was likely at church that day, and we might get to steal a glimpse. We also commented that whether there were police officers or Secret Service agents, we had our freedom to worship and go to church, and it was a privilege that couldn't have been denied.*

St. John's Episcopal Church on Lafeyette Square is nicknamed the "Church of the Presidents" since every President since James Madison has worshipped there.

*At the entrance to the old church Secret Service agents asked us to empty the metal from our pockets and then wanded us like at an airport. After passing through security we were greeted by ushers from the church, took a program, and shuffled inside. The service was already five or ten minutes underway, so we were anxious to quickly be seated.*

*It is a small chapel, with beautiful stained-glass windows. Maybe 100 people were attending that service. I noticed the President and his wife sitting in a middle pew about halfway up. There was only one other lady on the row, and she was on the opposite end with plenty of space between her and the First Family. I walked up to that row and asked the woman if it was okay to sit there, and she said yes. As I sat down, the President caught my eye, smiled, and nodded a hello.*

*I couldn't believe that we were there, attending church and sitting on the same pew as the President and First Lady! In our rush to get seated, Steve hadn't realized who was on our same row. When I told him to check out whose row we were sitting on he took the biggest double-take in the world!*

*But there we were, reading prayers together, listening to the sermon together as the reverend taught about God's faith in us, and our need to have faith in God and keep his commandments. We stood side by side with the First Family as we all recited the Lord's Prayer. You could tell the President is a God-fearing man. He often had his eyes closed during the prayers, even while many in the congregation simply followed along in the prayer book or printed program.*

*It was a conscious effort not to stare, and everyone in the congregation was as natural as could be.*

*At one point early in the service, the reverend invited everyone to "Greet one another in the name of the Lord." Everyone stood and began shaking hands with those around them saying "Peace of the Lord." I noticed the two Secret Service agents sitting behind the First Family and reached my hand to one saying "Peace of the Lord." He returned the greeting and the handshake. Then Laura Bush reached her hand to me, and said in her Texas drawl "Peace of the Lord." I returned the greeting and shook her hand. Then, as the congregation began to sit back down, President Bush caught my eye and reached his hand across his wife, and so I reached back. The forty-third President of the United States gripped my hand, looked at me, and said "Peace of the Lord." I returned the greeting. I've met vice presidents before (Dan Quayle and Dick Cheney), and even met Barbara Bush once, but this morning was my first experience meeting a President of the United States.*

*Later in the service a prayer was given by the reverend where he blessed some people by name in his congregation, including those who were in the service, those who were ill or have lost loved ones, and those who were having birthdays that week. In the midst of the prayer he added "and bless our President George" using the casual first name (George is a member of his congregation, after all). I have heard many prayers for our nation's President before, but never while sitting just a few feet from him in his "home ward."*

*Soon it was time for communion, and the congregation began filing up row by row to take the bread and wine. Steve and I did not, but George and Laura and everyone else did. After the First Family returned they glanced at us and probably wondered why we didn't go up with the rest of the church. Since we had a few minutes while we were waiting for the rest of the chapel to take communion, I wrote a little note on the back of my City Council business card:*

*"Pres. & Mrs. Bush,*
*Even us Mormons from Utah pray for you & are honored to worship God together.*
*—Mike"*

*I set my card down on the bench between Laura and I (the Secret Service behind us quickly glancing over the bench to see what I was doing), and she picked it up and read it. She smiled and seemed to get a kick out of it and showed her husband. He, too, got a big smile and seemed to enjoy it. He smiled back at us with an acknowledging nod. He took the card and studied the front of it for a minute. Then he pulled a black marker out of his suit coat and signed the front of the business card, and then handed it back to me:*

*"Thanks Mike—and God Bless. George Bush"*

Front and back of the author's business card after passing notes with the President in church. "Thanks Mike—and God Bless. George Bush"

*Toward the end of the service we all knelt to pray. Because we were in the "Church of the Presidents," there were prayer cushions of past presidents that we knelt on. I knelt on Woodrow Wilson's prayer cushion, Steve was on Calvin Coolidge's, Laura used Ronald Reagan's, and the President used his dad's. It was a humbling thing to connect to our nation's presidents' spiritual lives that way.*

*At the end of the service we all stood, and the First Family and Secret Service agents filed out the front door, shaking hands with the reverend on the way. After a couple minutes the rest of us were allowed to file out the back door.*

*As we left the church, Steve and I were marveling that there we were, a born-again-Christian President, a Methodist First Lady, and two Mormon city council members in an Episcopal church worshipping God together on a Sunday morning. Isn't America great?*

## ENDNOTES

1. *Pioneer,* Fall 1995, 21–24.

# GEORGE
# WASHINGTON

## *1789—1797*

America's first President died four years and one week before Joseph Smith Jr. was born. Therefore, he never had the opportunity in his lifetime to encounter the restored gospel of Jesus Christ. What would George Washington have thought of Mormonism? Examination of his own views of God and Jesus tell us that he was not very impressed with any organized religion of his day, but he did feel Americans should be a God-fearing people. He declared in his first inaugural address that "No people can be bound to acknowledge and adore the invisible hand, which conducts the affairs of men, more than the people of the United States."[1]

## WASHINGTON'S RELIGIOUS VIEWS

The first President was a lukewarm Anglican who rarely attended church and never took Communion. When George Washington did pray, he preferred not to kneel, but would rather stand.[2] "If he had a religious creed, it was much like the creed of ancient Stoicism," says Brigham Young University history professor Frank Fox. "He believed in God and in doing good, but not in religious participation."[3] Washington biographer Joseph Ellis agrees and points out that the first President was "never a deeply religious man, at least in the traditional Christian sense of the term. Washington thought of God as a distant, impersonal force, the presumed well-spring for what he called destiny or providence."[4] Consequently, says Ellis, the President "tended to talk about 'Providence' or 'Destiny' rather than God."[5] This viewpoint is seen through Washington's first inaugural address, where passages include his "fervent supplications to that Almighty Being," whose "providential aids can supply every human defect."[6]

George Washington did not endorse any particular articles of faith and unlike other founders was conspicuously silent in his writings and speeches regarding the divinity of Christ. Because Washington often referred to God without reference to the Savior, and because he neglected to defend or define what he regarded as the fundamental principles of Christianity, historians identify the father of our country with the non-Christian Deists of his age.[7]

Upon his deathbed, there were no prayers uttered or ministers present. In fact, some of his final thoughts were about his fear of being placed in a burial vault before they were absolutely sure he was dead. Washington was not convinced that Jesus was entirely dead when placed within the Garden Tomb, and he wished to avoid such a fate for himself.[8]

## WASHINGTON'S LEGACY AMONG THE SAINTS

George Washington has always been highly regarded by the Latter-day Saints. The grandfathers of the Prophet Joseph, Asael Smith and Solomon Mack, fought with the patriots in the Revolution, and when the Prophet organized the Nauvoo Legion, he gave himself the rank Washington had held—lieutenant general.[9] The mimicry of the Father of the Country was seen as very presumptuous by anti-Mormons and contributed to the animosity against him. After all, with the exception of George Washington, no other military officer held a rank that high until 1847 during the Mexican War.[10] When feeling most threatened by his enemies in Nauvoo, Lieutenant General Smith rallied his supporters in his sermons by invoking the courage of Davy Crockett, Captain Moroni, and George Washington.[11]

Wilford Woodruff said of Washington and his fellow founders that they were "the best spirits the God of Heaven could find on the face of the earth. . . . General Washington and all the men that labored for the purpose [of establishing this country] were inspired of the Lord."[12] President Lorenzo Snow said, "We look upon George Washington, the father of our country, as an inspired instrument of the Almighty; we can see the all-inspiring Spirit operating upon him."[13]

The Saints so admired Washington that when each state and territory was asked to donate stones for the interior walls of the Washington Monument, the Territory of Deseret sent a stone uniquely carved of limestone from Manti, Utah. This stone shows a symbolic beehive with the word *Deseret* and a phrase now used exclusively in LDS temples—"Holiness to the Lord."[14]

A book entitled *George Washington and the Mormons* was published in 1967 by Deseret Book. It praised the first President and his role in founding the nation that would someday be the host

## "LIEUTENANT-GENERAL" JOSEPH SMITH REVIEWING THE NAUVOO LEGION.

*When organizing the Nauvoo Legion, Joseph Smith gave himself the rank Washington had held—Lieutenant General. The mimicry of the Father of the Country was seen as very presumptuous by anti-Mormons and contributed to the animosity against him. After all, with the exception of George Washington, no other military officer outside Nauvoo held a rank that high until 1847 during the Mexican War.*

of Mormonism, and uses various scriptures to illuminate Washington's virtues. The author concludes, "George Washington was thus more than an American hero . . . he was a chosen instrument in the hand of God to help make possible not only the restoration of the Gospel of Jesus Christ in America, but the preaching of the restored Gospel 'in all the world for a witness unto all nations.'"[15]

A special family home evening supplement, including four lessons, was distributed to the Saints during the nation's bicentennial year. Entitled *The Great Prologue: A Prophetic History and Destiny of America,* the booklet included many points about George Washington's belief in Divine Providence and about Washington being foreordained before he came to earth to help establish the United States. It lauds the first President for refusing to be king since "General Washington knew, just as King Mosiah knew (Mosiah 29:16), that if a wicked man ever became king of the United States the freedom and liberty they had won during the war would be lost."[16]

President Ezra Taft Benson taught the divine role of the first President and pointed out Washington's belief in God: "When Washington was desperately hard pressed at Valley Forge, his men found him on his knees praying for guidance and aid. Yes, this nation has a spiritual foundation."[17] President Benson concludes, "From the life of our illustrious founder, George Washington, we have an example of rectitude worthy of emulation by all public servants, an example that demonstrates a consistency between his private morality and public behavior."[18]

*President Ezra Taft Benson taught of the divine role of the first President, and pointed out Washington's belief in God. "When Washington was desperately hard pressed at Valley Forge, his men found him on his knees praying for guidance and aid. Yes, this nation has a spiritual foundation."*

# WASHINGTON'S TEMPLE WORK

In Nauvoo, the Prophet Joseph revealed the doctrine that Saints could be baptized for the dead so that if the deceased so choose in the hereafter, they can accept the ordinance and progress. Joseph Smith's brother Don Carlos was consequently baptized on President Washington's behalf.[19] Later, these ordinances were confined to temples, but in the early 1840s they were done in the Mississippi River. Non-Mormon Charlotte Haven observed the following:

> We followed the bank toward town, and . . . spied quite a crowd of people, and soon perceived there was a baptism. Two elders stood knee-deep in the icy cold water, and immersed one after another as fast as they could come down the bank. We soon observed that some of them went in and were plunged several times. We were told that they were baptized for the dead who had not had an opportunity of adopting the doctrines of the Latter Day Saints. So these poor mortals in ice-cold water were releasing their ancestors and relatives from purgatory! We drew a little nearer and heard several names repeated by the elders as the victims were douched, and you can imagine our surprise when the name George Washington was called. So after these fifty years he is out of purgatory and on his way to the "celestial" heaven![20]

In August 1877, Elder Wilford Woodruff—then an Apostle and president of the St. George Temple—recorded being in the temple late one evening when "every one of those men that signed the Declaration of Independence with General Washington, called upon me, as an Apostle of the Lord Jesus Christ, in the Temple at St. George." Elder Woodruff said that they called upon him "two consecutive nights," and that they "demanded at my hands that I should go forth and attend to the ordinances of the House of God for them."[21] Elder Woodruff described how these individuals "pleaded with [me] as one man pleads with another to redeem them."[22]

He recounted them saying, "You have had the use of the Endowment House for a number of years, and yet nothing has ever been done for us. We laid the foundation of the government you now enjoy, and we never apostatized from it, but we remain true to it and were faithful to God." Elder Woodruff took immediate action. "I straightaway went into the baptismal font and called upon brother McAllister to baptize me for the signers of the Declaration of Independence, and fifty other eminent men, making one hundred in all, including John Wesley, Columbus, and others; I then baptized him for every President of the United States, except three; and when their cause is just, somebody will do the work for them."[23]

Wilford Woodruff held Washington in particularly high regard. For instance, during the performance of the endowment ordinance, men are usually ordained to the priesthood office of elder; yet Elder Woodruff had President Washington ordained to the higher office of high priest during the ordinances of 1877 in St. George. The remaining Presidents on his list that day were all ordained elders.[24] Also, George Washington was the only President at that time that had work done for not only himself, but for his wife's family, his parents, grandparents, and great-grandparents.

President Ezra Taft Benson bore testimony of Wilford Woodruff's vision. Having previously gone to the vault of the St. George Temple, he declared in LDS general conference, "I saw with my own eyes the record of the work which was done for the Founding Fathers of this great nation, beginning with George Washington. . . . The Founding Fathers of this nation, those great men, appeared within those sacred walls and had their vicarious work done for them."[25]

*The St. George Utah Temple in 1877, where Elder Wilford Woodruff—then an apostle and St. George Temple President—recalled "Every one of those men that signed the Declaration of Independence with General Washington, called upon me," and "demanded at my hands that I should go forth and attend to the ordinances of the House of God for them."*

# ENDNOTES

1    George Washington, "First Inaugural Address," *Harvard Classics,* 43:242.

2    Joseph J. Ellis, *His Excellency: George Washington,* 45.

3    Mark Eddington, "Sculpture Adds Fuel to Heated Debate Over Founding Fathers' Convictions," *Salt Lake Tribune,* 4 July 2002.

4    Ellis, *His Excellency,* 151.

5    Ellis, *His Excellency,* 45.

6    Washington, "First Inaugural Address," 242.

7    Paul F. Boller Jr., *George Washington and Religion,* 90–91. See also John C. McCollister, *God and the Oval Office: The Religious Faith of Our 43 Presidents,* 1–5.

8    Ellis, *His Excellency,* 269.

9    James B. Allen & Glen M. Leonard, *The Story of the Latter-day Saints,* 19. See also Joseph Fielding Smith, *Essentials in Church History,* 31.

10    Allen & Leonard, *The Story of the Latter-day Saints,* 168–69.

11    Richard Lyman Bushman, *Joseph Smith: Rough Stone Rolling,* 470.

12    Wilford Woodruff, in Conference Report, April 1898, 89.

13    Lorenzo Snow, *The Teachings of Lorenzo Snow,* 191.

14    The stone can be seen midway up the monument on the inside. Florian H. Thayn, "A Little Leavening," *BYU Studies* (Spring 1981): 221.

15    John J. Stewart, *George Washington and the Mormons,* 95.

16    *The Great Prologue: A Prophetic History and Destiny of America,* 12–13, 15.

17    Ezra Taft Benson, *Teachings of Ezra Taft Benson,* 570.

18    Benson, *Teachings,* 687.

19    Nauvoo Baptismal Record Index, microfilm #820155, Family History Library, Salt Lake City.

20    Charlotte Haven, letter to "My dear home friends," 2 May 1843, quoted in William Mulder & A. Russell Mortensen, eds., *Among the Mormons: Historical Accounts by Contemporary Observers,* 123.

21    Wilford Woodruff, in Conference Report, April 1898, 89–90.

22    Charles F. Middleton, "Notes from a Priesthood Meeting held in 1892," LDS Church Archives, Salt Lake City.

23    Wilford Woodruff, 16 September 1877, *Journal of Discourses,* 19:229. The three Presidents who Elder Woodruff was not baptized for were Van Buren (who had refused to help the Saints), Buchanan (who had sent the U.S. Army to replace Brigham Young as governor), and Grant (who was still alive in 1877).

24    Brian H. Stuy, "Wilford Woodruff's Vision of the Signers of the Declaration of Independence," *Journal of Mormon History,* Spring 2000, 71. Temple ordinances accessed by Church members at www.familysearch.org, 83. See also Benson, *Teachings,* 604.

25    Ezra Taft Benson, in Conference Report, October 1987, 5.

# JOHN ADAMS

## *1797–1801*

Like George Washington, America's second President died before The Church of Jesus Christ of Latter-day Saints was organized. Although his life overlapped Joseph Smith's by twenty years, at the time Adams died the young Prophet still had not yet removed the gold plates from the Hill Cumorah, and the Church was still four years away from being organized. Consequently, an examination of the religion of John Adams is the closest we can get to understanding what he might have thought of Mormonism.

## ADAMS'S RELIGIOUS VIEWS

John Adams was one of the more devout churchgoers of the Founding Fathers. "I have been a church-going animal for seventy-six years," quipped Adams, "and this has been alleged as proof of my hypocrisy."[1] He often attended two church services on Sundays and delighted in critiquing sermons. He was a Congregationalist, but his lifestyle was a far cry from what his Puritan forebears would have demanded. "He certainly enjoyed parties. He smoked, drank and went to the theater," Adams's biographer David McCullough says.

*When his wife, Abigail, died in 1818, Adams declared his belief that somehow marriage must be eternal: "And, if there be a future state, why should the Almighty dissolve forever the tender ties which unite us so delightfully in this world and forbid us to see each other in the next?"*

"He believed that the mind was the greatest of all the gifts of God and that he gave us our minds to use them." The nation's second President believed in an afterlife and disagreed with contemporaries who insisted that humans could learn everything through the scientific method.[2]

When his beloved wife, Abigail, died in 1818, Adams expressed his belief in eternal life and in being with his wife in the hereafter through a letter to Thomas Jefferson. Latter-day Saints, who have strong beliefs in life after death and the potential of eternal marriage, may find interest in these thoughts of John Adams:

I know not how to prove, physically, that we shall know each other in a future state; nor does revelation [i.e., the scriptures as they were interpreted by the clergy] as I can find give any positive assurance of such felicity. My reasons for believing it, as I do most undoubtedly, are that I cannot conceive such a being as the human, merely to live and die on this earth. If I did not believe in a future state, I should believe in no God. . . . And, if there be a future state, why should the Almighty dissolve forever the tender ties which unite us so delightfully in this world and forbid us to see each other in the next.[3]

John Adams periodically revealed in his private letters his dissatisfaction with American Christianity of the eighteenth century and expressed his approval of the general religious views of Thomas Jefferson. "The Ten Commandments and The Sermon on the Mount contain my Religion," Adams wrote to Jefferson.[4] Adams felt that in his day one Christian sect was as good as another. "Ask me not whether I am Catholic or Protestant, Calvinistic or Armenian," he said. "As far as they are Christians, I wish to be a fellow disciple with them all."[5]

*John Adams felt that in his day one Christian sect was as good as another. "Ask me not whether I am Catholic or Protestant, Calvinistic or Armenian," he said. "As far as they are Christians, I wish to be a fellow disciple with them all."*

## JOHN ADAMS'S LEGACY AMONG THE SAINTS

Like his predecessor in the White House, Adams has been well regarded posthumously by the Latter-day Saints. When he and Jefferson died on the same day—4 July 1826—a twenty-two-year-old Eliza Roxcy Snow wrote a poem honoring them that was published by the *Western Courier*, an Ohio newspaper.[6] She would later join the LDS Church and serve as general Relief Society president. President Wilford Woodruff taught, "Those men who laid the foundation of this American government and signed the Declaration of Independence were the best spirits the God of heaven could find on the face of

*Eliza R. Snow*

Adams, standing proudly with hand on hip, was among those described by President Wilford Woodruff: "Those men who laid the foundation of this American government and signed the Declaration of Independence were the best spirits the God of heaven could find on the face of the earth. They were choice spirits . . . noble spirits before God."

*"Our Constitution was made only for a moral and religious people. It is wholly inadequate to the government of any other." — John Adams*

the earth. They were choice spirits . . . noble spirits before God."[7]

Ezra Taft Benson and other LDS leaders have greatly admired Adams and his spirituality, often quoting the second President when he said, "Our Constitution was made only for a moral and religious people. It is wholly inadequate to the government of any other."[8] President Benson wrote, "We need more men like John Adams."[9]

# ENDNOTES

1    Adams, letter to Dr. Benjamin Rush, 28 August 1811, quoted in McCollister, *God and the Oval Office,* 9.

2    Mark Eddington, "Sculpture Adds Fuel to Heated Debate Over Founding Fathers' Convictions," *Salt Lake Tribune,* 4 July 2002.

3    Quoted in Alvin R. Dyer, *Who Am I?,* 12–13.

4    Milton V. Backman, Jr., *American Religions and the Rise of Mormonism,* 201.

5    Quoted in McCollister, *God and the Oval Office,* 9.

6    Eliza R. Snow, "Adams and Jefferson," *Western Courier* (Ravenna, Ohio), 5 August 1826. Photocopy available in LDS Church Archives, Salt Lake City.

7    Wilford Woodruff, in Conference Report, April 1898, 89–90.

8    Benson, *Teachings,* 621.

9    Benson, *God, Family, Country: Our Three Great Loyalties,* 405.

# THOMAS JEFFERSON

## *1801—1809*

With the same death date as Adams, Thomas Jefferson also never had an opportunity to know the Mormons in his lifetime. Shortly into Jefferson's second term, on 23 December 1805, Joseph Smith Jr. was born in Sharon, Vermont. Although the two would never cross paths in their twenty years as contemporaries, they would share similar uncertainty regarding the Christian sects of the day, and similar longings for a restoration of the primitive Christian church. At the very least, Jefferson would have likely tolerated the Latter-day Saints in a way that later Presidents did not. "It does me no injury for my neighbor to say there are twenty gods or no gods," he wrote in his *Notes on Virginia*. "It neither picks my pocket nor breaks my leg."[1]

## JEFFERSON'S RELIGIOUS VIEWS

Jefferson was accused by his political opponents of being an atheist, but he insisted that he was a Christian, just in his own way. "Say nothing about my religion," he declared. "It is known to my God and myself, alone."[2] The third President was a Deist who saw the Divine Creator as a distant and disinterested observer. Jefferson did not believe in the divinity of Christ or biblical miracles, but he greatly revered the teachings of Jesus and espoused Christian principles as important to good government. He took some scissors to the New Testament and cut out the teachings of Jesus and pasted them in a book, omitting what he felt were credulous stories about miracles, the Resurrection, and the Ascension. "It is a document in proof that I am a *real Christian*," he said. "That is to say, a disciple of the doctrines of Jesus." He titled his "Bible" as *The Life and Morals of Jesus of Nazareth*.[3]

Columbia University's Richard L. Bushman compared and contrasted Jefferson's version of the Bible and Joseph Smith's:

> Joseph's revision was more like Thomas Jefferson's treatment of the New Testament [as opposed to Noah Webster's 1836 Americanized version of the Bible]. Without referring to the ancient manuscripts, Jefferson altered the text to suit his own preferences, except that Jefferson pared back the text to the bare bones of Jesus's moral teachings, while Joseph added long passages and rewrote sentences according to his inspiration.[4]

Thomas Jefferson was unsatisfied with the traditional concept of the Trinity espoused by Catholics and most Protestants of the day. "Three are one and one is three, and yet the one is not three, and the three are not one," said Jefferson. "This constitutes the craft, the power and profit of the priests. Sweep away their gossamer fabric of factious religion, and they would catch no more flies."[5]

In a letter written to his friend F. A. Van Der Kemp in 1820, the year of Joseph Smith's First Vision, Jefferson waxed prophetic:

*Jefferson prophesied in 1820, "The genuine and simple religion of Jesus will one day be restored; such as it was preached and practiced by Himself."*

> The genuine and simple religion of Jesus will one day be restored; such as it was preached and practiced by Himself. Very soon after His death it became muffled up in mysteries, and has been ever since kept in concealment from the vulgar eye.[6]

*Benjamin Franklin and John Adams work with Thomas Jefferson on his draft of the Declaration of Independence. Latter-day Saints view Jefferson as a forerunner, who helped establish a land of religious freedom where the gospel could be restored.*

In a similar vein, Jefferson also wrote:

> The religion builders have so distorted and deformed the doctrines of Jesus, so muffled them in mysticisms, fancies and falsehoods, have caricatured them into forms so inconceivable, as to shock reasonable thinkers. . . .

> Happy in the prospect of a restoration of primitive Christianity, I must leave to younger persons to encounter and lop off the false branches which have been grafted into it by the mythologists of the middle and modern ages.[7]

Of course, Mormons also believe that the church organized by Jesus was distorted in the decades after his death—hence the need for the Prophet Joseph and the Restoration.

## JEFFERSON'S LEGACY AMONG THE SAINTS

LDS scholar John J. Stewart does well to summarize the Latter-day Saint perspective on

*Presiding Bishop Joseph J. Wirthlin declared, "This man of God, Thomas Jefferson . . . was raised up by the Lord to help establish this great republic."*

Thomas Jefferson: "The greatest role which Jefferson played has never been generally recognized as such, although in some future generation it most surely will be. This is his role as one who helped prepare the way for the great Latter-day Prophet Joseph Smith in the restoration of the true Gospel of Jesus Christ." He lays out the evidence of Jefferson's role as a forerunner to the Restoration in two separate books, citing his important roles in establishing a republic where new religious ideas could flourish in complete freedom.[8]

President Ezra Taft Benson had a love of Jefferson and his writings. He quoted the third President four times in his autobiography, for example.[9] President Benson taught, "The restoration of the gospel and the establishment of the Lord's Church could not come to pass until the Founding Fathers were raised up and completed their foreordained missions."[10] Former Presiding Bishop Joseph L. Wirthlin summarized the LDS view on Jefferson well when he praised him in LDS general conference as "this man of God, Thomas Jefferson, who was raised up by the Lord to help establish this great republic."[11]

# ENDNOTES

1    Quoted in Joseph J. Ellis, *American Sphinx: The Character of Thomas Jefferson,* 256.

2    Quoted in McCollister, *God and the Oval Office,* 17.

3    Letter from Jefferson to Charles Thomson, quoted in McCollister, *God and the Oval Office,* 19. Mark Eddington, "Sculpture Adds Fuel to Heated Debate Over Founding Fathers' Convictions," *Salt Lake Tribune,* 4 July 2002.

4    Richard Lyman Bushman, *Joseph Smith: Rough Stone Rolling,* 133.

5    Quoted in Leonard J. Arrington & Davis Bitton, *The Mormon Experience: A History of the Latter-day Saints,* 24.

6    Quoted in John J. Stewart, *Thomas Jefferson and the Restoration of the Gospel of Jesus Christ,* 85.

7    Thomas Jefferson, quoted in *The Great Prologue,* 4.

8    John J. Stewart, *Thomas Jefferson: Forerunner to the Restoration,* 11. See also Stewart's *Thomas Jefferson and the Restoration of the Gospel of Jesus Christ.*

9    Ezra Taft Benson, *Crossfire: The Eight Years with Eisenhower,* 3–4, 71, 426–27, 573.

10   Benson, *Teachings,* 604.

11   Joseph L. Wirthlin, in Conference Report, October 1946, First Day Morning Meeting, 31.

# JAMES MADISON

## *1809—1817*

When James Madison was inaugurated as Jefferson's successor, young Joseph Smith Jr. was a boy of three years old living in Vermont. While Madison was in the White House, the Smith family moved to Lebanon, New Hampshire (1811), where Joseph endured surgery on the bone in his leg. They were still residing in New England when Madison finished his second term.[1]

Unfortunately, the father of the Constitution never heard Joseph Smith preach—even though the Church had been established for six years by the time Madison died in Virginia in 1836. Very likely, he had heard of the Mormons in his lifetime, as there were occasional articles about them in the national press, and Madison was an avid reader of current events. The newspaper articles of the early 1830s had dismissed Joseph's visions and the Book of Mormon as interesting diversions. It is unknown if James Madison noticed or cared.[2]

## MADISON'S RELIGIOUS VIEWS

Madison, who had contemplated becoming a minister at one point in life, declared after the Consti-tution was written, "It is impossible for the man of pious reflection not to perceive in it a finger of that Almighty hand which has been so frequently and signally extended to our relief in the critical stage of the revolution."[3] Throughout his life, he read books on theology for relaxation but was never very impressed with any particular organized religion of his day. His wife, Dolley, was a Quaker, and the two occasionally attended St. John's Episcopal Church just across the square from the White House. Every President from Madison on has followed his example by also worshipping at St. John's. The fourth President was far more interested in advancing a clear separation of church and state, however, than in advancing any particular creed.[4]

As an ex-President, Madison attended the Virginia Constitutional

*In 1847, former First Lady Dolley Madison participated in a Washington charity dinner to raise money for the beleaguered Latter-day Saints.*

Convention of 1829, where the body was addressed by Alexander Campbell, a preacher of simple New Testament Christianity. Like Sidney Rigdon and many other early LDS leaders and members who were first Campbellites, Madison was impressed. He considered Campbell "the ablest and most original expounder of the Scriptures" he had ever heard.[5]

Dolley Madison outlived her husband, not dying until 1849, and in her lifetime heard more about the Mormons than her late husband. In late 1847, along with Washington's mayor, clergy, and other prominent socialites of the city, she attended a Washington charity dinner to raise money for the beleaguered Latter-day Saints.[6]

# MADISON'S LEGACY AMONG THE SAINTS

The Mormons have a high regard for James Madison—the "Father of the Constitution"— inasmuch as they proclaim the Constitution to be a "heavenly banner." The Prophet Joseph Smith taught:

> The Constitution of the United States is a glorious standard; it is founded in the wisdom of God. It is a heavenly banner; it is to all those who are privileged with the sweets of its liberty, like the cooling shades and refreshing waters of a great rock in a thirsty land. It is like a great tree under whose branches men from every clime can be shielded from the burning rays of the sun.[7]

President Gordon B. Hinckley said of Madison and his counterparts who were in Philadelphia in 1787, "There were men whom the God of Heaven had raised up who saw with a greater vision and dreamed a better and more inspired dream."[8] Even latter-day scripture proclaims the divinity of the Constitution and its authors. God revealed to Joseph Smith: "I established the Constitution of this land, by the hands of wise men whom I raised up unto this very purpose."[9] And principal among these wise men was James Madison.

*The Mormons have a high regard for James Madison—the "Father of the Constitution"— inasmuch as they proclaim the Constitution to be a "heavenly banner."*

# ENDNOTES

1   Lucy Mack Smith, *History of Joseph Smith by His Mother,* 48.

2   Bushman, *Joseph Smith: Rough Stone Rolling,* 399.

3   Benson, *Teachings,* 597. See also *The Federalist,* no. 37.

4   Quoted in McCollister, *God and the Oval Office,* 24–25.

5   Richard S. Van Wagoner, *Sidney Rigdon: A Portrait of Religious Excess,* 42.

6   *The Prophet of the Jubilee* (Welsh church periodical), January 1848, quoted in Givens, 92.

7   Joseph Smith, *History of the Church,* 3:304.

8   Gordon B. Hinckley, *Teachings of Gordon B. Hinckley,* 15.

9   Doctrine and Covenants 101:80.

# JAMES MONROE

## 1817–1825

James Monroe was the last of the Virginia dynasty of Presidents and last of the great Revolutionary generation to occupy the White House. It was during his presidency that America was said to be enjoying an "era of good feelings," as the young republic enjoyed relative peace and prosperity, gained national confidence, and began filling the fertile valleys west of the Appalachians. Regarding the Monroe era, President Ezra Taft Benson would later declare, "It is my conviction that God, who knows the end from the beginning, provided that period of time so the new nation could grow in strength to protect the land of Zion."[1] Indeed, important events in the beginning of the Restoration took place on Monroe's watch.

Joseph Smith Jr. was an eleven-year-old boy at the time James Monroe was inaugurated, and early in his first term (1818), the Smith family moved to Palmyra, New York. It was there that Joseph experienced his First Vision (spring 1820) and first visits from the angel Moroni (September 1823). The boy prophet was nineteen when Monroe moved out of the White House. James Monroe would die on 4 July 1831 in New York City—one year after The Church of Jesus Christ of Latter-day Saints was organized in another part of that same state.

# MONROE'S RELIGIOUS VIEWS

Madison said of the nation's fifth President, "His judgment was particularly good," and Jefferson declared of his fellow Virginian, "Monroe was so honest that if you turned his soul inside out there would not be a spot on it."[2] An Episcopalian who worshipped at St. John's, Monroe prayed at his first inauguration that "the Almighty . . . will be graciously pleased to continue to us this protection which He has already conspicuously displayed in our favor." Yet, besides such passing references to God in his inaugural addresses, Monroe seldom mentioned the Lord at all and was especially silent about his religious opinions. "Religion," he said, "is a matter between our Maker and ourselves."[3]

*Monroe's presidency was a time of peace in America known as the "Era of Good Feelings." It was during his presidency that Joseph Smith experienced his First Vision, and the seeds of the Restoration were planted.*

# MONROE'S LEGACY AMONG THE SAINTS

Latter-day prophets would later praise President Monroe for issuing the Monroe Doctrine, which forbade Europe from meddling in New World affairs. President Joseph Fielding Smith said that "the greatest and most powerful fortification in America is the 'Monroe Doctrine.' . . . It was the inspiration of the Almighty which rested upon John Quincy Adams, Thomas Jefferson and other statesmen, and which finally found authoritative expression in the message of James Monroe to Congress in the year 1823."[4] Ezra Taft Benson likewise believed Monroe was divinely inspired

*Political cartoon about the Monroe Doctrine.*

when he "formed and announced a policy which has profoundly influenced the development of our entire hemisphere."[5]

*Ezra Taft Benson, Joseph Fielding Smith, J. Reuben Clark, and other Church leaders taught that Monroe was inspired by God when he issued the Monroe Doctrine, forbidding Europe to meddle in the Western Hemisphere.*

President J. Reuben Clark Jr., formerly a member of the First Presidency, even acknowledged divine intervention in his highly acclaimed Monroe Doctrine memorandum, a secular government document published while Clark was under secretary of state:

Then came our GREAT Monroe Doctrine which placed us of the United States squarely behind efforts of Latin America to gain freedom and against those European states who would thwart it. God again moved us forward toward the destiny He has planned for us. He was preserving the blessings He had given to us.[6]

The presidency of James Monroe was consequentially a time when the rest of the world left America alone, and the restored gospel could begin to blossom in upstate New York.

# ENDNOTES

1    Ezra Taft Benson, "A Witness and a Warning," in Conference Report, October 1979, Saturday afternoon session.

2    Frank Freidel, *Our Country's Presidents*, 45.

3    Quoted in McCollister, *God and the Oval Office*, 29.

4    Joseph Fielding Smith, *The Progress of Man*, 466–67.

5    Ezra Taft Benson, in Conference Report, October 1960, Third Day Afternoon Meeting, 103.

6    Memorandum on the Monroe Doctrine, Dept. of State Publication #37, 17 December 1928.

# JOHN QUINCY ADAMS

## *1825–1829*

It was during the presidency of John Quincy Adams that Joseph Smith married Emma Hale (18 January 1827) and received the gold plates from the angel Moroni at the Hill Cumorah (22 September 1827).[1] Joseph was nineteen years old when the sixth President was sworn in and twenty-three when Adams left the White House. However, it is during Adams's post-presidency years, when he served as a congressman from the Plymouth District in Massachusetts, that he became the first U.S. President (albeit a former one) to have interactions with the LDS Church.

**December 1839:** While Joseph Smith is in Washington D.C. to meet with President Van Buren, he is introduced to "prominent members of Congress." It is unknown if the Prophet and ex-President Adams met, but they were in the U.S. Capitol together on the same days.[2]

**February 1844:** Joseph Smith meets with the Nauvoo City Council and dispatches Orson Pratt to Washington to call on the Illinois delegation for help. He also instructs, "Go to John Quincy Adams and ask him to call the delegates from Massachusetts separate from the Illinois delegation, and demand the same."[3]

**April 1844:** Orson Pratt arrives at the Capitol, and along with fellow Apostle John E. Page, has two meetings with Adams. The former President is polite and respectful toward them but is unable to help. He refers to the Mormons in his diary as a "new fanatical religious sect."

**May 1844:** John Quincy Adams's son, Charles Francis Adams, visits Nauvoo and writes of his impressions of the Prophet, the Nauvoo Temple, and the injustices done toward the Saints.

**February 1845:** After Illinois enemies have the Nauvoo City Charter revoked, Church leaders write to Adams asking for advice. It is not known if the ex-President ever responds.[4]

## THE VISITS OF TWO APOSTLES WITH THE SIXTH PRESIDENT

As mentioned, Apostles Orson Pratt and John E. Page of the Quorum of the Twelve Apostles arrived in the nation's capital in April 1844 to ask Congress for help. It is interesting that John Quincy Adams viewed Elder Pratt in political terms, as an agent of the mayor of Nauvoo, and Elder Page in religious terms, as a preacher, when both were Apostles. In his 3 April 1844 diary entry, Adams wrote of their visit:

*Elder Orson Pratt, one of the Twelve Apostles, met with John Quincy Adams as a representative of Joseph Smith to ask for help for the Saints.*

*Elder John E. Page, also one of the Twelve Apostles, was on a mission to the East in 1844, and joined Orson Pratt for his meetings with former President Adams.*

Pratt is a commissioned agent from Joseph Smith, the Mayor of the city of Nauvoo, in the State of Illinois, and Chief and Prophet of the Mormons, or Latter-day Saints, a new fanatical religious sect, who have occasioned great troubles and suffered great persecutions in the State of Missouri, from which they have been expelled by popular violence and the Government of the State. Page is a preacher of the gospel, of the same sect, now residing here. Pratt has two memorials from them to Congress, complaining of the injuries they have received, and claiming protection and redress. Pratt said he was instructed to ask an interview, first with the delegation from Illinois, and secondly with that from Massachusetts. I notified the members present from Massachusetts, who agreed to meet Pratt to-morrow morning in the chamber of the Committee of Manufactures, except Henry Williams, who declined to attend.

In his journal entry for the following day, Representative Adams discussed the meeting with the Mormon Apostles and the rest of his delegation. They concluded that there was really nothing the federal government could do to interfere with a state issues, and that any official request should go through the Illinois delegation anyway. He wrote:

At half-past ten this morning, with four other members of the Massachusetts delegation, I met in the chamber of the Committee of Manufactures the Mormon agent Pratt, and preacher Page, who set forth at large the grounds of their complaints against the Government and people of Missouri, and the persecutions for relief from which their memorials claim the interposition of Congress. The power of Congress to interfere is questionable; the right is doubtful. The memorials must be presented by a member from Illinois; and we agreed to act upon them as the proper sense of our duties would require.[5]

## THE PRESIDENT'S SON VISITS JOSEPH SMITH

Adams likely would have heard from his son, Charles Francis Adams, about his visit to the Prophet Joseph Smith in May 1844, a month before the martyrdom of the Prophet and a month after the meetings with Elders Pratt and Page. The younger Adams visited Nauvoo for two days with his

*John Quincy Adams considered the Latter-day Saints to be "a new fanatical religious sect, who have occasioned great troubles and suffered great persecutions in the State of Missouri, from which they have been expelled by popular violence and the Government of the State."*

cousin, Josiah Quincy, who was the mayor of Boston. A big fuss was made when word of the visitors reached Nauvoo, and Quincy noted the confusion upon their arrival:

It is probable that we owed the alacrity with which we were served to an odd blunder which had combined our names and personalities and set forth that no less a man than ex-President John Quincy Adams had arrived to visit Mr. Joseph Smith. Happily, however, Dr. Goforth [a fellow traveler with Quincy and Adams], who had got upon the road before us, divided our persons and reduced them to their proper proportions, so that no trace of disappointment was visible in the group of rough-looking Mormons who awaited our descent at the door.

As was mentioned, Joseph Smith thought highly of ex-President Adams. Josiah Quincy wrote: "As Dr. Goforth introduced us to the prophet, he mentioned the parentage of my companion. 'God bless you, to begin with!' said Joseph Smith, raising his hands in the air and letting them descend upon the shoulders of Mr. Adams. The benediction, though evidently sincere, had an odd savor of what may be called official familiarity, such as a crowned head might adopt on receiving the heir presumptive of a friendly court."[6]

Adams himself wrote that they "were introduced to the celebrated Joe Smith. A middle-aged man with a shrewd but rather ordinary expression of countenance, unshaved and in clothes neither very choice nor neat." For twenty-five cents each, the visitors were taken into Lucy Mack Smith's basement to see the Egyptian mummies and hear Joseph explain of the writings of Abraham found with them. Adams describes seeing the half-built Nauvoo Temple: "The architecture is original—and curious. It is built by the contribution of one-tenth of labor and goods. The prophet seems to have drawn his ideas largely from the Jewish system." Adams also expressed his sympathies upon hearing of the way the Mormons were driven from Missouri: "This is one of the most disgraceful chapters in the history of the United States, and shows that the spirit of intolerance, religious and political, can find a shelter even in the fairest professions of liberty."[7]

# ADAMS'S LEGACY AMONG THE SAINTS

President David O. McKay taught that Adams "sensed that the real John Quincy Adams was an immortal being, a son of a Father in heaven." To support this he related the following anecdote in several general conference talks and some of his books. Other LDS General Authorities also cited the following incident, upholding Adams as a prominent non-Mormon who sensed his immortality:

> Ex-President Adams was right, when he was accosted on the streets of Boston one day and was asked, "How is John Quincy Adams today?" and he answered, as he tottered along with his cane, "John Quincy Adams is well thank you, quite well. But the house in which he lives is tottering on its foundations, the windows are shaking, the roof is leaking, the doors are not hanging straight, and so on, and I think that John Quincy Adams will have to move out of it soon. But John Quincy Adams himself is quite well, I thank you, quite well."[8]

John Quincy Adams had served as secretary of state under President Monroe and was the principal architect of the Monroe Doctrine. President Joseph Fielding Smith taught that Adams received heavenly help during this time. "It was the inspiration of the Almighty which rested upon John Quincy Adams [at that time]," said President Smith.[9]

The Sixth President was the first President to hear of Joseph Smith and his small but growing group of followers. He met with Apostles and heard of the Saints' sufferings in Missouri, and in return was respected and admired by the Latter-day Saints for generations.

# ENDNOTES

1   *Deseret News 2003 Church Almanac*, 534.

2   B. H. Roberts, *A Comprehensive History of the Church*, 2:38n. See also John Quincy Adams, *Diary of John Quincy Adams*, entry for 30 November 1839. This shows John Quincy Adams arriving at the capital from Boston. Joseph Smith had arrived in Washington on November 28. They were both there during the first days of December. See also John Henry Evans, *Joseph Smith, an American Prophet*, 160.

3   Joseph Smith, *History of the Church*, 6:212.

4   Glen M. Leonard, *Nauvoo*, 468.

5   Charles Francis Adams, ed., *Memoirs of John Quincy Adams*, 7:3–5.

6   Josiah Quincy, *Figures of the Past from the Leaves of Old Journals*, 380–81.

7   Henry Adams, *Charles Francis Adams Visits the Mormons in 1844*, 20–22. See also Joseph Smith, *History of the Church*, 6:377 for the Prophet's account of this visit.

8   David O. McKay, in Conference Report, October 1959, Third Day Afternoon Meeting, 8. This anecdote was first shared at general conference in 1936. See Charles A. Callis, "The Present a Part of Eternity," in Conference Report, April 1936, First Day Afternoon Meeting.

9   Joseph Fielding Smith, *The Progress of Man*, 466–67.

# ANDREW JACKSON

## 1829–1837

Within a few months of Jackson's inauguration, Joseph Smith and Oliver Cowdery received angelic visits and priesthood ordinations from John the Baptist, and Peter, James, and John (spring 1829). That summer, the Three Witnesses and Eight Witnesses saw the gold plates, and in 1830 the Book of Mormon was published and the Church was organized. During Jackson's presidency, the Saints relocated to Ohio and built the Kirtland Temple. They also began settling Jackson County, Missouri (1831), which had been named after the popular President. By the time "Old Hickory" left the White House, the Saints had been expelled from both Jackson and Clay Counties and had regrouped at Far West in Caldwell County. Nonetheless, they dreamed of the day when they could return to the county named for the seventh President, to build their Zion.[1] Throughout Jackson's administration, the Saints were pro-Jackson, even though he was unable to help them.

**1830:** Jackson signs the Indian Removal Act. During his presidency, over 45,000 Native Americans are relocated west. Joseph Smith and the Saints praise Jackson and view this migration of the Indians as God's hand moving the Native Americans toward the promised land, where they could fulfill Book of Mormon prophesies and join in building Zion.[2]

Not fully understanding Jackson's forced relocation of 45,000 Native Americans, the Saints viewed what is now known as the "Trail of Tears" as God's hand moving the Native Americans toward the promised land, where they could fulfill Book of Mormon prophecies and join in building Zion.

**Fall 1832:** The Ohio Mormons endorse Jackson's reelection in their Kirtland newspaper, the *Northern Times*. They feel that the Whigs are corrupt and that Jackson will fight for the "common man." The Saints there are known as strong Jacksonian Democrats.[3]

**April 1834:** After the Mormon expulsion from Jackson County, Missouri, and in response to a revelation to "importune at the feet of the president" (D&C 101:86–89), Church leaders send a petition to President Jackson requesting help and protection.

**June 1834:** The Saints receive a disappointing response from the Jackson administration that the federal government will only intervene if asked to by

During the presidency of Andrew Jackson, the Saints were driven from Jackson County, Missouri. They dreamed of the day when they could return to the county named for the seventh President, to build their Zion.

the state of Missouri. While Jackson himself has sympathy for "the persecuted people," he deplores his "lack of power to interfere with the administration or non-administration of state laws."[4]

**Spring 1844:** During his campaign for the presidency, Joseph Smith fondly recalls the administration of Andrew Jackson, which he describes as the "Acme of American glory, liberty, and prosperity."[5]

**February 1845:** Like John Quincy Adams's, Andrew Jackson's advice is also sought by the Saints after the repeal of the Nauvoo Charter. By then, the seventy-eight-year-old Jackson is ailing from dropsy, old age, and a bad temper. He will die within a few months, never having responded to the Saints' second appeal for help.[6]

## JACKSON'S RELIGIOUS VIEWS

Andrew Jackson died at the Hermitage near Nashville, Tennessee, on 8 June 1845—fifteen years after the Church was organized and one year after the martyrdom of Joseph and Hyrum Smith. His Presbyterian faith was strong through the end. "I bequeath my body to the dust from whence it comes," he wrote in his last will and testament, "and my soul to God who gave it, hoping for a happy immortality through the atoning merits of our Lord Jesus Christ, the Saviour of the world."[7]

One of the great tragedies of Jackson's life was when his beloved wife, Rachel Donelson, died a premature death not long after he was elected President. Old Hickory sustained a hope that in the hereafter he could again be with his companion. "Heaven would not be heaven to me without my wife."[8]

Ezra Taft Benson and other Church leaders have often quoted Andrew Jackson when he said, "The Bible is the rock on which this Republic rests."[9] Gordon B. Hinckley has admired and quoted Jackson's statement that "no free government can stand without virtue in the people."[10]

## JACKSON'S LEGACY AMONG THE SAINTS

Despite Jackson's refusal to help during their time of need, Church leaders would fondly remember the seventh President. Eight U.S. Presidents after Jackson, when James Buchanan was sending Johnston's army to Utah at the behest of lying advisers, Brigham Young reminisced publicly about the days when the strong and independent Andrew Jackson was America's chief executive. "I wish that old Hickory Jackson was now our President," he said. "If we had a man in the chair who was really a man, and capable of magnifying his office, he would call upon his servants,

*In an 1861 sermon, President Brigham Young praised the courageous Jackson: "The administration of Andrew Jackson was as good as that of any one that ever occupied the presidential chair."*

and order them to kick those mean, miserable sneaks out of the presidential mansion, off from its grounds, and into the streets."[11]

In an 1861 sermon, President Brigham Young waxed nostalgic about Andrew Jackson once more: "The administration of Andrew Jackson was as good as that of any one that ever occupied the presidential chair, and he had a great many enemies. . . . You remember the struggle at the election of Andrew Jackson, and so do I. I repeat that his administration was as good as that of any man that ever administered the government. Some of his opponents did not like him very well for some of his political moves. I liked his moves, only he did not go far enough in removing the deposits and spoiling the United States Bank."[12]

One of the treasures of pioneer Utah was a cane made from the hickory grove at Andrew Jackson's estate, the Hermitage, that Jackson gave to Thomas Kane, a friend of the Mormons. Colonel Kane later gave this to John Smith, the first stake president in the Salt Lake Valley, who passed it to his son, Apostle George A. Smith, who gave it to his son, Apostle John Henry Smith, who gave it to his son, Church President George Albert Smith.[13]

Andrew Jackson had the support of the Mormons, both during his presidency and after. And yet he felt unable to help them in their struggles due to the principle of states' rights that prevailed in antebellum America. His administration, however, was held in high regard by the Latter-day Saints.

# ENDNOTES

1      *Deseret News 2003 Church Almanac,* 534–36.

2      Fawn M. Brodie, *No Man Knows My History,* 121. See also "Israel Will Be Gathered," *The Evening and Morning Star* 2, no. 13 (June 1833), 101; Monte S. Nyman & Charles D. Tate, Jr., eds., *Second Nephi: The Doctrinal Structure,* 334; Joseph Fielding Smith, *Church History and Modern Revelation,* 3:69–70.

3      Milton V. Backman, Jr., *Heavens Resound: A History of the Latter-day Saints in Ohio 1830–1838,* 24, 335. See also Brodie, *No Man Knows My History,* 64–65; Arrington and Bitton, *The Mormon Experience,* 50; Grant Underwood, "The Earliest Reference Guides to the Book of Mormon: Windows into the Past," *Journal of Mormon History* 12 (1985).

4      James E. Talmage, *Story and Philosophy of Mormonism,* 30. See also Richard S. Van Wagoner, *Sidney Rigdon: A Portrait of Religious Excess,* 146; Arnold K. Garr and Clark V. Johnson, eds., *Regional Studies in Latter-day Saint History: Missouri,* 247–48; Richard Abanes, *One Nation Under Gods: A History of the Mormon Church,* 119; "Officer's Arrival Bred Suspicion: Unfriendly Government Had Ignored," *Church News,* 8 June 1996.

5      Joseph Smith, *History of the Church,* 6:197–209.

6      Leonard, *Nauvoo,* 468. See also Phillip B. Kunhardt, Jr., Phillip B. Kunhardt III, & Peter W. Kunhardt, *The American President,* 356.

7      Preamble of his last will and testament, quoted in McCollister, *God and the Oval Office,* 37.

8      Elder Sterling W. Sill, BYU Speeches 1964, 3 March 1964, 6.

9      Ezra Taft Benson, in Conference Report, April 1963, Third Day Morning Meeting, 110. See also L. Tom Perry, "For the Time Will Come When They Will Not Endure Sound Doctrine," *Ensign,* November 1975, 85.

10     Gordon B. Hinckley, "An Honest Man: Gods Noblest Work," *Ensign,* May 1976, 60.

11     Preston Nibley, *Brigham Young: The Man and His Work,* 290.

12     Brigham Young, "Human Intelligence and Freedom—National Administrative Movements, &c.," in *Journal of Discourses,* 8:321.

13     George Albert Smith, "Walking Stick of Thomas L. Kane," in Conference Report, October 1947, First Day Morning Meeting, 2.

# MARTIN VAN BUREN

## *1837–1841*

The relationships between the presidents of the Church and the Presidents of the U.S. are all played out via letters and intermediaries in the eleven presidencies from Andrew Jackson through Andrew Johnson, with the significant exception of Martin Van Buren. The presidency of Van Buren is notable in this chronicle because of his face-to-face meetings with the Prophet Joseph. Such meetings did not take place again until Ulysses S. Grant visited Brigham Young nearly four decades later.

Van Buren's administration coincided with the Church's commencement of missionary work in the British Isles (1837), the Saints' abandonment of Kirtland and consolidation in Far West, Missouri (1838), and their ultimate expulsion from Missouri and reestablishment at Nauvoo (1839–40). It was because of this turmoil and suffering that Joseph Smith sought help wherever he could, even from the White House. But the relationship between the Church and Van Buren was ultimately a rough one.

**November 1836:** In an editorial of the Mormons' Kirtland publication, the *Northern Times,* Oliver Cowdery endorses Van Buren for President, saying his victory "would meet our mind, and receive our warm support." Kirtland Township votes 396 for Van Buren and only 116 for Whig nominee William Henry Harrison.[1]

**29 November 1839:** Joseph Smith and Elias Higbee have their first meeting with Van Buren in the White House. The President says he cannot help them.

**February 1840:** Joseph Smith meets a second time with Van Buren and is told "your cause is just, but I can do nothing for you. . . . If I take up for you I shall lose the vote of Missouri."

**November 1840:** Frustrated with Van Buren, Joseph Smith leads the Saints in reversing their political loyalties by supporting Whig William Henry Harrison. The Saints cast a decidedly anti–Van Buren vote and join the majority throughout the country in denying the eighth President a second term.[2]

**Fall 1843:** Joseph Smith writes to leading presidential candidates seeking their opinions on how they would protect persecuted groups like the Mormons. Van Buren is written to and asked "whether your views or feelings have changed since the subject matter of this communication was presented you in your then official capacity at Washington . . . and by you treated with a coldness, indifference, and neglect, bordering on contempt." The letter is ignored by the ex-President.[3]

**February 1844:** Missouri senator Thomas H. Benton makes a deal with Van Buren to help him reclaim the White House if, once elected, Van Buren will work to wipe out the Mormons. Likewise, Illinois governor Thomas Ford encourages Van Buren that month and tells him "the democrats can beat the Whigs, Mormons, Abolitionists."[4]

**Spring 1844:** Joseph Smith campaigns for the presidency and promises to restore the greatness of America, which he claims "began to decline under the withering touch of Martin Van Buren."[5] Van Buren is rejected by the Democratic Party, which nominates James K. Polk instead.

## JOSEPH SMITH'S VISITS TO PRESIDENT VAN BUREN

After the Latter-day Saints had been driven from the state of Missouri, Joseph Smith turned to the federal government for recourse. According to the Prophet's mother, Lucy Mack Smith, "He had been commanded of the Lord, while in prison [in Missouri], to pray for redress at the feet of the President."[6] So Joseph, counselor Sidney Rigdon, politically savvy Judge Elias Higbee, Dr. Foster, and bodyguard Porter Rockwell journeyed to Washington to call on the President. They left Illinois on 29 October 1839.

En route to the nation's capital, Rigdon took ill, and it was Joseph Smith and Judge Higbee that called upon Martin Van Buren, along with Representative John Reynolds of Illinois. On the morning of 29 November, the men walked up the front steps of the White House and knocked on the door, announced themselves, and requested to see the President. The Prophet described

*The White House as it appeared when Joseph Smith called upon President Van Buren. The Prophet described "the house of the President" as "a very large and splendid palace, decorated with all the fineries and elegance of this world."*

"the house of the President" as "a very large and splendid palace, decorated with all the fineries and elegance of this world."[7]

Congressman Reynolds described bringing Joseph Smith to the President:

> When we were about to enter the apartment of Mr. Van Buren, the prophet asked me to introduce him as a 'Latter-Day-Saint.' It was so unexpected and so strange to me, the 'Latter-Day-Saints,' that I could scarcely believe he would urge such nonsense on this occasion to the President. But he repeated the request, when I asked him if I understood him. I introduced him as a 'Latter-Day-Saint,' which made the President smile.[8]

Van Buren asked the men what difference there was between Mormonism and the other religions of the day. Joseph replied that the "mode of baptism, and the gift of the Holy Ghost by the laying on of hands" were the basic differences, remarking later, "we considered that all other con-

*Congressman John Reynolds of Illinois introduced Joseph Smith to President Van Buren and was surprised that he wanted to be introduced as a "Latter-Day-Saint."*

siderations were contained in the gift of the Holy Ghost, and we deemed it unnecessary to make many words in preaching the Gospel to him. Suffice it to say he has got our testimony."[9]

The topic then shifted to the treatment of the Mormons in Missouri, and the men demanded that the federal government intervene to allow the Saints to live there peacefully, or at the very least require the state of Missouri to compensate them for property lost. They handed the President letters outlining the atrocities the Saints had endured. "As soon as he had read one of them," related Joseph, "he looked upon us with a kind of half frown and said, What can I do? I can do nothing for you! If I do anything, I shall come in contact with the whole State of Missouri." Not backing down easily, Joseph asked for a formal hearing on the matter and a consideration of their constitutional rights.

The President, in Joseph's words, then "promised to reconsider what he had said, and observed that he felt to sympathize with us on account of our sufferings."[10]

In the end, they received little encouragement from Van Buren, so they resorted to attempting to persuade various senators and representatives in Washington.[11] LDS historian B. H. Roberts adds of their visit with Martin Van Buren, "Their presence seemed to be an annoyance to him."[12] Joseph summarized the meeting in his journal as follows:

*29 November 1839: Martin Van Buren meets with Joseph Smith in the White House, marking the first time—but not last—that a President of the United States would meet with the president of the LDS Church. "Your cause is just, but I can do nothing for you," was Van Buren's infamous response.*

> During my stay I had an interview with Martin Van Buren, the President, who treated me very insolently, and it was with great reluctance he listened to our message. . . . His whole course went to show that he was an office-seeker, that self-aggrandizement was his ruling passion, and that justice and righteousness were no part of his composition. I found him such a man as I could not conscientiously support at the head of our noble Republic.[13]

To his brother Hyrum, Joseph Smith did not hold back his disdain for the President. Calling the plump and extravagant Van Buren "His Majesty," Joseph scoffed:

> On the whole we think he is without body or parts, as no one part seems to be proportioned to another . . . to come directly to the point, he is so much a fop or a fool (for he judged our cause before he knew it) we could find no place to put truth into him. We do not say the Saints shall not vote for him, but we do say boldly . . . that we do not intend he shall have our votes.[14]

Early in February the Mormon leaders were able to have a second interview with the President. "It was with great reluctance [Van Buren] listened to our message," the Prophet later wrote.[15] Their "long efforts" were in vain, however. "Gentlemen," said Van Buren upon hearing their tale of mistreatment and injustice, "your cause is just, but I can do nothing for you. . . . If I take up for you I shall lose the vote of Missouri."[16]

Since the President was a Jacksonian Democrat—a party fiercely loyal to states' rights—his reply came as no surprise. For the federal government to intervene with a state in such a direct manner could have prematurely set off the powder keg that would later erupt into the Civil War. Yet the Mormons, who had been loyal Democrats, felt snubbed and betrayed.

"On my way home I did not fail to proclaim the iniquity and insolence of Martin Van Buren, toward myself and an injured people," wrote Joseph. "May he never be elected again to any office of trust or power."[17] The Prophet's curse of Van Buren would come to pass. Not long after his return to Illinois, the *Quincy Whig* interviewed a bitter Joseph, who contended that the President "was not as fit as my dog, for the chair of state; for my dog will make an effort to protect his abused and insulted master, while the present chief magistrate will not so much as lift his finger to relieve an oppressed and persecuted community of freemen."[18]

## VAN BUREN'S LEGACY AMONG THE SAINTS

The Saints in Utah did not have warm memories of the eighth President. In the April conference of 1861, Brigham Young lamented that Van Buren did not do more to help the Saints:

> When we made application to the General Government for a restoration of our property and rights in Missouri, if Martin Van Buren had said, "Yes, I will restore your lands to you, and will defend you in the possession of your rights, if I have power; and if

I have not, my name shall not remain as President of the United States," he could have reinstated us in our rights. A few words from the General Government to the Government of Missouri would have restored to us our lands and stayed the operations of the mob.[19]

In 1877 when Wilford Woodruff performed the temple work for the deceased Presidents, he purposely left Van Buren off his list, saying that when his cause is just, somebody will do the work for him. "Although he purposely left Martin Van Buren off his baptismal list as a form of posthumous payback," notes researcher Brian Stuy, "unbeknownst to him John M. Bernhisel had performed Van Buren's baptism the previous year in the Endowment House." Nonetheless, it was not until seventy-six years after Van Buren's death that his other temple ordinances were finally completed.[20]

*Joseph Smith was not impressed with Van Buren. In his opinion, the President "was not as fit as my dog, for the chair of state; for my dog will make an effort to protect his abused and insulted master, while the present chief magistrate will not so much as lift his finger to relieve an oppressed and persecuted community of freemen."*

# ENDNOTES

1  *Painseville Telegraph,* 20 February 1835 and 24 November 1836. See also Backman, *Heavens Resound,* 335; Thomas G. Alexander, *Things in Heaven and Earth: The Life and Times of Wilford Woodruff, a Mormon Prophet,* 42; James B. Allen, "The American Presidency and the Mormons," *Ensign,* October 1972, 48.

2  Allen & Leonard, *The Story of the Latter-day Saints,* 190.

3  *Doctrinal History of the Church* 6:63–65. See also Allen & Leonard, *The Story of the Latter-day Saints,* 202.

4  Roberts, *A Comprehensive History of the Church,* 3:101. See also Thomas Ford, letter to Martin Van Buren, 10 February 1844, Martin Van Buren Papers, Manuscript Division of the Library of Congress, Washington D.C. Microfilm Reel #27.

5  Joseph Smith, *History of the Church,* 6:197–209.

6  Lucy Mack Smith, *History of Joseph Smith by His Mother,* 305.

7  Joseph Fielding Smith, *Essentials in Church History,* 289.

8  Paul Simon, *Lincoln's Preparation for Greatness: The Illinois Legislative Years,* 266–67.

9  Joseph Smith, *History of the Church,* 4:42.

10  Van Wagoner, *Sidney Rigdon: A Portrait of Religious Excess,* 265–66, 269. See also Joseph Smith, *History of the Church,* 4:39.

11  Allen and Leonard, *The Story of the Latter-day Saints,* 158–59.

12  Joseph Smith, *History of the Church,* 2:30.

13  Quoted in Joseph Fielding Smith, *Essentials in Church History,* 292.

14  *Journal History,* 5 December 1839.

15  Joseph Smith, *History of the Church,* 4:80.

16  Joseph Smith, *History of the Church,* 4:203.

17  Joseph Smith, *History of the Church,* 4:89.

18  *Quincy Whig,* 17 October 1840.

19  Brigham Young, in Conference Report, April 1861.

20  Brian H. Stuy, "Wilford Woodruff's Vision of the Signers of the Declaration of Independence," *Journal of Mormon History* (Spring 2000): 71. Temple ordinances can be accessed by Church members at www.familysearch.org.

WILLIAM HENRY HARRISON,
9th President of the United States.
Born Febr. 9th 1773, died April 4th 1841.

By T. Campbell from the Original by J. H. Beard.    Printed by Klauprech & Menzel, Cincinnati.

# WILLIAM HENRY HARRISON

## *1841*

William Henry Harrison's brief presidency occurred at a time when the Saints were prospering in Nauvoo. The temple was under construction, the Nauvoo Legion had just been organized, and there was excitement about the newly announced principle of vicarious work for the dead. Although the Saints initially campaigned against Harrison, they ultimately supported him and mourned his premature death.

**November 1836:** In Harrison's first bid for the White House, the Saints support his Democratic opponent, Martin Van Buren. Kirtland Township votes against Harrison by a margin of four to one.[1]

**November 1840:** Frustrated by Van Buren's refusal to help, Joseph Smith leads the Saints in supporting a victorious Harrison. Mormons even participate in a pro-Harrison campaign parade in Springfield when the Whig nominee comes through the Illinois state capital.[2]

**Winter 1840–41:** With Harrison heading toward the White House, the Mormons are hopeful that the Whigs' traditional concern for property rights leads to more favorable treatment than the past administration's.[3]

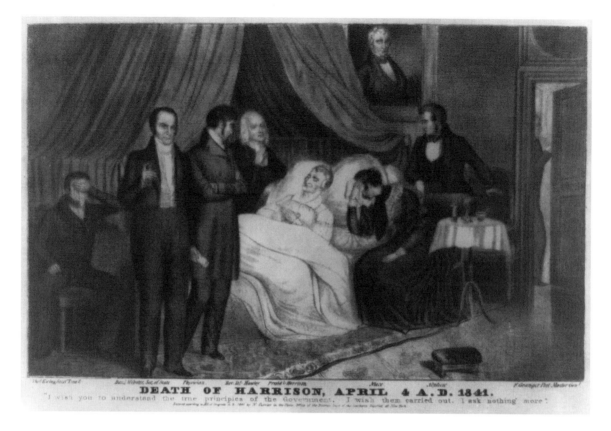

DEATH OF HARRISON, APRIL 4 A.D. 1841.

*The nation was stunned by Harrison's abrupt death one month into his presidency. "We voted for General Harrison because we loved him," remarked Joseph Smith. "He is now dead, and all his friends are not ours."*

**19 January 1841:** The Prophet Joseph receives by revelation a solemn proclamation directed toward various leaders including "the honorable President-Elect" Harrison. The revelation, later canonized as section 124 of the Doctrine and Covenants, encourages these leaders to assist the Saints in anticipation of the Second Coming.

**4 April 1841:** President Harrison dies of pneumonia just a month after giving the longest inaugural address in American history in a freezing rain without a coat. Joseph Smith remarks at the time, "We voted for General Harrison because we loved him—he was a gallant officer and a tried statesman; but this is no reason why we should always be governed by his friends—he is now dead, and all his friends are not ours."[4]

Now a presidential candidate himself, in April 1844, Joseph Smith includes praises for Harrison in his campaign literature: "General Harrison appeared, as a star among the storm-clouds, for better weather. The good man died before he had the opportunity of applying one balm to ease the pain of our groaning country."[5]

# ENDNOTES

1   *Painesville Telegraph,* 20 February 1835, 3.

2   Allen and Leonard, *The Story of the Latter-day Saints,* 190. See also Joseph Smith, *History of the Church,* 4:98; Larry Schweikart, "The Mormon Connection: Lincoln, the Saints, and the Crises of Equality," in *Western Humanities Review* 34, no. 1 (Winter 1980): 4; Rachel Grant Taylor, "A Hundred Years Ago," *Improvement Era* 36, no. 12 (October 1933).

3   Roberts, *A Comprehensive History of the Church,* 2:122.

4   Roberts, *A Comprehensive History of the Church,* 2:122.

5   *Times and Seasons* (Nauvoo, IL) 5, no. 8 (whole no. 92) (January 1844–1 January 1845), 15 April 1844, 511.

*Frustrated by Van Buren's refusal to help, the Saints supported the Harrison campaign in his victorious election of 1840.*

# JOHN TYLER

## *1841–1845*

When William Henry Harrison died suddenly, his vice president immediately insisted on assuming the full powers of a President rather than narrowly interpreting the constitutional provision to merely "act as President." Thus, "His Accidency," as John Tyler's detractors branded him, set a powerful precedent as the first vice president to assume the presidency upon the death of his predecessor. The Saints, who felt stung by Van Buren and were hopeful with Harrison, were initially unsure what to make of Tyler. His presidency overlapped a time when the Saints' situation in Nauvoo was becoming increasingly precarious and when Joseph Smith and other leaders were incarcerated in Carthage Jail. The martyrdom of Joseph and Hyrum Smith occurred during Tyler's administration, and Brigham Young and the Twelve Apostles began to lead the Church.

**April 1841:** The new President is annoyed with all the factions clamoring for his attention, and lists "Antimormons" as among the groups calling on him within days of taking office.[1]

**16 April 1843:** Joseph Smith is surprised to receive a letter from President John Tyler charging him with "high treason." It is soon found out that the letter is a farce.[2]

*Despite being asked, John Tyler never intervened to help the Saints. The martyrdom of Joseph and Hyrum Smith occurred on his watch.*

**26 March 1844:** The Prophet writes Tyler requesting to raise 100,000 men to extend protection to Americans settling in "Oregon and other portions of the United States."[3]

**25 April 1844:** Elder Orson Hyde has his first meeting with President Tyler when he presents the Prophet's request.

**April 1844:** In his presidential campaign literature, Joseph Smith denounces Tyler and claims it is time for a change from "President Tyler's three years perplexity and pseudo-whig-democrat reign."[4]

**May 1844:** The Prophet Joseph, when asked by visitors Josiah Quincy and Charles Francis Adams to make a prophecy, declares: "I will prophesy that John Tyler will not be the next president, for some things are possible and some things are probable; but Tyler's election is neither the one nor the other!"[5] Joseph's words prove prophetic.

**June 1844:** After Tyler is denied the Whig nomination, his supporters nominate him for President as a third party. Several newspaper editors suggest that he pick "Jo Smith" as his running mate. These suggestions are often made tongue-in-cheek, yet there is also recognition that Nauvoo is the swing vote in Illinois, whose electoral votes can tip the scales in a tight race.[6]

**20 June 1844:** Joseph Smith sends a desperate plea to President Tyler, requesting help from the mobs that are forming to exterminate the Mormon people.[7]

**22 June 1844:** Church leaders decide to send Joseph east to personally meet with Tyler regarding their dire situation. Two sons of powerful South Carolina senator John C. Calhoun convince the Prophet that appealing to Tyler will accomplish nothing, and he decides to flee to the West instead. After crossing the Mississippi River he changes his mind and returns to Nauvoo.[8]

## APOSTLES VISIT WITH TYLER

As was mentioned, Orson Hyde delivered the Prophet's memo to Washington, but neither Congress nor President Tyler acted upon it.[9] Elder Hyde described his 25 April visit with Tyler as follows:

> We were last evening introduced to President John Tyler at the White House by the politeness of Major Semple [Tyler's son-in-law], where we spent an hour very agreeably. The president is a very plain, homespun, familiar, farmer-like man. He spoke of our troubles in Missouri and regretted that we had met with such treatment. He asked how we were getting along in Illinois. I told him that we were contending with the difficulties of a new country, and laboring under the disadvantageous consequence of being driven from our property and homes in Missouri.[10]

Orson Pratt later joined Orson Hyde in appealing to Tyler and his cabinet for support.[11] In one interview, the two Apostles spoke with the President about American settlement in the Oregon area and the need to maintain a balance of power between the free states and the slave states.[12] Elder Hyde wrote on 9 June 1844 that they were ultimately unsuccessful in getting help directly from President Tyler.[13] In another letter two days later, Hyde reported that President Tyler spent a "good deal of time with [me]" and "was very frank." He explained that the President had remarked, "The general government cannot interfere with the laws and regulations of the states." Hyde also noted that "President Tyler seemed to feel that I should be satisfied with a few words because of the press of business." In conclusion, Hyde observed, "We are now thrown back upon our own resources. We have tried every department of government to obtain our rights, but we cannot find them."[14]

## EX-PRESIDENT TYLER AND THE MORMONS

One day ex-President Tyler visited a music store in Richmond, where he was impressed by one young man's ability to play the piano. The man was the future first president of Brigham Young Academy (later Brigham Young University), Karl Maeser, who was in Virginia on an LDS mission. The impoverished Elder Maeser was able to finance the remainder of his mission by giving piano lessons to John Tyler's daughters over the next six months.[15]

The ex-President's son and personal secretary, Robert Tyler, became one of the influential advi-

*As a young missionary in Virginia, future BYU president Karl G. Maeser financed some of his mission by giving piano lessons to former President Tyler's daughters.*

sors encouraging President Buchanan to send an army against the Mormons in Utah, principally as a diversion from the increasingly heated issue of slavery. "I believe that we can supersede the Negro-Mania with the almost universal excitements of an Anti-Mormon Crusade," he wrote to Buchanan 27 April 1857. "The Popular Idea is rapidly maturing that Mormonism should be put down and utterly extirpated." It is unknown if his father agreed with him, but it is that the two enjoyed a close friendship.[16]

John Tyler died in Richmond, Virginia, in 1862, at the height of the Civil War. At the time, he had been serving the Confederacy as a congressman. In his lifetime he had received correspondence from Joseph Smith, been visited by Apostles, and had personal interaction with a Mormon missionary. Yet John Tyler never extended his presidential influence to aid the beleaguered Latter-day Saints.

# ENDNOTES

1   Kunhardt, Kunhardt, & Kunhardt, *The American President,* 215.

2   J. Christopher Conkling, *A Joseph Smith Chronology,* 187.

3   *Improvement Era* 29, no. 12 (October 1926).

4   *Times and Seasons* 5, no. 8 (whole no. 92) (January 1844–1 January 1845), 15 April 1844, 511.

5   Leon R. Hartshorn, comp., *Classic Stories from the Lives of Our Prophets,* 24–25.

6   LeGrand L. Baker, *Murder of the Mormon Prophet: The Political Prelude to the Death of Joseph Smith,* 248–49. In addition to the *Clarkesville Jeffersonian* of 8 June 1844, Baker points to the *Rhode Island County Journal and Independent Inquirer* (Providence, RI), 2 February 1844; the *Haverhill Gazette* (Haverhill, MA), 1 June 1844; and the *Scioto Gazette* (Chilicothe, Ohio), 6 June 1844.

7   Joseph Smith, *History of the Church,* 6:508.

8   Roberts, *A Comprehensive History of the Church,* 2:246. See also Baker, *Murder of the Mormon Prophet,* 477.

9   Hyrum L. Andrus, *Joseph Smith and World Government,* 56–57.

10  *Improvement Era* 47, no. 6 (June 1944).

11  Andrew Jenson, *Encyclopedic History of the Church,* 1844.

12  H. Dean Garrett, ed., *Regional Studies in Latter-day Saint History: Illinois,* 194–95.

13  Clark V. Johnson, *The Mormon Redress Petitions: Documents of the 1833–1838 Missouri Conflict,* xxi–xxii.

14  Johnson, *The Mormon Redress Petitions,* 563. Also quoted in Garrett, *Regional Studies: Illinois,* 195.

15  Givens, 215. See also Andrew Jenson, *LDS Biographical Encyclopedia,* 1:707.

16  Philip Gerald Auchampaugh, *Robert Tyler, Southern Rights Champion 1847–1866,* 180–81.

# JAMES K. POLK

## *1845—1849*

The late 1840s saw both the presidency of James K. Polk and the Mormon migration across the plains to the Great Basin. Consequently, the Church's primary interaction with this President was in requesting assistance in their trek west—which resulted in the Mormon Battalion. Because of this, James K. Polk is considered to be the first President who could be called a "friend of the Mormons."[1] The President defended their right to practice their religion and to emigrate west and in return enjoyed their political support.[2] Yet in the end, he did not favor the Saints' appointing their own rulers in the West.

**May 1844:** As a result of a compromise at the Democratic national convention, Governor James K. Polk of Tennessee becomes the presidential nominee. Speculation soon flies that presidential candidate Joseph Smith might throw his support behind Polk in exchange for a cabinet position or ambassadorship.

**November 1844:** LDS support for Polk helps give him a 54 to 42 percent victory over Henry Clay in the state of Illinois.[3]

**Spring 1845:** Church leaders write President Polk, asking him to "convene a special session of congress and furnish us an asylum where we can enjoy our rights of conscience and religion unmolested."[4] This request is never granted.

**June 1846:** President Polk works with LDS representatives to commission what becomes the Mormon Battalion.

**Summer 1847:** Polk donates ten dollars to Charles C. Dana and Robert Campbell who are in Washington D.C. on a mission to raise money for the pioneers.[5] First Lady Sarah Polk also contributes toward the Saints at a benefit dinner held in Washington.[6]

**1848:** A friend to the LDS Church, Thomas Kane reports to the Saints that in a recent meeting with Polk "I found he did not feel disposed to favor your people, and he had his men of his own stamp picked out to serve as [Deseret's] governor and other officers. He would not appoint men from among yourselves."[7] Brigham Young declares "Polk would be damned for this act."[8]

*First Lady Sarah Polk contributed toward the Saints at a benefit dinner held in Washington in 1847.*

## POLK AND THE PROPHET IN THE ELECTION OF 1844

In writing to five candidates in the presidential race of 1844, Joseph Smith learned that there were none who would protect the Saints, so he announced his own candidacy for the presidency. Joseph likely realized that his campaign was a long shot at best, but felt it necessary since he had no other candidate he could support.[9] "Tell the people we have had Whig and Democratic Presidents long enough," the Prophet admonished his campaigners. "We want a President of the United States."[10]

THE PROPHET.

SATURDAY MORNING, JUNE 22, 1844.

SUPER HANC PETRAM ÆDIFICABO.

FOR PRESIDENT,
GEN. JOSEPH SMITH,
OF NAUVOO, ILLINOIS.
FOR VICE PRESIDENT,
SIDNEY RIGDON,
OF PENNSYLVANIA.

*Not seeing any candidate who would protect the Saints, Joseph Smith announces his candidacy for President of the United States. His death in June 1844 would end his campaign, and James K. Polk would become the nation's eleventh President.*

Political observers realized that although the Prophet was unelectable in 1844, he controlled the votes of Nauvoo—then the largest city in Illinois—which would likely determine where the state's nine electoral votes would go. A Georgia newspaper editor pointed out "the disciples of Joe undoubtedly hold the balance of power in Illinois."[11] Even more significant, the electoral votes of Illinois could tip the presidential scales in a tight race. "If the Whigs are beaten," concluded the *New York Daily Tribune*, "it will be by the votes of Nauvoo."[12]

As the real race began to crystallize around Democrat James K. Polk and Whig Henry Clay, speculation began to fly throughout the country about which direction the Mormons would throw their critical support. Regarding the Saints possibly supporting the Democrats, one newspaper editor asked, "Is it possible Joe [Smith] would withdraw from the canvass for the Presidency, if he could get to be secretary of state or Minister to Russia?"[13]

Immediately after James K. Polk was nominated, Tennessee congressman and Polk confidant Cave Johnson wrote to the candidate: "Several M.C. [Members of Congress] from Illinois desired me to say that you should answer no address from Joe Smith, which you may soon expect. I need not say to you, that the less said is the easiest word. You will be compelled to omit answering letters addressed to you. That we shall triumph I have not a doubt."[14]

However, the martyrdom of Joseph Smith in Carthage, Illinois, on 27 June 1844 brought the Prophet's presidential campaign to an abrupt halt. There would also be no opportunity to parlay his candidacy into a cabinet position or ambassadorship in the Polk administration. Polk went on to beat Henry Clay, becoming America's first "dark horse" President.

In the end, Polk was elected because he linked the Texas issue, attractive in the South, with the Oregon question, popular in the North, into a winning platform of national expansion.[15] Ironically, one of the Prophet's leading campaign issues was calling for the "annexation of Texas, Oregon, and any liberty-loving people." Similarly, President Polk pushed through the Walker Tariff Act and the Independent Treasury Act, which were along the lines of Smith's economic platform calling for a "judicious tariff whose revenues might foster economic expansion, and a federally owned national bank."[16]

Although it was not Joseph Smith but James K. Polk who ultimately triumphed in the campaign of 1844 and served as America's eleventh President, Polk was certainly a more desirable President in the Prophet's eyes than the five who snubbed his letters and caused him to run for the nation's highest office. Joseph Smith believed in a strong chief executive, and Polk would be the last strong President until Lincoln.

## PRESIDENT POLK CALLS UP THE MORMON BATALLION

In January 1846, Polk was warned by an advisor that the Mormons may be cooperating with agents of Great Britain or Mexico in a "treasonable movement" as they planned their western migration.[17] Four days after this letter was sent, Elder Orson Hyde of the Twelve in Nauvoo wrote to the President. "Your annual message has been received here, and its bold and patriotic tone in relation to Oregon and the west . . . has induced our people to direct their course to the valley of the 'Umqua,' and neighboring valley," Elder Hyde wrote, referring to the Umpqua River Valley of south-central Oregon. "In about nine mos. we hope to be there," the Apostle informed the President.[18]

Illinois Governor Ford saw no other way to resolve the Mormon question than to send the Saints west and wrote to President James K. Polk with a scheme to expedite the matter. Ford believed that if Polk ordered a military force to block the departure of the Saints, Brigham Young would order an immediate evacuation and Illinois would be rid of them sooner rather than later. The President rejected the proposal as inappropriate no matter how unacceptable the new religion was to the people of Illinois.[19] He penned the following in his diary:

Saturday, 31st January, 1846

> After night [Illinois] Senator [James] Semple called and held a conversation with me in relation to the intended emigration of the Mormons of Illinois to Oregon. I had examined Gov. Ford's letter on the subject, which he had delivered to me on the 30th Instant, & which I have placed on file, and informed him that as President of the U.S. I possessed no power to prevent or check their emigration; that the right of emigration or expatriation was one which any citizen possessed. I told him I could not interfere with them on the ground of their religious faith, however absurd it might be considered to be; that if I could interfere with the Mormons, I could with the Baptists, or any other religious sec; & that by the constitution any citizen had a right to adopt his own religious faith.[20]

As the Mormons began moving west from Nauvoo, Brigham Young instructed Jesse C. Little, the official Church agent in Washington, to seek government contracts in the West and "embrace any offer that would aid in the emigration." Using letters of introduction by Colonel Thomas L. Kane (a friend of the Mormons), Elder Little sought an audience with President Polk. After five days without a response, Little wrote to President Polk personally, threatening that lack of federal aid to help the Mormons migrate "under the outstretched wings of the American Eagle" might "compel us to be foreigners." The thought of an independent Mormon state in the West that was aligned with England was playing to the expansionist President's worst fears and likely facilitated an interview.[21] On 2 June Jesse Little was visited at his lodgings by Amos Kendall, the adviser to the President and former postmaster general, and informed that he would finally be granted an audience the very next day.[22]

Once the meeting was scheduled, the President wrote in his diary that he desired to make "a move to placate the Mormons and retain their loyalty." In the 2 June entry, Polk wrote "Col. Kearny was also

*Upon hearing that the Mormons were going to head West, Polk wrote in his diary that he desired to make "a move to placate the Mormons and retain their loyalty."*

authorized to receive into service as volunteers a few hundred of the Mormons who are now on their way to California, with a view to conciliate them, attach them to our country, & prevent them from taking part against us."[23]

On Wednesday, 3 June, at the Blue Room in the White House, Elder Little met with President Polk in company with Amos Kendall for three hours.[24] "The president said he had no prejudice against the Mormons, but believed us good citizens," wrote Little, "and was willing to do us all the good that was in his power consistently; said our people should be protected—that he had full confidence in me from information he had received. . . . He would do something for me, but did not decide [yet]."[25] That night the President wrote in his diary his version of the meeting:

> I told Mr. Little that b [sic] our constitution the mormons would be treated as all other American citizens were, without regard to the sect to which they belonged or the religious creed which they professed, and that I had no prejudices toward them which could induce a different course of treatment. Mr. Little said that they were Americans in all their feelings, & friends of the U. S. I told Mr. Little that we were at War with Mexico, and asked him if 500 or more of the mormons now on their way to California would be willing on their arrival in that country to volunteer and enter the U.S. army in that war, under the command of a U.S. Officer. He said he had no doubt they would willingly do so. . . .
>
> The mormons, if taken into the service, will constitute not more than ? of Col. Kearney's command, and the main object of taking them into service would be to conciliate them, and prevent them from assuming a hostile attitude toward the U.S. after their arrival in California.[26]

On 5 June, Elder Little met again with President Polk to hear the latter's decision regarding the Latter-day Saints. "He informed me," reported Little, "that we should be protected in California, and that five hundred or one thousand of our people should be taken into the service [to participate in the war with Mexico], officered by our own men; said that I should have letters from him, and from the secretary of the navy to the squadron [assigned to conquer California from the sea]." Elder Little considered the proposal throughout the afternoon and then sent a letter in the evening accepting the offer in behalf of the Church.[27]

At that meeting, Polk asked Little if the Mormons would offer five hundred volunteers to enlist *after* the Mormons reached the West. Polk was concerned that if Mormon volunteers were enlisted immediately and mixed with the existing Army of the West, there would be catastrophic results, since the existing army included a thousand Missouri volunteers, and Polk understood the

*LDS agent Jesse C. Little and Mormon-friend Thomas L. Kane were instrumental in persuading President Polk to commission the Mormon Battalion.*

antagonism between the Mormons and the Missourians. Little said that they would prefer immediate enlistment, but the President turned that down.[28] After Little left the meeting, the President explained his fears to Amos Kendall:

> If the mormons reached the country I did not desire to have them the only U. S. forces in the country. I told Mr. Kendall that the citizens now settled in California at Sutter's settlement and elsewhere had learned that a large body of mormons were emigrating to that country and were alarmed at it, and that this alarm would be increased if the first organized troops of the U. S. that entered the country were mormons. . . . Mr. Kendell assented to the wisdom of concealing these views from Mr. Little.[29]

On 8 June, Elder Little went to the White House again for his last interview with President Polk. The President assured Little that he regarded the Mormons as good citizens and had every intention to see that they were protected on the plains. He instructed the Department of War to make out the orders for a Mormon battalion. Colonel Thomas L. Kane helped work out the arrangements with Secretary of War W. L. Marcy.[30] Little later noted that Polk "expressed his good feelings to our people—regarded us as good citizens, said he had received our suffrages, and we should be remembered."[31]

Ironically, events played out contrary to Polk's vision. On 3 June, in anticipation of his meeting with Little, the President had sent orders to Colonel Stephen W. Kearny authorizing the enlistment of the Mormons, but in vague terms. While Polk anticipated the enlistment to take place once the Mormons arrived in the West, Kearny interpreted the instructions differently and on 19 June, sent Captain James Allen to Iowa with a "Circular to the Mormons," requesting five hundred volunteers immediately.[32] While some Latter-day Saints were skeptical, most shared Elder Wilford Woodruff's view, that "the President was very favorable to our people And had taken this course for our good. We were convinced that God had began to move upon the heart of the President . . . to begin to act for our interest and the general good of Zion."[33]

According to Young, President Polk's request was "the first offer we have ever had from the government to benefit us,"[34] and he was pleased that the Polk administration had "stretched its

*President Polk's call for a Mormon Battalion was in Brigham Young's words "the first offer we have ever had from the government to benefit us."*

arm to our assistance."[35] The battalion left Kanesville, Iowa, for Fort Leavenworth, Kansas, on 20 July and completed its march across the Southwest on 27 January 1847 at San Luis Rey, California, near San Diego.[36]

Brigham Young wrote Polk a letter dated 9 August 1846 in which he referred to the calling up of the Mormon Battalion as an act assuring the Saints "the personal friendship of the president."[37] Young also assured the President, "We have the fullest confidence in the friendly protection of President Polk," and that "our faith, prayers and blessing shall rest upon him."[38]

# ENDNOTES

1   Arnold K. Garr, "James K. Polk," in Garr, et al., *Encyclopedia of Latter-day Saint History,* 933–34.

2   Mark E. Byrnes, *James K. Polk: A Biographical Companion,* 139.

3   *Dave Leip's Atlas of U.S. Presidential Elections,* online at http://www.uselectionatlas.org. See also Byrnes, *James K. Polk: A Biographical Companion,* 139.

4   Roberts, *A Comprehensive History of the Church,* 2:523–24. See also Allen and Leonard, *The Story of the Latter-day Saints,* 223.

5   Richard E. Bennett, *We'll Find the Place: The Mormon Exodus 1846–1848,* 304.

6   *The Prophet of the Jubilee* (Welsh church periodical), January 1848, quoted in Givens, 92.

7   Roberts, *A Comprehensive History of the Church,* 3:445.

8   Susan Staker, ed., *Waiting for World's End: The Diaries of Wilford Woodruff,* 127.

9   Allen and Leonard, *The Story of the Latter-day Saints,* 204.

10  Scott Faulring, ed., *An American Prophet's Record: The Diaries and Journals of Joseph Smith,* 443.

11  *Columbus Enquirer* (Columbus, GA), 14 February 1844. See further discussion in Baker, *Murder of the Mormon Prophet,* 125–26.

12  *New York Daily Tribune* (New York, NY), 10 June 1844.

13  *Alton Telegraph* (Alton, IL), 11 May 1844. See also *Quincy Whig* (Quincy, IL), 11 May 1844. See discussion in Baker, *Murder of the Mormon Prophet,* 247–48.

14  Johnson letter, 31 May 1844, in Wayne Cutler, ed., *Correspondence of James K. Polk,* 7 (January–August 1844): 172.

15  Freidel, *Our Country's Presidents,* 77.

16  Allen and Leonard, *The Story of the Latter-day Saints,* 202.

17  Letter to Polk from John McNeely, 24 December 1845, *James K. Polk Papers,* Reel #43, Library of Congress Manuscripts Division, Washington, DC.

18  Letter from Hyde to Polk, 28 December 1845, in Cutler, *Correspondence of James K. Polk,* 442.

19  Leonard, *Nauvoo,* 509.

20  Polk, *The Diary of James K. Polk,* 1:205–6.

21  Allen and Leonard, *The Story of the Latter-day Saints,* 238–39.

22  "Camp of Israel: On the Pioneer Trail," *Church News,* 8 June 1996.

23  Polk, *James K. Polk, the Diary of a President 1845–1849,* 108–9.

24  William E.Berrett, *The Restored Church: Brief History of the Growth and Doctrines of The Church of Jesus Christ of Latter-day Saints,* 90.

25  "Camp of Israel: On the Pioneer Trail," *Church News,* 8 June 1996.

26  Polk, *The Diary of James K. Polk,* 1:444–46.

27  "Camp of Israel: On the Pioneer Trail," *Church News,* 8 June 1996.

28  Allen and Leonard, *The Story of the Latter-day Saints,* 239.

29  Polk, *The Diary of James K. Polk,* 1:450.

30  "Camp of Israel: On the Pioneer Trail," *Church News,* 8 June 1996.

31  Roberts, *A Comprehensive History of the Church,* 3:73–74.

32  Allen and Leonard, *The Story of the Latter-day Saints,* 239.

33  Staker, *Waiting for World's End: The Diaries of Wilford Woodruff,* 92.

34  Allen and Leonard, *The Story of the Latter-day Saints,* 238.

35  Norma Baldwin Ricketts, *The Mormon Battalion: U.S. Army of the West, 1846–1848,* 14.

36  *Church Almanac,* 539.

37  James R. Clark, comp., *Messages of the First Presidency of The Church of Jesus Christ of Latter-day Saints,* 1:300.

38  Roberts, *A Comprehensive History of the Church,* 3:90.

Brady          N.Y.

# ZACHARY TAYLOR

## *1849—1850*

When the Whigs nominated war hero Zachary Taylor for President, he was apolitical, having never voted in his life. As President, this Episcopal slaveholder from Virginia was determined to keep slavery from spreading to the territories, and for this reason, the future of the Great Basin—the Mormons' new home—became a matter of concern. The sixteen months of the Taylor administration saw the Mormons continuing to build their kingdom in the West, establishing the Perpetual Emigration Fund, commencing the Sunday School, beginning the *Deseret News,* and formally attempting to obtain statehood from the federal government for Deseret. It was during the course of these attempts that the Saints clashed with the twelfth President.

**Fall 1848:** While Elder Orson Hyde is traveling in the East and publishing a Church periodical, he is offered a free printing press if the Saints will publicly endorse Taylor's opponent, Democrat Lewis Cass. Hyde refuses and says he will support General Taylor, "press or no press."[1]

**Summer 1849:** Taylor launches his idea of allowing California and Deseret to enter the union together as a very large free state to offset the recent admission of the slave state Texas.

*Zachary Taylor considered "the exotic religious culture of the Mormons" to be "beyond redemption." Yet he hoped that a combined California and Deseret could join the Union and help end the debate of slavery in the territories, since they would all then be states.*

**1850:** As a result of receiving reports of Latter-day Saint polygamy and disloyalty (including a harsh anti-Mormon letter from the Prophet's brother William Smith), Taylor vows to never allow the Saints to have a state or territory of their own. Taylor considers "the exotic religious culture of the Mormons" to be "beyond redemption."[2]

**1850:** LDS representatives John M. Bernhisel and Almon W. Babbitt report of their meeting with Taylor, noting he "was not a friend of the Church" and that he refers to the Mormons as "a pack of outlaws."[3] An angry Brigham Young replies, "President Taylor you can't praise—you find nothing in him. Old General Taylor! What was he? A mere soldier, with regular army buttons on; no better to go at the head of brave troops than a dozen I could pick up between Leavenworth and Laramie."[4]

*Dr. John M. Bernhisel was sent east by Brigham Young to represent the Church's interests in Washington. He subsequently served as the Utah Territory's first delegate to Congress, during 1851–59 and 1861–63. As such, he represented Utah and the Saints with several U.S. Presidents, including Zachary Taylor, whom he found to be "not a friend of the Church" and who referred to Mormons as "a pack of outlaws."*

## TAYLOR'S PLAN FOR DESERET

During the previous presidential administration, Texas had become the twenty-eighth state. The recently sworn-in President Taylor worried that such a large slave state could be carved into several slave states, and saw the opportunity for a counterbalance out west. On 20 August 1849, General John Wilson arrived in Salt Lake City bearing word of Taylor's plan, which was to admit to the Union a large state including all of California, the proposed Mormon area of Deseret, and the remaining areas recently ceded by Mexico. This new "free state" would then automatically divide into two at the beginning of 1851—California and Deseret—thus offsetting the addition of slave state Texas.

Brigham Young was understandably excited about Zachary Taylor's scheme and sent Apostle Amasa M. Lyman to journey with General Wilson to California to help sell the idea there. However, snowstorms delayed the party from reaching California until late January 1850. By this time California had already adopted a constitution of its own, and the first legislature had been meeting in San Jose since 15 December. California Governor P. H. Burnett declared, "Texas and Maine might as well be made one state as Deseret and California," and much to the disappointment of the Mormons, the California legislature refused to support the President's proposal.[5]

Upon learning this, President Taylor instructed Congress that he "thought it best not to disturb that arrangement" and that it would not hurt to wait for a period to organize a state "of the territory which lies eastward of the new state of California." After all, he said, the area was "uninhabited, except in a settlement of our countrymen in the vicinity of Salt Lake."[6] Clearly he did not think much of the Mormons, except as part of his frustrated plan to simplify the issue of slavery in the territories.

## ENDNOTES

1    Peter Crawley, "The Constitution of the State of Deseret," *BYU Studies* 29, no. 4 (Fall 1989): 16.

2    Discussion in Elbert B. Smith, *The Presidencies of Zachary Taylor and Millard Fillmore.* See also Richard Neitzel Holzapfel and R. Q. Shupe, *My Servant Brigham: Portrait of a Prophet,* 51; Stanley B. Kimball, *Heber C. Kimball: Mormon Patriarch and Pioneer,* 197; "The Historians Corner," *BYU Studies* 12, no. 1 (Autumn 1971): 124; discussion on Deseret in K. Jack Bauer, *Zachary Taylor: Soldier, Planter, Statesman of the Old Southwest.*

3    John K. Carmack, *Tolerance,* 88.

4    Quoted in *Contributor* 4, no. 10 (July 1883). No. 10, Jedediah M. Grant, IV.

5    Roberts, *A Comprehensive History of the Church,* 3:437–40.

6    Zachary Taylor, Special Message to Congress, 23 January 1850, in *Message and Papers of the Presidents,* 5:26–30.

# MILLARD FILLMORE

## *1850–1853*

Millard Fillmore was born in 1800 in a log cabin near Moravia, in the Finger Lakes region of New York. He was reared there, only forty-five miles southeast of Joseph Smith's Palmyra, and had undoubtedly heard much about the Mormons. The Church of Jesus Christ was organized by Smith and his followers in 1830, in Fayette, New York—a mere twenty-five miles west of the Fillmore farm. Not only was he geographically close to the Saints, but he was also politically like-minded. After Joseph Smith published his presidential platform, for example, it was said by one newspaper editor that his views "do not differ very materially from those of . . . [then Congressman] Millard Fillmore."[1] In 1847, Fillmore was elected Comptroller of New York, where in 1848 he was selected by the Whigs to be General Zachary Taylor's running mate for the White House. Described as a peacemaker, quick to compromise, favoring moderation and conciliation, Fillmore emerged as a vice president and later a President who did his best to preserve the Union and keep peace with the Mormons.

**30 November 1849:** While in D.C. to lobby for the Saints' interest, Dr. John M. Bernhisel is introduced to Vice President Fillmore. "The vice-president kindly granted me the privilege of the floor of the senate during my sojourn in Washington," a pleased Bernhisel reported to Brigham Young.

**Summer 1850:** Fillmore appropriates $5,000 to territorial delegate Bernhisel to purchase a library for the new territory.[2] Another victory for the Latter-day Saints is Fillmore's decision to permit the retention of local bishops as government magistrates, which leaves the Church some official status in the territory.[3]

**September 1850:** President Fillmore signs into existence Utah Territory and appoints Brigham Young as territorial governor.

*The friendship of Millard Fillmore with the Saints is doubly honored by the territorial legislature when they name the new territorial capital Fillmore and the new county in central Utah Millard, where the capital would be located. Eventually the capital is returned to Salt Lake City, but the town and county remain a memorial to Millard Fillmore's friendship, as does the unfinished capitol there (shown here).*

**July 1851:** Due to negative newspaper reports, Fillmore is concerned about his choice of Brigham Young for governor. His concerns are assuaged by Thomas Kane.

**4 October 1851:** The friendship of Millard Fillmore to the Saints is doubly honored by the territorial legislature when they name the new territorial capital Fillmore and the new county in central Utah where the capital will be located Millard. Eventually the capital is returned to Salt Lake City, but the town and county remain a memorial to Millard Fillmore's friendship.

**Fall 1852:** First Presidency member Jedediah M. Grant and Apostle Orson Pratt call on President Fillmore.[4]

## FILLMORE CREATES UTAH TERRITORY AND APPOINTS YOUNG AS GOVERNOR

To facilitate Deseret's application for statehood, the Saints sent Dr. Bernhisel east once again to help lobby for its passage. On 9 September 1850, Congress refused Deseret's admission to the Union and instead created Utah Territory, which President Fillmore signed into existence. Dr. Bernhisel then began working with President Fillmore to ensure Latter-day Saint representation among the federal appointees, and to see about appointing Brigham Young as governor.[5]

*Thanks to the appointment by President Fillmore, Brigham Young became the first governor of the Utah Territory, an enormous victory in the Saints' desire for self-rule.*

Fillmore replied to Bernhisel "that officers, by all means, should be appointed among your members."[6] Fillmore, a Unitarian, was tolerant of other religions. He could see no reason to deny an office to a person because of his religious affiliation. He was further influenced by the pro-Mormon sentiments of Colonel Thomas L. Kane of Philadelphia.

Consequently, Fillmore took a moderate stance when making appointments for the new territory. On the one hand, he respected the advice given to him by Colonel Kane and Dr. Bernhisel. On the other, he did not want to see Utah operate as a total theocracy. Therefore, of the appointments made by Fillmore at that time, the territory's new secretary, chief justice, and associate justice were strangers to the Mormons from other states; but the second associate justice, the U.S. marshal, the U.S. attorney, and most importantly the governor, were members of the Church.[7]

## QUESTIONS OF UTAH'S LOYALTY RAISED TO FILLMORE

In the first week of July 1851, the *Buffalo Courier* printed a malicious attack on "Governor Brigham Young, of Utah Territory." It claimed that Young was levying unjust taxes, abusing democracy, and "leaguing with the Indians to harass people on the road to California." The New York newspaper found its way to a shocked and angered President, who fired off a letter to Thomas Kane on 4 July 1851:

> My Dear Sir:
> I have just cut the enclosed slip from the *Buffalo Courier*. It brings serious charges against Brigham Young, governor of Utah, and falsely charges that I knew them to be true. You will recollect that I relied much upon you for the moral character and standing of Mr. Young. You knew him and had known him in Utah. You are a Democrat, but I doubt not will truly state whether these charges against the moral character of Governor Young are true. Please return the article with your letter. Not recollecting your given name, I shall address this letter to you as the son of Judge Kane.
> I am in great haste,
> Truly yours,
> MILLARD FILLMORE

Colonel Kane responded with the following reply dated 11 July:

The President:

> My Dear Sir: I have no wish to evade the responsibility of having vouched for the character of Mr. Brigham Young, of Utah, and his fitness for the station he now occupies. I reiterate without reserve, the statement of his excellent capacity, energy, and integrity, which I made you prior his appointment. . . . I am ready to offer you this assurance for publication in any form you care to indicate, and challenge contradiction from any respectable authority.

I am, sir, with high respect and esteem, your most obedient servant,

THOMAS L. KANE

President Fillmore was satisfied with Kane's answer and never again questioned his appointment of Governor Young.[8]

Not long after arriving in Utah Territory in August, three of Fillmore's appointments returned to the East with negative reports about Brigham Young and the Mormons.[9] The Latter-day Saints' loyalty to the government was quickly reaffirmed in a letter from Governor Young to President Fillmore in September 1851: "Now sir, I will simply state that I know it to be true—that no people exist who are more friendly to the government of the United States than the people of this territory. The constitution they revere and the laws they seek to honor."[10] Similar letters were sent to the President from Jedediah M. Grant, mayor of Salt

*Thomas L. Kane was a stalwart friend of the Mormons and advocated for the Church's interests with Presidents Polk, Fillmore, and Buchanan. Even after successfully lobbying for Brigham Young's appointment as governor, Colonel Kane continued to defend him in correspondence with President Fillmore.*

Lake City, and again by Colonel Kane, supporting Young's position. President Fillmore backed up the Saints when he asked Secretary of State Daniel Webster to order the runaway officers to return to their positions or to resign. They resigned, and Fillmore appointed three new officials to Utah who were well received and became highly respected.[11] Dr. Bernhisel assured Governor Young that the new appointees were "gentlemen who were highly recommended for integrity and high, moral character, and as being unprejudiced." The delegate added that "President Fillmore was our friend and had done all he could for the interests of Utah."[12] On another occasion, Bernhisel said Fillmore was "a noble, high minded, accomplished gentleman, and the more intimately I become acquainted with him, the more he excites my respect and admiration."[13]

## FILLMORE'S LEGACY AMONG THE SAINTS

In the Whig convention of 1852, the delegates ignored the moderate incumbent, Millard Fillmore, and rallied behind General Winfield Scott. Scott went on to lose to Democrat Franklin Pierce in November, and Fillmore handed off the presidency to Pierce in March 1853. Later that year, at a Fourth of July celebration in Salt Lake City, Fillmore was celebrated by the Mormons. Daniel H. Wells—a legislator, future Salt Lake City mayor, and later counselor to Brigham Young—proposed, "*Ex-President Fillmore*: May his retirement be as happy and prosperous as his administration was successful and glorious; and the American people learn to know and appreciate their good men before they lose them."[14]

Later, in an 1856 general conference, Jedediah M. Grant derided the Buchanan administration for sending Johnston's army to Utah and declared that Millard Fillmore "would scorn to threaten an innocent people with the armies of the nation."[15] President Grant also suggested that the ideal pro-Mormon ticket for that year's presidential election would be Millard Fillmore for President and Stephen A. Douglas for vice president.[16] President Heber C. Kimball later remarked in a conference, "President Fillmore . . . he did us good. God bless him!"[17]

*President Fillmore, shown standing, was described by Utah's territorial delegate as a friend who "had done all he could for the interests of Utah . . . a noble, high minded, accomplished gentleman, and the more intimately I become acquainted with him, the more he excites my respect and admiration."*

# ENDNOTES

1   *Erie Observer* (Erie, PA), 23 March 1844.

2   Roberts, *A Comprehensive History of the Church,* 3:502–3.

3   Susan Easton Black and Larry C. Porter, eds., *Lion of the Lord: Essays on the Life and Service of Brigham Young,* 175.

4   Jenson, *Encyclopedic History of the Church,* "Washington (DC)."

5   Peter Crawley, "The Constitution of the State of Deseret," *BYU Studies* 29, no. 4 (Fall 1989). See also Roberts, *A Comprehensive History of the Church,* 3:509–10; Nibley, *Brigham Young: The Man and His Work,* 160–61.

6   Quoted in Carmack, *Tolerance,* 88–89.

7   Nibley, *Brigham Young: The Man and His Work,* 160.

8   Nibley, *Brigham Young: The Man and His Work,* 164–65. See also *Journal History,* 4 July 1851, LDS Church Archives, Salt Lake City.

9   Berrett, *The Restored Church,* 116.

10  Brigham Young to Millard Fillmore, *Manuscript History of Brigham Young,* 29 September 1851.

11  Berrett, *The Restored Church,* 116.

12  Roberts, *A Comprehensive History of the Church,* 3:543.

13  Quoted in Carmack, *Tolerance,* "Tolerant Friends."

14  *Deseret News,* 10 July 1853.

15  Conference Report, April 1856.

16  *Journal History,* 23 March 1856, 2.

17  Heber C. Kimball, "Organization—Destruction of Zion's Enemies—Oneness of Spirit in the Priesthood, Etc.," sermon, LDS Church Archives, Salt Lake City.

# FRANKLIN
# PIERCE

*1853—1857*

After Fillmore stepped down, there was some Mormon anxiety on whether or not Franklin Pierce would allow Brigham Young to remain the governor of Utah Territory. This single issue dominated the relationship between the Saints and the fourteenth President.

**19 June 1853:** Three months after Pierce's inauguration, Brigham Young expresses optimism that he will remain governor. "I have no fears whatever of Franklin Pierce excusing me from office, and saying that another man shall be the Governor of this territory," he remarks in the Tabernacle.[1]

**September 1854:** President Pierce secretly appoints Colonel Edward J. Steptoe as Utah's new governor. Once arriving in Utah and recognizing Brigham Young's preeminent position in the community, he joins other prominent "Gentiles" in Salt Lake City who send a petition to Pierce urging Young's continuation as governor.

**Early Spring 1855:** Apostle John Taylor, John Bernhisel, and Nathaniel Felt call on Pierce to lobby for the continuation of Brigham Young as governor.

**May 1855:** After concluding that "wisdom and the public peace demanded that Brigham Young be left undisturbed," Pierce reappoints Brigham Young to a second term as governor of Utah.[2]

**March 1856:** Apostles John Taylor and George A. Smith go to Washington, where they have several interviews with President Pierce to lobby for statehood and commend the decision of keeping Brigham Young as governor.[3]

**31 January 1857:** Although Pierce is a lame duck that will leave the White House within weeks, Brigham Young writes Orson Pratt: "It is expected by some that . . . a [new] Governor, will be appointed before Franklin Pierce leaves the White House."[4] His fears are unfounded.

## PIERCE ATTEMPTS TO REPLACE GOVERNOR BRIGHAM YOUNG

The year following the 1853 Indian murders of members of the U.S. Topographical Survey, President Pierce ordered Lieutenant Colonel Edward J. Steptoe and three hundred men to Utah to capture the murderers. Secretly, however, Steptoe carried sealed orders from Pierce to replace Brigham Young as governor of the territory.[5] Steptoe arrived in the territory on 31 August 1854 and observed how well Young was governing Utah.[6] Recognizing Young's preeminent position in the community, Steptoe declined Pierce's offer and joined the non-Mormon chief justice, other federal officials, and prominent "Gentile" businessmen in Utah in signing a petition urging the President to reappoint Brigham Young.[7] Utah delegate Bernhisel met with the President shortly after these letters were received:

*Appointed by President Pierce to replace Brigham Young as Utah's governor, Edward J. Steptoe eventually declined after seeing firsthand Young's popularity in the territory.*

> The President seems quite friendly and stated at a recent interview that he had received letters from Colonel Steptoe and Chief Justice Kinney, speaking in high terms of the Governor and the people of Utah, and added that if he did not appoint Governor Young he would appoint no one but a man of the highest character, believing that it would be better for our people that such a one should be appointed, for he would do us justice, and speak well of us, which would do much toward removing the prejudice against us, but I still urged the reappointment of Governor Young. The President has no idea of interfering with the domestic relations of our Territory.[8]

For a while the Saints believed that Young would not be reappointed, but having liked Colonel Steptoe, they concluded that "President Pierce made the best appointment for us that our enemies would let him."[9] At a time when Dr. Bernhisel in Washington D.C. thought that Steptoe was going to replace Young, he wrote the following to Franklin D. Richards, an Apostle who was then in England:

> His Excellency [Pierce] spoke in the most exalted terms of Colonel Steptoe, saying that he was a gentleman and a scholar, and the most amiable and just man he ever knew. The Colonel sustains a high character here and numbers among his friends the Hon. Secretary of War. Since Governor Young's reappointment could not be secured, which is a source of profound regret to us all, I know of no one whom I suppose would be more acceptable than Colonel Steptoe.[10]

## JOHN TAYLOR'S VISIT WITH PRESIDENT PIERCE

In the early spring of 1855, Apostle John Taylor went to Washington to lobby President Pierce about retaining Governor Young. Along with Dr. Bernhisel and Nathaniel Felt, Elder Taylor called on the White House, where the President admitted that he wanted to replace Young as governor more out of popular sentiment rather than acting from any relish he had for the undertaking.[11]

> Gentlemen, you are well acquainted with the immense outside pressure that popular prejudice has arrayed against your people; this obliges me as Chief Magistrate to make some show in responding to it, so I have appointed Colonel Steptoe as Governor of Utah; but you will readily conceive that Colonel Steptoe, holding an honorable position in the United States army, will not be willing to resign that position for the uncertain tenure of a four years Governorship of that distant Territory.

Pierce went on to speak "very highly of the urbanity, wise conservatism and honor of Colonel Steptoe."[12] Taylor told the President that they were pleased Colonel Steptoe was so honorable a gentleman and that the people of Utah had been frequently abused by ambitious politicians "who seemed determined to make a hobby of the Mormon question whereon to ride into power." Pierce assured him that Colonel Steptoe would not resort to such meanness.

The White House as it appeared in the mid 1850s when LDS leaders John Taylor, John M. Bernhisel, and Nathaniel Felt called upon Franklin Pierce.

Elder Taylor took the occasion to tell the President about the pioneer trek west, how Utah was settled, and how Brigham Young was the undisputed leader of the territory as a result. Taylor told Pierce that if he believed in the principle of popular sovereignty, then he ought to recognize that "Brigham Young would be the universal choice of the people." Nonetheless, the Apostle assured the President that if he felt compelled to appoint a new governor, the Saints "recognized the authority of the President of the United States, and would submit to any legal or constitutional enactment."[13]

Future Church president John Taylor had a significant discussion with President Pierce in 1855, where he boldly defended keeping Brigham Young as Utah's governor, and the scriptural basis for plural marriage.

"Well," said President Pierce, "what about your polygamy?"

"Mr. Pierce," said Elder Taylor, "we read about such a man as Abraham," and he proceeded to outline the marital status of Abraham, Jacob, Moses, and David as given in the Bible. "Mr. Pierce," said Taylor, "it is possible that we of the nineteenth century have not been able to instruct the Lord very much in regard to these matters. Probably He knew just as much about them then as we do now, and that in regard to our marital laws, we may have made some mistakes." To which the President replied, "Well, I cannot say."[14]

In the end, Franklin Pierce was neither the friend to the Latter-day Saints that his predecessor was, nor the enemy of Utah that his successor would be.

# ENDNOTES

1 An address delivered by President Young in the Tabernacle, Salt Lake City, 19 June 1853.

2 Roy Franklin Nichols, *Franklin Pierce: Young Hickory of the Granite Hills,* 402–3. See also Nibley, *Brigham Young: The Man and His Work,* 230.

3 Francis M. Gibbons, *John Taylor: Mormon Philosopher, Prophet of God,* 146. See also B. H. Roberts, *Life of John Taylor,* 265; Blaine M. Yorgason, *Courageous Defender of Truth: The Story of John Taylor,* 297–98.

4 Brigham Young to Orson Pratt, 31 January 1857, quoted in Nibley, *Brigham Young: The Man and His Work,* 269.

5 Stanley B. Kimball, *Heber C. Kimball: Mormon Patriarch and Pioneer,* 260–61.

6 Richard Neitzel Holzapfel, et al, *On this Day in the Church: An Illustrated Almanac of the Latter-day Saints,* 169.

7 Alexander, *Things in Heaven and Earth,* 176–77.

8 Bernhisel letter to Franklin Richards, quoted in Nibley, *Brigham Young: The Man and His Work,* 227.

9 *Deseret News,* 8 March 1855.

10 Bernhisel letter to Franklin Richards, quoted in Nibley, *Brigham Young: The Man and His Work,* 227.

11 Roberts, *Life of John Taylor,* 264.

12 Jenson, *LDS Biographical Encyclopedia,* 2:380.

13 Roberts, *Life of John Taylor,* 264–65.

14 John Taylor, "Discourse of 10 February 1884," LDS Church Archives, Salt Lake City.

# JAMES
# BUCHANAN

## *1857–1861*

Although Franklin Pierce did not replace Brigham Young as governor of Utah Territory, his successor James Buchanan would exert tremendous military and political muscle to successfully make that change. He referred to the mixture of church and state in the territory as "a strange system of terrorism" that had to be stopped.[1] The resulting "Utah War" would shatter the Mormon's fragile faith in the American presidency that had been carefully crafted during the Fillmore and Pierce administrations and sour their federal relations for decades to come. Ironically, the Saints' initial relations with James Buchanan were positive.

**7 June 1846:** After Elder James C. Little, president of the Eastern States Mission, and Mormon friend Thomas Kane meet with President Polk to discuss what would later be known as the Mormon Battalion, the two meet with then-Secretary of State Buchanan to discuss the matter.[2]

**Summer 1847:** While in the nation's capital on a "begging mission," Latter-day Saints Charles C. Dana and Robert Campbell meet with Secretary Buchanan, who donates ten dollars to the beleaguered Saints.[3]

**November 1856:** Buchanan defeats the first Republican Party presidential candidate, John C. Fremont, who campaigns against "those twin relics of barbarism—Polygamy and Slavery." The Saints are thrilled with the news. "We learn that Buchanan is elected as President of the United States," wrote Elder Woodruff, "which we would far prefer that he be our President than Fremont."[4]

**28 May 1857:** Responding to complaints by disgruntled federal officials fleeing Utah, the newly sworn-in President calls up 2,500 troops to escort non-Mormon Alfred Cumming of Georgia to Utah to replace Brigham Young as territorial governor.[5] It is the largest military action in the United States between the Mexican War and the Civil War.

**24 July 1857:** Brigham Young and the Saints are panicked to receive word that the President is sending the army to Utah. They fear being driven from their homes once again, as has happened in Ohio, Missouri, and Illinois. The guerilla tactics to slow the advancing troops become known as the "Utah War."

**26 June 1858:** The army sent by Buchanan and led by General Albert Sidney Johnston peacefully enters the Salt Lake Valley. They stay in Cedar Valley, west of Utah Lake, until they are called back east in 1861 to fight the Civil War.

**2 March 1861:** Two days before Lincoln's inauguration as Buchanan's successor, Buchanan fires a final parting shot at the Mormons by signing a bill dividing Utah Territory and creating Nevada Territory out of Utah's western half.[6]

## THE "UTAH WAR"

After word reached Utah in 1857 that the U.S. Army was advancing, elaborate military defense preparations began. Later that year, guerilla warfare took place on the plains of Wyoming as Mormon scouts attempted to delay the troops. The beleaguered U.S. Army finally made it to Fort Bridger but had been greatly taxed due to destruction of wagon trains, ambushes, theft of oxen, and early snowfall. "It was a scene," said the *Atlantic Monthly,* "which could be paralleled only in the retreat of the French from Warsaw."[7] Meanwhile, Brigham Young had the Saints retreat south to Utah Valley and prepare for the worst. Back east, President Buchanan was receiving severe criticism for sending such a large expedition without first investigating the charges and for sending an army west so late in the season. "Buchanan's Blunder," as the little war began to be called, was becoming a sore spot for the administration.

At the height of the tensions, President Young sized up the fifteenth President, laying much of the blame on those ill-advising him:

James Buchanan, who is now sitting in the chair of state, and presiding over this great republic, is naturally a passive, docile, benevolent, and good man—that is his natural disposition, I will venture. Arouse him, and he has been a man who could make flaming speeches. He is now bound up; they have the fetters upon his feet; he is handcuffed; his elbows are pinioned; he is bound on every side; and they make him do as they please. . . . The President hearkens to the clamour around him; and, as did Pontius Pilate, in the case of Jesus Christ, has washed his hands, saying, "I am clear of the blood of those Latter-day Saints. Gentlemen, you have dictated, and I will order a soldiery and officials to Utah."[8]

During the height of the Utah War, President Buchanan was in Washington negotiating the U.S. purchase of Alaska (the Russians ultimately thought his price of $5 million too low, and it fell to later officials to finish the deal). In the fall of 1857, he discussed the purchase with Russian minister, Baron de Stoeokl. According to one Buchanan biographer, "since the Mormons seemed determined to set up an independent nation in Utah, Buchanan toyed with the idea of colonizing them in Alaska. There was a rumor that they might go there, anyway; and when Stoeokl asked the President whether they would go as conquerors or colonists, Buchanan

*Albert Sidney Johnston carried out President Buchanan's orders by leading the U.S. Army's expedition to Utah. Johnston's Army, as the 2,500 troops were sometimes called, was the largest military action in the United States between the Mexican War and the Civil War. Johnston eventually died at the Battle of Shiloh during the Civil War as one of the most revered Confederate generals.*

replied with a laugh that it mattered little to him, provided he got rid of them." Needless to say, Buchanan was unable to carry out his fantasy of running the Mormons to Alaska—or anywhere else for that matter.[9]

Earlier, adventurer Walter Murray Gibson (who later joined the LDS Church, served a mission to Hawaii and was excommunicated for selling priesthood offices there) approached James Buchanan with a plan to relocate the Mormons to the island of New Guinea. He thought the Buchanan administration would like the idea, but Buchanan considered the project too expensive and impractical and refused to support it further.[10]

In Buchanan's first annual message to Congress, which he submitted 8 December 1857, he declared that

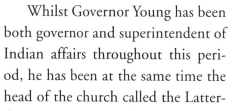

*James Buchanan not only sent the U.S. Army to Utah to replace Brigham Young as governor, but he also plotted in vain with the Russian government to buy Alaska and banish the Mormons there.*

Whilst Governor Young has been both governor and superintendent of Indian affairs throughout this period, he has been at the same time the head of the church called the Latter-day Saints, and professes to govern its members and dispose of their property by direct inspiration and authority from the Almighty. His power has been, therefore, absolute over both church and State.

The people of Utah, almost exclusively, belong to this church, and believing with a fanatical spirit that he is governor of the Territory by divine appointment, they obey his commands as if these were direct revelations from Heaven. If, therefore, he chooses that his government shall come into collision with the government of the United States, the members of the Mormon church will yield implicit obedience to his will.[11]

Later in the message he lamented that the federal appointees in Utah had fled in disgust, and that "there no longer remains any government in Utah but the despotism of Brigham Young." Buchanan wanted to emphasize that sending the army to Utah was not about the Mormons' religious belief so much as it was about insubordination:

With the religious opinions of the Mormons, as long as they remained mere opinions, however deplorable in themselves and revolting to the moral and religious sentiments of all Christendom, I had no right to interfere.[12]

Along these lines he later said in his missive to the Saints:

Do not deceive yourselves nor try to mislead others by propagating the idea that this is a crusade against your religion. The Constitution and laws of this country can take no notice of your creed, whether it be true or false. That is a question between your God and yourselves, in which I disclaim all right to interfere. If you obey the laws, keep the peace, and respect the just rights of others, you will be perfectly secure and may live on in your present faith or change it for another at your pleasure.[13]

## THE RESOLUTION OF "BUCHANAN'S BLUNDER"

Thomas L. Kane offered the White House to go to Utah as a mediator, and his offer was gratefully accepted, although he would travel at his own expense and without official position.[14] "I come as an ambassador from the chief executive of our nation," Kane took the liberty to declare. He successfully persuaded Young that the Saints should let the new governor enter Utah without incident. He also pointed out to Brigham that "so far he [Buchanan] has made an excellent president. He has an able cabinet. They are more united and work together better than some of our former cabinets have done."[15] Kane then traveled through the snow to Fort Bridger, where he persuaded Governor Cumming to return with him to Salt Lake City without a military escort.[16] Colonel Kane, regarded as "Buchanan's friend" by the President's biographers, returned to Washington and "convinced the president that the Mormons were a peace-loving people and that Brigham Young would cooperate in any honest program of the Administration."[17]

Buchanan sent Major Ben McCullock and U.S. Senator-elect Isaac Powell as peace commissioners to Utah, along with an offer of pardon if the Saints reaffirmed their loyalty to the United States. The commissioners arrived in Salt Lake City on 6 June 1858, and a copy of President Buchanan's "Proclamation to the People of Utah" was presented to Brigham Young. The pompously worded document charged the Mormons with treason and rebellion. "I, James Buchanan, President of the United States, have thought proper to issue this, my proclamation . . . offering to the inhabitants of Utah, who shall submit to the laws, a free pardon for the seditions and treason

*Alfred Cumming of Georgia was James Buchanan's choice to replace Brigham Young as governor of Utah Territory. He was escorted to Utah by the U.S. Army in 1858 and remained as governor there until 1861.*

heretofore by them committed."[18] As one might expect, the Saints were indignant at the idea that they needed to be pardoned, for they had never been disloyal, but they accepted it in order to establish peace.[19] Brigham Young remarked:

As far as I am concerned, I thank President Buchanan for forgiving me, but I really cannot tell what I've done. I know one thing, and that is that the people called Mormons are a loyal and law-abiding people, and have ever been. Neither President Buchanan nor any one else can contradict that statement.[20]

Wilford Woodruff wrote of Buchanan, "He had got into a bad scrape and wished to get out of it the best he could. . . . The Lord has heard our prayers," he added, "and the President of the United States has been brought to a point where he has been obliged to ask for peace."[21]

After hearing word that Governor Cumming had arrived peacefully in Salt Lake City, President Buchanan sent a message to Congress declaring "our difficulties with the Territory of Utah have terminated, and the reign of the Constitution and the laws have been restored."[22]

## CONTINUED ENMITY BETWEEN THE SAINTS AND BUCHANAN

Brigham Young remained upset at the President in the months that followed. "I will say, in reference to President Buchanan, that, for his outrageous wickedness in this movement, he shall wear the yoke as long as he lives; he shall be led about by his party with the yoke on his neck, until they have accomplished their ends, and he can do no more for them; and his name shall be forgotten."[23]

Buchanan's distaste for the Mormons also remained. On 8 April 1859 he even requested of Lord Clarendon, "I would thank you to keep your Mormons at home." He informed the British secretary of foreign affairs that "the English Mormon is a strange article. Although the glories of Brigham have faded, yet he believes him still, with unfaltering fidelity, to be a prophet sent from God to reform & regulate the affairs of all mankind in this lower world. The American Mormons are fast losing their faith."[24] Clarendon could clearly do nothing to stem emigration to America, and by the end of the decade nearly 20,000 British Latter-day Saints had crossed the Atlantic en route to Zion.[25]

According to Thomas Kane, who met with Buchanan several times in March and April 1860, "the old gentleman" seemed to have learned his lesson from the Utah War and had taken up a stance of "leave the Mormons alone." Buchanan feared a polygamy bill would soon pass both houses of Congress and insisted he did not want the Mormons disturbed. He claimed he "would use his influence with his friends to have unfriendly and unjust legislation arrested." According to Kane's report to George Q. Cannon, Buchanan "among all his colleagues thinks he is our best friend," and Kane thought it best the Saints "encourage him in the feeling to some extent, as with his peculiar turn he thinks . . . a sense of pride in being thought of as our protector." Kane added that "the old man has done well in several instances, better almost than he could have expected, having manifested interest on several occasions in our affairs and on our behalf."[26]

"The administration of King James Buchanan, what an administration!" declared Brigham Young in February 1861, summing up the lame-duck President mere weeks before his term expired. "What is the difficulty with King James? His high position and exalted opinion of himself so addled and bewildered him, that he said, 'I am the greatest man in the nation! I am the Chief Magistrate!!'"[27] George Q. Cannon also saw Buchanan as a hypocrite. When a New York newspaper reported of a scandalous free-love household, Cannon wrote, "Where are James Buchanan and the U.S. Army, those knights-errant of morality?"[28] Thus the Mormons had a great dislike of James Buchanan, a dislike brought on by his mistrust of their religion and its leaders.

*Unfriendly to the Saints throughout his administration, President Buchanan asked the British government to "keep your Mormons at home" and chopped the Utah Territory in half two days before leaving office.*

# ENDNOTES

1   James Buchanan, *The Works of James Buchanan,* 10:202–3.

2   Roberts, *A Comprehensive History of the Church,* 3:74.

3   Bennett, *We'll Find the Place: The Mormon Exodus 1846–1848,* 304, quoted in Givens, 92–93.

4   Scott G. Kenney, ed., *Wilford Woodruff's Journal, 1833–1898,* 5:5.

5   *Church Almanac,* 542.

6   *Church Almanac,* 542–43.

7   Quoted in Philip Shriver Klein, *President James Buchanan: A Biography,* 316.

8   Nibley, *Brigham Young: The Man and His Work,* 290.

9   Klein, *President James Buchanan: A Biography,* 325.

10  R. Lanier Britsch, *Unto the Islands of the Sea: A History of the Latter-day Saints in the Pacific,* 119.

11  James Buchanan, *The Works of James Buchanan,* 10:152.

12  Buchanan, *The Works of James Buchanan,* 10:152.

13  Buchanan, *The Works of James Buchanan,* 10:204.

14  Roberts, *A Comprehensive History of the Church,* 4:347–48.

15  Nibley, *Brigham Young: The Man and His Work,* 321.

16  Allen and Leonard, *The Story of the Latter-day Saints,* 315.

17  Klein, *President James Buchanan: A Biography,* 316–17.

18  Nibley, *Brigham Young: The Man and His Work,* 335–36. The proclamation in its entirety is found in *Messages and Papers of the Presidents,* 5:493–95.

19  Allen and Leonard, *The Story of the Latter-day Saints,* 317.

20  Spencer and Harmer, *Brigham Young at Home,* 106. Also quoted in Susan Evans McCloud, *Brigham Young: An Inspiring Personal Biography,* 216.

21  Quoted in Francis M. Gibbons, *Wilford Woodruff: Wondrous Worker, Prophet of God,* 209.

22  "Message on Affairs in Utah," 10 June 1858. Printed in James Buchanan, *The Works of James Buchanan,* 10:217.

23  Remarks by Brigham Young delivered in the Bowery, Salt Lake City, 6 September 1857, in *Journal of Discourses,* 5:211–12.

24  Buchanan, *The Works of James Buchanan,* 10:317–18.

25  *Church Almanac,* 428.

26  Davis Bitton, *George Q. Cannon: A Biography,* 98.

27  Brigham Young, "Human Intelligence and Freedom—National Administrative Movements, &c." in *Journal of Discourses,* 8:321–22.

28  Bitton, *George Q. Cannon,* 92.

# ABRAHAM LINCOLN

## 1861—1865

As a young legislator in Illinois, Abraham Lincoln knew the Mormons, likely met Joseph Smith, and helped approve the Nauvoo Charter. His path crossed with the Mormons later during his presidency when he signed the first antipolygamy legislation into law, but he also gained popularity with the Saints through a "let them be" philosophy. In many ways, Lincoln's laissez-faire attitude toward the Mormons was an oasis from the harshness of Presidents from Pierce through Arthur, a thirty-two-year period.

**Winter 1838–39:** A tall thirty-year-old Whig legislator named Abraham Lincoln writes of a "strange new sect" called "Mormons" that are moving into the state.[1]

**1839:** For five days, Lincoln and Joseph Smith are both in the Illinois capital at the same time and possibly meet. This occurs again in 1842 and 1843.[2]

**1 March 1840:** Intrigued with the political support the Mormons could give, Lincoln writes to a Whig ally of a conversation he's had recently with Joseph Smith when the latter passed through Springfield. "We will procure the names of some of his people here and send them to you before long," he writes to his friend.[3] Lincoln also remarks that "Joseph Smith is an admirer of mine, and that a few documents had better be mailed to the Mormon people."[4]

**November 1840:** Lincoln's name is on the ballot to be chosen as a presidential elector for Whig candidate William Henry Harrison but he does not receive the votes of Nauvoo. The Saints claim no ill feeling toward Lincoln, but rather, they desire to divide their vote to "show kindness to the Democrats, for the part they took in welcoming the saints."[5]

**December 1840:** Lincoln assists the Saints in getting the Nauvoo Charter approved in the Illinois legislature.

**December 1842:** The Lincolns live in the same boarding house as Willard Richards and other Church leaders who are preparing for the Prophet's visit to Springfield, and undoubtedly dine and converse with them.[6]

*In the famous Lincoln–Douglas debates, Lincoln tried to pin the Mormons on the Democrats, arguing that if Stephen Douglas is for a state's right to self-determination on slavery, then logically he must also support self-determination on polygamy.*

**1 January 1843:** Mary Todd Lincoln attends Joseph Smith's extradition hearing, held in the Tinsley Building—the same building that houses Lincoln's law office.[7]

**1844:** Following the publication of caustic accusations of Joseph Smith written by an excommunicated member of the First Presidency, Lincoln writes to a friend, "[John C.] Bennett's Mormon disclosiers are making some little stir here, but not very great."[8]

**June 1844:** Lincoln confesses to be "keeping abreast of the Mormon situation." He serves two legislative terms with Mark Aldrich, who is later one of the mob indicted for the murder of Joseph and Hyrum Smith; his cousin, Abram, serves on the grand jury which indicts Smith's murderers;[9] and his longtime secretary, John Hay, is familiar enough with the martyrdom to write an account of it for the *Atlantic Monthly*.[10]

[Continued on page 342]

RECEIVED of the Librarian of Congress, the following Books, which I promise to return, undefaced, to the said Librarian, within the time hereinafter specified, or to forfeit and pay twice the value thereof; as also twenty cents per day for each day's detention beyond the limited time of a Folio Volume; ten cents per day for the detention of a Quarto Volume; and five cents per day for the detention of an Octavo or smaller Volume.

*President of the U.S.*

| WHEN RECEIVED. | WHEN RETURNED. | FOLIO. To be returned in three weeks. | QUARTO. To be returned in two weeks. | OCTAVO OR SMALLER VOLUME. To be returned in one week. | LAWS, STATE PAPERS. To be returned five days before the close of the Session. |
|---|---|---|---|---|---|
| '61 Aug 5 | Oct 3 | | | ✓ Oeuvres de Victor Hugo, 9th v. Le Roi s'Amuse | |
| Oct 3 | Nov 16 | | | ✓ Do | — 13th V — |
| Nov 18 | 1862 July 29 | | | ✓ Do vol 11. | |
| " " | " " " " | | | ✓ Gunnison's Mormons | |
| " " | " " " " | | | ✓ Hyde's Mormonism | |
| " " | " " " " | | | ✓ Book of Mormon | |
| " 22 | 1861. Dec 6 | | | ✓ U. S. Constitution 8vo. 1783. | |
| " " | " " | | | ✓ Do 8vo 1856. | |
| " " | 1862 July 29 | | | ✓ Mormonism in all ages | |
| " " | " Dec 24 | | | ✓ Mormons, or Latter Day Saints | |
| " " | " Dec 6 | | | ✓ Jefferson. Wks Vols 4.7.8.9. | |
| Dec 6 | 1862 Feb 17 | | | ✓ Museum Volksmaaden | |
| " 13 | " July 29 | | | ✓ Mountains Display of Heraldry | |
| " 30 | s | | | Constitutions 1783. | |
| " " | | | | Do 1856 nov. | |

As seen by these ledgers from the Library of Congress, President Lincoln checked out the Book of Mormon and several books relating to the Latter-day Saints. He kept the Book of Mormon for eight months.

---

**1857:** In the famous Lincoln-Douglas debates, Lincoln tries to pin the Mormons on the Democrats, arguing that if Stephen Douglas is for a state's right to self-determination on slavery, then logically he must also support self-determination on polygamy.[11]

**November 1860:** After election day, Brigham Young tells Wilford Woodruff, "I hope that Abel Lincoln was Elected President of the United States yesterday."[12] President Young and Lincoln know each other from their Illinois years.[13]

**18 November 1861:** In preparation for making an appointment of Utah's new territorial governor, Lincoln checks out the Book of Mormon from the Library of Congress (not returning it until 29 July 1862).[14] Over the next few weeks he also borrows *Mormonism in All Ages;* John Hyde's 1857 book *Mormonism: Its Leaders and Designs;* and Lieutenant Gunnison's 1856 book *The*

*During the Civil War, Lincoln recognized Brigham Young as the principal leader in Utah and bypassed the territorial governor by wiring Young directly to request a cavalry company to protect the telegraph and mail routes.*

*Mormons or Latter-day Saints, in the Valley of the Great Salt Lake: A History of their rise and progress, peculiar doctrines, present condition, and prospects.*[15]

**Spring 1862:** Recognizing Brigham Young as the prime force in Utah, the President bypasses the territorial governor by wiring Young directly, authorizing him to "raise, arm and equip a company of cavalry for ninety days service, to protect the property of the telegraph and overland mail companies."[16]

**9 June 1862:** Apostle George Q. Cannon and Utah delegate William H. Hooper lobby Lincoln for Utah statehood.

**8 July 1862:** Abraham Lincoln signs the Morrill Bill into law, which defines polygamy as bigamy, declares it a crime, unincorporates The Church of Jesus Christ of Latter-day Saints, and prohibits any religious organization in the territories from owning real estate valued at more than fifty thousand dollars.[17] Even though Lincoln signs the first antipolygamy legislation into law (he rarely uses the veto power), he avoids enforcing it.

**June 1863:** Lincoln heeds the petitions of the Mormons and removes from office Stephen S. Harding, the anti-Mormon governor of Utah who has known the Smith family in Palmyra and has persecuted the Saints ever since.[18] Harding's replacement, James Duane Doty, is purposely sent by Lincoln to Utah since he has a reputation as a "very discreet gentleman" and is supportive of Lincoln's policy of letting the Mormons alone.[19]

**April 1865:** Brigham Young grieves the untimely death of the President, well aware of how few friends the Saints have in government.[20] A day of mourning is declared, all Salt Lake City businesses close, and a memorial service is held in the Old Tabernacle.[21]

*As a young Illinois legislator, Abe Lincoln assisted the Saints with the passage of the Nauvoo Charter, had frequent interactions with the Mormons, and boasted, "Joseph Smith is an admirer of mine."*

## LINCOLN'S ASSISTANCE WITH THE NAUVOO CHARTER

Abraham Lincoln was a pivotal figure in helping the Mormons secure the Nauvoo charter, which granted the city unprecedented autonomy. Future counselor to Joseph Smith and mayor of Nauvoo, John C. Bennett, wrote the following in the *Times and Seasons* in December 1840, upon the approval of the charter:

Many members of the House were warmly in our favor, and with only one or two dissenting voices, every representative appeared inclined to extend to us all such powers as they considered us justly entitled to, and voted for the law; and here I should not forget to mention that Lincoln . . . had the magnanimity to vote for our act, and came forward after the final vote to the bar of the House and congratulated me on its passage.[22]

The young legislator was not showing favoritism to Nauvoo, however, for it was said "Lincoln helped cities such as Nauvoo as a matter of course."[23] Yet such assistance was greatly appreciated by the Saints.

## PRESIDENT LINCOLN VISITED BY LDS LEADERS

*The White House in the early 1860s, as it would have looked when approached by LDS leaders George Q. Cannon and William H. Hooper en route to their meetings with Lincoln. "He received us very kindly," reported Elder Cannon.*

George Q. Cannon and territorial delegate William H. Hooper, who had been elected senators from the proposed state of Deseret, called upon Lincoln on 9 June 1862. Amazingly the chief executive found time to receive them. "The President has a plain, but shrewd and rather pleasant face," wrote Cannon. "He is very tall, probably 6 feet 4 inches high, and is rather awkwardly built, heightened by his want of flesh. He looks much better than I expected he would do from my knowledge of the cares and labors of his position, and is quite humorous, scarcely permitting a visit to pass without uttering some joke. He received us very kindly and without formality. Conversed some little upon Utah affairs and other matters." Lincoln asked about the population of Utah Territory and "appeared to be satisfied" upon learning that the population had surged from 11,000 in 1850 to over 40,000 in 1862. However, he would not commit himself on the subject of Utah statehood.[24]

A year later, Thomas B. H. Stenhouse, an LDS representative in Washington, met with Lincoln. In a letter to Brigham Young dated 7 June 1863 he reported the Great Emancipator as saying:

> Stenhouse, when I was a boy on the farm in Illinois there was a great deal of timber on the farm which we had to clear away. Occasionally we would come to a log which had fallen down. It was too hard to split, too wet to burn, and too heavy to move, so we plowed around it. You go back and tell Brigham Young that if he will let me alone I will let him alone.[25]

*In a conversation with LDS representative Thomas B. H. Stenhouse, Lincoln declared his hands-off approach to managing the Saints: "You go back and tell Brigham Young that if he will let me alone I will let him alone."*

"Lincoln's policies demonstrated remarkable political practicality," notes historian Larry Schweikart. "Lincoln apparently made two assumptions when dealing with the Mormons: the leader could maintain order without the help of the federal government, and Lincoln could deal directly with the leader, circumventing the traditional territorial systems."[26] Another historian, George U. Hubbard, asserts that Lincoln's pronouncement of his "let them alone" policy was the real turning point in the Latter-day Saint view toward Lincoln. It was "the kind of governmental policy which the Mormons had sought in vain for the past thirty-three years"—no special privileges, but freedom to worship God without unjust interference.[27]

## LINCOLN'S LEGACY WITH THE SAINTS

"I always had a liking for Abe Lincoln," related Brigham Young in his later years, "and if he had come out here and known us, he would have understood us and liked us, and I'd have told him 'another' [story] to match his every time, and then we wouldn't have heard so much rot about our ways."[28]

The admiration and respect for the Great Emancipator continued to grow after his death. It seemed, both among the Latter-day Saints and America in general, that the longer Lincoln was dead, the larger he loomed as a heroic figure. LDS officials have publicly praised Lincoln or quoted reverently from his words over two hundred times in general conference.[29] For example, Elder Hyrum M. Smith, an Apostle, taught in a 1905 general conference, "I believe Abraham Lincoln was raised up to do God's will."[30] President Heber J. Grant referred to the sixteenth President as "that great and wonderful man, Abraham Lincoln, who all Latter-day Saints believe firmly was raised up and inspired of God Almighty."[31] He added, "Perhaps no other people in all the world look upon Abraham Lincoln as an inspired servant of God, a man raised up by God to occupy the presidential chair, as much as do the Latter-day Saints."[32]

*President Heber J. Grant declared, "Perhaps no other people in all the world look upon Abraham Lincoln as an inspired servant of God, a man raised up by God to occupy the presidential chair, as much as do the Latter-day Saints."*

On Lincoln's one hundredth birthday, 12 February 1909, former Apostle Matthias F. Cowley participated in the proxy sealings for the President and Mary Todd Lincoln in the Salt Lake Temple. He also had Lincoln sealed to his former sweetheart that day, Ann Mayes Rutledge, whose early death had broken young Lincoln's heart.[33]

In the nation's bicentennial year, the LDS First Presidency reminded the Saints that "Abraham Lincoln, our sixteenth president, taught that God rules in the affairs of men and nations." They provided a copy of and asked members to read Lincoln's 30 March 1863 proclamation entitled "God Rules in the Affairs of Men."[34]

Today Lincoln continues to emerge in LDS conference talks, lesson manuals, and anecdotes. President James E. Faust once told about a meeting of the Brigham Young University board of trustees where he was trying to make the point that academic grades shouldn't be the sole criteria for entrance into the university. "Even Abraham Lincoln couldn't qualify for admission to the J. Reuben Clark Law School," President Faust exclaimed. Then-BYU president Rex Lee quipped, "He showed up one day, but he had a beard."[35]

## ENDNOTES

1   Simon, *Lincoln's Preparation for Greatness,* 209.

2   Cyril D. Pearson, "Abraham Lincoln and Joseph Smith," in *Improvement Era* 48, no. 2 (February 1945).

3   Roy P. Basler, ed., *The Collected Works of Abraham Lincoln,* 1:206–7.

4   Charles A. Callis, in Conference Report, October 1938, 24–25.

5   Roberts, *A Comprehensive History of the Church,* 2:54n.

6   R. Scott Lloyd, "Land of Lincoln," *Church News,* 7 May 2005. See also in Byron Andreason, "Latter-day Saint Connections to Abraham Lincoln-era Springfield" (address to the Sangamon County Historical Society), 26 April 2005.

7   Paul Angle, *Here I Have Lived,* 126. See also Lloyd, "Land of Lincoln," *LDS Church News,* 7 May 2005.

8    Schweikart, "The Mormon Connection: Lincoln, the Saints, and the Crises of Equality," 6. See also Basler, *The Collected Works of Abraham Lincoln,* 1:291.

9    Dallin Oaks and Marvin Hill, *The Carthage Conspiracy,* 48, 315.

10   John Hay, "The Mormon Prophet's Tragedy," in *Atlantic Monthly* 24 (1869):669–78.

11   Basler, *The Collected Works of Abraham Lincoln,* 2:399.

12   Staker, *Waiting for World's End: The Diaries of Wilford Woodruff,* 256.

13   George Albert Smith, "Remarks and Prayer Given at the Unveiling Ceremonies of the Brigham Young Statue, Held in the Rotunda of the Capitol Building, Washington, D.C., Thursday, 1 June 1950," in *Improvement Era* 53 (September 1950).

14   Library of Congress, Presidents Collection. See also Cyril D. Pearson, "Abraham Lincoln and Joseph Smith," in *Improvement Era* 48, no. 2 (February 1945).

15   *Lincoln Lore: Bulletin of The Lincoln National Life Foundation,* 2. Hyde's book was published by W.P. Fetridge & Co., New York. Gunnison's book was published by J.B. Lippincott & Co., Philadelphia.

16   *Deseret News,* 30 April 1862.

17   Arrington and Bitton, *The Mormon Experience,* 172. See also Bitton, *George Q. Cannon,* 123.

18   Roberts, *A Comprehensive History of the Church,* 2:346.

19   McCloud, *Brigham Young: An Inspiring Personal Biography,* 233.

20   McCloud, *Brigham Young: An Inspiring Personal Biography,* 236.

21   Preston Nibley, "Lincoln and the Latter-day Saints," manuscript, LDS Church Archives, Salt Lake City. See also Arrington and Bitton, *The Mormon Experience,* 173; Davis Bitton and Maureen Ursenbach Beecher, eds., *New Views of Mormon History: Essays in Honor of Leonard J. Arrington,* 320; Holzapfel, et al., *On this Day in the Church,* 75.

22   *Times and Seasons* 2:267, quoted in Nibley, *Brigham Young: The Man and His Work,* 368.

23   Schweikart, "The Mormon Connection: Lincoln, the Saints, and the Crises of Equality," 4.

24   Bitton, *George Q. Cannon,* 120.

25   Arrington and Bitton, *The Mormon Experience,* 170. See also Stenhouse to Young, 7 June 1863, in Brigham Young Correspondence, LDS Church Archives, Salt Lake City; Nibley, *Brigham Young: The Man and His Work,* 369.

26   Schweikart, "The Mormon Connection: Lincoln, the Saints, and the Crises of Equality," 13–14.

27   George U. Hubbard, "Abraham Lincoln As Seen by the Mormons," *Utah Historical Quarterly* 31 (Spring 1963): 91–108.

28   Protea [Gentile governess of Brigham Young's children], "Brigham Young at Home, the Ways and Words of the Prophet in His Household: His Conversations about Himself, the Government, Mormons," *The Weekly Sun* [daily newspaper of New York], 19 September 1877.

29   For examples, see *LDS Conference Reports,* Spring 1905, Fall 1919, Fall 1924, Spring 1942 (twice), and Fall 1941. A full list is indexed in the LDS Collectors Library 2005 (software).

30   Conference Report, Spring 1905, 47.

31   James R. Clark, *Messages of the First Presidency,* 5:263.

32   *Improvement Era* 47, no. 2 (February 1944); *Lincoln Douglas and Joseph Smith,* Heber J. Grant.

33   Temple ordinances can be accessed by Church members in the International Genealogical Index (IGI) at www.familysearch.org.

34   *The Great Prologue,* 13, 17.

35   "Funeral Speakers Laud Life of Rex E. Lee," *Church News,* 23 March 1996.

# ANDREW JOHNSON

## *1865–1869*

Vice President Andrew Johnson, a native of North Carolina, became President of the United States following Lincoln's assassination in Ford's Theater. His administration was preoccupied with the aftermath of the Civil War and with fending off political enemies that succeeded in impeaching him, although he was acquitted by the Senate. Consequently, Johnson had little time for interacting with the Mormons.

William H. Hooper, Utah's territorial delegate to Congress from 1859–61 and 1865–73, later recalled that "Prest. Andrew Johnson was a friend to the Mormons."[1] Johnson was known for his relaxed attitude toward the Saints.[2]

**June 1865:** Johnson ignores a petition signed by 250 prominent Latter-day Saints asking him to appoint Colonel O. H. Irish, the very popular superintendent of Indian affairs for the territory, as their next governor.[3]

**14 March 1866:** En route to a mission in England, John W. Young (Brigham Young's son and a future counselor in the First Presidency), calls on President Johnson in the White House. He writes to his father that while he and his companion, John T. Caine, waited to see the President,

William H. Hooper represented the Utah Territory as its delegate to Congress during 1859–61 and 1865–73. As such, he had interactions with several U.S. presidents, including Andrew Johnson, whom he recalled as "a friend to the Mormons."

En route to a mission in England, John W. Young (Brigham Young's son and a future counselor in the First Presidency), called on President Andrew Johnson in the White House. During the same trip, Elder Young also visited with General Ulysses S. Grant.

"Republicanism was beautifully illustrated, for I could see from diamonds of the millionaire down to the greasy coat of the poor artisan brushing side by side with equal rights to be introduced to the President, and to promenade in the grand salons." When the third son of Brigham Young is presented to the President, it "excited a great deal of curiosity and caused many a stare." John writes to his father that "the feeling of hatred toward us is intensely strong with the majority of the head men at Washington."[4]

Andrew Johnson simply did not have much interaction with the Mormons. This would be unheard of in the many administrations to come as the Mormons became an increasingly important part of the American political agenda.

# ENDNOTES

1    John Henry Smith, *Church, State, and Politics: The Diaries of John Henry Smith,* 75.

2    Gibbons, *John Taylor,* 165.

3    Roberts, *A Comprehensive History of the Church,* 5:179–80.

4    Brigham Young, *Letters of Brigham Young,* 103.

# ULYSSES S. GRANT

## 1869–1877

The hero of the Union Army was the natural choice for the Republican nomination in 1868, promising peace to a healing nation. Yet, in relations with the Latter-day Saints, Grant's desire for peace would conflict mightily with Victorian morality that regarded monogamy as imperative. Moreover, with accusations of corruption in the Grant administration and criticisms of how he was managing reconstruction in the South, attacking polygamy would make a good diversion for the Methodist President that few in the East could argue with. In the end, Grant did make the first visit of any U.S. President to Utah, but he also stepped up the antipolygamy persecutions that would continue through his presidential successors until the 1890 Manifesto. The presidency of U.S. Grant was "trying for both the Mormons and the federal government," wrote historian Thomas Alexander. "Not since the Utah War of 1857–58 had conditions been so tense; and not until 1885, when the final push to eradicate polygamy and Church control began, were they to become so again."[1]

**1865:** Following the conclusion of the Civil War, General Grant receives word from Major General John Pope that the Mormons are threatening to stir up the Indians in rebellion against the Union.[2] Patrick Connor, commander of

Fort Douglas in Salt Lake City, also sends the general negative reports about the Saints, to which he responds, "It is not believed that an institution like Mormonism can exist permanently in force and close communication with the civilized world."[3]

**14 March 1866:** John W. Young (Brigham's son and future First Presidency member), John T. Caine, and Utah's territorial delegate, William Hooper, call upon the popular general at his Georgetown headquarters. Young finds Grant "a perfect stoic, and I think his great forte lies in him knowing just enough to hold his tongue. However, he shook hands very cordially when we took our leave."[4]

**April 1869:** Newly sworn-in Grant removes Robert T. Burton, the only Mormon federal appointee in Utah Territory, from his post as collector of internal revenue.[5]

**Fall 1869:** Grant sends Vice President Schuyler Colfax to Salt Lake City to assess the situation and warn the Mormons to obey the law.[6] Colfax reports that "the golden moment has arrived" to appoint tough officials for the territory to subdue the Saints.[7] Brigham Young is clearly not impressed with the new administration and quips, "Who goes to the White House these days? . . . A gambler and a drunkard. And the Vice-President is the same."[8]

**1870:** Anti-Mormon William S. Godbe calls on the President and suggests sending more troops to Utah. Grant disagrees and states that if "more troops were sent to Utah they would be merely designed as a moral force." He notes that while he expects Mormon leaders "to understand that the Nation intended to enforce her laws in Utah," he hopes to be "as solicitous as you can possibly be to preserve the Mormon people."[9]

**1871:** Grant names Judge James B. McKean as chief justice of the territorial supreme court, appointing him to "take the lead in vigorously fulfilling the Republican pledge to end 'plural marriage.'"[10] McKean tells Grant, "Mr. President, in my endeavors to perform my duty in Utah I may become embroiled with the Mormons," to which Grant replies, "If civil process will not restrain lawlessness, I will support you with the army of the United States."[11]

**December 1871:** In his third annual message to Congress, Grant declares that while the Mormons will be "protected in the worship of God according to the dictates of their consciences," the law will be enforced to rid the nation of "a remnant of barbarism repugnant to civilization, decency and the laws of the United States."[12]

**January 1872:** In his famous diary entry, Elder Wilford Woodruff calls down the "wrath & indignation of the Lord of Hosts" on President Ulysses S. Grant. He also records his dream that "a tattered United States flag passed in the sky from north to south. The Constitution then followed,

*A member of the LDS First Presidency, George Q. Cannon also represented Utah Territory as a delegate to Congress from 1873 to 1883. As such, President Cannon had interactions with several U.S. Presidents, including Ulysses S. Grant, whom he lobbied in vain for statehood. When Grant visited Utah, Cannon introduced the President to Brigham Young and other leaders throughout his tour.*

tied in ropes to keep it from falling to pieces. After these two images came an immense eagle carrying Ulysses S. Grant in its talons by the hair."[13]

**Spring 1872:** Apostle George Q. Cannon and other Utah leaders meet with Grant to lobby for Utah statehood.

**December 1872:** Grant declares to Congress, "It has seemed to be the policy of the legislature of Utah to evade all responsibility to the government of the United States, and even to hold a position in hostility to it. I recommend the enactment of a law as will secure peace, the equality of all citizens before the law, and the ultimate extinguishment of polygamy."[14]

**14 February 1873:** Grant insists again to Congress that "the Territory of Utah requires special legislation by Congress" and that if legislation is not enacted soon, he will put his troops in Utah "and nail the thing by that means."[15]

**7 March 1874:** Apostles Joseph F. Smith and George Q. Cannon meet with President Grant to lobby against harsher antipolygamy legislation.[16] Ignoring their pleas, the President signs the Poland Bill into law that June.[17]

**October 1875:** Ulysses S. Grant becomes the first U.S. President to visit Utah.

**1885:** In his dying days, former-President Grant writes the first presidential memoir and includes one passage about the Mormons—one that aptly summarizes his views toward the Latter-

*In his presidential memoirs, Grant aptly summarized his views towards the Latter-day Saints: "There are now people who believe Mormonism and Polygamy to be ordained by the Most High. We forgive them for entertaining such notions, but forbid their practice."*

day Saints: "There are now people who believe Mormonism and Polygamy to be ordained by the Most High. We forgive them for entertaining such notions, but forbid their practice."[18]

## GRANT LOBBIED FOR UTAH STATEHOOD

On 18 March 1872, Utahns ratified a constitution for statehood, and Frank Fuller, Apostle George Q. Cannon, and non-Mormon Thomas Fitch were selected to carry the proposal to Washington to lobby for approval. When the petitioners met with President Grant they were disappointed that although he was courteous, he wanted to talk about farming instead of statehood. They eventually learned that even if an admission bill were to pass Congress, Grant would veto it. "He would never consent to admission," Cannon wrote back to Salt Lake after the White House visit, "until the people had forsaken polygamy."[19]

About this time, the *Cincinnati Commercial* printed the following anecdote submitted by their Washington correspondent. Entitled "Wasted Argument," it exhibits Grant's feelings about Utah and the Mormons:

> Senator-elect [Thomas] Fitch, from the embryo "State of Deseret," called upon the president a few days ago to talk over Utah affairs. He found the president enjoying a cigar.
>
> "Mr. President," said the colonel, "I want to try and convince you of the advisability of admitting Utah into the sisterhood of states."
>
> "I am unalterably opposed to the admission of Utah," answered the president.

THE MORMON PROBLEM SOLVED.

In November 1871, Frank Leslie's illustrated newspaper captured the public stereotype of Brigham Young with hundreds of wives and children, as well as referencing President Grant's reputation of political corruption and aggressive patronage. Entitled "The Mormon Problem Solved," it has Brigham Young telling Grant, "I must submit to your laws—but what shall I do with these." Grant replies, "Do as I do—give them offices."

"Yes, but you have been prejudiced against the people out there by unfair advisers," said Fitch.

"I am unalterably opposed to the admission of Utah," was the reply.

"But our population is sufficient; we have made a fair Constitution, and it would be a great relief to the people out there to get into the Union."

"I am unalterably opposed to the admission of Utah," again replied the firm man.

"Under any terms?"

"Yes, upon any terms. At least they should not come in until they learn how to behave themselves."

"If you refer to polygamy, they will no doubt surrender that for the sake of admission and peace, although it is one of the doctrines of their church."

"And murder is one of the doctrines of the church, ain't it?"

"No, indeed; there are less murders committed there than in any of the surrounding territories. As I said before, you have been very much misinformed about the true condition of affairs. You surely don't believe everything you hear against the Mormons?"

"Where there is so much smoke there must be some fire," answered the president.

"Suppose we should say the same about all the lies told about you?"

Silence and smoke . . .

"Is your mind, Mr. President, so firmly made up, that whatever arguments might be addressed to you would be useless?"

"I am unalterably opposed to the admission of Utah," replied our firm president, and the charming interview ended.[20]

## FIRST PRESIDENTIAL VISIT TO UTAH

On Sunday, 3 October 1875, Ulysses S. Grant became the first President of the United States to visit Utah. En route to Denver, he took a detour to Utah Territory to confer with his new appointee, Governor George W. Emery. Federal officials and Church leaders competed to host Grant, resulting in a rather clumsy meeting at the train station in Ogden. There, George Q. Cannon said to Grant, "Mr. President may I have the pleasure of introducing to you President Brigham Young." They then shook hands, but Young did not understand at first who it was and had to be quickly told by Cannon that it was President Grant. Both presidents removed their top hats in respect, and Brigham Young then exclaimed, "President Grant, this is the first time I have ever seen a President of my country."[21] Wilford Woodruff penned in his diary that it was notable to witness the meeting of "the Presidet [sic] of the Kingdom of God on the Earth & a law giver unto Israel . . . & . . . the Presidt [sic] of the United States and of this Great Nation."[22]

While traveling by train from Ogden to Salt Lake, President Grant, Governor Emery, and Elder Cannon stood on the platform to view the countryside, while Brigham Young remained inside conversing with the First Lady.[23] En route, Julia Grant told Brigham that she admired the accomplishments of the Mormons, though she objected to the practice of polygamy.

*Brigham Young welcomed Ulysses S. Grant to Utah in 1875, the first time a U.S. President had ever visited. "President Grant, this is the first time I have ever seen a President of my country," he remarked upon being introduced. It was the first meeting between the presidents of the Church and nation since Joseph Smith had called on Martin Van Buren thirty-six years prior.*

When a carriage took the presidential party from the railroad station to Grant's Salt Lake City hotel, South Temple Street was lined with throngs of white-clad children singing and throwing flowers before the President's carriage. Grant asked Governor Emery, "Whose children are these?" When he learned that they were Mormon children, he reportedly murmured to himself, "I have been deceived!"[24]

The following day, 4 October, the presidential party visited the Temple Block and the Tabernacle. From here, President Grant left in a buggy to visit one of the nearby hills where he could have a view of the city.[25] Grant gave some advice to Governor Emery, urging him to identify himself with Utah's non-Mormon community and not try to ally himself with the Mormons. Emery ended up being a moderate Grant appointee, neither antagonizing nor siding with the Mormons.[26]

Meanwhile, Elder Cannon was left to entertain Mrs. Grant and her son at an organ recital at the Tabernacle, where the First Lady offered a prayer for the Mormons. She was deeply moved by what she saw and heard, and told ex-delegate William H. Hooper, "Oh, I wish I could do something for these good Mormon people." The group later reunited and left on the train for Ogden, escorted once more by Brigham Young and a delegation of LDS leaders.[27]

After the presidential visit, President Young wrote about it to his son Alfales, who was in Ann Arbor, Michigan:

> We have had a pleasant little excitement this week in the visit of Pres. Grant and party to our city and territory. The ring [of anti-Mormons] attempted to corral him but signally failed, and he very impartially bestowed his attentions on all persons and parties alike, at which they, fancying themselves his especial pets, feel very much chagrined. The party—the ladies especially—expressed themselves very much delighted with their visit to the home of the Latter-day Saints.[28]

## ULYSSES S. GRANT REMEMBERED BY HEBER J. GRANT

The eighteenth President died 23 July 1885 in Mount McGregor, New York. When his funeral procession went through Manhattan, a future president of the Church, twenty-nine-year-old Heber J. Grant, looked on. "I took some pride in looking out of a window on Broadway at the four-mile-long procession which was the funeral of President Ulysses S. Grant, and seeing a grandson of Brigham Young riding on horseback at the head of the funeral procession," recalled Heber. He was referring to his friend Richard W. Young, a West Point graduate then commissioned as a major in the U.S. Army.[29] Heber J. Grant was pleased to note that President Grant treated the Saints much differently after visiting them in the Great Basin:

> I rejoice in the friendship of Ulysses S. Grant. He sent out a lot of officials whose work and only object seemed to be to destroy our people politically and to take away from us the franchise, and do everything against us that they possibly could. But he came here himself and met the people. . . . He went home and chopped off

*Grant's funeral procession down the streets of Manhattan. A young Heber J. Grant admired the sight, and was impressed to see Richard W. Young, a West Point graduate and grandson of Brigham Young, riding on horseback at the head of the procession.*

the heads of the officials, figuratively speaking, whom he had sent out here, and then sent us some good men. To everybody who undertook to tell him untruths about us he said: "I have been there. I have met them. I know."[30]

# ENDNOTES

1     Thomas G. Alexander, "A Conflict of Perceptions: Ulysses S. Grant and the Mormons," *Ulysses S. Grant Association Newsletter* (Carbondale, IL) 8, no. 4 (July 1971): 40.

2     John Y. Simon, ed., *The Papers of Ulysses S. Grant,* 15:573.

3     E. B. Long, *The Saints and the Union,* 264.

4     Brigham Young, *Letters of Brigham Young,* 103.

5     *New York Times,* 14 July 1869

6     Alexander, "A Conflict of Perceptions," 33.

7     Schuyler Colfax to Ulysses S. Grant, 18 August 1870, San Francisco, quoted in John Y. Simon, *The Papers of Ulysses S. Grant,* 21:105–6.

8     Young, quoted in Stanley P. Hirshon, *The Lion of the Lord: A Biography of the Mormon Leader, Brigham Young,* 278–79.

9     Edward W. Tullidge, *History of Salt Lake City and Its Founders,* 469.

10     Holzapfel and Shupe, *My Servant Brigham,* 18.

11     Quoted in Francis M. Gibbons, *Brigham Young: Modern Moses, Prophet of God,* 242–43.

12     Third Annual Message, MS, Grant Papers, Library of Congress.

13     Alexander, *Things in Heaven and Earth,* 227.

14     John Y. Simon, *The Papers of Ulysses S. Grant,* 23:299–300.

15     Fourth Annual Message, MS, Grant Papers, Library of Congress. See also John Y. Simon, *The Papers of Ulysses S. Grant,* 24:36; Roberts, *A Comprehensive History of the Church,* 5:435.

16     Joseph F. Smith, *From Prophet to Son,* 22–23.

17     *Church Almanac,* 544.

18     Ulysses S. Grant, *Personal Memoirs of U.S. Grant,* 1:217–18.

19     Bitton, *George Q. Cannon,* 171–72.

20     Reprinted in Roberts, *A Comprehensive History of the Church,* 5:467–68.

21     Nibley, *Brigham Young: The Man and His Work,* 518.

22     Alexander, *Things in Heaven and Earth,* 228. See also Staker, *Waiting for World's End: The Diaries of Wilford Woodruff,* 309; Roberts, *A Comprehensive History of the Church,* 5:503.

23     Bitton, *George Q. Cannon,* 195.

24     Roberts, *A Comprehensive History of the Church,* 5:504–5. See also Nibley, *Brigham Young: The Man and His Work,* 518; Alexander, "A Conflict of Perceptions," 39.

25     Staker, *Waiting for World's End: The Diaries of Wilford Woodruff,* 310.

26     Alexander, "A Conflict of Perceptions," 39–40.

27     Staker, *Waiting for World's End: The Diaries of Wilford Woodruff,* 310. First Lady quoted in Roberts, *A Comprehensive History of the Church,* 5:505.

28     Brigham Young, *Letters of Brigham Young,* 224.

29  Heber J. Grant, in Conference Report, October 1934, 123.

30  Heber J. Grant, in Conference Report, April 1930, 186–87.

# RUTHERFORD
# B. HAYES

*1877—1881*

The election of 1876 was close and controversial. Samuel Tilden, governor of New York, won the popular vote. Pleased that a Democrat was finally heading to the White House, Brigham Young sent Apostle George Q. Cannon to meet with the presumed winner. Tilden was very friendly in his interview with Elder Cannon and in his attitude toward the Mormons. "He seems confident that he will be inaugurated, talks very hopefully about our affairs," wrote Cannon, pleased that he had won goodwill from the President-Elect. The Church leaders felt that "a new day had dawned" in their relationship with the White House and that statehood was nigh. However, when double returns from South Carolina, Louisiana, and Florida were discovered, a special commission was assembled to decide the election. Fearing that their good fortune would evaporate, Church leaders watched the events with great interest, and Cannon went to Washington to personally observe the proceedings. The panel of five Supreme Court justices, five senators, and five House members ruled that Tilden had 184 electoral votes and that Rutherford B. Hayes had 185. "One imagines his dismay when the final count was announced," wrote a Cannon biographer. "The Republican Hayes, no friend of the Latter-day Saints, was elected." It was a despondent Apostle that watched Hayes—not

Tilden—sworn in as the nineteenth President.[1] And it was Hayes who went on to become one of the most anti-Mormon of Presidents.

**January 1878:** Elder Cannon meets with Hayes for the first time. "His Fraudulency," as his enemies called him after his dubious election, is polite but unwilling to back down from his view that federal law should be firmly enforced in Utah Territory.[2]

**January 1879:** Through their affiliation with the National Women's Suffrage Association, Relief Society leaders Emmeline B. Wells and Zina Young Williams (daughter of Brigham Young) secure a meeting with President and Mrs. Hayes. They request that children of plural marriage be legitimized and that the 1862 Morrill Anti-Bigamy Act not be enforced, as it would tear families apart.[3]

*Emmeline B. Wells, wife of church leader Daniel H. Wells, represented Utah in the National Women's Suffrage Association for nearly thirty years. There she became associated with national suffrage leaders Susan B. Anthony and Elizabeth Cady Stanton, and was able to secure a meeting with President and Mrs. Hayes to lobby against the Morrill Anti-Bigamy Act.*

*Zina Presendia Young Williams, daughter of Brigham Young, joined Emmeline Wells to represent Utah at a National Women's Suffrage convention in 1879. Both women ended up meeting with the President and First Lady to express the views of many Utah women.*

**June 1879:** Elder George Q. Cannon meets with Hayes and negotiates a deal that will grant amnesty to all who entered plural marriage before 1879. President John Taylor rejects it, however, as he does not trust Hayes and feels that agreeing to such a deal would ultimately result in an abandonment of polygamy.[4]

**October 1879:** President Hayes asks European nations to keep their Mormons from emigrating to America.

**1 December 1879:** In his annual message to Congress, Hayes strongly denounces polygamy. "It is the duty and purpose of the people of the United States to suppress polygamy where it now exists in our Territories, and to prevent its extension," he explained. "The Mormon sectarian organization which upholds polygamy has the whole power of making and executing the local legislation of the Territory. . . . The political power of the Mormon sect is increasing; it controls now one of our wealthiest and most populous Territories." Hayes asks Congress to end or at least decrease the role of the territorial legislature and to limit the rights to vote, hold office, or sit on juries to those "who neither practice nor uphold polygamy."[5] Upon hearing of the request to Congress, President John Taylor says, "This proposal branded Hayes as the greatest ignoramus of all times."[6]

**January 1880:** Hayes appoints anti-Mormon Eli H. Murray as governor of Utah Territory.

**September 1880:** President and Mrs. Hayes visit Utah.

**6 December 1880:** In his annual presidential message to Congress, given after Garfield has been elected his successor, Hayes declares, "Polygamy will not be abolished if the enforcement of the law depends on those who practice and uphold the crime. It can only be supposed by taking away the political power of the sect which encourages and sustains it." He once again recommends that the "right to vote, hold office, and sit on juries in the territory of Utah be confined to those who neither practice nor uphold polygamy."[7] Not many years after, Congress passes legislation to this effect. In response to Hayes' address, Cannon writes, "I cannot express the contempt I have for his character."[8]

**March 1881:** The outgoing President lists developing a "true policy with respect to Mormonism and polygamy" as one of the great successes of his administration.[9] Before leaving office, Hayes has a farewell reception at the White House for diplomats and members of Congress. George Q. Cannon, Utah's lone delegate, declines to attend.[10]

# HAYES ASKS EUROPE TO KEEP THEIR MORMONS AT HOME

In 1879 President Hayes and his secretary of state, William M. Evarts, discussed how to halt the flood of Mormons pouring into the United States from Europe. As a result of such White House meetings, on 9 October, Evarts issued a proclamation to the American ambassadors in Britain, Germany, Norway, Sweden, and Denmark asking them "to seek aid of these governments in stopping any further Mormon departures for the United States." The Hayes administration felt this action was justified since the Latter-day Saint converts were "potential violators" of the laws against polygamy. Mixed reactions in Europe resulted. While the Scandinavian countries promised to discourage emigration if they could, the English ridiculed the action. The *London Times* denounced the very idea of curtailing the emigration of those "who have contravened no law," and the *London Examiner* likewise was critical.[11]

# HAYES SEEKS TOUGH ANTI-MORMON GOVERNOR FOR UTAH

On 9 January 1880, the President wrote in his diary:

> [Utah] is virtually under the theocratic government of the Mormon Church. The Union of Church and State is complete. The result is the usual one[:] usurpation or absorption of all temporal authority and power by the Church. . . . Laws must be enacted which will take from the Mormon Church its temporal power. . . . [A]s a system of government it is our duty to deal with it as an enemy to our institutions, and its supporters and leaders as criminals.[12]

At that time Hayes was considering whom to appoint as the new territorial governor of Utah. Ten days later it was announced that the President had ignored the other forty applicants and the wish of every cabinet officer by appointing the corrupt and harsh Eli H. Murray of Kentucky. Governor Murray's actions made it clear that "President Hayes had personally determined a hostile policy toward the Church of the Latter-day Saints."[13]

On 13 January the President wrote in his diary:

> Two things that may be important considered. . . . The other affair is the appointment of a Governor for the Territory of Utah. This under ordinary circumstances is an ordinary Administrative

*Former Civil War general Eli H. Murray of Kentucky was appointed governor of Utah by President Hayes, and charged to toughly prosecute Mormon polygamists. Murray's philosophy echoed the President's in that he believed that no man could be a faithful Mormon and a loyal citizen of the United States. He served as governor during 1880–86, and in 1883 the South Cottonwood Post Office was renamed in his honor, eventually resulting in the city of Murray, Utah, carrying his name.*

act. But an appointment in the place of the present reputable governor means a change of policy toward the Mormons. Now the territory is virtually under the theocratic government of the Mormon Church. . . . Polygamy and every other evil sanctioned by the Church is safe. To destroy the temporal power of the Mormon Church is the end in view. This requires agitation. . . . Laws must be enacted which will take from the Mormon Church its temporal power. Mormonism as a sectarian idea is nothing, but as a system of government it is our duty to deal with it as an enemy to our institutions, and its supporters and leaders as criminals.[14]

# HAYES VISITS UTAH

*President Hayes visited Salt Lake City in 1880, where he met with President John Taylor and other Church leaders. He spent most of his visit with Governor Murray and the non-Mormons of the city.*

Upon hearing that President Hayes would be making a trip to the West, Governor Murray wrote him, "I am glad to know of your proposed [visit] to the west and write now in advance to express the hope that you will stop, take a look at this great Territory and dwell for awhile within the gates of the City of the Saints." The governor argued, "Salt Lake City is a good halfway place, a sojourn here would prove both refreshing and interesting." The President agreed and added the "City of the Saints" to his itinerary.[15]

President and Mrs. Hayes visited Salt Lake City on 5–6 September 1880, where it was hoped by the Saints that his opinions of the Mormons might soften. The presidential party was greeted at the train station in Ogden by the Ogden Brass Band, an enthusiastic crowd, and various Utah dignitaries. Hayes recognized George Q. Cannon, who introduced him to LDS Church President John Taylor and Elder Daniel H. Wells. The VIPs transferred to the two coaches of John Taylor's train and traveled south to the capital.

Upon arrival in Salt Lake, thousands of Sunday School children lined the streets from the depot to the Walker House, where the presidential party would stay. From the portico of the hotel, Governor Murray introduced the guests to the crowd. Besides a few words of greeting to the crowds below, General William Tecumseh Sherman, who was traveling with the presidential party, was the only one to say much: "The president will in due time on all proper occasions recognize your kindness to him—not here but elsewhere; . . . he is so familiar with the history of this people, that when the time comes that he can say a kind word for you, he will do it." The crowd then cheered but realized within months the hypocrisy of such a statement.[16]

The largely LDS Salt Lake City Council's efforts to host President Hayes and give him a balanced view of the affairs in Utah were preempted by Governor Murray and his group of federal appointees and anti-Mormons. Church officials were notified that the President would be the exclusive guest of the Governor, who made a great effort during the remainder of the presidential visit to keep Hayes away from LDS officials and have him meet only with the anti-Mormons of the city. Historian B. H. Roberts believed that "this visit, under the conditions prevailing when it was made, and the president's association with the anti-Mormon party while in the city—deepened his prejudices, and led to his determination to make recommendations of his subsequent message to congress."[17]

When the presidential party left the city, three special train cars of business and LDS leaders accompanied Hayes to Ogden. Shortly after leaving Salt Lake, President Hayes entered the rear cars, shook hands with all present, and then took a seat near President John Taylor, where the two presidents conversed until they reached Ogden. The *Deseret News* reported their conversation as follows:

> The conversation was on a variety of topics, secular and religious, mostly pertaining to Utah, and at the close President Hayes on rising to leave shook hands warmly with President Taylor, assured him that he had much enjoyed the interview, and for himself and associates declared that the impressions received during their visit to Utah had been of the most favorable character, and as such would long be remembered. Mrs. Hayes also left her car and entering the others at the rear of the train, held extended conversations with several of the "Mormon" ladies.[18]

President Taylor said of his conversation with Hayes: "I told him that . . . we had received the doctrine of plural marriage as a part of the Gospel, and that it was only for pure men and pure women, that class, and that class only, could receive it and practice it, and make it honorable; it was . . . for those who feared God and worked righteousness, who were true to themselves and true to the female sex, and who would stand by and sustain them and preserve them in purity and honor."[19] However, in spite of Taylor's efforts, "Hayes was not willing to change his anti-Mormon attitude."[20]

## REMAINING VOCAL AGAINST THE SAINTS POST PRESIDENCY

On 10 December 1881, Hayes wrote a journal entry expressing harsh criticism for the new Arthur administration's stance on the issue of "the Utah question." He wrote very harsh comments not just on polygamy, but also on the Church's dominance of local government:

> On the Mormon question he strikes in the back. He deals with it as if polygamy were the beginning and end of the affair.

Polygamy is one of the evils attendant upon a system which is utterly inconsistent with our republican institutions. Utah is now governed by an irresponsible priesthood. It is a hierarchy. The Mormon Church is the government. It controls Utah and is likely if unchecked to govern other Territories which will soon become States. The remedy—the only remedy—is to destroy the political power of the Mormon Church. No union of church and state is one of the foundation stones of our system. Utah is governed by the church—and such a church! Take from it political power, and it falls and polygamy with it within five years. How to do this? The measure should be radical. Half-way measures have been tried for twenty-five years. They have failed. Let the territorial government of Utah be reorganized. Let all power, I mean of course all the power that it is deemed wise to entrust [to] a merely territorial government, be vested in the registered voters of the Territories. Let them alone hold office, vote, and sit on juries. Allow no one to be registered who does not prove affirmatively to the satisfaction of United States courts, or other United States officials, that he neither practices the crime of polygamy, nor belongs to or supports any church or other organization which upholds it.[21]

On 29 March 1886 Hayes sent a letter to Eli H. Murray, commending him on his tough stance on the Saints while Murray served as governor of Utah. "The failure of Congress to adopt radical measures for the destruction of the political power of the Mormon priesthood only serves to emphasize and attract attention to the merits of your administration," Hayes wrote. "Personally, I feel grateful to you, and therefore hasten to thank you."[22]

Despite meetings with LDS leaders— male and female—and his amicable visit to

*Rutherford B. Hayes was no fan of the Latter-day Saints. "Utah is now governed by an irresponsible priesthood," he wrote. "The remedy—the only remedy—is to destroy the political power of the Mormon Church."*

Utah in 1880, Rutherford Hayes remained tough on the Saints until he went to the grave. The practice of plural marriage and the blurred lines between church and state in Utah had become personal crusades he pursued until his death.

# ENDNOTES

1   Bitton, *George Q. Cannon,* 203–5.

2   Bitton, *George Q. Cannon,* 216.

3   Beverly Beeton, "The Hayes Administration and the Woman Question," *Hayes Historical Journal* 2, no. 1 (1978): 54–55. See also *Encyclopedia of Mormonism,* 1313.

4   Bitton*, George Q. Cannon,* 223–24.

5   Richardson, 7:559–60. See also *Messages and Papers of the Presidents,* 7:559–60.

6   Wayne Stout, *The Mighty John Taylor,* 117.

7   *Messages and Papers of the Presidents,* 7:605–6.

8   Bitton, *George Q. Cannon,* 241.

9   Rutherford B. Hayes, *Diary and Letters of Rutherford Birchard Hayes,* 3:597.

10  Bitton, *George Q. Cannon,* 242.

11  Allen and Leonard, *The Story of the Latter-day Saints,* 397–98.

12  Hayes, *Diary and Letters of Rutherford Birchard Hayes,* 258–59.

13  Roberts, *A Comprehensive History of the Church,* 5:608–9.

14  Hayes, *Diary and Letters of Rutherford Birchard Hayes,* 258–59.

15  Governor Eli H. Murray to President Rutherford B. Hayes, 14 August 1880, Correspondences of President Hayes, Hayes Presidential Center, Spiegel Grove, Ohio.

16  Roberts, *A Comprehensive History of the Church,* 5:611–13. See also *Journal History,* 6 September 1880.

17  Roberts, *A Comprehensive History of the Church,* 5:611–12.

18  *Deseret News,* 7 September 1880.

19  Quoted in Hyrum L. Andrus, *Doctrines of the Kingdom,* 489, footnote 143.

20  Yorgason, *Courageous Defender of Truth,* 370.

21  Hayes, *Diary and Letters of Rutherford Birchard Hayes,* 4:52–55.

22  Hayes, *Diary and Letters of Rutherford Birchard Hayes,* 4:278–79.

# JAMES A. GARFIELD

## *1881*

James A. Garfield—the last of America's log cabin Presidents—was born near the town of Orange, Cuyahoga County, Ohio, on 19 November 1831. Growing up a mere twelve miles south of Kirtland, which served as LDS Church headquarters for much of the 1830s, young Garfield had numerous contacts with the Mormons. As a boy, he became acquainted with prominent Mormon leaders Sidney Rigdon and Parley P. Pratt, had Mormon neighbors, and had LDS relatives, including cousin John Farnham Boynton, who was one of the original Twelve Apostles.[1] Later, Garfield attended functions at the Western Reserve Teachers Seminary and Kirtland Institute, which was housed in the Kirtland Temple for a year and later located a few feet north of the temple.[2]

"He knew better concerning us than any man in public life, that is, he knew more of us," said George Q. Cannon of Garfield. "He was brought up in Ohio, near where our people had lived in the days of his childhood. He was familiar with men who had been members of our Church, and I believe was connected remotely by marriage with some of our people; and while he had no sympathy with some of our doctrines, nevertheless he had opportunities of knowing many things concerning us which others did not know."[3] This background gave Garfield some sympathies for the Saints, and yet he was strongly against polygamy and vocalized in his inaugural address that the eradication of plural marriage would be pursued vigorously.

**1858:** Garfield marries Lucretia Rudolph, daughter of Disciples of Christ leader and anti-Mormon Zeb Rudolph.[4] Earlier, Mr. Rudolph had been taught Latin and Greek by Sidney Rigdon,[5] and later claims that Rigdon has forged the Book of Mormon.[6]

**19 April 1872:** Congressman Garfield writes in his diary that he dined with "G. Q. Cannon, a Mormon Apostle."[7] Cannon, who will be elected this August as delegate for Utah Territory, will build a close bond with Garfield.[8] Garfield in return likes and admires Cannon. At one point, he introduces the Apostle and territorial delegate in this manner: "Mr. Cannon is the most remarkable man in Congress, in some respects. He has a speaking acquaintance with nearly all the diplomats and with every man in Congress and the Senate."[9]

**11 August 1872:** Representative Garfield stops in Salt Lake City while on a western rail tour and records in his diary that he "immediately went out to one of the Ward meetings and heard Taylor, one of the Apostles, preach." The following day he records, "After breakfast G. Q. Cannon, one of the 12 Apostles and the Delegate-elect to Congress, took us in a carriage to the various points of interest in the city. The Tabernacle, the Temple, Brigham's house and Camp Douglas. After dinner he took us to the depot, where we met Brigham just coming in from Ogden. Mr. Young held our train 15 minutes for a chat."[10]

**Summer 1873:** Garfield joins an old friend in his buggy for a pleasure ride to visit some of the familiar sites of his childhood, including the Kirtland Temple. Garfield writes, "In looking at this deserted temple, I can not repress a

*James A. Garfield grew up in the Kirtland area, and attended school in or near the Kirtland Temple. Years later he wrote, "In looking at this deserted temple, I can not repress a feeling of regret at the monument of failure they left. Yet they deserve a grander failure than this."*

feeling of regret at the monument of failure they left. Yet they deserve a grander failure than this. Their origin was curiously connected with the early history of the Disciples [of Christ/Campbellites]. Indeed the theological doctrines of the two are almost identical in every thing except in reference to spiritual gifts and polygamy. Sidney Rigdon must have stamped his own ideas very strongly upon the movement. I never think of that strange people without a mixture of admiration and contempt. Admiration for the boldness of the attempt they made in the world of ideas and actions, and contempt for what appears to be the hollow shams and deceptions by which they carried out their objects."[11]

**January 1875:** George Q. Cannon and Congressman Garfield hold a long conversation as they sit together on a train from Washington to Philadelphia.[12] "He has been one of my allies in Congress," Cannon later writes. "I have appealed to him a number of times when I needed help." The future President helps look out for the plight of the Mormons, in Cannon's view, and "was well acquainted with our circumstances."[13]

**June 1875:** Garfield visits Utah a second time and enjoys sailing on the Great Salt Lake with President Cannon and other Church leaders.[14] "He had visited this city twice; he had become acquainted with the people, seen them at their homes, and had frequently conversed upon our doctrines," says Cannon later. "I know therefore, he understood our question probably better than any man in public life."[15]

**4 March 1881:** James A. Garfield is sworn into office and becomes the only President to utter the phrase "Mormon Church" in an inaugural address.

**2 July 1881:** President Garfield is shot by a disgruntled office seeker. While he hovers between life and death, the Saints pray for him in the Tabernacle and cancel that year's Pioneer Day festivities on July 24. "I feel in my heart a strong sympathy for President Garfield," remarked John Taylor at the time.[16]

*White House mourning the death of Garfield.*

**19 September 1881:** Garfield finally dies from his gunshot wound. In Salt Lake City, bells throughout the city toll in mourning until late in the night, and a memorial service for the slain President is held in the Tabernacle.[17]

**October 1881:** Rumors begin to spread throughout the nation that the Mormons were behind Garfield's assassination. To prove there is no ill will, the Utah Legislature later names a county after the late President.

# THE ANTI-MORMON INAUGURAL ADDRESS

James Abram Garfield was elected the twentieth President of the United States, and when he was sworn into office on Friday, 4 March 1881, he became the only President to utter the phrase "Mormon Church" in an inaugural address. His comments on plural marriage and LDS hindrance with the law were not complimentary:

> The Territories of the United States are subject to the direct legislative authority of Congress, and hence the General Government is responsible for any violation of the Constitution in any of them. It is therefore a reproach to the Government that in the most populous of the Territories [Utah] the constitutional guaranty is not enjoyed by the people and the authority of Congress is set at naught.

> The Mormon Church not only offends the moral sense of manhood by sanctioning polygamy, but prevents the administration of justice through ordinary instrumentalities of law. In my judgment it is the duty of Congress, while respecting to the uttermost the conscientious convictions and religious scruples of every citizen, to prohibit within its jurisdiction all criminal practices, especially of that class which destroy the family relations and endanger social order. Nor can any ecclesiastical organization be safely permitted to usurp in the smallest degree the functions and powers of the National Government.[18]

Cannon, who was at the ceremony along with the other members of Congress, felt betrayed. "I felt hurt at his words concerning Utah, just as I would at the turning of a friend to meanness and wickedness."[19] He later tried to justify why his friend would say such things in a public setting: "But for fear, as I fully believe, that he would be suspected of cherishing sympathy for us, he uttered expressions which I thought were exceedingly unwise and unstatesmanlike in his inaugural address. But notwithstanding this, I must bear testimony to the man and to the largeness of his soul and the breadth of his mind."[20]

Even non-Mormon observers were somewhat taken aback by the section of the inaugural address about the Mormons. "The only jarring note was a passionate and unexpected denunciation of the Mormons," read one record of the speech. "Otherwise, all was bland and inoffensive."[21]

Just one week after the inauguration, Delegate Cannon was in the new President's office complaining about some of the unjust federal appointments made by Garfield's predecessor,

WASHINGTON, D.C.— THE INAUGURATION OF PRESIDENT GARFIELD—CHIEF JUSTICE WAITE ADMINISTERING THE OATH OF OFFICE.— FROM SKETCHES BY OUR SPECIAL ARTISTS.—SEE PAGE 98.

On 4 March 1881, James A. Garfield became the only U.S. President to utter the phrase "Mormon Church" in an inaugural address. Among his remarks he asserted, "The Mormon Church not only offends the moral sense of manhood by sanctioning polygamy, but prevents the administration of justice through ordinary instrumentalities of law."

Rutherford B. Hayes. Garfield "listened attentively" and promised to look into the matter, later encouraging Cannon to further his complaint by filing a report with the attorney general. Before the Delegate's departure, however, the inevitable topic of the remarks toward Utah were brought up. "He said he felt as he had done about polygamy," reported Cannon. "Was not in favor of harshness, but polygamy must cease."[22]

By May it was increasingly clear that the President was taking up the abolition of polygamy as a personal crusade. "The President is quite anxious to consider some practical and speedy plan of dealing with the Mormon question," reported the *New York Times*. Early in his administration, President Garfield observed hundreds of Mormon immigrants arriving in New York and the departure of forty missionaries from the same port, who were heading into the world "with a view of increasing the flood of polygamous immigration." Such a sight, according to the *Times,* "intensified in his mind the desire expressed in his inaugural."[23]

## MORMONS BLAMED FOR GARFIELD'S ASSASINATION

In an October 1881 sermon in Brooklyn, New York, Reverend T. DeWitt Talmage declared that Garfield's assassin, Charles Guiteau, was a Mormon and had "the Mormon ugliness." Reverend Talmage said that Guiteau "had the spirit of Mormon licentiousness; of Mormon cruelty; of Mormon murder." He asserted that he "should not wonder if in the great day, when all

*As if to help show the rest of the nation that there were no ill feelings among the Mormons toward the late President, early in 1882 the LDS-dominated Utah legislature changed the name of a proposed new county from Snow County to Garfield County. Above is a view of Panguitch, the county seat.*

such things are revealed, it should be found that he was a paid agent of that old hag of hell [i.e., the Mormon Church] who sits making mouths to heaven between the Rocky Mountains and the Sierra Nevada." The anti-Mormon reverend added that "while all good people throughout the world were praying for the President's recovery, the Mormons were praying for his death."[24]

That same Sunday in Dayton, Ohio, a Baptist preacher, Reverend J. H. Parks, told his congregation that the "Mormons rejoiced over the death of President Garfield, because in his inaugural address he favored the adoption of some means of abolishing this infamous practice of polygamy."[25]

Eastern newspapers reported on both of these sermons and spread the story that the news of the President being shot was received in Salt Lake City "with joy and satisfaction." The *Boston*

*Watchman,* for example, asserted that on the national day of prayer for Garfield's recovery, "the 'praying circle' of the Mormon church was engaged in continual supplication for the death of President Garfield."[26] The nation, having only buried an assassinated President Lincoln sixteen years prior, was hurt and many looked for a scapegoat in the Mormons.

Even Garfield's official biographer, writing the following year, assumed that the Latter-day Saints welcomed the President's death. He wrote, "All classes, parties and sects, except some Mormons and Socialists, appeared to feel deeply the calamity to the nation, and to indulge the most heartfelt desire that the President's life might be spared."[27]

As if to help show the rest of the nation that there were no ill feelings among the Mormons toward the late President, early in 1882 the LDS-dominated Utah legislature changed the name of a proposed new county from Snow County to Garfield County—a tract of land comprising over 5,200 square miles and boasting what would later be known as Bryce Canyon National Park. Shifting the honor from Mormon Apostle and southern Utah pioneer Erastus Snow to James A. Garfield was a move first suggested by the non-Mormon governor Eli H. Murray but quickly embraced by Elder Snow himself and the other LDS leaders in the legislature.[28]

Despite his disappointment in Garfield's anti-Mormon actions as President, apparently First Presidency member George Q. Cannon eventually forgave him. In March 1900, President Cannon would be baptized on Garfield's behalf in the Salt Lake Temple.[29] In the end, it appeared the Mormons forgave him too as there were no hard feelings toward James A. Garfield.

# ENDNOTES

1   Roberts, *A Comprehensive History of the Church,* 6:32. See also *Deseret News* clipping, in *Journal History,* 27 March 1896, 8; Allan Peskin, *Garfield,* 6, 9; *Church Almanac,* 70.

2   Lachlan E. Mackay, interview by author.

3   George Q. Cannon, "Remarks by President George Q. Cannon—3 July 1881," in *Journal of Discourses,* 22:137.

4   Peskin, *Garfield,* 29, 55. See also Joseph, 10–12.

5   Mentioned in the October 1881 issue of *Scribner's Magazine,* quoted in William Alexander Linn, *The Story of the Mormons: From the Date of their Origin to the Year 1901.*

6   Quoted in James H. Kennedy, *The Early Days of Mormonism,* 70.

7   James A. Garfield, *The Diary of James A. Garfield: Volume II 1872–1874,* 43.

8   Bitton, *George Q. Cannon,* 242–43, 460. See also Cannon, *Journal of Discourses,* 22:137.

9   Quoted in Beatrice Cannon Evans and Janath Russell Cannon, eds., *Cannon Family Historical Treasury,* 100.

10  Garfield, *The Diary of James A. Garfield,* 75–76.

11  Garfield, *The Diary of James A. Garfield,* 215–16.

12  Bitton, *George Q. Cannon,* 120.

13  Bitton, *George Q. Cannon,* 247.

14  *Deseret News* article, in *Journal History,* 4 June 1875, 1. See also *Journal History,* 5 June 1875, 1.

15  Cannon, *Journal of Discourses,* 22:137.

16  John Taylor, "Remarks by President John Taylor—3 July 1881," in *Journal of Discourses,* 22:139–44. Full text of the letter found in *Journal History,* 2 July 1881, 3.

17  John Henry Smith, *Church, State, and Politics,* 66–67.

18  Paragraphs 33 and 34 of James A. Garfield's Inaugural Address, online at http://www.bartleby.com/124/pres36.html.

19  Bitton, *George Q. Cannon,* 243.

20  Cannon, *Journal of Discourses,* 22:157.

21  Peskin, *Garfield,* 539.

22  Bitton, *George Q. Cannon,* 243.

23  *NY Times* clipping, in *Journal History,* 7 May 1881, 4.

24  Roberts, *A Comprehensive History of the Church,* 6:27.

25  Roberts, *A Comprehensive History of the Church,* 6:28.

26  Roberts, *A Comprehensive History of the Church,* 6:28–29.

27  William M. Thayer, *From Log Cabin to White House,* 416.

28  Linda King Newell and Vivian Linford Talbot, *A History of Garfield County,* 170.

29  Temple ordinances can be accessed in the International Genealogical Index (IGI) at www.familysearch.org.

# CHESTER A. ARTHUR

## *1881—1885*

Like Joseph Smith, Chester Alan Arthur was born in Vermont and reared in New York State. As vice president, he was elevated to the presidency upon the assassination of James A. Garfield. One of his early acts as President was to appoint anti-Mormon Eli Murray to a second term as governor of Utah Territory.[1] Arthur shared his predecessor's disdain for the LDS practice of polygamy and therefore became one of the Church's harshest enemies to date.

**6 December 1881:** In a formal message to Congress, Arthur vigorously urges measures to be taken against the polygamists of the West: "In my judgment it is the duty of congress, while respecting to the uttermost the conscientious convictions, and religious scruples of every citizen, to prohibit within its jurisdiction all criminal practices, especially of that class which destroy the family relations and endanger social order."[2]

**11 March 1882:** Elder John Henry Smith of the Twelve, who is sent by Church leaders to the capital to help lobby against hostile legislation, meets with the President. Although the Apostle and the chief executive disagree,

Elder Smith is impressed with his dignified bearing and notes in his report, "Chester A. Arthur is a fine looking man."[3]

*President Arthur, shown standing, was lobbied on behalf of the Church by Elder John Henry Smith of the Twelve. After their meeting, Elder Smith reported being impressed with the President's dignified bearing and wrote, "Chester A. Arthur is a fine looking man."*

**22 March 1882:** Arthur signs the Edmunds Bill into law, which defines polygamous living as "unlawful cohabitation" and makes punishable the contracting of plural marriage as well as disenfranchisement of those who continue to live it.[4] Apostle John Henry Smith, who is still in Washington, pens in his diary, "President C. A. Arthur had signed the Edmunds bill. I am feeling like the weather looks and that rather blue."[5]

**1884:** Apostles Charles W. Penrose and Brigham Young Jr. meet with President Arthur in a futile attempt to persuade him to back off the government's antipolygamy persecutions.[6] Instead, Arthur appoints Charles S. Zane, a harsh prosecutor of polygamists, to be chief justice of Utah.[7]

Although Chester Arthur's dealings with the Church were few, they were harsh. His signature on the Edmunds Bill and his unpopular appointments were enough to dissolve any affection the Saints may have felt for him.

## ENDNOTES

1   "The Governors of Utah: Eli H. Murray," *Improvement Era* 4, no. 9 (July 1901).

2   *Messages and Papers of the Presidents,* 7:11.

3   Entry for Saturday, 11 March 1882, in John Henry Smith, *Church, State, and Politics,* 75–76.

4   Yorgason, *Courageous Defender of Truth,* 381.

5   Entry for Friday, 24 March 1882, in John Henry Smith, *Church, State, and Politics,* 77.

6   Michael K. Winder, comp., *Counselors to the Prophets,* 199.

7   "Passing Events," *Improvement Era* 18, no. 8 (June 1915).

*In the winter of 1881–82, debate raged inside the United States Capitol as antipolygamy legislation, encouraged by President Arthur was debated and advanced into law.*

# GROVER CLEVELAND

## *1885—1889* AND *1893—1897*

As a result of the antipolygamy stances of the previous six Republican administrations, the Mormons saw a flicker of hope as Grover Cleveland became the first Democratic presidential victor in twenty-eight years. In the campaign of 1884, the Republican platform was harsh in its stance against the Mormon Church, while the Democratic platform was not only silent on the Mormon question, but also advocated that territorial officers should be selected locally.[1] Cleveland would talk tough against polygamy, but in deed became the Saints' best friend in the White House since Millard Fillmore. Utah statehood would be the result, albeit not until Cleveland's second term.

**4 March 1885:** "The conscience of the people demands," booms the new President in his inaugural address, "that polygamy in the Territories, destructive of the family relation and offensive to the moral sense of the civilized world, shall be repressed."[2]

**13 May 1885:** Church leaders meet with Cleveland to protest the enforcement of the unjust Edmunds Act.

*The Saints were initially wary of Grover Cleveland due to his tough speech at his swearing in. "The conscience of the people demands," boomed the new President in his inaugural address, "that polygamy in the Territories, destructive of the family relation and offensive to the moral sense of the civilized world, shall be repressed."*

**Summer 1885:** LDS Apostles Charles W. Penrose and Brigham Young Jr. meet with President Cleveland to lobby their cause, and develop a good friendship.[3]

**November 1885:** George L. Miller is dispatched from President Cleveland to meet the Mormons. In a secret late-night visit with George Q. Cannon, Miller assures him that "Grover Cleveland was someone who could be dealt with," for Cleveland wants "Utah to be a state and a Democratic one." However, Miller implores, the Saints must abandon polygamy. Just as Abraham Lincoln insisted the nation could not exist part slave and part free, Cleveland claims it cannot exist part polygamous and part monogamous.[4] During this time, Mormon Apostles publicly pray in conferences for the success of Grover Cleveland and hold him up as a standard of an honest politician.[5]

**December 1885:** In Cleveland's first annual message to Congress he again expresses his disdain for polygamy. He even adds, "Since the people upholding polygamy in our Territories are re-enforced by immigration from other lands, I recommend that a law be passed to prevent the importation of Mormons into the country." This proposal never materializes, but the Perpetual Emigration Fund, which assists the LDS immigration efforts, is dissolved shortly thereafter by federal law.[6]

**February 1887:** As more antipolygamy legislation makes its way through Congress, LDS lobbyists and President Cleveland favor the Scott Amendment, which will not be as harsh. But in the end, harsher legislation prevails.[7] The Edmunds-Tucker Act passes Congress and is sent to President Cleveland. Included in the stringent provisions is the disenfranchisement of The Church of Jesus Christ of Latter-day Saints, and the confiscation of practically all Church property. The President feels the bill is too harsh but realizes that he will be jeopardizing his political future and angering both political parties if he vetoes it. However, he doesn't want to sign it and endanger future negotiations with the Church, so Cleveland diplomatically does nothing. Since no action is taken within ten days, it becomes law without his signature.[8]

**1887:** Former First Presidency member John W. Young meets with the President and reassures Church headquarters, "He is kindly disposed to act as fair and far as possible."[9] Cleveland proves this that year when he pardons polygamist Apostle Rudger Clawson, replaces "Mormon-hater" Utah governor Eli Murray, withdraws his nomination of an anti-Mormon judge, and encourages light sentences for polygamists.[10]

**December 1888:** In his fourth annual message to Congress, the President boasts of his administration's "vigilant execution of these laws" and that under his watch, "polygamy within the United States is virtually at an end." The statistics he gives are impressive: prior to his inauguration in March 1885 there have only been six convictions of unlawful cohabitation in Utah and Idaho, but during his first four years in the White House there have been nearly six hundred convictions. Rather than backfiring, President Cleveland's soft-handed strategy with the Mormons makes him appear on paper to be tougher than ever. Because Cleveland-appointed judges give drastically less severe sentences than their Republican predecessors, many Mormon polygamists (including First Presidency member George Q. Cannon) simply turn themselves in.[11]

**27 August 1894:** Cleveland grants pardons to those who have been disfranchised under antipolygamy laws.[12]

*Grover Cleveland was ingenious when it came to prosecuting polygamists. By greatly lightening their prison sentences, most LDS men guilty of unlawful cohabitation simply turned themselves in and served their time, including President George Q. Cannon (seated in center). This allowed Cleveland to boast to Congress of six hundred convictions, compared with his six Republican predecessors' total of six.*

**4 January 1896:** Cleveland admits Utah as the forty-fifth state.

**28 March 1896:** Cleveland signs an act returning property to the Church that has been confiscated as a result of the Edmunds-Tucker Act.[13]

# CHURCH LEADERS PROTEST EDMUNDS ACT

Less than two months after Cleveland's inauguration, a mass meeting was held in the Tabernacle in Salt Lake City, where a "Statement of Grievances and Protest" regarding the antipolygamy Edmunds Act was drafted and approved. John T. Caine (Utah's delegate to Congress), John W. Taylor (Apostle and son of then-Church president John Taylor), and John Q. Cannon (son of President George Q. Cannon) were sent to present their statement to President Cleveland. The Associated Press related the 13 May meeting at the White House as follows:

The president listened courteously and attentively, to the address and upon its conclusion, said: "Well, gentlemen, so far, of course, as the Edmunds law is concerned, I had nothing to do with that. Of course it is my duty to see that it is enforced, as well as all other laws. You are entitled to fair consideration and to have the law impartially administered, as you have asked, and, so far as any appointments which I shall make are concerned, I will endeavor to give you a character of men who will see that the law is impartially administered. I hope soon to be able to get at these matters, but it will require a little time."

The president's face broke into a smile as he concluded, "I wish you out there could be like the rest of us."

"All we ask," rejoined Mr. Caine, "is that the law shall be impartially administered."

"You are entitled to that," said the president, "and, so far as I am concerned, I shall see that it is done. I will give these matters my attention as carefully as possible."[14]

*"I wish you out there could be like the rest of us," Grover Cleveland once told a delegation from Utah. The only President to serve two nonconsecutive terms balanced both interests when he let the anti-Mormon Edmunds-Tucker Act become law without his signature. He didn't want to sign it and upset the Mormons, and he could not veto it and upset Congress.*

# GROVER CLEVELAND AND UTAH'S STATEHOOD

Even while out of the White House between his two terms, Cleveland kept an eye on Utah and the Mormons. He was pleased to see the Manifesto denouncing polygamy in 1890, and in 1891 he wired his congratulations to Church leaders for dissolving the Mormon's People's Party and encouraging their members to embrace the national political party of their choice.[15] Clearly he was hoping to keep the Church leaning toward the Democrats. As the 1892 election approached, Cleveland once again sent national Democratic leader George Miller to Utah, and Miller met with George Q. Cannon in September. Miller told Cannon that if the Saints helped Idaho and Wyoming vote Democratic in November, then the new Cleveland administration would give Utah "the full benefit of it"—meaning statehood.[16]

Cleveland was returned to the White House in the election of 1892, a return that was optimistically viewed by the Mormons. President Cannon called on the newly inaugurated President in the White House just days after the March ceremony. The Church leader explained that the Saints were doing the best they could to obey the law regarding plural marriage and put in a plug for Utah statehood. If Utah became a state during Cleveland's term, Cannon said to him, "It will be a cause of gratulation to you throughout your life."[17]

In a later interview, Cannon explained to the chief executive that the

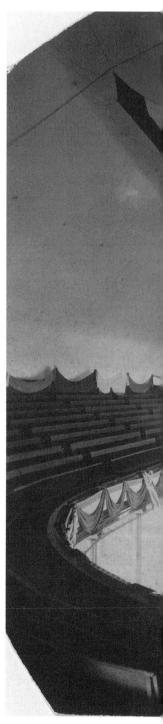

When President Cleveland signed the act allowing Utah to join the sisterhood of states, celebrations spilled onto Salt Lake City's Main Street despite the January cold (below, left), and formal commemorations took place inside a patriotically decorated Tabernacle on Temple Square (below).

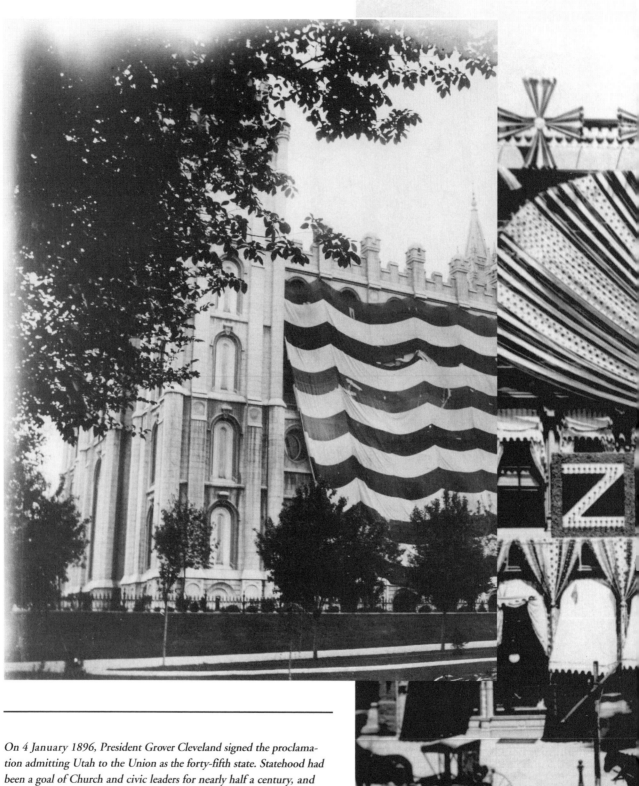

On 4 January 1896, President Grover Cleveland signed the proclamation admitting Utah to the Union as the forty-fifth state. Statehood had been a goal of Church and civic leaders for nearly half a century, and celebrations included parades in the streets of Salt Lake City, and patriotic decorations in the Tabernacle, on Z.C.M.I., and even on the Salt Lake Temple.

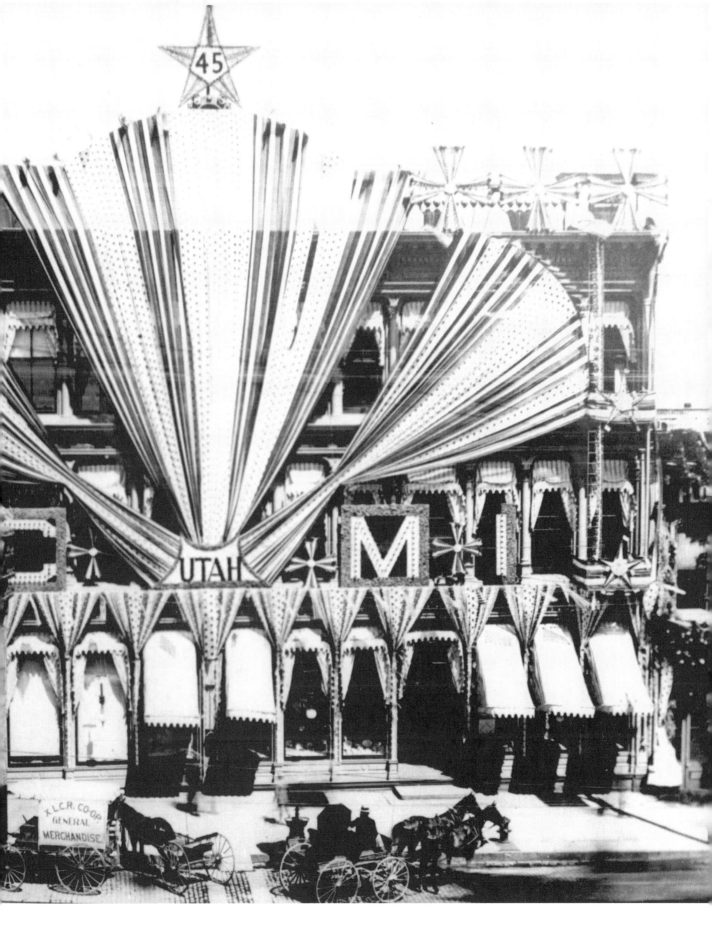

Saints in Utah Territory, including himself, were doing their best to obey the laws against cohabitation. Cannon told Cleveland of the common dining room his family once enjoyed, but he explained that now he dined only with his deceased wife's children, never daring to dine at the home of one of his other wives. "That is pretty hard," said Cleveland. Cannon said that the Saints generally had obeyed the Manifesto but that "there may be violations of the law, sporadic cases." Cleveland replied, "There are in every community." Cannon felt that his meetings with the President helped keep Cleveland sympathetic to the Mormons and continuously supportive of Utah statehood.[18]

Cleveland soon began preparing Utah for statehood. For the first time in decades, local residents—including Latter-day Saints—were appointed by the President to federal positions within

Utah Territory.[19] In July 1894 Cleveland signed the Utah Statehood Bill, which authorized Utah to hold a constitutional convention.[20] In March 1895 the Utah Constitutional Convention met in Salt Lake City, and the resulting state constitution was overwhelmingly approved by the people of Utah. On 4 January 1896, President Grover Cleveland signed the proclamation admitting Utah to the Union as the forty-fifth state.[21]

Democrat Grover Cleveland accomplished what his six Republican predecessors could not. On one hand, the Edmunds-Tucker Act was created under his administration and prosecutions of polygamists increased one hundred fold. On the other, local officials were appointed in Utah, pardons were issued, and statehood finally authorized. Remarkably, both the Latter-day Saints and their antagonists were satisfied.

# ENDNOTES

1    Roberts, *A Comprehensive History of the Church,* 6:123.

2    Paragraph 14 of Grover Cleveland's first inaugural address, online at http://www.bartleby.com/124/pres37.html.

3    Winder, *Counselors to the Prophets,* 199, 291.

4    Bitton, *George Q. Cannon,* 275.

5    See Moses Thatcher's address delivered in the Logan Tabernacle, in *Journal of Discourses,* 26:335. See also George Q. Cannon's address delivered in the Provo Tabernacle, in *Journal of Discourses,* 26:17.

6    Grover Cleveland, *The Writings and Speeches of Grover Cleveland,* 338–40.

7    Bitton, *George Q. Cannon,* 283–84.

8    *Church Almanac,* Ibid; Allen and Leonard, *The Story of the Latter-day Saints,* 412–13.

9    Bitton, *George Q. Cannon,* 285.

10   Allen and Leonard, *The Story of the Latter-day Saints,* 404. See also Yorgason, *Courageous Defender of Truth,* 410; Roberts, *A Comprehensive History of the Church,* 6:175.

11   Roberts, *A Comprehensive History of the Church,* 6:210–12.

12   *Church Almanac,* 548. See also Allen and Leonard, *The Story of the Latter-day Saints,* 422–23.

13   Holzapfel, et al., *On this Day in the Church,* 59.

14   Roberts, *A Comprehensive History of the Church,* 6:151–52. He states that the AP account "appeared in practically all the newspapers of the country."

15   Alexander, *Things in Heaven and Earth,* 275–76.

16   Bitton, *George Q. Cannon,* 328–29.

17   Bitton, *George Q. Cannon,* 335–36, 11 March 1893.

18   Bitton, *George Q. Cannon,* 356–57.

19   Alexander, *Things in Heaven and Earth,* 282.

20   *Church Almanac,* 547. See also Holzapfel, et al., *On this Day in the Church,* 140.

21   *Church Almanac,* Ibid.

# BENJAMIN HARRISON

## *1889–1893*

Between the two friendly terms of Democrat Grover Cleveland came Republican Benjamin Harrison. Harrison initially took a harsh stance against the Latter-day Saints due to the polygamy issue, but the Manifesto of 1890 officially ceasing the practice and Harrison's 1891 visit to Utah helped soften his views. In the end, he began pardoning the Saints but did not go as far in this as they had hoped, and they would have to wait for Cleveland's second term to achieve their long-sought goal of Utah statehood.

**November 1888:** Benjamin Harrison is elected President on a Republican platform that pledges to "stamp out the . . . wickedness of polygamy" among the Mormons and that declares, "The political power of the Mormon church . . . is a menace to free institutions and dangerous to be longer suffered."[1]

**1889:** Mormon attorney Franklin S. Richards meets with the newly elected President and Secretary of State James G. Blaine to urge "the appointment of conservative men of high character who would enforce the law fairly." President Harrison replies that he expects to make no appointments of vindictive or unfriendly officials. However, he soon appoints anti-Mormon Arthur L. Thomas as governor and supports antipolygamy federal officials for Utah Territory.[2]

**1890:** Harrison is initially suspicious upon hearing of President Woodruff's Manifesto officially ceasing plural marriages.

**May 1891:** Benjamin Harrison visits Utah.

**7 September 1891:** Harrison grants amnesty to First Presidency member Joseph F. Smith. For the first time in seven years he is now able to speak publicly in the Tabernacle: "I spoke briefly, for I was so overcome by my feelings that I could scarcely restrain them."[3]

**October 1892:** Moderating his views somewhat due to his Utah visit and the Manifesto, Harrison instructs newly appointed U.S. marshal Irving Benton to "do as he was directed by the heads of the Mormon Church if he desired to retain his position."[4]

**13 October 1892:** Harrison asks LDS leaders for their prayers on behalf of his ill and dying wife, Caroline. "Who even heard," President Woodruff wrote in his diary, "of such a thing in this generation as President of the United States asking their [the First Presidency's] prayers for himself & wife? May God grant it." The Mormon leaders obliged, but Carrie Harrison died on 25 October.[5] A telegram of condolence was sent that afternoon to the grieving President from President Woodruff and his counselors.[6]

**4 January 1893:** After years of lobbying by George Q. Cannon, as well as James S. Clarkson (chairman of the Republican National Committee), and Secretary of State James G. Blaine, Harrison finally issues a proclamation of amnesty weeks before leaving office. However, it was a pardon only for polygamists "who have, since November 1, 1890, abstained from such unlawful cohabitation." Thus, the long-sought amnesty was of no protection to any whose plural wives had borne children since 1890.[7]

---

*The First Presidency during Harrison's administration (George Q. Cannon, Wilford Woodruff, and Joseph F. Smith) was asked by the President to pray on behalf of his ill and dying wife, Caroline. "Who even heard," President Woodruff wrote in his diary, "of such a thing in this generation as President of the United States asking their [the First Presidency's] prayers for himself & wife? May God grant it."*

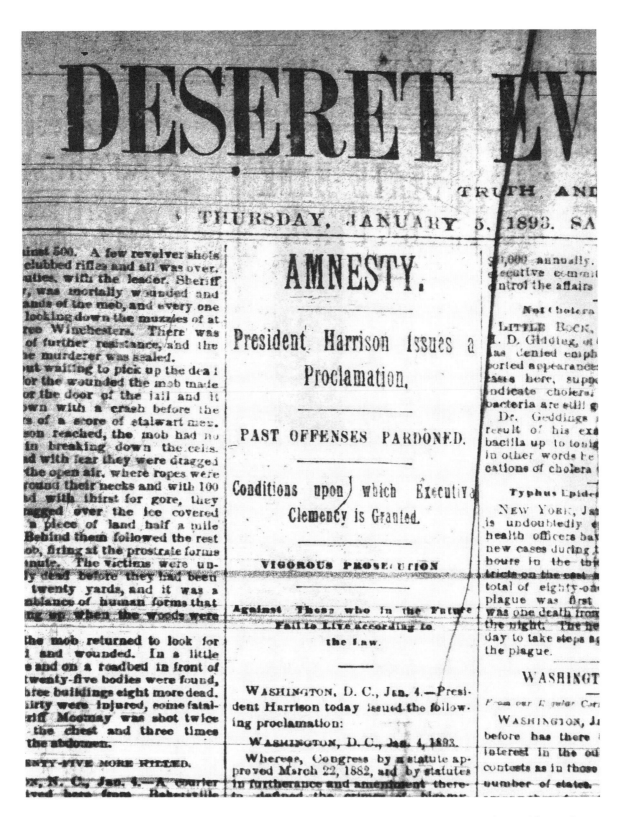

# DESERET EV

TRUTH AND

THURSDAY, JANUARY 5, 1893. SA

## AMNESTY.

### President Harrison Issues a Proclamation.

### PAST OFFENSES PARDONED.

### Conditions upon which Executive Clemency is Granted.

### VIGOROUS PROSECUTION

### Against Those who In the Future Fail to Live According to the Law.

WASHINGTON, D. C., Jan. 4.—President Harrison today issued the following proclamation:

WASHINGTON, D. C., Jan. 4, 1893.

Whereas, Congress by a statute approved March 22, 1882, and by statutes in furtherance and amendment thereof defined the crime of bigamy

*Benjamin Harrison announces a limited amnesty for polygamists "who have, since November 1, 1890, abstained from such unlawful cohabitation."*

## HARRISON'S INITIAL REACTION TO THE MANIFESTO

After the Manifesto was issued in 1890, President Harrison suspected that it was merely a trick to win statehood. He warned against granting statehood too hastily. In his second annual message to Congress, he declared,

> President Woodruff does not renounce the doctrine, but refrains from teaching it and advises against the practice of it because the law is against it. Now it is quite true that the law should not attempt to deal with the faith or belief of anyone; but it is quite another thing, and the only safe thing, to so deal with the Territory of Utah as that those who believe polygamy to be rightful shall not have the power to make it lawful.[8]

## BENJAMIN HARRISON'S VISIT TO UTAH

Despite his initial suspicions regarding the Manifesto, Harrison gradually assumed a more moderate attitude toward the Saints and announced in 1891 that he would visit Utah. In Salt Lake City, the Gardo House, Beehive House, and other Church-owned buildings were "profusely decorated" with flags and patriotic bunting. Signs covered the *Juvenile Instructor* building declaring "Welcome to the Grandson of Tippecanoe" and "Under Harrison freedom dawned on Utah." Even the temple had a huge banner covering an entire side of the building that said, "Fear God, Honor the President."[9]

On 9 May 1891, President Benjamin Harrison arrived, where he met with Presidents Woodruff, Cannon, and others.[10] A parade formed behind the presidential procession and along South Temple Street, the

*The Salt Lake Temple, shown draped with a flag to celebrate Utah's statehood, was also decorated for the 1891 visit of Benjamin Harrison. A huge banner covered an entire side of the building and pronounced, "Fear God, Honor the President."*

*In his 1891 visit to Utah, President Harrison was especially impressed with what he saw as he traveled through Utah Valley. "It has been very pleasant to-day to ride through this most extraordinary valley, and to notice how productive your fields are and how genial and kind your people are."*

VIPs passed a large group of children cheering and waving flags. President Harrison was touched and stopped and talked with them.[11] "I have not seen in all this long journey," the President later said, "anything that touched my heart more than . . . when the children from the free public schools of Salt Lake City, waving the one banner that we all love and singing an anthem of praise to that beneficent Providence . . . , gave us their glad welcome."[12] He later added, "I have seen nothing more beautiful and inspiring than this scene which burst upon us unexpectedly. The multitude of children bearing waving banners makes a scene which can never fade from our memories."[13]

At Liberty Park, the First Presidency sat on the stand within feet of the President during his address.[14] "We are a people organized upon principles of liberty," Harrison told the cheering crowd, "but, my fellow countrymen, it is distinguished from license; its liberty within and under the law. I have no discord as a public officer with men of any creed, religious or political, if they will obey the law."

A host of LDS Sunday School children and the Mormon Tabernacle Choir waited patiently for hours in the Tabernacle to perform patriotic music for the President. However, the anti-Mormons of the city, including Governor Thomas, worked hard to keep the President far away from Temple Square, to the disappointment of many Saints.[15] The presidential train continued south, making stops and brief speeches in Lehi, American Fork, Provo, and Springville. "It has been very pleasant to-day to ride through this most extraordinary valley," Harrison said in Springville after a day traveling through the Mormon settlements of Utah County, "and to notice how productive your fields are and how genial and kindly your people are."[16]

# ENDNOTES

1   Roberts, *A Comprehensive History of The Church,* 6:283.

2   Alexander, *Things in Heaven and Earth,* 251.

3   Joseph Fielding Smith, comp., *Life of Joseph F. Smith,* 299–300.

4   Alexander, *Things in Heaven and Earth,* 278.

5   Alexander, *Things in Heaven and Earth,* 274.

6   Staker, *Waiting for World's End: The Diaries of Wilford Woodruff,* 393–94.

7   Among Clarkson's papers (articles and speeches folder, Box 4) in the Library of Congress is a report, as of 1910, which includes, "Then after Harrison's election as president, Mr. Blaine and Mr. Clarkson induced the President to pardon the hundreds of Mormons still in prison for polygamy and restore all Mormons to citizenship." See also Garr, et al., *Encyclopedia of Latter-day Saint History,* Ibid.; *Church Almanac,* 547; Bitton, *George Q. Cannon,* 325–26, 331.

8   Richardson, *Messages and Papers of the President,* 9:118.

9   Bitton, *George Q. Cannon,* 318.

10   Alexander, *Things in Heaven and Earth,* 278.

11   Bitton, *George Q. Cannon,* 318.

12   Benjamin Harrison, *Speeches of Benjamin Harrison,* 431.

13   Harrison, *Speeches of Benjamin Harrison,* 433–34.

14   Bitton, *George Q. Cannon,* 318.

15   *Deseret News,* 16 May 1891. See also Bitton, *George Q. Cannon,* 318.

16   Harrison, *Speeches of Benjamin Harrison,* 434–36.

# WILLIAM MCKINLEY

## *1897–1901*

Many presidential scholars regard McKinley's presidency as the beginning of America's transformation to the modern age, when the U.S. moved beyond old Civil War Era issues and emerged as a world power through the Spanish-American War. Likewise, in the relationship between the Mormons and the White House, McKinley's presidency represented the beginning of a transformation toward modernity. For decades, the relationship between the Saints and the Presidents was defined by Utah's quest for statehood and the various chief executives' quests to eradicate polygamy. However, with McKinley we began to move beyond these issues and into the twentieth century where Presidents recognized the Church as a potential ally and where the Church worked to cultivate positive personal relationships with Presidents for the benefit of its members and programs.

**November 1896:** William McKinley wins the White House. In the first presidential election for the new state of Utah, a rousing 83 percent goes to William Jennings Bryan and a mere 17 percent to McKinley.[1]

**May 1897:** First Presidency member George Q. Cannon travels to Washington and calls on McKinley three times. He invites the President to attend the pioneer jubilee in Utah on 24 July 1897 and urges him to not exclude Mormons from federal appointments. McKinley agrees and asks for a list of names.[2] "If I can, I shall go," promises the President regarding the jubilee. In the end he is unable to.[3]

**June 1897:** McKinley makes his first federal appointment of a Latter-day Saint when he appoints Charles Kingston to be register of the U.S. Land Office at Evanston, Wyoming.[4]

**January 1898:** McKinley appoints future Church president George Albert Smith—age twenty-seven at the time and not yet ordained an Apostle—to serve as receiver of public monies and disbursing agent in the U. S. Land Office in Utah. McKinley says he feels "that a member of The Church of Jesus Christ of Latter-day Saints was entitled to a federal appointment."[5]

**January and February 1900:** Elder John Henry Smith of the Twelve and Hiram B. Clawson, then a bishop, have a couple of meetings with the President. They report having "a pleasant talk on Utah affairs" and insisted that the Mormon people had kept their word regarding polygamous marriages, which continue to decrease.[6] They also talk political strategy for the upcoming reelection. "I told him I would do all I could for him but that he must not overestimate my strength," reports Elder Smith. "We had a good handshake and he seemed very happy."[7]

**November 1900:** McKinley wins reelection against his previous rival, William Jennings Bryan. This time, LDS-dominated Utah backs McKinley 51 to 48 percent thanks to McKinley's fair treat-

ment of the Saints and Bryan's focusing less on the silver issue and more on an anti–Spanish-American War stance.[8] The day after McKinley is reelected, President Joseph F. Smith and Elder John Henry Smith telegram the White House: "We rejoice to say that Utah is again in the Republican column."[9]

**December 1900:** Apostle Reed Smoot visits McKinley in Washington. The President seems "much in favor of his becoming a senator from Utah."[10]

*Although William McKinley lost Utah's votes in their first presidential election 17 percent to 83 percent, he exhibited friendship toward the Church and won their votes in 1900 when he was up for reelection.*

*Future Church president George Albert Smith, then 31, reported he "heard the shot that killed McKinley." Both were in the Music Hall at the Pan-American exposition in Buffalo, New York, when President McKinley was assassinated.*

**26 May 1901**: President McKinley stops briefly at the rail depot in Ogden, Utah, while returning from California. He greets the crowd gathered to meet him, including Church and government leaders, but declines giving a speech since it is the Sabbath.[11]

**6 September 1901:** While in the Music Hall at the Pan-American exposition in Buffalo, New York, President McKinley is shot. The President has just given a little girl the red carnation from his buttonhole when an anarchist named Leon Czolgosz shoots him twice.[12] George Albert Smith, who is also visiting the expo, reports that he was in the hall and "heard the shot that killed McKinley."[13]

**8 September 1901:** President Snow declares it is the duty of the Latter-day Saints to pray for McKinley's recovery. He teaches that McKinley has been "called of the Lord to do the work assigned him. He will receive a great reward in the future life for that which he has accomplished in the interest of the nation."[14] The President dies six days later.

## UTAH REJECTS McKINLEY IN THE ELECTION OF 1896

Voters in predominately Mormon Utah gave William Jennings Bryan over four times the votes as McKinley in 1896. Such a lopsided vote for the Democratic nominee was a result of Mormon

*Elder John Henry Smith of the Twelve Apostles was active in campaigning for GOP presidential candidates William McKinley and Theodore Roosevelt. George Albert Smith said of him, "My father did more to establish the Republican Party in Utah than any other man."*

gratitude for Democrat President Cleveland making statehood possible, Bryan's free silver stance that was immensely popular in the Mountain West, and the personal connection Bryan had forged with the Saints. Bryan had attended an LDS general conference in Salt Lake City while on the campaign trail and commented that the world would benefit more from what was said in conference than they would gain from his own speeches. Heber J. Grant, then an Apostle, recalled, "I remember saying to my family that William Jennings Bryan ought to be a Latter-day Saint, because many of his views were in perfect harmony with our faith."[15]

Elder John Henry Smith of the Twelve and father of George Albert Smith had campaigned for McKinley in various western states.[16] George Albert Smith said of him, "My father did more to establish the Republican Party in Utah than any other man. He devoted his time and means to accomplish the desired end. I did all I could, going out on the stump, and helping the unpopular cause along."[17] Embarrassed by Utah's strongly Democratic vote on election day, Elder Smith and his cousin, President Joseph F. Smith, quickly penned a letter to Republican National Committee Chair, Mark Hanna, apologizing for Utah's behavior.[18]

## McKINLEY'S MEMORIES OF LORENZO SNOW

Elder John Henry Smith called upon President McKinley in 1901 and carried with him official greetings from Church President Lorenzo Snow. As a young man in Ohio, Lorenzo Snow was an acquaintance of William McKinley. While meeting with Elder Smith, the President recalled that he had "known President Snow from his boyhood." He remembered as a boy being introduced formally to Lorenzo Snow who was "in the heyday of his young manhood, erect in person, and with a graceful, dignified bearing." McKinley said he had "remembered him very distinctly ever since."

Regarding his old acquaintance, the President instructed Elder Smith, "I desire you, upon your return to your mountain home, to bear to him my kind regards; for I esteem him as a man devoted to the interests and wellbeing of his fellowmen, who loves his God and his country." Elder Smith said he

*Having both grown up in Ohio, President McKinley had warm memories of Church president Lorenzo Snow [right] as a young man. "In the heyday of his young manhood," remembered McKinley, Snow was "erect in person, and with a graceful, dignified bearing. [I have] remembered him very distinctly ever since."*

was moved by the President's affection for the Church President. "I had little doubt of the possibilities for the accomplishment of good in the interests of the Latter-day Saints through the ministrations and efforts of the man whom Providence had placed at the head of His people and the man whom Providence had placed at the head of our nation."[19] Thus, although the Mormons didn't give their vote to McKinley, they later realized the good in him and voted to reelect him. They considered him a good President.

# ENDNOTES

1   *Dave Leip's Atlas of U.S. Presidential Elections.*

2   Bitton, *George Q. Cannon,* 419.

3   *Deseret News,* 15 May 1897.

4   Jenson, *LDS Biographical Encyclopedia,* 1:331.

5   Francis M. Gibbons, *George Albert Smith: Kind and Caring Christian, Prophet of God,* 39. See also George Albert Smith, in Conference Report, April 1949, 84.

6   John Henry Smith, *Church, State, and Politics,* 445.

7   John Henry Smith, *Church, State, and Politics,* 448.

8   *Dave Leip's Atlas of U.S. Presidential Elections.*

9   John Henry Smith, *Church, State, and Politics,* 468.

10  Stan Larson, ed., *A Ministry of Meetings: The Apostolic Diaries of Rudger Clawson,* 232.

11  "President Visits Ogden," *Ogden Standard-Examiner,* 27 May 1901.

12  Freidel, *Our Country's Presidents,* 147.

13  Gibbons, *George Albert Smith,* 39.

14  Larson, *A Ministry of Meetings,* 314–15.

15  Conference Report, Fall 1925, 3–4.

16  John Henry Smith, *Church, State, and Politics,* 361.

17  Gibbons, *George Albert Smith,* 37.

18  Letter to Mark Hanna from John Henry Smith and Joseph F. Smith, 16 November 1896, in the John Henry Smith Letters, Special Collections, Marriott Library, University of Utah, Salt Lake City.

19  John Henry Smith, in Conference Report, November 1901, Afternoon Session, 1.

# THEODORE ROOSEVELT

## *1901—1909*

In the ever-changing relationship between the White House and the Mormons, it would not be an exaggeration to say that no President did more than Theodore Roosevelt to bestow national legitimacy on the LDS Church. It would have been unthinkable just a few administrations prior to see the nation's chief intervene to help a Mormon Apostle secure his Senate seat or to visit Salt Lake City—not as a host of the "gentiles" of the state, but as one fully embracing her inhabitants and even speaking at the pulpit in the Tabernacle. While Cleveland and McKinley privately showed some warmth toward the Saints, it was Teddy who first openly associated with them and praised their virtues in speeches and in an op-ed piece written to a popular national magazine. The presidency of Theodore Roosevelt also marks the beginning of Apostle-Senator Reed Smoot's many presidential relationships—and his becoming the chief face of the Mormon–White House interchanges during six presidencies and over thirty years. Not until Ezra Taft Benson became active in politics would a Mormon play such a role among America's leaders.

**Fall 1900:** While campaigning for the vice presidency in Idaho and Utah, Governor Roosevelt develops relationships with Apostles John Henry Smith, and George Albert Smith, and mission president Ben E. Rich.

**5 September 1901:** George Albert Smith meets with Roosevelt in Buffalo, New York, and spends the afternoon with him in the home of Anthony Wilcox.[1] Remarkably, the visit took place on the day before President McKinley's assassination, an event which elevates Roosevelt to the White House.

**19 March 1902:** Elder John Henry Smith and Ben E. Rich call upon President Roosevelt. "He received us with open arms and expressed his personal regard for us," writes Elder Smith, "and said he would do anything he could for us."[2]

**January 1903:** Apostle Reed Smoot is elected to the Senate and successfully enlists the help of President Roosevelt to gain his protested seat.

**29 May 1903:** Teddy Roosevelt visits Utah and becomes the first U.S. President to speak in the Tabernacle.

**April 1904:** Roosevelt honors LDS President Joseph F. Smith and Apostles John Henry Smith and Reed Smoot by having them join him on the reviewing stand at the World Fair's parade in St. Louis, Missouri. During the social event, the brethren discuss with the President a current problem of missionaries being restricted in Kaiser Wilhelm II's Germany. Roosevelt volunteers that "it was his intention to do what he could for the Mormon missionaries who were suffering persecution in Germany."[3]

**Fall 1904:** Because of his unprecedented support for the Saints, the Church hierarchy works to see Roosevelt elected. Samuel O. Bennion recalls, "I was preparing to go on my mission. I called on President Joseph F. Smith, and told him I was ready to go. He said to me, 'Brother Bennion, you stay here and help elect Theodore Roosevelt, and then go.' And I did."[4] George Albert Smith campaigns for him full-time, and other Apostles speak out in favor of Roosevelt.[5] In Utah, Roosevelt wins easily with 61 percent to Alton Parker's 33 percent.[6]

**April 1905:** During the annual general conference, Elder Hyrum Mack Smith reports, "We believe that in President Roosevelt we have an unprejudiced friend; and we know that in the Latter-day Saints President Roosevelt will find loyalty to the government and the greatest friendship toward him." He praises Roosevelt's courage and claims, "There are no people in the nation more friendly to him. . . . I believe he is a man who so long as he believes our cause just, will be willing to do something for us."[7]

**February 1906:** Elder John Henry Smith and his wife are warmly received by the President on two separate occasions.[8] Their son George Albert Smith also goes to see "Teddy," but when he sees the large crowd waiting, he decides not to intrude and merely leaves his card with the clerk.

However, before he can exit the White House, the clerk overtakes him and says that the President wants to see him. "I am very glad to see you," says the dynamic President, "and I never want you to come to Washington while I am president of the United States without coming to see me."[9]

*Theodore Roosevelt (left) visits the Saltair resort on the shores of the Great Salt Lake with Utah's first governor, Heber M. Wells (center) and others as part of his May 1903 visit. Governor Wells was the son of First Presidency member Daniel H. Wells. Note the two Secret Service agents on the right. Roosevelt was the first President to receive full-time Secret Service protection, a response to McKinley's assassination.*

*In his 1900 campaign swing, Roosevelt struck up a friendship with Ben E. Rich (above)—a charismatic LDS mission president who spent an entire railway trip explaining the doctrines and history of the Church to Roosevelt. The future President walked away from his discussion with Elder Rich with a copy of the Book of Mormon in hand and saying he had "never listened to a more interesting account of a great people and a great religion."*

**September 1907:** Mary Harmston names her family's Uinta Basin settlement Roosevelt City, after the pro-Mormon President.[10] Today the Utah town has 8,000 residents.

**October 1907:** While Roosevelt is in a parade in Chattanooga, Tennessee, he is called to by Ben Rich, the Southern States mission president. Roosevelt leaves his place at the head of the parade to walk over and talk to his old friend for a moment. Newspapers report the event, and thereafter Rich and the Mormons have much greater respect in the community.[11]

**April 1909:** A month after Roosevelt hands the reins over to Taft he is praised by several leaders in LDS general conference. "I believe that, in the writings of historians of the future," declares Elder John Henry Smith, "one of the brightest names in the history of the race will be that of the man who has served this nation so faithfully and well—Theodore Roosevelt." Ben E. Rich reports "that this people never had a better friend in the White House than Theodore Roosevelt. There has never been a man there that understood this people as he understood them. He has been, and he is your friend. Many a conversation have I had with him concerning the struggles of this people, and the building up of this land."[12]

**April 1911:** The former President writes a letter, published by *Collier's,* a prominent national magazine, refuting anti-Mormon charges.

**November 1912:** Despite Teddy Roosevelt's popularity with the Mormons and his second-place finish nationally, in Utah he comes in third with 22 percent of the vote, compared to 33 percent for Wilson and 37 percent for Taft.[13] Apostle-Senator Smoot had convinced the members of the Church that Taft would likely win and that it would be better to support him.[14]

## ROOSEVELT MEETS THE MORMONS IN THE 1900 CAMPAIGN

While the forty-one-year-old Theodore Roosevelt campaigned as William McKinley's running mate in the election of 1900, he was aided by Elder John Henry Smith of the Twelve and his son George Albert Smith, a future Apostle and Church president. The Smiths and Roosevelt developed a strong friendship as they toured Utah and Idaho together.[15]

That fall Roosevelt also became acquainted with the Latter-day Saints while speaking in Rexburg, Idaho. There, Ben E. Rich, who had returned home for a break while serving as president of the Southern States Mission, introduced him to the audience with great eloquence and even declared that Roosevelt would be the next President of the United States. Roosevelt was very pleased with the introduction and invited Rich to join him in his private car on the railway trip from Idaho Falls to Utah. The candidate said he had some questions concerning the LDS Church, and the mission president was happy to answer them. They spent the better part of the night talking about the Church and its teachings, Rich giving Roosevelt a copy of the Book of Mormon. In the early morning hours when Rich left Roosevelt's private car, Roosevelt thanked him and said he had "never listened to a more interesting account of a great people and a great religion."[16]

In Utah Roosevelt spoke to the Saints at the Logan Tabernacle, at Brigham City, and at the Salt Lake Tabernacle on Temple Square. On 21 September, he met with LDS Church President Lorenzo Snow.[17] Although the Mormons of Utah and Idaho delivered a strong anti-McKinley vote in 1896, with Roosevelt on the ticket in 1900, they committed their electoral votes to the Republicans.[18]

# ROOSEVELT AND APOSTLE-SENATOR REED SMOOT

Elder Reed Smoot of the Quorum of the Twelve was elected a U.S. senator by the Utah Legislature on 21 January 1903. This caused an immediate uproar in the East, as many argued that a high-ranking clergyman from the formerly polygamist Mormons should not be allowed a Senate seat. Early on, however, Theodore Roosevelt met with Smoot privately and became convinced of his innocence.[19] Smoot reported that when he first called on the President, "He came across a crowded room to shake hands with me, and received me warmly and bade me welcome to Washington."[20] They then left the crowd for a private discussion. By the conclusion, the President declared, "Mr. Smoot, you are a good enough American, or Gentile for that matter, for me."[21] Later, Roosevelt related that Smoot had "[come] to me of his own accord, and not only assured me that he was not a polygamist, but, I may add, assured me that he had never had any relations with any woman excepting his own wife. . . . I looked into the facts very thoroughly, became convinced that Senator Smoot had told me the truth, and treated him exactly as I did all other Senators—that is, strictly on his merits as a public servant."[22]

Part of Roosevelt's investigation was an interview with non-Mormon C. E. Loose, a colonel who had been stationed in Utah.

Roosevelt asked, "Is Smoot a polygamist?"

"No," Loose replied.

"Are Mormons good Americans?" Roosevelt continued.

"Yes, and I know because I know them," said Loose.[23]

Roosevelt became convinced and later declared, "By all that's holy, I say to you that Reed Smoot is entitled to his seat in the Senate under the Constitution, and the fact that he is a high church officer makes no difference. I shall do all in my power to help him retain his seat."[24]

"If Mr. Smoot," President Roosevelt wrote later, "or anyone else for that matter had disobeyed the law, he should, of course, be turned out, but if he had obeyed the law and was an upright and

Reed Smoot (R-UT) faced a hostile Senate when he arrived in Washington, who did not like the idea of an LDS apostle holding a Senate seat. His successful weathering of the hearings to seat him is due in large part to his ally in the White House, Theodore Roosevelt. "Mr. Smoot, you are a good enough American, or Gentile for that matter, for me," Smoot was told by the President.

reputable man in his public and private relations, it would be an outrage to turn him out because of his religious belief."[25]

The President's support of Reed Smoot was a major turning point in the development of the relationship between the Church and the American public, and Roosevelt took some heat for the courageous act. "The President of the United States is an open friend of the Senator from Utah," declared Senator Frank Dubois to a group of GOP congressmen. "You Republicans join with the President in wanting the Mormon vote. You have got it. They are with you. . . . But it has cost you moral support of the Christian women and men of the United States."[26] It was reported that protestors of the President's pro-Mormon stance "were cussing Roosevelt up-hill and down-dale" over the matter.[27] However, an editorial in the *Wilmington* [Delaware] *News* asked sympathetically, "Why shouldn't he support a Mormon Republican as well as any other Republican? . . . To suggest that President Roosevelt sanctions polygamy is to go wild."[28]

In February 1903, when Smoot first came to Washington, Teddy Roosevelt's prospects of becoming the Republican nominee in 1904 were uncertain. Ohio senator Marcus Hanna thought T.R. a "damned cowboy" who was an undeserving, accidental President, and he sought the GOP nomination himself. Smoot quickly told the President "that I will stand or fall with you." Roosevelt accepted Smoot's word with the expectation that Smoot could deliver the Mormon vote, which would be essential in a close convention fight and in the final election. Theoretically, a Mormon Apostle could deliver Utah, and Idaho, and could help turn the tide in Colorado, Wyoming, Montana, and Arizona. Smoot worked hard to deliver support for Roosevelt, and Roosevelt in turn agreed to assist Smoot.[29] In a letter to the Church president, Smoot pled, "The President is counting on a Roosevelt delegation, and I ask you to help me to accomplish the same, for if I do not, I may just as well go home as far as influence with the administration is concerned."[30] When Hanna died unexpectedly in February 1904, Smoot wrote the Church president, "I am very thankful that I had an understanding with President Roosevelt before this happened."[31]

Socially, Reed Smoot and his family were always snubbed in the capital until the night in 1907 when President Theodore Roosevelt spent most of a party conversing with Mrs. Smoot. Later, when leaving the reception, he turned and said graciously and loudly, "Good night, Mrs. Smoot." That subtle and respectful gesture broke the ice and marked the turning of the tide.[32]

Salt Lake Herald *cartoonist Alan L. Lovey caricatured Roosevelt's delight in Church president Joseph F. Smith's testimony before Congress in the Smoot Hearings, and in learning of his very large family. Lovey played off of Roosevelt's strong encouragement of large families as one more reason why the President liked the Mormons. Theodore Roosevelt spoke vigilantly against the "race suicide" he felt was taking place when many children were not produced in American homes.*

Roosevelt provided support throughout the Smoot hearings until the Senate voted to officially seat the Apostle in 1907.[33] One tactic tried by the President during the hearings was to appoint R. W. Taylor, the chief counsel for the anti-Mormons, to a federal judgeship in Ohio in an attempt to throw Smoot's opposition into confusion.[34] Roosevelt was proud of his influence in saving Reed Smoot, "and inferentially the Mormon Church." Smoot's daughter and a friend were attending a White House reception in 1908 when President Roosevelt held up the line upon hearing the name Smoot. He informed the entire company with pride that he "was responsible for the favorable vote."[35]

When Roosevelt decided to challenge Taft in 1912, Apostle-Senator Smoot agonized over the situation personally since he could not simultaneously support Taft as a loyal Republican and also reward Roosevelt for the assistance and friendship shown during the Smoot Hearings. As a result, he remained relatively quiet that campaign but officially backed Taft.[36] Roosevelt knew of Smoot's support for Taft in the campaign, but they nonetheless "parted as friends."[37] Even after Wilson defeated both Taft and Roosevelt, the latter kept in touch with Elder Smoot. He sent his support to Smoot during a fight over the Ship Purchase Bill in 1915,[38] lunched with him at the Waldorf Astoria in New

*When Roosevelt visited Salt Lake City, he led a troop of shouting Rough Riders on a wild dash up South Temple Street.*

York in 1916,[39] and invited Smoot to visit him at his home in Oyster Bay in November 1917. After the afternoon together, Smoot confided in his diary, "The Colonel is aging a little and I don't believe his mind is as quick as it used to be."[40] He later related the visit in a general conference address:

> The last time I visited Theodore Roosevelt he was a very, very sick man. It was some time before his death. In our conversation he expressed the opinion that the time was near at hand when he would be taken to the Beyond. He said: "I have tried to live a Christian life, I believe in God, I have tried to wrong no man. I expect to continue my work beyond."[41]

## ROOSEVELT'S UTAH VISIT

On 29 May 1903, hundreds of Latter-day Saints gathered to greet President Roosevelt when he arrived for a visit in Salt Lake City. He spoke to school children on the lawn of the City and County Building and "led the troop of shouting Rough Riders on a wild dash up the street" (South Temple).[42] Upon entering the Tabernacle, the band in the loft struck up "Hail to the Chief," and the vast audience "rose, cheered, stamped, clapped and made every manner of noise." The youngest President bowed and waved to the congregation and then greeted President Joseph F. Smith, his counselors John R. Winder and Anthon H. Lund, and the other Church authorities. "He received me with open arms as an old time friend," John Henry Smith wrote of the occasion.[43] From the pulpit of the Tabernacle Roosevelt declared, "It is not so much what you Mormons did as where you did it that distinguished you."[44] He went on:

> Here in this state the pioneers, and those who came after them, took the land that would not ordinarily be chosen as a land that would yield returns for little effort. You took a territory which at the outset was called after the desert, and you literally—not figuratively—you literally made the wilderness blossom as the rose. The fundamental element in building up Utah has been the work of the citizens of Utah.[45]

## ROOSEVELT DEFENDS THE SAINTS IN A NATIONAL MAGAZINE

Even after leaving the White House, Roosevelt continued to be a friend to the Mormons. During an anti-Mormon propaganda surge in 1910–11, the Rough Rider stepped in to help defuse the situa-

DESERET EVENING NEWS.
THURSDAY, MAY 28, 1903, SALT LAKE CITY, UTAH.

Theodore Roosevelt, President of the United States

THE NATION'S CHIEF—UTAH'S GUEST TOMORROW.

*The people of Salt Lake City were in high anticipation for the May 1903 visit by President Roosevelt, as shown by this newspaper that appeared the day before the presidential visit.*

tion. In the 18 April 1911 issue of *Collier's*, a popular magazine published in New York, a letter appeared from Theodore Roosevelt refuting charges made against Senator Reed Smoot and the Church. Therein he publicly lauded the Latter-day Saints for their profamily stances, their morality, and their chastity:

**ES UTAH PEOPLE A TASTE OF THE**

PRESIDENT ROOSEVELT SPEAKING IN THE TABERNACLE.

BRILLIANT STREET PAGEANT.

(Continued on page 195.)

*Roosevelt was very complimentary toward the Saints in his speech in the Tabernacle: "You took a territory which at the outset was called after the desert, and you literally—not figuratively—you literally made the wilderness blossom as the rose."*

I have known monogamous Mormons whose standard of domestic life and morality and whose attitude toward the relations of men and women was as high as that of the best citizens of any other creed; indeed, among these Mormons the standard of sexual morality was unusually high. Their children were numerous, healthy, and well brought up; their young men were less apt than their neighbors to indulge in that course of vicious sexual dissipation so degrading to manhood and so brutal in the degradation it inflicts on women.[46]

Roosevelt also denounced any prejudice toward the Saints but was quick to point out that the Church must forever leave plural marriage behind if it were to prosper:

> The Mormon has the same right to his form of religious belief that the Jew and the Christian have to theirs; but like the Jew and the Christian, he must not practice conduct which is in contravention of the law of the land. . . . Any effort, openly or covertly, to reintroduce polygamy in the Mormon Church would merely mean that that Church had set its face toward destruction. The people of the United States will not tolerate polygamy. . . . In so far as the Mormons will stand against all hideous and degrading tendencies of this kind, they will set a good example of citizenship.[47]

*At the heart of the Church's political efforts in the early nineteenth century were Church president Heber J. Grant [left], and the apostle-senator, Reed Smoot [right]. Five years after Theodore Roosevelt's death, President Grant reminisced to Smoot, "I believe that Roosevelt felt that we were right. I think he was nearer converted to the truth than any man who ever occupied the presidential chair."*

## TEDDY ROOSEVELT'S LEGACY AMONG THE SAINTS

Upon Roosevelt's death in January 1919, it was Reed Smoot that gave the Associated Press a statement on the late President's life and character. Smoot was also one of the few friends invited to the simple and private funeral, where the only song was Roosevelt's favorite hymn, "How Firm a Foundation." "His death is a great loss to America and the world," penned Smoot in his diary. "He was among the greatest Americans."[48]

In the general conference following Roosevelt's death, Elder Richard R. Lyman proclaimed from the pulpit, "I recognized, long before the death of Theodore Roosevelt, that the Lord raised him up to stir the hearts of men to civic righteousness, as perhaps no man could have stirred them."[49]

Many LDS leaders felt that Roosevelt was "seriously interested in Mormonism," and one of the Presidents "most receptive" of the LDS theology.[50] Five years after Roosevelt's death, President Heber J. Grant reminisced to Smoot, "I believe that Roosevelt felt that we were right. I think he was nearer converted to the truth than any man who ever occupied the presidential chair."[51] Elder Smoot must have agreed, for in 1925 he began to do the temple work for his presidential friend, where he personally served as Roosevelt's proxy.[52]

# ENDNOTES

1   Gibbons, *George Albert Smith,* 39.

2   John Henry Smith, *Church, State, and Politics,* 505.

3   John Henry Smith, *Church, State, and Politics,* 521. See also Larson, *A Ministry of Meetings,* 593–94.

4   Samuel O. Bennion, in Conference Report, October 1944, 65.

5   Gibbons, *George Albert Smith,* 39. See also Larson, *A Ministry of Meetings,* 775.

6   *Dave Leip's Atlas of U.S. Presidential Elections.*

7   Conference Report, Spring 1905, 49.

8   5 February 1906 and 28 February 1906 entries in John Henry Smith, *Church, State, and Politics,* 561, 564.

9   Gibbons, *George Albert Smith,* 125–26.

10  Roosevelt History on the Roosevelt City website, online at http://www.rooseveltcity.com/history.html. See also Jenson, *Encyclopedic History of the Church,* s.v. "Roosevelt Ward."

11  C. Michael Norton, "Theodore Roosevelt's 1907 Nashville Visit," online at http://pages.prodigy.net/nhn.slate/nh00050.html. See also "That Missionary Ben E. Rich," *Improvement Era* 55, no. 6 (June 1952).

12  Conference Report, Spring 1909, 47–48, 117.

13  *Dave Leip's Atlas of U.S. Presidential Elections.*

14  Milton R. Merrill, *Reed Smoot: Apostle in Politics,* 133.

15  Gibbons, *George Albert Smith,* 39, 125.

16  "That Missionary Ben E. Rich,"*Improvement Era* 55, no. 6 (June 1952). See also Carmack, *Tolerance,* 91; "Presentation of the Book of Mormon to Rulers of the World," *Improvement Era* 43, no. 7 (July 1940).

17  John Henry Smith, *Church, State, and Politics,* 464.

18  *Dave Leip's Atlas of U.S. Presidential Elections.*

19  Abanes, *One Nation Under Gods,* 343.

20  Larson, *A Ministry of Meetings,* 572–73.

21  Reed to Smoot to Joseph F. Smith, 10 November 1903, quoted in Merrill, *Reed Smoot: Apostle in Politics,* 41.

22  "Theodore Roosevelt Refutes Anti-Mormon Falsehoods: His Testimony as to Mormon Character; Advice Concerning Polygamy," pamphlet, 9.

23  Harlow E. Smoot, interview, September 1949, quoted in Merrill, *Reed Smoot: Apostle in Politics,* 28.

24  Quoted in Carmack, *Tolerance,* 91.

25  Quoted in "A Mormon in the New Cabinet," *Improvement Era* 56, no. 3 (March 1953).

26  *Congressional Record,* 41:3408.

27  *Salt Lake Herald,* 16 April 1906.

28  *Wilmington News,* 6 December 1906.

29  Merrill, *Reed Smoot: Apostle in Politics,* 83–85.

30  Reed Smoot to Joseph F. Smith, 5 February 1904, quoted in Merrill, *Reed Smoot: Apostle in Politics,* 85.

31  Reed Smoot to Joseph F. Smith, 16 February 1904, quoted in Merrill, *Reed Smoot: Apostle in Politics,* 86.

32  Richard N. Ostling & Joan K. Ostling, *Mormon America: The Power and the Promise,* 130–31. See also Julian C. Lowe and Florian H. Thayn, eds., *History of the Mormons in the Greater Washington Area,* 6.

33  Arrington and Bitton, *The Mormon Experience,* 248.

34  William E. Berrett and Alma P. Burton, *Readings in L.D.S. Church History,* 3:202.

35  Merrill, *Reed Smoot: Apostle in Politics,* 83.

36  Harvard S. Heath, ed., *In the World: The Diaries of Reed Smoot,* 136 n14.

37  Heath, *In the World,* 46 n9.

38  10 February 1915 entry in Heath, *In the World,* 261.

39  31 March 1916 entry in Heath, *In the World,* 310–11.

40  27 November 1917 entry in Heath, *In the World,* 376.

41  Reed Smoot, in Conference Report, October 1935, 117.

42  "The Achievement of Civilization, Recollections of East Brigham Street," *Improvement Era* 18, no. 9 (July 1915).

43  John Henry Smith, *Church, State, and Politics,* 522. See also William W. Slaughter, "Teddy in the Tabernacle," *Pioneer,* Fall 1995, 21–24.

44  Melvin J. Ballard, in Conference Report, October 1935, 46.

45  Quoted in *Improvement Era* 13, no. 11 (September 1910).

46  "Theodore Roosevelt Refutes Anti-Mormon Falsehoods," 10–11.

47  Ibid.

48  Heath, *In the World,* 407–8, including n1. See also Morris, *Theodore Rex,* 533.

49  Richard R. Lyman, in Conference Report, October 1919, 120.

50  Merrill, *Reed Smoot: Apostle in Politics,* 155.

51  Heber J. Grant to Reed Smoot, 16 December 1924, quoted in Merrill, *Reed Smoot: Apostle in Politics,* 132.

52  Baptism, 26 October 1925 (Salt Lake Temple); and Endowment, 29 September 1926 (Salt Lake Temple). Temple ordinances can be accessed through the International Genealogical Index (IGI) at www.familysearch.org.

# WILLIAM HOWARD TAFT

## *1909–1913*

During the Taft years, the Church further established its modern pattern of interaction with the White House—hosting the President in Salt Lake City on several occasions (Taft broke a new record by visiting Utah six times); having the Church president visit the White House (Joseph F. Smith was the first to do so since Joseph Smith called on Van Buren); involving the Tabernacle Choir as a tool of goodwill (they had their first performance in the White House); and utilizing prominent Mormon politicians to build the Church's reputation with the President. Reed Smoot was the epitome of this relationship building, but in the Taft administration future First Presidency member J. Reuben Clark Jr. also came on the scene. Apostle-Senator Smoot "got along famously" with Taft, as they shared the same positions on nearly every major issue. The President often had the Smoots to dinner at the White House, where there would be long discussions on Utah affairs and LDS beliefs.[1]

**November 1908:** Roosevelt's hand-picked successor, William Howard Taft, defeats William Jennings Bryan, carrying 52 percent of the vote to the Democrats' 43 percent. Despite Bryan's earlier popularity in Utah, he only garners 39 percent there compared to 56 percent for Taft.[2]

**April 1909:** Elder John Henry Smith praises the recently inaugurated President during general conference: "The coming into power of [Taft] as the executive of our nation, fully equipped for the discharge of his duties, with extended experience, and a body of able men around him, I believe presages to our country continued glorious growth and development."[3]

**September 1909:** Taft makes his first visit to Utah.

**6 October 1909:** Latter-day Saints from the Mexican colonies travel to El Paso to hear President Taft, who has come to the border to meet with Mexican President Porfiri Diaz. "It was an event of great pageantry, with bands and a parade," remembers Camilla Kimball, future wife of President Spencer W. Kimball, who is there with her family. "The meeting of these two presidents had special significance to the colonists, because it symbolized our double loyalty to the United States and to Mexico."[4]

**1 July 1910:** Taft appoints future First Presidency member J. Rueben Clark Jr. to be solicitor of the Department of State. Clark has been serving as the assistant solicitor.[5]

*Utah welcomed President Taft for his first visit in September 1909. He would later visit the state five more times.*

*In his October 1911 visit to Utah, President Taft spoke to a crowd of 40,000 at the state fairpark. Reed Smoot remarked afterward, "The President has made many friends. . . . A great day for Utah."*

---

**1911:** As the Mexican Revolution heats up, President Taft takes advice on the issue from J. Reuben Clark Jr., who is particularly concerned for the plight of the Saints who live in the northern Mexican colonies and who are often in the middle of the conflict.[6] President Joseph F. Smith, clearly concerned about the LDS colonies, strongly supports the Taft administration's Mexican policy, which includes sending 20,000 troops to the Mexican border as a show of force.[7]

**Summer 1911:** After testifying to Congress in the Smoot Hearings, Church resident Joseph F. Smith is welcomed at the White House by William Howard Taft, after an introduction by Senator Smoot.[8]

**5 October 1911:** Taft makes a second visit to Salt Lake City, which includes a stay in the new Hotel Utah. The press picks up Taft's compliments about the extraordinary hospitality of the new hotel, which helps build its reputation. Every President through Ronald Reagan follows Taft's lead by staying at Hotel Utah at least once.[9] After an address to an assembly of senior citizens at Hotel Utah, Taft lunches at the Alta Club, visits Fort Douglas, speaks to 40,000 people at the state fair-park, and takes dinner at the Commercial Club. Smoot concludes, "The President has made many friends . . . and was pleased with his visit. . . . A great day for Utah."[10]

**18 October 1911:** Taft makes a third presidential visit to Utah while returning from California. He stops again in Salt Lake, and speaks in Ogden, Brigham City, and Logan to great crowds.[11]

**15 November 1911:** The Mormon Tabernacle Choir performs for the President, the First Lady, and invited guests in the East Room of the White House. The choir happens to be in town as part of their midwestern and eastern U.S. tour, and Senator Smoot is able to arrange it just two days prior. Smoot writes in his diary that it "has been a great day for Utah and the choir's visit has done much good."[12]

**October 1912:** Although Joseph F. Smith personally favors Taft, in general conference various talks are given reminding the Saints that they are free to make their own political judgments and that they should rely on prayer to do so.[13]

**November 1912:** Woodrow Wilson wins the election, with Theodore Roosevelt in second. Only in Vermont and predominantly LDS Utah does President Taft come in first place, due to the support by Church leaders.[14] The Saints still consider Taft a friend, and President Joseph F. Smith sends him a kind letter after Wilson took office.[15]

**August 1915:** To make a speech at a gathering of the American Bar Association, Taft makes his fourth visit to Utah, and his first as an ex-President. The Church gives him lodging in Hotel Utah's presidential suite and holds a reception for him at the hotel upon his arrival on the 18 August. He also has a private meeting with Joseph F. Smith and his counselors, along with Presiding Bishop Charles W. Nibley.[16]

**February 1919:** Taft makes a fifth visit to Utah, this time to speak at the Tabernacle and address a Mountain Congress to promote the League of Nations.[17]

**1920:** Former President Taft travels to Utah a sixth time to encourage voters to return Reed Smoot to the Senate and to campaign for Warren G. Harding.[18] Church President Heber J. Grant reflects on the visit: "I remember when ex-President Taft was here he said, with that little chuckle of his that made us all laugh, 'And to think that when he [Reed Smoot] first came down to

*William Howard Taft enjoyed his many visits with the Mormons through the years. "There is in my heart a warm feeling for your people," he once told President Heber J. Grant.*

Washington nearly everybody tried to keep him out of the senate. Now I have come all the way to Utah to plead with the people to be sure and send him back again.'"[19]

**24 October 1921:** President Heber J. Grant and Elder Smoot call on now-Chief Justice Taft. "There is in my heart a warm feeling for your people," he tells the prophet. "I have great respect for them, and I want you to call on me whenever you are here." President Grant presented Taft with a copy of the Book of Mormon.[20]

**13 May 1922:** Apostles Reed Smoot and George Albert Smith are invited to spend an evening in the Tafts' home, an evening which they enjoy.[21]

**8 March 1930:** William Howard Taft dies. Elder Smoot represents the Church at the funeral, calling Taft a "remarkable American."[22]

## TAFT'S FIRST UTAH VISIT

In June 1909, Senator Reed Smoot requested that President Taft make a stop in Utah as part of his autumn trip west, which Taft agreed to do.[23] The Apostle later worked with the President to schedule the details.[24] Upon Taft's September arrival in Provo, he was greeted by cheering crowds. Academy Avenue was lined with school children shouting for the President. Taft stopped in the Provo Tabernacle for a brief program, and then went on to Salt Lake.

Taft's train stopped in American Fork, Lehi, and Bingham Junction so he could make brief remarks to the assembled crowds before arriving in Salt Lake. The following morning, Taft was introduced to the First Presidency and Quorum of the Twelve at a breakfast at the Commercial Club. They proceeded to admire the Great Salt Lake at Saltair, attend an organ recital in the Tabernacle, have lunch at the Salt Lake Country Club (where Taft taught Reed Smoot how to

*Senator and Apostle Reed Smoot joins the President on the stand at a program in the Provo Tabernacle during Taft's 1909 visit.*

drive a golf ball), speak to a large crowd at Liberty Park, and address prominent Church and civic leaders at the Alta Club.[25]

The Sunday morning of 26 September, President Taft arrived to a Temple Square packed with people. Inside the Tabernacle, Apostle-Senator Smoot introduced the President, who gave a forty-minute sermon to the congregation on the proverb "A soft answer turneth away wrath, but grievous words stir up anger." During the address, the American President pled for cooperation between Mormons and non-Mormons. Smoot wrote, "I never heard a better sermon. . . . The President was delighted with the meeting and so were the people."[26]

As the entourage traveled from the Tabernacle, they observed some 20,000 children lining the street, waving flags and cheering for the President. Taft made a brief visit to the YMCA, attended the eleven o'clock service at the Unitarian church, and then boarded the train for Ogden. There he spoke in the City Park, and traveled on to make brief stops to speak in Brigham City and Cache Valley, where thousands came out in the rain to hear from the Republican President. As he was

*The whirlwind visit of Taft's first visit to Utah was caricatured in the front page of the 25 September 1909 edition of the Salt Lake Tribune.*

UTAH PEOPLE EXTEND WELCOME T

# The Salt Lake T

COMMERCIAL TRAVELERS
KNOW THE PULSE
of the business world. They are, as a class, keen observers; hence, when a dozen or so each unknown to the other gives it out as his individual judgment that Salt Lake is commercially the best town in his territory, one is liable to believe it, and the same time look for the reason—the AMERICAN PARTY. Building permits are today almost double the entire September permits of 1908.

VOL. LXXIX, NO. 164.    WEATHER TODAY—Cloudy.    SALT LAKE CITY, UTAH, SATURDAY MORNING, SEPTEMBE

## PRESIDENT TAFT IS GUEST OF THE STATE OF UTAH

### Nation's Chief Executive Met at Helper by Apostle Smoot's Committee and Welcomed to Commonwealth.

### SPEAKS IN MORMON TABERNACLE IN SENATOR SMOOT'S HOME TOWN

### Presidential Train is Met at D. & R. G. Station in Salt Lake by Prominent Citizens and Escorted to Fort Douglas.

Saturday, September 25.

8:30 to 9:30 a. m.—Breakfast at Commercial club.
9:30 to 11:00 a. m.—Trip to Saltair and return.
11:00 to 11:45 a. m.—Organ recital at tabernacle.
11:45 a. m. to 3:15 p. m.—At Country club.
3:30 to 5:30 p. m.—At Liberty park for public reception.
5:30 to 6:45 p. m.—At Knutsford hotel.
6:45 to 8:00 p. m.—University club for reception of Ohio society and Yale graduates.
8:00 p. m. and balance of evening—Alta club.

William Howard Taft, president of the United States, made a triumphal entry into Utah early Friday morning, and when he was greeted by the Utah party at Helper and a number of school children and citizens of that place, the students singing "America," President Taft, in the language of his predecessor, was "de-lighted."

The sun was shining brightly and the evidence of [...] when President Taft and his party rolled into Helper promptly at 8:45 a. m., Friday. Senators Smoot and Sutherland, Governor Spry, Congressman Howell, Col. C. E. Loose, Col. D. C. Jackling of the governor's staff, and Capt. Conrad of the Fifteenth infantry at Fort Douglas traveled to Helper on Thursday night. They were the guests of D. C. Jackling in his private car, and Mr. Jackling acted as host to the local newspaper men on their return journey, and he is certainly a prince of hosts.

Preceding the presidential special, a special Rio Grande train pulled into Helper. On board of it were Assistant

Ogden. The governor also stated that there would be a three-minutes' stop at Springville, American Fork and Lehi, and a three-minute stop at Brigham City, Sunday, and fifteen minutes at Cache Junction. The governor and his staff will accompany the party as far north as Cache Junction.

At Springville there was a stop of three minutes. The school children were lined up, waving American flags and singing the national anthem, with a band in attendance. Just before the president began to make a few remarks, bouquets were presented to him by little twin girls. He was asked the question: "Which is which?" Both were dressed alike; they were alike as two peas, as the saying goes, and after looking at them, President Taft said: "I can't say which is which. Both girls, the observed of all observers, were as shy as could be, and one of them coyly hid her face in her arms. Wherever the president met a little girl, his address was: "How are you, dear?"

In his brief speech at Springville the president remarked on the evident prosperity of the people. He said they were well dressed, and being properly educated and having those conditions, there was no fear or doubt as to their welfare otherwise.

#### On to Provo.

[...] enthusiastic reception. As the train pulled into the depot the Provo band discoursed patriotic airs. There was no delay. Automobiles were in waiting and the entire party was taken to Temple Heights, or rather, Capitol Hill. Every precaution was taken for the safety of the president. He was accompanied not only by his personal bodyguard, but a mounted escort of patrolmen and deputy sheriffs never left his car.

At Temple Heights, or Capitol Hill, the beauties of the valley, of which a splendid view can be obtained, were pointed out to President Taft by Senator Smoot, and Professor Brimhall of the B. Y. U., president of the institution, was introduced to the president. A quick return journey was made to the tabernacle, where President Taft

"SEEING SALT LAKE"

## BITTER ATTACK TO BE MADE ON COOK

### To Be Claimed Now That He Did Not Ascend Mt. McKinley.

### THIS IN ADDITION TO THE POLE CONTROVERSY

### Friend of Commander Peary Is Checking Up Doctor's Data.

NEW YORK, Sept. 24—For the first time since his arrival here, Frederick A. Cook took into his confidence today one of the leading American geographical authorities, Archer M. Huntington, president of the American Geographical society, with whom he had an hour's

WOULD [...] HUDSON, THE [...]

New York [...] cities of the Hu [...] are just now cel [...] achievements of [...] ton. In view [...] Vantyne has [...] about Hudson [...] usual interest. [...] The Sunday Tri [...]

BLACKBEA [...]

The fourth [...] of the remarkable [...] ton Cortina, tell [...] strange adventures [...] John Dare. Ar [...] will appear in th [...] the tomorrow [...]

CATTLE [...] THRILLI [...]

Those who live [...] along the cattle [...] York lead lives [...] ally strenuous, [...] know about the [...] day's Tribune. W [...] ston contributes [...] three men that i [...] esting.

MILLION [...] FIFTEEN [...]

[Above] Taft in Provo, Utah.

[Right] William Howard Taft was loved by the Latter-day Saints. George Albert Smith recalled shaking hands with him during his visits and remembered Taft's "goodly girth and walrus mustache."

leaving Utah, Taft told his entourage that his visit there "was one continual round of pleasure and a continual revelation . . . the people so healthy and prosperity was evident on all sides."[27]

Future Church President George Albert Smith (then a thirty-nine-year-old Apostle) was the chairman of the entertainment committee for the presidential visit. He recalled the organ recital held in the President's honor, shaking hands with him afterward and noting his "goodly girth and walrus mustache."[28]

William Howard Taft visited Utah five more times and continued to build positive relationships with Church members.

# ENDNOTES

1   Heath, *In the World,* 3, including n2; see also 21, 42, 49, 91, 98, 172, 175.

2   *Dave Leip's Atlas of U.S. Presidential Elections.*

3   John Henry Smith, in Conference Report, April 1909, 117.

4   Caroline Eyring Miner and Edward L. Kimball, *Camilla: A Biography of Camilla Eyring Kimball,* 24.

5   David H. Yarn, Jr., "Biographical Sketch of J. Reuben Clark Jr., *BYU Studies* 13, no. 3 (Spring 1973), 238.

6   Winder, *Counselors to the Prophets,* 350.

7   Heath, *In the World,* 162.

8   Gibbons, *Dynamic Disciples,* 150–51.

9   "Hotel Utah: Colorful History of Elegance," *Church News,* 26 June 1993.

10  Heath, *In the World,* 119.

11  Heath, *In the World,* 123.

12  Allen and Leonard, *The Story of the Latter-day Saints,* 478. See also Heath, *In the World,* 128–29; "Music and the Spoken Word," *Improvement Era* 32, no. 7 (July 1939).

13  Allen and Leonard, *The Story of the Latter-day Saints,* 490–91.

14  Merrill, *Reed Smoot: Apostle in Politics,* 133.

15  Heath, *In the World,* 180.

16  Heath, *In the World,* 285–86. See also "Passing Events," *Improvement Era* 18, no. 11 (September 1915).

17  *Improvement Era* 22, no. 6 (April 1919): footnotes.

18  Merrill, *Reed Smoot: Apostle in Politics,* 228. See also "Passing Events," *Improvement Era* 25, no. 3 (January 1922): [page number?].

19  Heber J. Grant, "Glimpses of Famous Contemporaries, Reed Smoot and William Howard Taft," in *Gospel Standards*: *The Ministry of Heber J. Grant.*

20  Heath, *In the World,* 480. See also "Presentation of the Book of Mormon to Rulers of the World," *Improvement Era* 43, no. 7 (July 1940); Heber J. Grant, *Gospel Standards,* 90.

21  Gibbons, *George Albert Smith,* 126. See also Heath, *In the World,* 502; 21 May 1922 entry; Preston Nibley, *The Presidents of the Church,* 285.

22  Heath, *In the World,* 721.

23  Heath, *In the World,* 19.

24  Heath, *In the World,* 20, 22–23, 29–30.

25  Heath, *In the World,* 31–32.

26  Heath, *In the World,* 32, 35 n127. Visit also noted in *Church Almanac,* 550.

27  Heath, *In the World,* 32–33.

28  Gibbons, *George Albert Smith,* 66, 126.

# WOODROW WILSON

## *1913—1921*

As mentioned, the rift between William Taft and Teddy Roosevelt in the 1912 presidential election resulted in victory for New Jersey Governor Woodrow Wilson. On the one hand Wilson's administration brought about the appointment of the first Mormon to a subcabinet position, and on the other, in the words of Reed Smoot, it was as if a "no Mormon need apply" policy was put in place by the administration.[1] Later, Wilson's crusade for the League of Nations would greatly divide Church leadership, where top officials argued passionately and publicly on both sides. Historian James Allen concluded, "Perhaps at no time in [Church] history had there been such divergence of opinion among its leaders."[2]

**14 March 1913:** Wilson gives his inaugural address, which Elder Reed Smoot considers "a well written moral lecture." However, the Apostle-senator soon considers the new President "autocratic and bull-headed" as well as "arrogant, sanctimonious, hypocritical, and a poor statesman." He and other GOP Apostles also complain that the Church-owned *Deseret News* is too sympathetic toward Wilson.[3]

*James Henry Moyle became the first Latter-day Saint ever appointed by a U.S. President to a subcabinet position in 1917. Moyle, who served as Wilson's assistant secretary of the Treasury, had been a past candidate for governor of Utah, candidate for U.S. senator, and the Democratic national committeeman from Utah. He had also been president of the Eastern States Mission.*

**Summer 1913:** Regarding the Mexican Revolution, Elder Smoot meets with Wilson on behalf of the Church to encourage him to stay his course in not having the United States enter the conflict. Smoot relays that the Saints in Mexico "had suffered more in number and loss of property than any other and [yet] they were not demanding intervention."[4] Wilson responds by declaring a policy of "watchful waiting" in regards to Mexico.

**June 1916:** Future president of the Church Spencer W. Kimball attends all four days of the Democratic National Convention in St. Louis, where Woodrow Wilson is nominated for a second term. The twenty-one-year-old missionary is impressed with Wilson's speech, and writes that the convention is "the most wonderful & beautiful sight and the loudest noise of yells & whistles that I have ever heard."[5]

**November 1916:** Wilson wins reelection, with the help of Utah, where 59 percent vote for him, compared to the 38 percent who support Charles Evans Hughes.[6] A disappointed Joseph Fielding Smith writes in his diary, "In my judgment the Latter-day Saints show a wonderful lack of good sense in elections."[7] Yet, Mormon laboring and railroad men appreciate Wilson's eight-hour workday law, and Utah's many farmers enjoy relative prosperity under Wilson's first term.[8]

**20 September 1917:** Wilson becomes the first U.S. President to appoint a Latter-day Saint to a subcabinet position in his administration when he names Democrat James Henry Moyle to serve as assistant secretary of the U.S. Treasury. Moyle has been a past candidate for governor of Utah, candidate for U.S. senator, and the Democratic national committeeman from Utah. He's also been president of the Eastern States Mission.[9]

**October 1917:** Democrat Stephen L Richards of the Twelve praises Wilson for his faith in Christ and for his recent letter endorsing the Bible, which was placed in the front of 27,000 Bibles that were distributed to U.S. servicemen.[10] Years later, Ezra Taft Benson, Elder Mark E. Peterson, and other LDS leaders would quote Wilson, who said, "Our civilization cannot survive materially unless it is redeemed spiritually. It can be saved only by becoming permeated with the Spirit of Christ."[11]

**January 1918:** Wilson announces the League of Nations. While sixty-five nations join, the Senate ultimately refuses to ratify the treaty and forbids U.S. membership. The national debate over Wilson's Nobel Prize–winning concept deeply divides the LDS leadership.

*Emmeline B. Wells, who had called on President Hayes in her younger years, was visited by Woodrow Wilson during his 1919 visit to Utah. President and Mrs. Wilson visited the Hotel Utah apartment of Sister Wells—the ninety-one-year-old, bedridden general Relief Society president—to thank the Relief Society for providing 205,000 bushels of wheat to the government during World War I.*

**23 September 1919:** President and Mrs. Wilson visit Utah as part of the President's national tour to drum up support for the League of Nations. He is welcomed with a great street parade, speaks in the Tabernacle, meets with the First Presidency, and even visits the Hotel Utah apartment of the general Relief Society president—ninety-one-year-old, bedridden Emmeline B. Wells—to thank the Relief Society for providing 205,000 bushels of wheat to the government during World War I.[12]

**27 November 1919:** Having just suffered a major stroke, Wilson becomes the only President blessed by name in a temple dedicatory prayer. In Hawaii, President Heber J. Grant prays, "We pray Thee to bless Woodrow Wilson, the president of these United States. Touch him with the healing power of Thy Holy Spirit and make him whole. We pray that his life may be precious in Thy sight, and may the inspiration that comes from Thee ever abide with him."[13]

## CHURCH DIVIDED OVER WILSON'S LEAGUE OF NATIONS

Woodrow Wilson was "raised up of the Lord" according to Elder George F. Richards of the Twelve, who also declared, "I believe that the League of Nations is inspired of God."

The debate over American participation in the League of Nations raged heavily in Utah, and prominent Church leaders jumped in to support or oppose President Wilson. Elder Smoot disagreed with Wilson and even suggested that the Book of Mormon opposed the idea of the League of Nations. Seventy B. H. Roberts avidly supported the League and declared that the scriptures supported the idea.[14] State Department official (and future First Presidency member) J. Reuben Clark Jr. traveled and spoke passionately against it.[15] BYU's faculty and student body vocally supported the League,[16] as did Elder George F. Richards of the Twelve, who at the July 1919 Pioneer Stake conference declared,

I believe that the president of the United States was raised up of the Lord. I believe that the Lord has been with him. He is regarded in Europe as one of the greatest men—a man with one of the greatest minds in the world—Woodrow Wilson. . . . I believe that the League of Nations is inspired of God.[17]

*Woodrow and Edith Galt Wilson converse in the car with some of their Utah hosts during their 1919 visit to the Saltair resort on the shores of the Great Salt Lake.*

---

On 21 September, President Heber J. Grant firmly endorsed the League of Nations at a quarterly conference of the Salt Lake Stake. However, he made it clear that he was speaking as an individual and not as a Church leader; that scriptures were not to be used on either side of the argument; that neither side represented an official Church position; and that the issue should not divide the Church.[18] Two days later, Wilson himself, along with the First Lady, visited Utah to rally support for the League. Following the President's address on Temple Square, the Church's official magazine, *The Improvement Era,* editorialized, "Was not this a great message? Is it not one worthy our closest consideration?"[19]

The arguments continued in the October 1919 general conference, which Presiding Bishop Charles W. Nibley, a Republican, lamented "had more politics talked in this one conference than all the seventeen years of Joseph F. Smith's administration." One historian called the 3–5 October event a "League of Nations rally," where "speaker after speaker praised the League, lauded Wilson . . . and inferred [sic] in degree that opposition to the League was opposition to the Church."[20]

On this controversial issue, Woodrow Wilson had divided many Americans and had sparked a lively debate among the Latter-day Saints. Ultimately, with the help of Reed Smoot, who felt that Wilson was overly ambitious and power hungry, the U.S. Senate blocked American membership in the League of Nations.[21] Yet he was a president whom the Mormons still saw as a friend.

*While in Salt Lake City for a visit in 1919, President Wilson spoke to a large gathering of Boy Scouts on the steps of the state capitol. Earlier in the year the President had declared, "The Boy Scout movement should not only be preserved, but strengthened. It deserves the support of all public-spirited citizens."*

# ENDNOTES

1    Heath, *In the World,* 295.

2    James B. Allen, "Personal Faith and Public Policy: Some Timely Observations on the League of Nations Controversy in Utah," *BYU Studies* 14, no. 1 (Autumn 1973): 83.

3    Merrill, *Reed Smoot: Apostle in Politics,* 141. See also Heath, *In the World,* 180, 224 n26, 232 n36, and 261 n11.

4    Heath, *In the World,* 190.

5    Edward L. Kimball and Andrew E. Kimball, Jr., *Spencer W. Kimball: Twelfth President of The Church of Jesus Christ of Latter-day Saints,* 79. See also "The Mission Experience of Spencer W. Kimball," *BYU Studies* 25, no. 4 (Fall 1985): 134.

6    *Dave Leip's Atlas of U.S. Presidential Elections.*

7    Joseph Fielding Smith, Jr., and John J. Stewart, *The Life of Joseph Fielding Smith,* 198.

8    Heath, *In the World,* 332, 334–35.

9    Holzapfel, et al., *On this Day in the Church,* 183. See Gene A. Sessions, ed., *Mormon Democrat: The Religious and Political Memoirs of James Henry Moyle.*

10   Conference Report, Fall 1917, 144.

11   Benson, *Teachings,* 605. See also Mark E. Petersen, in Conference Report, April 1968, Second Day Morning Meeting, 60.

12   *Encyclopedia of Mormonism,* 1560. See also William Mulder, "A Glance At Heber J. Grant's Twenty-Five Years as President of the Church," *Improvement Era* 49, no. 11 (November 1943); Bryant S. Hinckley, *Sermons and Missionary Services of Melvin J. Ballard,* 73–74.

13   N. B. Lundwall, *Temples of the Most High,* 148.

14   Allen and Leonard, *The Story of the Latter-day Saints,* 513.

15   James B. Allen, "Personal Faith and Public Policy: Some Timely Observations on the League of Nations Controversy in Utah," *BYU Studies* 14, no. 1 (Autumn 1973): 83.

16   Heath, *In the World,* 424.

17   Allen, "Personal Faith and Public Policy," *BYU Studies* 14, no. 1 (Autumn 1973): 83.

18   Allen and Leonard, *The Story of the Latter-day Saints,* 513.

19   "Visit of President Wilson," *Improvement Era* 23, no. 1 (November 1919).

20   Merrill, *Reed Smoot: Apostle in Politics,* 261–62.

21   See Reed Smoot to George H. Brimhall, 17 November 1919, George H. Brimhall papers, Brigham Young University Library. See also *The Paysonian,* 29 October 1920, Newspaper of Payson, Utah; Merrill, *Reed Smoot: Apostle in Politics,* 247–48.

# WARREN G. HARDING

## *1921–1923*

Of the half-dozen Presidents that Apostle-Senator Reed Smoot was acquainted with, few had the close relationship with him as did Warren Gamaliel Harding. This positive personal relationship would result in President Harding meeting with various Apostles and even with President Heber J. Grant. It also would result in numerous discussions about the Church, a gift of a Book of Mormon, and the President asking Elder Smoot to come to the White House to give the First Lady a priesthood blessing. Harding would also visit the Saints in Utah on the western trip that ended with his fatal heart attack in San Francisco.

**1914:** Harding is elected a U.S. senator from Ohio and begins his close friendship with fellow Republican Reed Smoot. "I hold Senator Smoot to be the most valuable member of the United States Senate," Harding would conclude. While in the Senate, Harding supports causes popular with LDS leadership, including the Volstead Act's provisions for enforcing prohibition, women's suffrage, and antistrike legislation.[1]

**June 1920:** Elder Smoot is one of the early backers of Harding for President and is part of the famous "smoke-filled room" of the Chicago GOP convention this year that helps to engineer the noncontroversial Harding as the party's nominee. After receiving the nomination, Harding tells Smoot he can be secretary of the Treasury. "I told him I would prefer to remain in the Senate," remarks the Mormon Apostle.[2]

**November 1920:** Harding wins, thanks in part to Utah's electoral votes. In the heart of Mormon country, Harding receives 56 percent of the vote to Democrat James Cox's 39 percent.[3] The President-Elect relies on Smoot for help in assembling his cabinet and setting his agenda. "I was to come to the Whitehouse [sic] at any time and at any hour," Smoot is told.[4]

**March 1921:** Harding is sworn in as President, and Smoot continues his role as unofficial advisor. The close friendship leads to conversations about the Church.

**12 May 1922:** Reed Smoot brings Elder George Albert Smith to meet the President. Later, Elder Smith returns to the White House for a visit, along with Elder Stephen L Richards. Another Apostle, Melvin J. Ballard, is also introduced to the President by Smoot. "I told the President we were pleased with his work and blessed him to be successful, and he thanked me," records Elder Ballard.[5]

**26 June 1923:** President and Mrs. Harding visit Utah.

**2 August 1923:** Harding dies of a heart attack in San Francisco. "The report made me sick," writes Smoot. "A great, wise and good man called home. One of my dearest friends." Despite the friendship between President Harding and the Mormon Apostle, Harvard Heath asserts that "perhaps Smoot was unaware of his philandering, drinking, and party-going with the Ohio gang in Washington. . . . Historians have found little that was complimentary in Warren G. Harding."[6] Nonetheless, a few years later, Reed Smoot is baptized for his friend, and Heber J. Grant serves as Harding's proxy for his temple endowment.[7]

## SMOOT SHARES THE RESTORED GOSPEL WITH HARDING

As Senator-Apostle Smoot grew closer to the President, he began to discuss Latter-day Saint beliefs. Learning of this, Heber J. Grant wrote to Smoot, "With all my heart I thank the Lord for your splendid standing with President Harding."[8] The prophet also looked forward to sharing LDS scriptures with Harding and wrote to Elder Smoot:

> I note with much interest the visit you and your good wife had
> with President Harding, his wife and his sister, and I am grateful for
> the opportunity you had of presenting some gospel truths to these

First Lady Florence Harding received a priesthood blessing of healing from Apostle and Senator Reed Smoot late one night when she lay ill. Her husband, President Harding, had recalled Elder Smoot's description of priesthood blessings and had telephoned him and requested that he come to the White House to bless his ill wife.

prominent people and that you succeeded in interesting them.

It will certainly be a great pleasure to present President Harding with a set of Church works in the best form they are gotten out. The new edition of the "Book of Mormon" is now ready for delivery. We are having "The Doctrine and Covenants" and "Pearl of Great Price" gotten out in the same shape but it will be a month or six weeks before they are ready for delivery. Brother Talmage seems to think that the "Book of Mormon" in full Morocco binding, printed on a heavier paper would be more desirable than the India paper for presentation to the President.[9]

When the new 1921 edition came off the press, Smoot delivered a copy of the Book of Mormon to the First Family.[10] The President and Mormon senator apparently discussed LDS beliefs on several more occasions, and Harding seemed "most receptive" to the Latter-day Saint theology. Historian Milton Merrill shares the following anecdote, unique among the relationships between Mormons and the occupants of the White House:

On one occasion, Harding telephoned Smoot late at night. He stated that Mrs. Harding was very ill, and recalling Smoot's description of the Mormon healing ceremony, he requested the Senator to come to the White House and perform the rite. Smoot went immediately, taking a bottle of consecrated olive oil, a necessary accessory. He was shown to Mrs. Harding's bedroom by the president, and he then and there administered to her. (Administration is a prayer spoken by authority of the priesthood, coupled with an application of a small quantity of oil on the head of the one receiving the blessing.) Under the circumstances, Smoot could not doubt that President Harding was at least moderately impressed with Mormonism.[11]

After hearing about the blessing, President Grant wrote excitedly back to Smoot: "Sister Grant and I have read with interest your remarks about Mrs. Harding." The Church President was also thrilled to hear of President Harding's remark: "I do not know but what Brigham Young was right in his religion."[12]

## HARDING'S VISIT TO UTAH

As part of their 1923 western tour, President Harding and his wife visited Utah. They arrived in Ogden and were driven south to Salt Lake, where they observed en route that every house in Davis County had a flag flying in honor of Harding's visit. A crowd of 100,000 people cheered as

*While on his 1923 tour through Utah, President Harding stands in his automobile to speak to a group. His LDS friend and confidant, Reed Smoot, stands two to the right of the car.*

*During his Utah visit, Warren G. Harding (left) visited the Salt Lake Country Club. There, President Harding and Heber J. Grant played golf against the club's golf pros. According to Reed Smoot, who walked around with the players, "The two Presidents won."*

the entourage entered Salt Lake City, and when the entourage stopped at Liberty Park for a speech, President Harding was visibly moved, "Words are unable to express my appreciation of the warm friendly spirit of this reception."[13] Among the children who lined the streets and cheered was thirteen-year-old Gordon B. Hinckley, who remembers standing with his siblings and waving flags as the President's motorcade drove by. This was the first, but by no means the last, presidential encounter for the future Church president.[14]

The President was impressed with Utah. "I have found a new slogan in your wonderful country, which I am delighted to adopt, namely, the one which refers to 'Utah's best crop.' I do not know when I have seen so many happy, smiling, sturdy children in so short a period of travel. A thousand delights have come to us in getting more intimately acquainted with your wonderful country . . . but I love, above all else, the boyhood and girlhood of marvelous Utah."[15]

After lunch, they drove around the state capitol and over to the Salt Lake Country Club. There, President Harding and Heber J. Grant played golf against the club's golf pros. According to Reed Smoot, who walked around with the players, "The two Presidents won."

President and Mrs. Harding went to a special organ recital in the Tabernacle, then to the Church Administration Building, and left from the Union Pacific Depot for Cedar City, where they spent 27 June visiting Zion National Park and dining with President and Mrs. Heber J. Grant, Apostle-Senator Smoot, Governor and Mrs. Mabey, former Utah Governor and Mrs. Spry, and General Mac Alexander.[16] Golfing, touring, and dining with President Harding gave the LDS prophet time to get to know the President and to make a positive impression of the Church.

President Harding had come to know not only Church members, but even Church doctrines in a way that few Presidents have. His death a mere two months after his Utah visit left the Church to mourn a true friend.

*27 June 1923: President Warren G. Harding and LDS and Utah state leaders enjoy viewing Zion National Park on horseback. (L–R) Utah Governor Charles R. Mabey, President Harding, Salt Lake City Mayor Charles C. Nelsen, Senator Reed Smoot, President Heber J. Grant.*

# ENDNOTES

1   Heath, *In the World,* 313. See also Warren G. Harding to Henry Welch, 27 July 1920, quoted in Merrill, *Reed Smoot: Apostle in Politics,* 229; W. Paul Reeve, "President Harding's 1923 Trip to Utah," *History Blazer,* July 1995, online at http://history-togo.utah.gov.html.

2   Heath, *In the World,* 440–42. See also Freidel, *Our Country's Presidents,* 175; Merrill, *Reed Smoot: Apostle in Politics,* 267.

3   *Dave Leip's Atlas of U.S. Presidential Elections.*

4   Heath, *In the World,* 463; see also 464–66, 468–69, 474–75, 478, 483–84, 507, 509, 517, 522.

5   Preston Nibley, *The Presidents of the Church,* 285. See also Heath, *In the World,* 517; Hinckley, *Sermons and Missionary Services of Melvin J. Ballard,* 79.

6   Heath, *In the World,* 554, 555 n39.

7   Temple ordinances can be accessed by Latter-day Saints through the International Genealogical Index (IGI) at www.family-search.org.

8   Heber J. Grant to Reed Smoot, 4 February 1921, quoted in Merrill, *Reed Smoot: Apostle in Politics,* 132.

9   Heber J. Grant to Reed Smoot, 12 October 1921. Reed Smoot files, Brigham Young University Archives, Provo, Utah, quoted in James R. Clark, *Messages of the First Presidency,* 5, 206.

10  Merrill, *Reed Smoot: Apostle in Politics,* 151.

11  Merrill, *Reed Smoot: Apostle in Politics,* 155–56. Smoot shared this incident in a July 1939 interview.

12  Letter, 16 December 1924, in James R. Clark, *Messages of the First Presidency,* 5:238.

13  Heath, *In the World,* 540. See also *Deseret News,* 25, 26, 27, 28 June 1923, 10 August 1923; *Salt Lake Tribune,* 27 June 1923; *Millennial Star,* 2 August 1923.

14  Sheri L. Dew, *Ezra Taft Benson: A Biography,* 41.

15  *Salt Lake Tribune,* 27 June 1923, 1.

16  Heath, *In the World,* 540–41. See also program for "Special organ recital tendered to President and Mrs. Warren G. Harding on the occasion of their visit to Salt Lake City," in LDS Church Archives, Salt Lake City.

# CALVIN COOLIDGE

## 1923–1929

Apostle Reed Smoot had a remarkable relationship with President Harding, but his friendship with President Calvin Coolidge was also very strong. He frequently dined, traveled, and even stayed at the White House with Coolidge. Partially as a result of this friendship, the General Authorities developed very positive views of Coolidge and greatly respected his faith and good Puritan example. Shortly before his death, an ailing Coolidge had Elder Smoot give him a priesthood blessing. Calvin Coolidge also promoted future First Presidency member J. Reuben Clark Jr. to be undersecretary of state.

**1920:** Warren G. Harding and vice presidential running mate Calvin Coolidge are popular in Utah, where they win 56 percent of the vote in the mostly Mormon state.[1]

**August 1923:** Upon hearing of Harding's death, Smoot wires Heber J. Grant, "We thanked God that he was at the helm," referring to Coolidge.[2] The Apostle-Senator meets, dines, and travels with the President frequently.

**October 1923:** Heber J. Grant prays specifically for Coolidge in general conference. He does so again the following April.[3]

*In 1928, Coolidge appointed future First Presidency member J. Reuben Clark Jr. as his undersecretary of state. While Secretary of State Frank Kellogg was away on business, Clark was the one interacting with the President on international affairs. Dissatisfied at times with Kellogg's management of the State Department, Coolidge remarked that he would have preferred Clark as secretary of state.*

**November 1924:** Coolidge is elected to a full term. In Utah, the tally stands at 49 percent for Coolidge, 30 percent for Democrat John Davis, and 21 percent for Progressive Robert LaFollette. On election night, Coolidge asks Elder Smoot to join him and Mrs. Coolidge at the White House to receive election returns. Once the landslide is official, Smoot is sent outside at 1:30 AM to deliver a statement to the newspapers.[4]

**1928:** Coolidge appoints J. Reuben Clark Jr. as his undersecretary of state. While Secretary of State Frank Kellogg is away on business, Clark is the one interacting with the President on international affairs. Dissatisfied at times with Kellogg's management of the State Department, Coolidge remarks that he would have preferred Clark as secretary of state.[5]

**November 1928:** Following the death of Smoot's wife, the President invites the widower to stay at the White House for a week or so in order to provide the Apostle with a change and to spend quality time with him.[6]

**1933:** Coolidge is blessed by Elder Smoot shortly before the ex-President's death.

## REED SMOOT AND CALVIN COOLIDGE'S FREQUENT INTERACTIONS

As chair of the powerful Senate Finance Committee, Smoot was consulted frequently by President Coolidge. For example, within days of becoming President, Coolidge asked Elder Smoot

to join him for dinner to brief him on matters foreign and domestic. On a couple of occasions, President Coolidge also invited the Mormon Apostle to join him aboard his boat, the *Mayflower,* for weekend cruises. Later, when Senator Smoot turned 63, he had several close friends to dinner at his home, including the President and First Lady. On occasion, Smoot would dine at the White House alone with the President and First Lady, and the secretary of commerce Herbert Hoover and Mrs. Hoover. The President also had Smoot and one other senator join him for a trip to his boyhood home in Plymouth, Massachusetts, in August 1925.[7]

At various times Elder Smoot was able to introduce Church leaders to Coolidge, including George Albert Smith—who presented him with a copy of the Young Men's Mutual Improvement Association Diamond Jubilee booklet—and President Heber J. Grant.[8]

*For thirty years, Reed Smoot served as both a United States senator and as a member of the Quorum of the Twelve Apostles. During Calvin Coolidge's presidency, when Smoot was especially influential, Church President Heber J. Grant paid him this compliment: "I feel, Brother Smoot, that Roosevelt, Taft, Harding and Coolidge have been made friends of Utah more through your personal influence . . . than any other single influence."*

President Grant once wrote to Smoot:

> I feel, Brother Smoot, that Roosevelt, Taft, Harding and Coolidge have been made friends of Utah more through your personal influence and devotion to your duty and at the same time your strong championship of the Gospel of Jesus Christ than any other single influence.[9]

Once as an ex-President, Coolidge had a "very pleasant visit" with Apostle-Senator Smoot in Washington. Later in the day Coolidge remarked to his Secret Service driver, "Senator Smoot is a darling. America owes him a debt of gratitude for his wonderful services as United States Senator."[10] Later, Smoot related the following experience that took place during his final visit with Calvin Coolidge in the winter of 1932:

> The last time I visited him was shortly before his death. I sat by his bedside. We talked over conditions existing in our country, and when I was about to leave, the President said to me: "Senator, there is some plan in your Church, isn't there, where men administer to the sick and pray for them?" I said, "Yes, Mr. President. We call that administering to the sick." He said, "Can anyone in the Church administer to anyone outside of the Church?" I told him "Yes." He said, "Reed, I wish you would administer to me." I did so, and I want to say to you, my brothers and sisters, I never felt happier in my life than when I laid my hands upon him and asked God to bless him.[11]

Coolidge brought a conservative simplicity, and God-fearing outlook to the White House that was later admired by LDS prophets. "We do not need more material development, we need more spiritual development," he said. "We do not need more law, we need more religion."

# COOLIDGE'S LEGACY WITH THE SAINTS

The thirtieth President has been quoted numerous times by Church authorities, due to his wit and his religious values. Joseph Fielding Smith relayed Coolidge's thoughts that "our government rests upon religion. It is from that source that we derive our reverence for truth and justice, for equality and liberality and for the rights of mankind." He remarked that these words were "just as good as scripture."[12]

President Benson often quoted Coolidge's remark:

> We do not need more material development, we need more spiritual development. We do not need more intellectual power, we need more moral power. We do not need more knowledge, we need more character. We do not need more government, we need more culture. We do not need more law, we need more religion.[13]

Both President Harold B. Lee and President Gordon B. Hinckley enjoyed retelling in conference the time "Silent Cal" Coolidge returned from church one Sunday, and his wife asked him what the preacher spoke about. He replied, "Sin." "What did he say?" she asked. "He was against it," was his reply.[14]

*Coolidge was known for being friendly but also a man of few words and a dry wit. Both President Harold B. Lee and President Gordon B. Hinckley enjoyed retelling in conference the time "Silent Cal" Coolidge returned from church one Sunday, and his wife asked him what the preacher spoke about. He replied, "Sin." "What did he say?" she asked. "He was against it," was his reply.*

# ENDNOTES

1    *Dave Leip's Atlas of U.S. Presidential Elections.*

2    Heath, *In the World,* 554.

3    Heber J. Grant, in Conference Report, April 1924, 160. See also Conference Report, October 1923, 2–3.

4    *Dave Leip's Atlas of U.S. Presidential Elections.* See also Heath, *In the World,* 581.

5    Winder, *Counselors to the Prophets,* 352–54.

6    Heath, *In the World,* 701–4.

7    Heath, *In the World,* 556, 572, 585, 601, 607–8, 616–18, 626, 641, 647, 650, 674, 678–79.

8    Gibbons, *George Albert Smith,* 126. See also *Encyclopedia of Mormonism,* 634.

9    Letter of Grant to Smoot, 16 December 1924, quoted in James R. Clark, *Messages of the First Presidency,* 5, 238.

10   24 July 1929 entry in Heath, *In the World,* 711.

11   Reed Smoot, in Conference Report, April 1939, 56.

12   Joseph Fielding Smith, in Conference Report, April 1943, 15. See also Joseph Fielding Smith, *Doctrines of Salvation,* 3:317.

13   Ezra Taft Benson, "Watchman, Warn the Wicked," *Ensign,* July 1973, 38.

14   Harold B. Lee, in Conference Report, April 1956, 108–9. See also Gordon B. Hinckley, "Gambling," *Ensign,* April 2005.

# HERBERT HOOVER

## 1929–1933

During his long career of public service, Herbert Hoover developed very positive impressions of The Church of Jesus Christ of Latter-day Saints. From his years as chair of the American Relief Committee, he developed an appreciation for the Church's welfare efforts and self-sufficiency. From his time as secretary of commerce and President, Hoover developed a strong friendship with Reed Smoot—even allowing the Apostle to spend his honeymoon at the White House and traveling to Utah to campaign for Smoot's reelection. Also from his time in the White House, and especially in his thirty-one-year post-presidency, Hoover became close and corresponded often with First Presidency member J. Reuben Clark Jr., whom he had appointed as ambassador to Mexico. Finally, the former President developed a good friendship with Elder Ezra Taft Benson during the future Church president's years in Eisenhower's cabinet, and Hoover even wrote the foreword to one of Benson's books.

In 1960, at the request of LDS bishop Loftis J. Sheffield, Herbert Hoover gave a public statement on his feelings toward the Church:

> I have had the great privilege of association
> with the leaders of the Church of Jesus Christ of
> Latter-day Saints for more than 43 years. I have

witnessed their devotion to public service and their support of char-
itable efforts over our country and in foreign lands during all these
years. I have witnessed the growth of the Church's communities over
the world where self-reliance, devotion, resolution and integrity are
a light to all mankind. Surely a great message of Christian faith has
been given by the Church—and it must continue.[1]

**August 1917:** U.S. food administrator Herbert Hoover works with Presiding Bishop Charles
W. Nibley at a sugar conference. In the months to follow he interacts often with Bishop Nibley
and Elder Smoot regarding sugar issues—an important product of many key LDS-owned businesses.[2]

**June 1918:** Herbert Hoover, then chair of the American Relief Committee, asks that his appreciation to the Relief Society of the Church for donating wheat during the Great War be proclaimed from the floor of the House of Representatives.[3]

**1920:** Smoot convinces President-Elect Harding that Hoover be named secretary of commerce. In this capacity, Hoover works and socialized often with Smoot, visits Utah twice (including a 1926 trip to assist in Smoot's reelection), meets with George Albert Smith, and is visited by
President and Mrs. Heber J. Grant.[4]

**Winter 1927–28:** Smoot begins to build support for Hoover's presidential bid among fellow
senators. "I thought a great deal of Hoover," writes Smoot, "and that he would make a good
President."[5]

**November 1928:** Hoover campaigns in Utah to cheering crowds. He wins on election day,
thanks in part to Utah—where he wins 54 percent to Alfred Smith's 41 percent. Apostle Reed
Smoot is troubled by Utah's weaker numbers for Hoover. "A great humiliation," he writes. "I cannot understand it as to Hoover. The balance of the country supported Hoover splendidly. . . . I
am ashamed for Utah." Elder George Albert Smith writes, "We have elected a wonderful man to
be president, a God fearing, courageous, capable executive. Being personally acquainted with
Herbert Hoover, I do not hesitate to say I believe he will be one of our greatest presidents."[6]

**1928–29:** President-Elect Hoover utilizes Elder Smoot in deciding the makeup of his cabinet,
in writing his inaugural address, and the two relax on a fishing vacation in Florida before his inauguration. Once President Hoover is sworn in, Smoot continues as a key advisor. President Hoover
once tells a visitor that "there was one Senator he could rely on and that was Sen Smoot." This
fierce loyalty insures Hoover's support for Utah's sugar beet industry and other projects important
to the Mormon leadership.[7]

**1929:** George Albert Smith calls on President Hoover while on assignment in Washington and sees "signs of worry and concern in the new chief executive," who is already feeling the nation's economic stress that will soon spiral into the Great Depression. Elder Smoot, who dines frequently with Hoover at the White House, also notes that the "President looks very much worried." In the October 1929 general conference, President Grant's counselor Charles W. Nibley prays for the President: "I bless Herbert Hoover in the great effort that he is making now."[8]

**July 1930:** Apostle-Senator Reed Smoot and his new bride, Alice Sheets Smoot, spend their two-week honeymoon as guests of the Hoovers at the White House.

**1930:** Hoover invites Elder David O. McKay to participate in the White House Conference on Child Health and Protection.[9]

**30 October 1930:** Hoover appoints Latter-day Saint J. Reuben Clark Jr. to be his ambassador to Mexico—one of only fifteen U.S. ambassadors in the world. Later, Heber J. Grant invites Ambassador Clark to serve as his counselor, but Clark worries that President Hoover will consider him a "deserter" if he leaves his administration to take a Church job, so he waits until Hoover is out of office to resign. This concern for President Hoover keeps the First Presidency as a two-man quorum for nearly a year and a half.[10]

**November 1932:** In return for Smoot's continuous loyalty, Hoover visits Salt Lake City on the day before the election to campaign for Smoot. Despite a warm reception in the Tabernacle, both the President and the Apostle-Senator lose their election the following day (Utah voted 57 percent for FDR and 41 percent for Hoover). "It was rather satisfying, however," reflects Smoot "to have the President of the United States make a strenuous effort in support of an Apostle of the Mormon Church."[11]

**February 1940:** The former President telegrams President Grant to thank the Church for contributing toward the Finnish Relief Drive. "I think I realize the many problems of relief which the Mormon Church faces among its own people and the whole country knows of and admires the effective way in which it is solving its serious problems at home. I can therefore on this occasion pay sincere tribute to the Mormon Church."[12]

**1946:** As he was leaving from a meeting with the President of Mexico, President George Albert Smith meets former President Hoover, who happens to be President Camacho's next appointment. Mr. Hoover warmly shakes hands with the LDS delegation and asks them to give his best to President J. Reuben Clark Jr., "for whom he had real affection." President Smith wrote, "He looks well. . . . I have a very high regard for Mr. Hoover."[13]

**April 1949:** Hoover, now chair of the Hoover Commission to identify government waste, calls on George Albert Smith to ask about his thoughts on the topic.[14]

**1952:** The former President meets with incoming Secretary of Agriculture Ezra Taft Benson, and they begin a friendship that lasts until Hoover's death in 1964.

*As he was leaving from a meeting with the President of Mexico in 1946, President George Albert Smith met former President Hoover, who happened to be President Camacho's next appointment. Mr. Hoover warmly shook hands with the LDS delegation and asked them to give his best to President J. Reuben Clark Jr., "for whom he had real affection." President Smith wrote, "He looks well. . . . I have a very high regard for Mr. Hoover." George Albert Smith is pictured in the center, with Herbert Hoover to the right, and Joseph L. Anderson (Secretary to the First Presidency) at the far right.*

# AN APOSTLE'S WHITE HOUSE HONEYMOON

The strong friendship between Herbert Hoover and Reed Smoot is evidenced in the fact that when Smoot remarried after his first wife's death, he canceled his honeymoon to Hawaii and instead returned to Washington D.C. with his bride to help secure the passage of the Naval Treaty.

Hoover thought it "an act of loyalty . . . and duty without equal" and insisted the newlyweds stay at the White House for their two weeks in the nation's capital (10–24 July 1930). As the personal guests of President and Mrs. Hoover, they were given a wedding breakfast on the south porch of the White House for friends and family, several dinners in their honor, and a weekend with the Hoovers at their summer home on the Rapidan River in Virginia.[15] The wedding breakfast was described as "Quaker-plain and Mormon-simple": melon, bacon and eggs, whole wheat muffins, toast, and without coffee or

*The south porch of the White House during the Hoover administration. It was here that Reed Smoot and his bride were given a "Quaker-plain and Mormon-simple" wedding breakfast in their honor by President and Mrs. Hoover.*

tea. Lou Henry Hoover was dressed in light blue, and the President in a white linen suit. Sitting at the head table, the chief executive raised a stemmed crystal goblet and said, "A toast to the bride and bridegroom; May every hour, of every day, of every year, bring you health and happiness." The guests murmured, "Hear, hear," and drank. President Hoover lowered his glass to the table and studied it, twisting the stem between his thumb and forefinger. "A good glass of water," he said. "The greatest stimulant in the world."[16]

Reed Smoot later explained to the Saints in general conference:

> It has given me unbounded pleasure to explain to all the Presidents of the United States, from Theodore Roosevelt down, our attitude, our belief in the Word of Wisdom. On two occasions

*Alice Sheets Smoot and her new husband Reed. President Hoover was so pleased that they would cancel their honeymoon to Hawaii and return to Washington for some important Senate votes that he invited the Mormon couple to honeymoon at the White House for two weeks.*

---

I have lived at the White House, I have slept there, and taken part in all the exercises that were held, and I want to say to you, my brethren and sisters, that there never was a morning or a night that I did not bow before my Heavenly Father in that place and thank him for the knowledge I had of him and his great work.[17]

The *New York Evening Graphic*'s headline declared "Romance Turns White House into Cozy Love Nest," and described how the Senator and his wife were put up in the Rose Suite, and the bed of Andrew Jackson.[18] Upon returning to Utah from Washington, Mrs. Smoot gave an account of the unique honeymoon trip published in the Church magazine the *Improvement Era*.

It is needless to say that every dignified, sweet, graceful thing that could be done to make our stay pleasant, was done. When we reached Washington one of the President's cars took us immediately to the White House. We were presented to Mrs. Hoover and assigned to the Rose Room suite. It is hardly necessary to say that President and Mrs. Hoover are probably the best educated, most traveled, and best read occupants the White House has ever had.

At my first dinner in the White House the program of guests was most imposing. President Hoover escorted me and Senator Smoot escorted Mrs. Hoover. During the course of the dinner I had the privilege of telling the President of some of the work that is being done by our Church and particularly by the Primary Association in which I have been interested particularly in our programs commemorating "Child Health Day."

While there we frequently had breakfast on the large front porch with the President and Mrs. Hoover and Mrs. Stark McMullan of Palo Alto, California, who was also a White House guest. After the first morning, when it was found that the Senator and I did not use tea or coffee, milk was added to the menu. And furthermore I did not see a single woman smoke while I was in the White House.[19]

# EZRA TAFT BENSON'S FRIENDSHIP WITH HOOVER

When Ezra Taft Benson of the Twelve was nominated to serve as secretary of agriculture in 1952, he called on ex-President Hoover for advice. "This was my first meeting with Mr. Hoover," said Benson, "though I later became quite well acquainted with him. I don't believe anyone could really know Hoover without recognizing him as a truly great American. . . . A heavy-set man, of more than average height, Hoover at seventy-eight still conveyed an impression of great strength—like one of the sturdy trees in my beloved West."[20] The ex-President stepped forward on a couple of occasions to applaud Benson's efforts to reorganize the department and offer his help.[21] Years later, after another meeting with Hoover, Elder Benson recalled, "Here is a grand character, a true American, and a valued friend; the stuff that has made this country great."[22]

In 1960, former President Hoover penned the foreword to the Deseret Book publication *So Shall Ye Reap*, a collection of the speeches of Ezra Taft Benson. In it he includes his thoughts on the LDS Church and on Elder Benson, a future president of the Church. Some excerpts include:

> During more than thirty-five years it has been my good fortune to have many associations with the leaders and the members of the faith to which Secretary Ezra Taft Benson was born and to which he adheres.
>
> The religious faiths in our country—all of them—maintain great principles in common. They believe in God. They command the virtue of loyalty to our country. They demand the highest standards of morals, of truth and integrity; the highest performance of public office; a willingness to self-sacrifice for the common good. These principles have in no way been suspended by our gigantic discoveries in science and invention. Secretary Benson is the embodiment of these principles and this faith.
>
> With these principles the religion to which Secretary Benson belongs has pioneered and builded a great industrious, law-abiding community. Within it are the highest standards of education and comfort.
>
> From that community have come many of our great religious leaders and statesmen. From them have come a member of the Supreme Court, members of the Cabinet, eminent Senators and Congressmen.

*When Apostle Ezra Taft Benson (above) was named Eisenhower's Secretary of Agriculture, he called on former-President Hoover for advice. "Here is a grand character, a true American," remarked Benson of Hoover, "and a valued friend; the stuff that has made this country great." Hoover would later write of Benson, "Ezra Taft Benson is today the great contribution of this community to America statesmanship and a leader of the Christian faith."*

The Church has a special distinction. In times of unemployment and war they have taken care of their own people without charge on the Treasury of the United States. The Church has stood adamant for the Constitution both in business and education. It has also been a staunch supporter of every other basic freedom.

Ezra Taft Benson is today the great contribution of this community to America statesmanship and a leader of the Christian faith.[23]

# ENDNOTES

1 Quoted in Spencer Howard (Archives Technician, Herbert Hoover Presidential Library), email to author, 25 July 2005.

2 Heath, *In the World,* 365, 381, 400.

3 "Recognition of Noble Work," *Improvement Era* 21, no. 10 (August 1918).

4 Heath, *In the World,* 466, 466 n3, 468, 526, 633–34. See also "Services and Liberties of Our Great and Glorious Country," *Improvement Era* 25, no. 8 (June 1922); Hoover's Daily Calendar, 23 May 1926 and 26 April 1926 items, Herbert Hoover Presidential Library.

5 Heath, *In the World,* 668, 688. See also Merrill, *Reed Smoot: Apostle in Politics,* 166.

6 "Passing Events," *Improvement Era* 32, no. 2 (December 1928). See also *Dave Leip's Atlas of U.S. Presidential Elections;* Heath, *In the World,* 695; Gibbons, *George Albert Smith,* 126.

7 Heath, *In the World,* 698, 701, 704–5, 722. See also Merrill, *Reed Smoot: Apostle in Politics,* 312.

8 Gibbons, *George Albert Smith,* 126–27. See also Heath, *In the World,* 748; Conference Report, October 1929, 119.

9 Jeanette McKay Morrell, *Highlights in the Life of President David O. McKay,* 77.

10 Ambassadors listed in *Register of the Department of State, January 1, 1931,* 321–37. Clark's concerns expressed in letter to Heber J. Grant and Anthony W. Ivins, 19 December 1931, J. Reuben Clark Jr. Papers, Special Collections, Harold B. Lee Library, Brigham Young University.

11 Merrill, *Reed Smoot: Apostle in Politics,* 230. See also Heath, *In the World,* 779; Herbert Hoover, Address in the Mormon Tabernacle, Salt Lake City, Utah, on 7 November 1932, in John Woolley and Gerhard Peters, *The American Presidency Project,* online at http://www.presidency.ucsb.edu/site/docs/sou.php. See also *Dave Leip's Atlas of U.S. Presidential Elections.*

12 "Church Contributes to Finnish Relief," *Improvement Era* 43, no. 2 (February 1940).

13 Joseph Anderson, *Prophets I Have Known,* 109. See also George Albert Smith to Harry S Truman, 27 May 1946, Truman Presidential Museum and Library.

14 Gibbons, *George Albert Smith,* 350.

15 Heath, *In the World,* 728–30.

16 Robert O'Brien, *Marriott: The J. Willard Marriott Story,* 144–45.

17  Reed Smoot, in Conference Report, October 1935, 116–17.

18  O'Brien, *Marriott: The J. Willard Marriott Story,* 145–46.

19  Mrs. Reed Smoot, "A Guest at the White House," *Improvement Era* 33, no. 12 (October 1930).

20  Benson, *Crossfire,* 24.

21  Francis M. Gibbons, *Ezra Taft Benson: Statesman, Patriot, Prophet of God,* 180, 185.

22  Benson, *Crossfire,* 116.

23  Benson, *So Shall Ye Reap,* i.

# FRANKLIN D. ROOSEVELT

## *1933–1945*

The four terms of Franklin Delano Roosevelt were vastly different for the Mormons than the previous six administrations, where Senator Reed Smoot had paved positive relations between the White House and the Church. With FDR's 1932 landslide victory, Smoot and other Republicans were swept from power, Prohibition was soon repealed, Communist Russia was officially recognized, and the New Deal was unrolled. These elements led to bitter anti-Roosevelt sentiment among many Church leaders, most especially President Heber J. Grant, who left the Democratic Party over it.[1] Yet, among some General Authorities and most rank-and-file Latter-day Saints, FDR was a hero who was making decisive moves to combat the Great Depression. Despite open editorials from the Church president, the Saints would continue to support Roosevelt. For his part, Roosevelt would involve some Latter-day Saints in his administration, take an interest in the Church's welfare program, visit the Hawaii Temple, and would develop—in his words—"a very high opinion of the Mormons."

**1880s:** Roosevelt first hears about the Mormons. "I shall never forget a stop, which my Father and Mother made in Salt Lake City, when I was a very small boy," he later recalls in a letter to Winston Churchill. "They were walking up and down the station platform and saw two young ladies each wheeling a baby carriage with youngsters in them, each about one year old. My Father asked them if they were waiting for somebody and they replied 'Yes, we are waiting for our husband. He is the engineer of this train.'" Roosevelt then quips, "Perhaps this was the origin of the Good Neighbor policy!"[2]

**1906:** Young Roosevelt flunks a difficult contracts course at Columbia Law School that his LDS classmate J. Reuben Clark Jr. passes. Years later, President Roosevelt summons his former law school classmate to Washington to help on special projects.[3]

**1920:** FDR runs unsuccessfully for vice president on the Democratic ticket with James Cox. The pair are unpopular in Mormon Utah, where they only win 39 percent.[4]

**2 July 1930:** President Heber J. Grant presents a copy of the Book of Mormon to Roosevelt, who has been elected governor of New York in 1928.[5]

**1932:** FDR wins the presidency, with 57 percent of the Utah vote. His platform includes the repeal of the Eighteenth Amendment (Prohibition). Frustrated General Authorities declare, "The ground already gained ought not to be surrendered."[6] George Albert Smith scoffs, "The attitudes of the President of the United States and his wife toward the use of liquor has acted like an invitation to many heretofore temperate people to become guzzlers."[7]

**1933:** Church leaders have mixed reactions to the New Deal.

**4 November 1933:** Through President Clark's Washington contacts, a White House meeting with Roosevelt is arranged for the entire First Presidency, Apostle and former senator Reed Smoot, and pro-Roosevelt Apostle Stephen L Richards.[8]

**Summer 1934:** FDR becomes the first President to visit Hawaii, where he visits the LDS community at Laie and is treated to a Polynesian dance show on the temple grounds. William M. Waddoups, president of the Hawaii Temple, reports, "The president told me he was highly delighted with the reception and very much pleased with the work we as a Church are doing among the people here."[9]

**1 September 1936:** The President and First Lady arrive in Salt Lake City for the funeral of Roosevelt's secretary of war (and former Utah governor), George H. Dern.

**Fall 1936:** Heber J. Grant and other Church leaders publicly encourage the Saints to vote against Roosevelt—but he wins anyway. Similar tension is again seen in the 1940 election.

*1 September 1936: The President and First Lady arrive in Salt Lake City for the funeral of Roosevelt's secretary of war (and former Utah governor), George H. Dern. Also appearing on the rail car with the Roosevelts was Utah Governor Henry H. Blood. Governor Blood, who had served as president of the LDS North Davis Stake for twenty-two years, obtained an important endorsement from FDR, which helped him win reelection that fall.*

**4 January 1944:** Roosevelt discusses genealogy and the Mormons in a letter to Winston Churchill and to his wife.

**November 1944:** FDR wins a fourth term and posts big numbers in Utah: 60 percent compared to only 39 percent for Thomas Dewey.[10]

**12 April 1945:** Roosevelt dies in office. Elder Joseph Fielding Smith writes, "There are some of us who have felt that it is really an act of providence."[11] President J. Reuben Clark Jr. quips, "The Lord gave the people of the United States four elections in order to get rid of him, that they failed to do so in these four elections, so He held an election of His own and cast one vote, and then took him away."[12]

## MORMONS REACT TO THE NEW DEAL

When FDR announced the New Deal, President Heber J. Grant, J. Reuben Clark Jr., David O. McKay, and other Church leaders became outspoken critics of what they felt was socialism.[13] However, Anthony W. Ivins, Stephen L Richards, B. H. Roberts, and Presiding Bishop Sylvester Q. Cannon applauded the President for applying the federal government more deeply in economic and social affairs, and encouraged the Saints to accept the help offered in the New Deal.[14] President Ivins endorsed FDR's National Recovery Administration (NRA) at the October 1933 general conference. Democrat Apostle Stephen L Richards also urged members to rally behind Roosevelt as "in an emergency an army follows its commander."[15]

When the First Presidency announced the new Church Security Program (later Church Welfare Program) in April 1936, it was initially viewed by national newspapers and Mormon New Dealers as an attempt to undermine and supplant the New Deal's relief programs.[16] However, the program caused anti–New Deal Americans to look on the independent Mormons with new respect. Privately, the Roosevelt administration scoffed at it, and the entire program was declared "fictitious" by one FDR agent.[17] As a result of such attention Elder Melvin J. Ballard of the Twelve (and chair of the Church Relief Committee) was invited to the nation's capital to explain to President Roosevelt the Church's new "security" program. "I told him our program," said Elder Ballard of the fifteen-minute visit. "The President said that the Mormon Church could do it. They have something that no other Church has." The President claimed to be pleased with the Church's efforts and pledged his full cooperation in continuing to battle the Depression. FDR expressed hope that the Mormons' effort would inspire other groups to launch similar programs of their own. He then asked Elder Ballard to see his relief administrator, Harry Hopkins, which resulted in an hour-long discussion the Church Welfare Program.[18]

*The First Presidency of Heber J. Grant, J. Reuben Clark Jr., and David O. McKay were strongly opposed to Franklin Roosevelt. They were concerned about his support for repealing Prohibition, fearful that the New Deal would be the beginning of socialism in the United States, and viewed Roosevelt's runs for three and four terms, along with his attempt to increase the number of Supreme Court justices so that he could pack it with his supporters, as troubling attempts to augment his power.*

## LATTER-DAY SAINTS IN THE ROOSEVELT ADMINISTRATION

Roosevelt involved a few Mormons in his administration. Future General Authority Franklin D. Richards was named by President Roosevelt as the first head of Utah's Federal Housing Administration in 1934. The President promoted him to head the national FHA in 1947.[19] Other Latter-day Saints tapped by Roosevelt include James Henry Moyle, a mission president who had served in the Wilson administration, to be Commissioner of Customs.[20] Marriner S. Eccles, a

Latter-day Saint banker who had served a mission in Scotland, was appointed by Roosevelt to a post in the Treasury Department. He served there briefly until the President appointed him to chair the Federal Reserve in 1934, which he led until 1948.[21] In July 1933, Presiding Bishop Sylvester Q. Cannon accepted an appointment to an advisory committee for Roosevelt's Public Works Administration (PWA).[22]

In 1933, the President asked his old law school classmate J. Reuben Clark Jr. to serve as a delegate to the upcoming Pan-American Conference in Uruguay. The First Presidency member accepted and took leave of his Church duties for the four-month assignment. Roosevelt would later enlist President Clark's help again to serve as president of the Foreign Bondholders' Protective Council (FBPC).[23]

Washington Stake President Ezra Taft Benson represented the National Council of Farmer Cooperatives as one of four national agriculture leaders who met with President Roosevelt regularly. The future Apostle and Church president made a positive impression. "Who was that fine-looking young man?" FDR asked of him after one of their early committee meetings. "If they will make him their spokesman, I will talk with him anytime." However, Benson's impression of Roosevelt was less rosy: "Roosevelt always seemed to feel he knew all the answers. . . . He didn't seem to want advice unless it agreed with his own opinions."[24]

## ROOSEVELT OPPOSED BY THE PROPHET, SUPPORTED BY SAINTS

Church President Heber J. Grant was vocal in his disapproval of the policies of the thirty-second President, especially after the death of his pro-Roosevelt first counselor, Anthony B. Ivins, in September 1934. He would often become upset when discussing FDR, and in one heated discussion slammed his cane on the desk of Franklin J. Murdock, shattering the glass desktop in his anti-Roosevelt fury.[25]

It comes as no surprise, then, that in the election of 1936, President Grant openly endorsed the Republican candidate for President, Alf Landon. However, he pointed out that he was speaking for himself and not for the Church.[26] First Counselor J. Reuben Clark Jr. was not only anti-Roosevelt, but he was very much in favor of Landon. "Governor Alf M. Landon of Kansas will make a great president," he told reporters gathered in the First Presidency's office. President Clark traveled the West stumping for Landon, helped write the GOP platform that year, and was privately assured by Governor Landon that he would be appointed secretary of state if the Republicans succeeded in defeating Roosevelt.[27]

As the 1936 election drew near, an unsigned, front-page editorial in the Church-owned *Deseret News* accused FDR of knowingly promoting unconstitutional laws and advocating Communism. However, the "other candidate [Landon] has declared he stands for the Constitution and for the American system."[28] Although many Roosevelt-loving Mormons were upset over the editorial, one future Church leader was persuaded. Future First Presidency member Marion G. Romney, a staunch Democrat committed to vote for Franklin Roosevelt, was deeply torn. When the editorial appeared, Romney's biographer said, "He felt as if his political life had collapsed around him." After fasting and three hours of prayer Marion concluded that the editorial was inspired and given through the Lord's prophet. He then reversed his political loyalties and labored to dissuade his friends from voting for Roosevelt.[29]

In 1936, Roosevelt won every state in the Union except Maine and Vermont. As convincing as the victory was nationally, it was even more so in Utah, where FDR had over 69 percent of the vote.[30]

Determined that Utah should not support FDR's bid for a third term in 1940, the General Authorities once again drafted a joint anti-Roosevelt statement but settled on issuing a less dramatic unsigned editorial.[31] President Grant deferred to those who thought too bold a statement would cause problems for the Church without much hope of changing votes and came to the horrified conclusion that "about half the Latter-day Saints almost worship him [Roosevelt]." He regarded the strong LDS support for the President and his "neo-socialism" as "one of the most serious conditions that has confronted me since I became President of the Church."[32]

In 1940, Utah was one of the strongest pro-Roosevelt states, giving him over 62 percent of the

*Despite* Deseret News *editorials endorsing Roosevelt's opponents, and the Church president and other authorities encouraging his defeat, Franklin Delano Roosevelt garnered enormous electoral wins in Utah—even at higher percentages than he received nationally.*

vote and opponent Wendell Willkie under 38 percent.[33] When the pro-FDR tallies came in on election night in Utah, President Grant saw the total and was "dumbfounded."[34] Part of the explanation was the fact that up to three-fourths of the population of rural Utah received federal relief, and a higher proportion of LDS Utahns obtained federal relief than did non-LDS Utahns.[35] At election time it was a simple financial decision that no editorial could sway.

*In a candid letter between friends, Franklin Roosevelt wrote Winston Churchill about Mormon genealogists discovering that they were distantly related. "I have a very high opinion of the Mormons—for they are excellent citizens," he wrote to the British Prime Minister.*

## ROOSEVELT'S LETTER TO CHURCHILL ON THE MORMONS

On 4 January 1944, Roosevelt wrote an informal note to Winston Churchill and his wife, Clementine, regarding genealogy and the Mormons. He seemed delighted to learn that Churchill was his distant cousin and expressed some genuine admiration for the Latter-day Saints. This letter is significant in that we see FDR's true opinion of the Mormons as expressed in a casual note to friends. The compliments he pays the Saints in this context are infinitely more meaningful than if he had said the same words on a visit to Temple Square, for example, when expressing such pleasantries would simply be expected:

> I find the enclosed clipping on my return home. Evidently, from one of the paragraphs, the Dessert News [sic] of Salt Lake City claims there is a direct link between Clemmie and the Mormons. And the last sentence shows that, Winston is a sixth cousin, twice removed, All of this presents to me a most interesting study in heredity.

> Hitherto I had not observed any outstanding Mormon characteristics in either of you—but I shall be looking for them from no[w on].

> I have a very high opinion of the Mormons—for they are excellent citizens.[36]

So FDR caused a rift within the Mormon community, but he did have a high opinion of the Church—and many in the Church had a high opinion of him.

# ENDNOTES

1     Sessions, *Mormon Democrat,* 283. See also Richard O. Cowan, *The Church in the Twentieth Century,* 136.

2     Franklin D. Roosevelt to Winston and Clementine Churchill, 4 January 1944, Letter, Franklin D. Roosevelt Presidential Library and Museum, online at http://www.fdrlibrary.marist.edu/psf/box37/t335b01.html. The "Good Neighbor" policy was the policy of the Roosevelt Administration in relation to Latin America and Europe from 1933 to 1945, when the active U.S. intervention of previous decades was moderated in pursuit of hemispheric solidarity against external threats.

3     Winder, *Counselors to the Prophets,* 350, 355.

4     *Dave Leip's Atlas of U.S. Presidential Elections.*

5     "Presentation of the Book of Mormon to Rulers of the World," *Improvement Era* 43, no. 7 (July 1940).

6     Allen and Leonard, *The Story of the Latter-day Saints,* 526.

7     Gibbons, *George Albert Smith,* 127.

8     Hinckley, *Heber J. Grant,* 128.

9     *Church News,* 11 August 1934, 1, 8.

10     *Dave Leip's Atlas of U.S. Presidential Elections.*

11     Joseph Fielding Smith typed diary, 12 April 1945. See also Smith and Stewart, *The Life of Joseph Fielding Smith,* 326.

12     J. Reuben Clark to Preston D. Richards, 7 May 1945, fd 11, box 372, J. Reuben Clark Jr. Papers, Department of Archives and Special Collections, Harold B. Lee Library, Brigham Young University.

13     Francis M. Gibbons, *Heber J. Grant: Man of Steel, Prophet of God,* 198–99. See also Gregory A. Prince and Wm. Robert Wright, *David O. McKay and the Rise of Modern Mormonism,* 349.

14     Allen and Leonard, *The Story of the Latter-day Saints,* 526. See also Sylvester Q. Cannon diary, annual summary for 31 December 1933, LDS Church Archives, Salt Lake City.

15     Conference Report, October 1933, 64–65, 89.

16     Leonard J. Arrington, Feramorz Y. Fox, and Dean L. May, *Building the City of God: Community and Cooperation among the Mormons,* 348–50.

17     Ostling and Ostling, *Mormon America,* 109.

18     Church Education System, 512. See also Bryant S. Hinckley, *Sermons and Missionary Services of Melvin J. Ballard,* 119; "Church Security Program Indorsed by Pres. Roosevelt," *Deseret News,* 9 June 1936, 1.

19     "Franklin D. (Dewey) Richards," Grampa Bill's G.A. Pages, online at http://personal.atl.bellsouth.net/w/o/wol3/richafd2.htm.

20     See Sessions, *Mormon Democrat.*

21     Wikipedia.com, s.v. "Marriner Stoddard Eccles."

22     Sylvester Q. Cannon diary, annual summary for 31 December 1933, LDS Church Archives, Salt Lake City.

23     Frank W. Fox, *J. Reuben Clark: The Public Years,* 36. See also J. Reuben Clark office diary, 25 September 1933; "Plan to Aid Bondholders Outlined," *New York Times,* 21 October 1933.

24     *Improvement Era* (January 1953): 27. See also Gibbons, *Ezra Taft Benson,* 120–21, 131; Benson, *Crossfire,* 123.

25     Heber J. Grant journal sheets, 9 June 1936, 17 June 1940; see also Sessions, *Mormon Democrat,* 288; Franklin J. Murdock oral history, 1973, Typescript 52, LDS Church Archives, Salt Lake City.

26     Allen and Leonard, *The Story of the Latter-day Saints,* 526–27.

27  J. Reuben Clark office diary, 24 May 1958. See also Donald R. McCoy, *Landon of Kansas,* 349 n19.

28  "An Editorial, The Constitution," *Deseret News,* 31 October 1936:1, repeated in full on page 2.

29  F. Burton Howard, *Marion G. Romney: His Life and Faith,* 96.

30   *Dave Leip's Atlas of U.S. Presidential Elections.*

31  Ostling and Ostling, *Mormon America,* 109. See also "The Third Term Principle," *Deseret News,* 1 November 1940, 4.

32  Heber J. Grant journal sheets, quoted in D. Michael Quinn, *Elder Statesman: A Biography of J. Reuben Clark,* 57, 74, and 95.

33  *Dave Leip's Atlas of U.S. Presidential Elections.*

34  Heber J. Grant journal sheets, 5 November 1940.

35  Garth Mangum and Bruce Blumell, *The Mormons' War on Poverty: A History of LDS Welfare, 1830–1990,* 97, 113.

36  Franklin D. Roosevelt to Winston and Clementine Churchill, 4 January 1944, Letter, Franklin D. Roosevelt Presidential Library and Museum, online at http://www.fdrlibrary.marist.edu/psf/box37/t335b01.html.

# HARRY S TRUMAN

## *1945–1953*

The relationship between the Mormons and the White House advanced to a higher plane during the presidency of Harry S Truman. Whereas previous Presidents developed close ties with key Church leaders (i.e., George Q. Cannon, Reed Smoot, and J. Reuben Clark Jr.), beginning with Truman, we see chief executives developing personal relationships with Church presidents themselves. Truman—who hailed from Independence, Missouri, and had a grandfather who was once saved from financial ruin by Brigham Young—had already heard much about the Mormons by the time he reached the White House. Visits paid him by President George Albert Smith, and several visits he himself made to Salt Lake City, built a foundation of friendship between Truman and the Mormon prophet. The two presidents corresponded frequently, sharing ideas about politics and religion, and even sharing fruits and vegetables. And although Truman did not develop a similar friendship with President Smith's successor, David O. McKay, he still had positive personal contact with the prophet.

**1922:** Truman is elected judge of the county court of Jackson County, Missouri, where he officiates from the old log courthouse where Mormon leader Algernon Sidney Gilbert had his store in the 1830s. Judge Truman is befriended by the Central States Mission's president, future General Authority Samuel O. Bennion.[1]

**1944:** Senator Truman wins big as FDR's running mate. In Utah they receive 53 percent of the vote.[2]

**26 June 1945:** The new President stops in Salt Lake City for a night's sleep while returning east from San Francisco, where earlier in the day he participates in the founding of the United Nations and the signing of the U.N. Charter. He is met at the airport by President George Albert Smith and Governor Herbert B. Maw, who ride to the hotel with the President.[3]

**September 1945:** Truman invites the Mormons to join in a day of prayer and thanksgiving to mark the end of World War II. When the President learns of their prayers, he writes to George Albert Smith, "That you and the members of your Church have remembered me in special prayers has touched me deeply. It is extremely gratifying to know that I have your confidence."[4]

**3 November 1945:** President George Albert Smith surprises Truman with the Church's ambitious plans to aid post-war Europe.

**4 January 1946:** To celebrate Utah's fiftieth anniversary, Truman sends congratulations: "I like to believe that the hardy pioneer spirit survives in Utah."[5]

**December 1946:** While George Albert Smith is in New York for Boy Scout meetings, he receives a wire advising him that President Truman wants to see him. He immediately cancels his appointments and takes the train south to Washington. Ironically, there is no special reason why the President wants to meet with the LDS leader, but he has heard Smith is on the East Coast and simply wants to shake his hand and wish him a "Merry Christmas."[6]

**24 July 1947:** On the pioneer centennial, Truman sends compliments of Brigham Young and the pioneers. "Through their labors was fulfilled the prophecy of scripture and the desert was made to blossom like the rose."[7]

**14 May 1948:** Harry S Truman becomes the first head of state to officially recognize the state of Israel. According to LDS scholar Michael Benson, "Truman's recognition of the nation of Israel in May 1948 might be viewed as a partial fulfillment of [Elder Orson] Hyde's 1841 dedicatory prayer." Truman has been viewed by Latter-day Saints as a "Modern Day Cyrus" and as a facilitator of the literal gathering of Israel.[8]

**21 September 1948:** Truman's campaign rolls through Utah.

*President Truman visited Utah twice, in 1948 and 1952. He was cheered by large crowds on one of these visits as the presidential motorcade headed north past the Brigham Young Monument on Salt Lake City's Main Street. "I like to believe that the hardy pioneer spirit survives in Utah," Truman once said.*

**November 1948:** Truman garners 54 percent in Utah, compared to 45 percent for Thomas Dewey. Many Mormons across the nation admired Truman for his "small-town, heartland virtues: simplicity, honesty, self-acceptance, and his indomitable, scrappy, game-cock spirit."[9]

**1949:** Truman compliments Brigham Young in an address to the American Society of Engineers: "There isn't a city in the United States that was properly planned to begin with. I know of only one whose streets were laid out in anticipation of the automobile, and that was Salt Lake City, Utah. The man that laid out that city really had vision."[10]

**June 1949:** President Smith and Elder Ezra Taft Benson send Truman a Book of Mormon and other Church literature.

**October 1951:** Truman invites the new Church president, David O. McKay, to participate in a White House conference. The day after the conference, President and Sister McKay have a brief and pleasant visit with the President.[11]

**6 October 1952:** Truman visits Utah and speaks at BYU.

## THE NEW PRESIDENT AND GEORGE ALBERT SMITH

George Albert Smith and Harry Truman became pen pals of sorts, exchanging several dozen letters with one another throughout the late 1940s. Often the topic was Utah produce, of which the prophet would send the President exceptional samples. For example, in October 1945 he sent Truman an apple grown in St. George, Utah, weighing 1 3/4 pounds with a circumference of fifteen inches. The President thanked him for "that fine apple—truly the most beautiful one I have ever seen." Later the President thanked the prophet for sending him "that beautiful pear—it is the largest one I ever saw." In the fall of 1947, Truman again thanked President Smith, this time for "that fine celery for our Thanksgiving dinner. I need hardly assure you that it was enjoyed by all." Other items sent included cherries and peaches.[12]

George Albert Smith also invited Truman to attend a great youth conference, the pioneer centennial celebration, and the dedication of the Brigham Young statue at the U.S. Capitol's Statuary Hall, although in all cases the President was unable to attend. Also, at various times the Mormon leader would send the President the pioneer centennial edition of the Church magazine, the *Improvement Era;* the October 1947 general conference edition of that magazine; and his book, *Sharing the Gospel with Others.*[13]

On one occasion President Truman had heard that President Smith was in the hospital recuperating from an illness, and he quickly sent a letter to the prophet wishing him well. Upon President Smith's turning eighty, he received a kind note of congratulations from the President.[14] Their letters continued back and forth until President Smith's death in 1951, when Truman sent a letter of condolence to the late prophet's daughter, Emily Smith Stewart, which read:

*George Albert Smith and Harry S Truman mailed each other frequent letters. In addition, President Smith would also send outstanding specimens of Utah produce to the White House for the Trumans to enjoy.*

The death of your father causes me great personal sorrow. He not only was my friend and the grandson of a friend of my grandfather, but I looked upon him as one of our country's great moral leaders. Mrs. Truman joins me in extending sympathy in your bereavement.[15]

## TRUMAN AND THE LDS PLANS TO AID POST-WAR EUROPE

On 3 November 1945, President George Albert Smith met with President Truman in the White House, where he presented the Church's plans to use its welfare facilities to help relieve the suffering of Latter-day Saints in Europe. Accompanying President Smith to Washington for the six-day trip were Joseph Anderson (secretary to the First Presidency), Elder John A. Widtsoe of the Twelve, and Elder Widtsoe's assistant, Thomas E. McKay. Also included in the White House interview were representatives of the press.

President Smith began the twenty-minute meeting by retelling the story of Brigham Young saving Truman's grandfather from financial ruin. "Now the head of the Church is seeking the cooperation of the merchant's grandson to ship supplies to Saints in Europe," President Smith said.[16] The prophet described the visit in his own words as follows:

> When I called on him, he received me very graciously—I had
> met him before—and I said: "I have just come to ascertain from you,
> Mr. President, what your attitude will be if the Latter-day Saints are
> prepared to ship food and clothing and bedding to Europe."

He smiled and looked at me, and said: "Well, what do you want to ship it over there for? Their money isn't any good."

I said: "Of course; we would give it to them. They are our brothers and sisters and are in distress. God has blessed us with surplus, and we will be glad to send it if we have the cooperation of the government."

He said, "You are on the right track," and added, "we will be glad to help you in any way we can."

I have thought of that a good many times. After we had sat there a moment or two, he said again: "How long will it take you to get this ready?"

I said: "It's all ready."[17]

President Smith ended the visit by giving Truman a personalized, leather-bound copy of *A Voice of Warning,* one of the Church's classic proselyting pamphlets authored by Parley P. Pratt. As he gave him this gift, President Smith informed the President that the Latter-day Saints prayed for him regularly. Truman "expressed his appreciation and said that he very much needed the faith and prayers of the people."[18]

Three years later President Smith wrote a report to Truman about the Church's humanitarian efforts in Europe since the two had met. This included ninety carloads of food, clothing and bedding; thousands of cartons of supplies sent by mail; and $210,000 raised from a fast day. President Smith explained the LDS custom of fast Sundays and noted that if all the people of the U.S. had a similar Fast Day for the needy in Europe, it would raise over fifty million dollars. President Truman was impressed and replied, "It certainly is a wonderful work you have done for the welfare and feeding of starving people in Europe and I congratulate you on it."[19]

## TRUMAN'S WHISTLE STOP TRAIN STOPS IN UTAH

In July 1948, as the presidential election neared, George Albert Smith wrote to Truman, "I realize that you are in the midst of a political campaign. I hope that you will conserve your strength and come through it in a satisfactory way."[20] Truman replied to the Mormon prophet, "I am, as you suggest, trying to get myself in good physical condition for the coming campaign. It will be a tough one I can assure you. I intend to put everything possible into it."[21] And he did.

That fall Harry Truman made a thirty-five-day journey across the nation by train, making as many as sixteen speeches a day. Although the incumbent, he was viewed as the underdog and vowed to "fight hard" and "give 'em hell" on the campaign trail.[22]

As the train entered Utah on 21 September it pulled into Price, where the President gave a speech from the rear platform of the train. "Congressman [Walter K.] Granger paid me a very high

*21 September 1948: Harry Truman's famous whistle stop train makes a stop in Utah to campaign. Exiting the train (L–R): Presidential daughter Margaret Truman, First Lady Bess Truman, President George Albert Smith, and President Harry S Truman.*

compliment when I was out here as a Senator," said the President and native of Independence, Missouri. "He told me that he had become so fond of me that when the Mormons moved back to Independence, he was going to let me stay. I thought that was the greatest compliment that could be paid to anybody."

Later that evening in Salt Lake City, Truman was introduced by Governor Herbert B. Maw and then said a few words in the Empire Room of Hotel Utah. "Governor Maw, President [George Albert] Smith: I noticed very carefully that when the Governor addressed you, he said 'Fellow Democrats.' That included President Smith. [Laughter] That made me very happy."

Following the short speech there, the entourage crossed Main Street to Temple Square, where Truman gave a stirring speech to a Tabernacle audience, outlining some of his relationship to Utah and the Mormons. "You don't know what a great pleasure it is to see this magnificent auditorium," Truman said of the Tabernacle, "one of the historic ones in the world. . . . There is no story in our history more typical of the free American spirit than that of the Mormon settlers who founded this great city," declared the President. He continued:

> I have a close personal interest in the history of this great city. My grandfather, who lived in Jackson County, Mo., was a freighter across the plains, in the early days, and on occasion he brought an ox trainload of goods and merchandise here to Salt Lake City. My grandfather, whose name was Young, went to see Brigham Young, and told him his troubles, and Brigham Young gave him advice and told him to rent space down on the main street here in Salt Lake City, place his goods on display, and he would guarantee that my grandfather would lose no money. And he didn't.

> Today, I am most cordially received by the President of the Mormon Church, the successor of Brigham Young. I wish my old grandfather could see me now! Those pioneers had faith, and they had energy. They took the resources that Nature offered them, and used them wisely. Their courage and fighting spirit made them secure against enemies. They have left you a great heritage.[23]

"Everybody in Utah was at that meeting," crowed the President upon returning to his native Missouri the next day. "We had the meeting in the Mormon Tabernacle. It holds 11,000 people,

*21 September 1948: (L–R) First Lady Bess Truman, Utah Governor (and Latter-day Saint) Herbert B. Maw, President Harry S Truman, and President George Albert Smith enjoy dessert in the Empire Room of Hotel Utah.*

and there were about 12,500 at the place. And when I got through with them I don't think there was a Republican in Utah that didn't feel like he wanted to vote the Democratic ticket."[24]

## HARRY TRUMAN AND THE BOOK OF MORMON

In the spring of 1949, Elder Ezra Taft Benson and his wife called on Truman, where during the visit the President expressed his desire to receive a copy of the Book of Mormon.[25] A Book of Mormon, which had been signed by both President Smith and Elder Benson, was mailed to the White House that June. In addition, Elder James E. Talmage sent a pamphlet entitled "The Book of Mormon: An Account of its Origin, With Evidences of its Genuineness and Authenticity," and President Smith sent a three-page letter outlining various archeological evidences that correspond with the Book of Mormon account of American history, along with his testimony. "I hope you will pardon this long letter," wrote the prophet, "but my regard for you is so sincere that I am anxious that your administration shall be all that the Lord would have it be."[26] Truman's prompt reply upon receiving the book was, "I appreciate it very much and I want to thank you most sincerely for your thoughtfulness in sending it to me."[27]

When President George Albert Smith visited Washington D.C. to dedicate the Brigham Young statue in the Capitol, he and his secretary, D. Arthur Haycock, called on Truman. During the brief 1 June 1950 visit, Truman opened his desk drawer in the Oval Office and said, "Look, President Smith, I've got my Book of Mormon right here." A Haycock biographer noted, "Arthur wasn't sure whether that book of scripture was always so handy. He thought perhaps President Truman had a secretary who understood how to make visitors feel welcome."[28]

# TRUMAN'S VISIT TO BYU

On 6 October 1952, while President Truman was campaigning for Democratic nominee Adlai Stevenson, he made a stop in Utah. The previous day in general conference, President McKay took the occasion to squelch rumors that the General Authorities favored the Republican Party by reminding the congregation of the Church's policy of political neutrality and declaring, "The report is not true, and I take this opportunity here, publicly to denounce such a report without foundation in fact."[29]

As if to seal his words with his actions, President McKay was particularly gracious when Truman arrived the next morning. Instead of waiting for the President to come see him at the Church Administrative Building, as was customary, McKay took his private car to meet Truman at the train depot. There the two presidents enjoyed breakfast together and then traveled to Provo, where Truman was scheduled to speak at a rally in Brigham Young University's stadium.[30] President McKay described the train ride in his diary:

> President Truman then came in and said: "Oh, President McKay, you honor me in coming down!" I thanked him for his invitation: The President then introduced me to his daughter Margaret. The President then invited me to come out to the platform with him to have pictures taken, stating that if having the picture taken would embarrass me for me not to do it. I, however, accepted his invitation. . . .

> I had a very pleasant thirty minutes or so with the President, during which time, I saw the better Truman, and got a glimpse of his better nature—the cockiness was gone. He referred to the fact that this is his last official tour before retiring, saying, "When I get through with this, it is my last." He then told me what he wanted to do; viz. to spend his time instructing the youth of America in loyalty and American ideals. He mentioned some other men whom he would like to have join him in this project. I commended him for this desire, and told him that I think that is just what we need. I then gave him a few of my ideas on the subject, emphasizing the freedom of the individual; that that must be maintained at all cost. . . .

> On the train, President Truman made the remark to me that he did not have hatred in his heart for any man, and said: "I am campaigning—that is politics."[31]

*Brigham Young University President Ernest L. Wilkinson, President Truman, and President David O. McKay during Truman's 6 October 1952 visit to BYU.*

At the BYU stadium, the prophet sat by the President for all to see. During his address Truman announced that just that morning he had appointed Latter-day Saint Eugene H. Merrill as chairman of the Federal Communications Commission (FCC). During his vigorous campaign speech, he also charged that the Republican Party was "ruled by a little group of men who have calculating machines where their hearts ought to be."[32] After he had delivered his harshly partisan speech, he sat down next to President McKay and asked innocently, "I wasn't so hard on them was I?" McKay seemed to appreciate Mr. Truman's friendliness and candor and recorded in his diary of the thirty-third President, "I had a higher opinion of him today."[33]

# MORMONS IN TRUMAN'S POST-PRESIDENCY

During the 1950s, a young Neal A. Maxwell served as a staff economic analyst with a government intelligence department. One highlight for the future Apostle was attending a group meeting with former President Truman, who gave his perspective on several current international issues. Maxwell was impressed with Truman's grasp of detail and with his candor.[34]

Harry S Truman maintained his high regard for the Mormons. He regarded the Mormon exodus to the West as "the most remarkable march in the history of civilization" and fondly recalled Salt Lake City as one of the most beautiful cities in the country. He was saddened that a violent prejudice against Mormons survived in his hometown of Independence, Missouri, into the 1960s. Longtime residents wouldn't "have anything to do with Mormons" the ex-President said. "It's prejudice," Truman said, "and it doesn't make any sense, but it's there."[35]

# ENDNOTES

1   "Finding History in Modern Jackson County," *Church News,* 9 May 1998. See also "Samuel O. Bennion of the First Council of the Seventy," *Improvement Era* 48, no. 4 (April 1945): [page number?].

2   *Dave Leip's Atlas of U.S. Presidential Elections.*

3   "The Church Moves On," *Improvement Era* 48, no. 8 (August 1945).

4   Gibbons, *George Albert Smith,* 286. See also Harry S Truman to George Albert Smith, 25 October 1945, Truman Presidential Museum and Library.

5   "The Church Moves On," *Improvement Era* 49, no. 2 (February 1946).

6   Gibbons, *George Albert Smith,* 325.

7   "'This Is the Place Monument' Dedication, A Message From Harry S Truman President of the United States," *Improvement Era* 50, no. 9 (September 1947).

8   See Michael T. Benson, "Harry S Truman as a Modern Cyrus," *BYU Studies* 34 (1994), 6–7.

9   *Dave Leip's Atlas of U.S. Presidential Elections.* See also O'Brien, *Marriott: The J. Willard Marriott Story,* 207.

10   *Improvement Era* 53, no. 1 (January 1950).

11   David O. McKay Diaries, 22–23 October 1951.

12   George Albert Smith to Harry S Truman, 31 July 1948. Also Harry S Truman to George Albert Smith, 25 October 1945; 11 August 1948; 14 October 1947; 11 December 1947; 17 September 1948, Truman Presidential Museum and Library.

13   George Albert Smith to Harry S Truman, 27 May 1946; 9 June 1947; 22 November 1947; 24 April 1950, Truman Presidential Museum and Library.

14   Harry S Truman to George Albert Smith, 13 April 1949; 17 April 1950, Truman Presidential Museum and Library.

15   Shared by David O. McKay, in Conference Report, April 1951, 161.

16   *Church Almanac,* 556. See also "This Week in Church History," *Church News,* 11 November 1995; Gibbons, *George Albert*

*Smith,* 297–98.

17  Robert B. Day, *They Made Mormon History,* 332–33.

18  Gibbons, *George Albert Smith,* 298–99. See also Anderson, *Prophets I Have Known,* 105.

19  George Albert Smith to Harry S Truman, 7 January 1948; also Harry S Truman to George Albert Smith, 13 January 1948, Truman Presidential Museum and Library.

20  George Albert Smith to Harry S Truman, 31 July 1948, Truman Presidential Museum and Library.

21  Harry S Truman to George Albert Smith, 11 August 1948, Truman Presidential Museum and Library.

22  Freidel, *Our Country's Presidents,* 207–8.

23  Harry S Truman, "Speech in the Mormon Tabernacle," 21 September 1948; in Woolley and Peters, *The American Presidency Project.* See also Truman, *Miracle of '48,* 85; Gibbons, *George Albert Smith,* 344–45.

24  Harry S Truman, "Rear Platform and Other Informal Remarks in Oklahoma and Missouri," 29 September 1948, Neosho, Missouri (Rear platform, 8:10 p.m.), in Woolley and Peters, *The American Presidency Project.*

25  George Albert Smith to Harry S Truman, 5 May 1949; Harry S Truman to George Albert Smith, 11 May 1949; Ezra Taft Benson to Harry S Truman, 13 June 1949, Truman Presidential Museum and Library. See also Dew, *Ezra Taft Benson,* 236.

26  George Albert Smith to Harry S Truman, 20 June 1949, Truman Presidential Museum and Library.

27  George Albert Smith to Harry S Truman, 20 June 1949; Harry S Truman to George Albert Smith, 29 June 1949, Truman Presidential Museum and Library.

28  Heidi S. Swinton, *In the Company of Prophets,* 38.

29  Conference Report, October 1952, 129.

30  Francis M. Gibbons, *David O. McKay: Apostle to the World, Prophet of God,* 312.

31  David O. McKay Diaries, 6 October 1952.

32  *Salt Lake Tribune,* 7 October 1952. See also "Address at Brigham Young University, Provo, Utah, 6 October 1952," Truman Presidential Museum and Library.

33  Gibbons, *David O. McKay,* 313.

34  Hafen, Bruce C., *Neal A. Maxwell: A Disciple's Life,* 205.

35  Will Bagley, "The Man from Independence, Truman Changed Washington—Not Vice Versa," *Salt Lake Tribune,* 29 October 2000, B1.

# DWIGHT D. EISENHOWER

## 1953–1961

It was one thing to have an Apostle as a United States senator and confidant to several Presidents as Reed Smoot did in the early decades of the twentieth century, but it was quite another for a President to have an LDS Apostle and future Church president in his cabinet for eight years. Such was the case when Dwight David Eisenhower appointed Ezra Taft Benson as his secretary of agriculture. This led to the thirty-fourth President's attendance at a family home evening, a Tabernacle Choir concert in the White House, and opportunities for Church President David O. McKay to get to know the nation's chief. These experiences resulted in Eisenhower's appreciation of the Mormons and in his immense popularity among the Saints.

**1951:** "Draft Ike" movements begin to spring up around the country, with Ivy Baker Priest, a Utah woman and Republican activist, as one of the leaders. When Eisenhower wins the nomination, Priest is named assistant chair of the campaign committee. The Latter-day Saint woman travels throughout the country for Eisenhower and is rewarded after Ike's victory by being appointed U.S. treasurer. Ivy Baker Priest's signature appeared on all U.S. currency for the next eight years.[1]

*Ivy Baker Priest, a Latter-day Saint Utahn, was appointed as Eisenhower's assistant chair of the campaign committee. Following Eisenhower's victory, Priest was appointed U.S. treaserer, where she served for eight years.*

**10 October 1952:** General Eisenhower visits Salt Lake City and makes the customary courtesy call on the First Presidency. President McKay is visibly thrilled to have the famous general with him in the Tabernacle.[2]

**November 1952:** On election day, 59 percent of Utahns vote for Ike. David O. McKay pens in his diary, "We were all thrilled with the News. In my opinion, it is the greatest thing that has happened in a hundred years for our country." He told one reporter that Ike's election "is the turning point in United States, if not world, history." The prophet promptly sent a congratulatory letter to the President-Elect, noting that his election is "a manifestation of Providential watchfulness over the destiny of this land of America."[3]

**25 November 1952:** Eisenhower appoints Elder Ezra Taft Benson to be his secretary of agriculture.

**21 December 1954:** The Eisenhowers join the Benson and Marriott families for a family home evening.

**May 1955:** The President dines with President McKay and is thoroughly charmed by the Mormon prophet.

**November 1956:** Elder Benson travels the country to campaign for Eisenhower. On election day, every county in Utah voted for Ike; where statewide he received 65 percent.[4]

**Summer 1957:** First Lady Mamie Eisenhower undergoes surgery, and the First Presidency and Twelve pray for her in their regular Thursday meeting. Touched by the gesture, Ike tells Secretary Benson that it was a Thursday when his wife took a turn for the better.[5]

**26 October 1958:** The Mormon Tabernacle Choir presents a concert for the Eisenhowers in the Gold Room at the White House. The President thanks each choir member individually and leads them into the State Dining Room for refreshments, where he mingles with them for over an hour. "Ezra, I never enjoyed music before as I have tonight," he says to Secretary Benson. He is especially moved by two of his favorite numbers, "Battle Hymn of the Republic" and "A Mighty Fortress Is Our God."[6]

**March 1969:** Eisenhower dies, and the Church holds a memorial service for him in the Tabernacle on Temple Square. Harold B. Lee praises the late President's virtues.[7]

# A MORMON APOSTLE IN IKE'S CABINET

By the 1950s Ezra Taft Benson of the Quorum of the Twelve was a nationally regarded leader in agriculture. When Ike was elected, strong recommendations from U.S. senator Robert Taft (R-Ohio) and the President-Elect's brother—agriculture leader Milton S. Eisenhower—put the Mormon Apostle at the top of the list for the position of secretary of agriculture.[8] Elder Benson's first impression of Ike, when they met for the first time at the Hotel Commodore in New York for the Apostle's interview, was very positive:

> I saw a powerfully built person, a little under six feet, with a smile fresh and warm as a sunny summer's day, a face that seemed almost to glow with health and vigor. I liked him immediately. He looked younger than his pictures indicated. As vigor was his dominant quality, the lively, blue, direct eyes were his most striking fea-

*21 January 1953: Elder Ezra Taft Benson of the Quorum of the Twelve Apostles (left) is sworn in by Chief Justice Frederick M. Vinson (right) as Secretary of Agriculture in the Cabinet of President Dwight D. Eisenhower (center).*

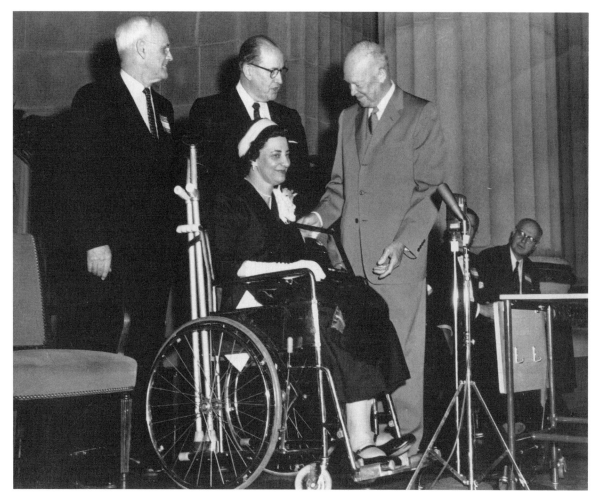

*President Dwight D. Eisenhower (at right) with LDS Senator Arthur Watkins (R-UT; left), Secretary of Agriculture (and LDS Apostle) Ezra Taft Benson (center top), and Utahn Louise Lake (center bottom) (the "Handicapped American of the Year") in September 1958.*

ture. You knew in an instant they mirrored the inner man, that they would reveal all his quick changing moods: interest, welcoming warmth, delight, icy rebuke or cold anger. . . . My next impression was that he was decisive and confident, too; he inspired an immediate faith in his ability and leadership.[9]

In that initial meeting between Benson and Eisenhower, the LDS Apostle asked, "I wonder about the wisdom of calling a clergyman, a Church official, to be a Cabinet member? What will be the reaction from other religious groups, from people generally?" The general thought for a moment, and then looking directly at Benson, replied, "Surely you know that we have the great responsibility to restore the confidence of our people in their own government—that means we've got to deal with spiritual matters. I feel your Church connection is a distinct asset."[10]

On 25 November 1952 the announcement of Benson's appointment was made public.[11] President McKay felt inclined to approve the appointment out of a sense of obligation to his country and because he felt that it would have a "beneficial effect" on the nation to have "an ordained Apostle functioning at the center of the government."[12] Many members of the Church had a sense of euphoria when the announcement came and viewed having a General Authority in the President's cabinet as "a vindication of the Church."[13]

Elder Benson suggested to General Eisenhower that the preinaugural cabinet meeting of 12 January be opened with prayer. At the appointed time, the President-Elect called on the Mormon Apostle to offer a prayer. The prayer included, in part, the following special supplication for Dwight David Eisenhower:

> Our Heavenly Father bless, richly, we pray thee, thy son and servant who has been chosen by the sovereign people of this great nation, to serve as their Chief Executive. Our Father, wilt thou endow him, and all of us, with a deep spirit of humility and devotion. . . . Bless in a special manner thy servant, our leader, with wisdom, understanding, and the inspiration of thy spirit to guide him in his heavy and all-important duties. Bless him with unbounded energy, health, and strength. And may he always be blessed with wisdom and a constant spirit of discernment in his leadership.[14]

However, at the next cabinet meeting, the Friday after the inauguration, Ike conducted the meeting without a prayer. "I was deeply disappointed," recalled Benson. Later, Secretary Benson sent Eisenhower a memo asking that all cabinet meetings begin with prayer. At a subsequent meeting, Ike announced that all cabinet meetings would commence with prayer, and to the gratification of his secretary of agriculture, this practice continued throughout Eisenhower's two terms. The prayers, however, were usually moments of silence rather than a vocal invocation.[15]

President McKay attended the 1953 inaugural as a VIP guest of the incoming Secretary of Agriculture, marking the first time a prophet had attended an inauguration. The day after the inaugural, Eisenhower looked on as Elder Ezra Taft Benson was sworn in as his Secretary of Agriculture. Three months later in general conference, Elder Benson encouraged the Church members to pray for President Eisenhower.[16]

In 1957, Secretary Benson asked Eisenhower to be relieved of his duties so that he could return to the life of a full-time Apostle. The President replied, "If I have to, I'll go to Salt Lake City and appeal to President McKay to have you stay on with me." Not long after Labor Day, the General Authorities were contemplating a reorganization of the leadership of the young men's program (YMMIA) and President McKay envisioned using Elder Benson, if he could be spared from the government. Not being able to get a hold of the President by phone to discuss it, McKay was inspired to hop on a plane to Washington in hope that Eisenhower could squeeze him in for a few

*President Eisenhower (far left) engages in a discussion with three LDS leaders (L–R): Senator Arthur Watkins (R-UT), President David O. McKay, and Elder Ezra Taft Benson.*

moments. Once in Washington, President McKay spoke with numerous White House secretaries in an attempt to get an appointment to see President Eisenhower. The White House staff called a surprised Secretary Benson to get his recommendation on whether the two should meet. "I indicated that I felt sure President Eisenhower would want to see President McKay since I knew he was rather fond of him." The President fit President McKay in at 11:30 that morning.

In the meeting between the two presidents, McKay discussed Elder Benson's timetable in Washington. "Mr. Eisenhower indicated to me that you and he have been very close," related the Mormon prophet to Apostle-Secretary Benson afterward. "In fact, the President told me 'Ezra and I have been just like this'—and he interlocked the fingers of his hands. Then he said, 'I just don't know where I could turn to get someone to succeed him.'" It was decided that Benson should remain in the cabinet for the duration of Eisenhower's administration. "We want to support President Eisenhower," stressed President McKay to Elder Benson later. "He is a noble character, a fine man. In this case our country comes first. . . . Please tell President Eisenhower that we want to help him in every way possible." Upon hearing all this, Ike was pleased with the Mormon prophet's comments. "His visit was most gracious," he later told Benson. "I can appreciate that your Church is anxious to have you back . . . and I will not go against the wishes of your Church if they feel it imperative that you should leave. But I wish to emphasize the word imperative."[17]

Elder Benson and Postmaster General Arthur Summerfield would be the only members of Eisenhower's cabinet to serve all eight years of Ike's presidency.[18] Eisenhower and Benson generally got along well, but he noted that the bold Ezra did not always express his views with "the maximum of tact."[19] Post-presidency, Eisenhower felt somewhat betrayed by his Mormon friend. Elder Benson was very supportive of the ultraconservative John Birch Society, and when society founder Robert Welch accused Eisenhower of being a Communist plant "for the purpose of *throwing the game*," Benson refused to defend the ex-President. Eisenhower "supported me in matters of agriculture," he said when asked point-blank about the statement in September of 1963. "In other areas we had differences." The general was hurt and perplexed by his former cabinet member's apparent disloyalty. "Whatever happened to Ezra?" he later asked BYU's President Ernest Wilkinson and L. Ralph Mecham.[20]

## IKE'S FIRST FAMILY HOME EVENING

On 21 December 1954, the President of the United States participated in his first Mormon family home evening. "The President knew of our custom of having a family hour one night during the week, and he had expressed a wish to see how it was done. So we put one on just as if we were at home," reported Elder Benson. In this case, President and Mrs. Eisenhower, her mother, sister, and brother-in-law joined the LDS families of Elder and Sister Benson and J. Willard Marriott at the Marriotts' ranch for an evening of dinner, singing, religious readings, and comic skits. "The President and his party participated and seemed to enjoy it," wrote Benson. "There was a roaring fire in the fireplace, because it was a bitter cold and wintry night, and this helped make the evening especially cozy. Our only regret was for the Secret Service men who had to stand at their posts in the cold. For that reason, the President called things to a halt at a reasonable hour, and a little reluctantly it seemed, we all started back to Washington." The program had ended with a hymn and a family prayer.[21]

## DINNER WITH THE PROPHET

Eisenhower used to host "stag" (all-male) dinners at the White House, and Secretary Benson suggested to the President that he invite David O. McKay to one. So in early May 1955, David

*The large LDS family of Ezra Taft Benson visits with President Eisenhower in the Oval Office. The Eisenhowers would join the Bensons and the family of J. Willard Marriott for a family home evening at the Marriotts' ranch on 21 December 1954.*

O. McKay joined nineteen other invited guests for a relatively intimate dinner at the White House, hosted by President Eisenhower. President McKay was given the seat of honor directly across from the American President. Eisenhower called on McKay to say grace and was very struck with the charm and wit of the eighty-one-year-old prophet. President McKay sensed toward the end of the evening that President Eisenhower was tired and suggested that the guests leave so as not to wear out their welcome. The President retorted jokingly that it was his, not President McKay's, prerogative to indicate when the festivities were at an end. This humorous incident became a Washington legend and was even used by Lyndon Johnson years later for some gentle ribbing of President McKay.[22]

Secretary Benson reported that President McKay had made a great impression on Eisenhower at that dinner:

The Friday morning after the Thursday night dinner, President Eisenhower referred to the dinner. As I recall, it was the only time he ever singled out one individual. He said to the Cabinet, Friday morning, "Among the group was President David O. McKay, head of the Mormon Church." Then he added, "He was the life of the party." On another occasion President Eisenhower said to me he considered David O. McKay the greatest spiritual leader in the world.[23]

Ezra Taft Benson's secretary relayed the following incident to David O. McKay, which confirmed Ike's great regard for him:

> After your visit in the White House with President Eisenhower as his dinner guest, the following morning Mamie Eisenhower phoned Sister Flora Benson and remarked: "Flora, I just wanted to call you this morning to let you know that my husband was profoundly impressed by President McKay. After he returned last night, he spent most of the night talking to me about this singular and enjoyable experience."

> Then Mrs. Eisenhower said: "Flora, we know that you folks pray for us every day and we wanted you to know that we feel of the strength which comes to us through those prayers. In fact," she continued, "we frankly don't know what we would do without this strength."[24]

*In May 1955, President McKay was one of the few guests at one of President Eisenhower's "stag dinners." The President was struck by the LDS prophet's spirituality and charm. "Among the group was President David O. McKay, head of the Mormon Church," Eisenhower related the next day. "He was the life of the party."*

# ENDNOTES

1   Ivy Baker Priest's biography is online at wikipedia.com, s.v. "Ivy Baker Priest," and historytogo.utah.gov.

2   Gibbons, *David O. McKay*, 313–14.

3   *Dave Leip's Atlas of U.S. Presidential Elections.* See also David O. McKay Diaries, 5 November 1952, quoted in D. Michael Quinn, *The Mormon Hierarchy: Origins of Power,* 360; Letter from McKay to Eisenhower, 6 November 1952, David O. McKay Scrapbook #22.

4   Gibbons, *Ezra Taft Benson,* 214. See also *Dave Leip's Atlas of U.S. Presidential Elections.*

5   Benson, *Crossfire,* 359.

6   Benson, *Crossfire,* 412–13.

7   Harold B. Lee, "[Address at] Memorial Service for President Dwight D. Eisenhower, March 31, 1969," located at 921 E36L 1969, in the LDS Church Archives, Salt Lake City.

8   Benson, *Crossfire,* 7–9

9   Benson, *Crossfire,* 11.

10  Benson, *Crossfire,* 12.

11  *Church Almanac,* 558.

12  Francis M. Gibbons, *Harold B. Lee: Man of Vision, Prophet of God,* 299.

13  Gibbons, *Ezra Taft Benson,* 178.

14  Benson, *Crossfire,* 37.

15  Benson, *Crossfire,* 49, 60, 246. See also Gibbons, *Ezra Taft Benson,* 184.

16  David Lawrence McKay, 242. See also Gibbons, *David O. McKay,* 317; Gibbons, *Ezra Taft Benson,* 190.

17  Benson, *Crossfire,* 359–61. See also David O. McKay Diaries, 3 September 1957.

18  Gibbons, *Ezra Taft Benson,* 233.

19  Eisenhower, *The White House Years,* 354.

20  Prince and Wright, *David O. McKay and the Rise of Modern Mormonism,* 295, 297.

21  Benson, *Crossfire,* 221–22. See also "LDS Home Night Demonstrated to President and Mrs. Eisenhower," *Church News,* 12 February 1955, 6; O'Brien, *Marriott: The J. Willard Marriott Story,* 231–32.

22  Gibbons, *David O. McKay,* 351–52, 378–79. See also Prince and Wright, *David O. McKay and the Rise of Modern Mormonism,* 351.

23  Ezra Taft Benson to Clare Middlemiss, 28 May 1966, David O. McKay Scrapbooks #169.

24  Handwritten letter, 21 August 1958, from Frederick W. Babel, former secretary to Ezra Taft Benson, to President McKay regarding the impression President McKay made on President Eisenhower. David O. McKay Scrapbooks #169.

# JOHN F. KENNEDY

## *1961–1963*

Kennedy's relationship with the Church was the most positive of the Democratic administrations to that point but lacked the depth of relationship that many of the other twentieth-century chief executives had with the Church. This was simply because there was no Apostle in his cabinet or Apostle-senator as his confidant. There were, however, several positive visits by Kennedy to Church headquarters and by lay-member Mormons employed in his administration, and there was a reaching out by the Kennedy White House to involve the Church in civil rights discussions. And like most Americans, the Church deeply mourned his assassination.

**1952–60:** Kennedy serves as a U.S. senator, a post in which he is supportive of Ezra Taft Benson's agriculture efforts.[1] A young future Apostle, Neal A. Maxwell, is on the staff of Senator Wallace Bennett (R-UT) at the time. One day while Maxwell is in a Senate corridor, the voting bell rings, calling all senators back to the main floor. Senator Kennedy rushes past him in the hallway, stops, looks around, then turns to the future Apostle and asks, "Which way am I supposed to vote?" Maxwell calmly replies that he believes the Democrats are voting "aye" on this one, so Kennedy proceeds to the floor and votes "aye" on the legislation.[2]

**12 November 1957:** Senator Kennedy meets President David O. McKay, who says to the forty-year-old senator, "You are younger than I thought." During the visit, they discuss the recent launch of *Sputnik* and the future of the Soviet Union. President McKay prophetically predicts that the Soviet Union will eventually collapse from within: "They are fundamentally wrong. Free agency is inherent in every individual. Rule of force has been fought against by men throughout history." Kennedy disagrees and expresses his belief that the USSR will never break up on its own: "They have the power to continue. Their prospects for the immediate future are bright." President McKay was initially underwhelmed with Kennedy and suspicious of his religion. "I enjoyed my visit with him, although not too much impressed with him as a leader," he writes in his diary.[3]

**6 March 1959:** Senator Kennedy and his wife Jacqueline visit with the First Presidency in their offices. This time around President McKay is more impressed. "Mr. Kennedy seems to be a very fine young man," records the prophet in his diary.[4]

**1959:** As Senator Kennedy's presidential campaign heats up, he calls and asks Oscar W. McConkie Jr., a young stake president and Democratic legislator, to be his Utah representative. "I'm nervous about representing a Roman Catholic for President," recalls McConkie. "And so I say to him, 'Yes, I like you, but let me check and get back to you.' So I went over to see the First Presidency, to see if it would be okay with them to have me represent John F. Kennedy in his attempt." It takes some time to get an answer back, but "finally, President McKay said yes, he thought that I ought to do it because the time may come when the Church needs a friend in court, and they'd like me to be there just in case."[5]

**1960:** Kennedy calls on Church headquarters two more times. In November, Kennedy squeaks past Nixon, but in Utah, 55 percent poll for Nixon. After the outcome is known, someone remarks to President McKay, "Doesn't it worry you that a Catholic has been elected President?" The Church President replies, "You know, all I thought about on election day was how wonderful it is that in this great country everybody can go to the polls and vote for a Catholic or a Quaker just as they please and not have to worry about it."[6]

**March 1962:** Brigham Young University president Ernest Wilkinson, a staunch Republican, is not a fan of Kennedy's New Frontier, which he feels is socialistic. "I informed President McKay we had a member of our faculty who adamantly felt the government should engage in all of the new ventures that were being proposed for it, and which together have been characterized as the welfare state," writes Wilkinson. "President McKay emphatically told me to have him locate elsewhere."[7]

**August 1962:** Congressman Ralph R. Harding of Idaho meets with Kennedy in the Rose Garden to present to him a first edition copy of the Book of Mormon and to give a brief history of the book and the Church. The gift is in response to Mrs. Kennedy's announced plans to assemble a White House library of first editions.[8]

*26 September 1963: President Kennedy delivering a major foreign policy speech in the Tabernacle. He is applauded by Utah Governor George Dewey Clyde (left of Kennedy), Senator Frank E. "Ted" Moss (left of Clyde), President David O. McKay (far left, front), and the Mormon Tabernacle Choir (background). Robert F. Kennedy would later remark that his brother felt it was "one of the best speeches he had ever given."*

**June 1963:** President McKay declines an invitation to a White House meeting of religious leaders to discuss civil rights legislation. However, he encourages general Relief Society president Belle S. Spafford to attend a civil rights meeting in the White House with other presidents of leading women's organizations.[9]

*Democrat and First Presidency member Hugh B. Brown (left) joins President David O. McKay in applauding President John F. Kennedy after his address in the Tabernacle on Temple Square.*

**Summer 1963:** President Kennedy makes his historic trip to Germany. When the missionaries in Cologne find out his motorcade is passing through their city they create a forty-foot-long banner which announces, "The 1,100 Mormon Missionaries in Germany Welcome Pres. Kennedy." The press reports that the President is welcomed in many ways, "but none more enthusiastically and dramatically" than in the missionaries' way. Kennedy sees it and "turn[s] his head to make a complete reading of the sign as his car rounded the curve."[10]

**26 September 1963:** JFK delivers a major foreign policy speech in the Tabernacle, spends the night at Hotel Utah, and has breakfast with President McKay.

**22 November 1963:** The Church, along with the rest of the nation, is shocked to hear of the assassination of President Kennedy.

## CANDIDATE KENNEDY'S 1960 VISITS TO SALT LAKE

By 30 January 1960, Senator Kennedy was in full pursuit of his party's presidential nomination and called a third time on David O. McKay and his counselors, this time with Briton and Oscar McConkie Jr. and other Utah Democrats.[11] Of the visit, President McKay wrote,

> We had a very pleasant interview with Senator Kennedy, talking on various domestic and international subjects. I was very much impressed with him, and think that the country will be in good hands if he is elected as he seems to be a man of high character. He comes from a home where he has received good training, and his father, a wealthy man, has seen to it that the children have had to work and take responsibility. Our interview lasted for nearly an hour.[12]

Oscar McConkie Jr. reported of the meeting:

> I took Senator Kennedy, Candidate Kennedy, in to see President McKay. And they had a really significant conversation, a lot more so than most political people, where you just bring them in and they kind of pass pleasantries, and this sort of thing. They had a serious talk about how it was going to be possible to bring democratic governments throughout the world. They discussed, for instance, such things as the fact that the difficulty the President

would have in doing this was that there isn't any middle class in the rest of the world. The third world has extremely few very wealthy people, and then there is huge poverty. But President Kennedy was saying that it takes a middle class in order to make a democratic system work. It was a significant talk.

As we walked out of President McKay's office, Senator Kennedy turned to me and said, "I have never met a man as ideally suited and qualified to be the spiritual leader of his people." That's a pretty good statement from Senator Kennedy and his assessment when he first met President McKay.[13]

Later, during the heat of the 1960 campaign, Kennedy made yet another visit to Utah. During this 23 September visit, the Mormon prophet had his photograph taken with the charismatic senator and accompanied him to the Tabernacle to hear him speak.[14]

## KENNEDY ADMINISTRATION INCLUDES LATTER-DAY SAINTS

President Kennedy named a Mormon congressman from Arizona, Stewart Udall, as his secretary of the interior. He also had other Latter-day Saints in his administration, including Education Commissioner Sterling M. McMurrin and Assistant Secretary of Labor Esther Peterson. Future First Presidency member James E. Faust, then a Democratic state legislator, was appointed by Kennedy to be a member of the Lawyers' Committee for Civil Rights and Racial Unrest. Marion D. Hanks, a member of the First Quorum of the Seventy, had a heavy traveling and speaking schedule as a member of Kennedy's Council of Physical Fitness.[15]

*Stewart Udall, Kennedy's LDS Secretary of the Interior.*

*John F. Kennedy and David O. McKay having breakfast together. Later, when Robert Kennedy came by to visit President McKay, he noted, "My brother enjoyed the breakfast with you and Mrs. McKay, and admired all of the fine things you and your Church stand for."*

## PRESIDENT KENNEDY'S 1963 UTAH VISIT

On 26 September 1963, President Kennedy scheduled a special trip to Utah to deliver a major foreign policy address. He had planned to visit Utah a year before, but it had been cancelled because of the Cuban Missile Crisis. More than 20,000 people showed up on the streets of Salt Lake City to catch a glimpse of his motorcade. At some intersections, the crowd stood ten persons deep.[16] The Church invited him to speak in the Tabernacle, where he was met beforehand by President and Sister McKay in the General Authorities' lounge beneath the choir loft.

"Hello, Mr. President!" exclaimed President McKay upon greeting Kennedy. "Hello, Mr. President!" was Kennedy's reply to the Church leader. With the prophet and other Church authorities on the stand, the President gave his address.[17] "I take strength and hope in seeing this monument [the Tabernacle], hearing its story retold by [Utah Senator] Ted Moss, and recalling how this State was built, and what it started with, and what it has now," said Kennedy in his address. His ninety-minute remarks also included the following statements about the Church:

> Of all the stories of American pioneers and settlers, none is more inspiring than the Mormon trail. The qualities of the founders of this community are the qualities that we seek in America, the qualities which we like to feel this country has, courage, patience, faith, self-reliance, perseverance, and, above all, an unflagging determination to see the right prevail. . . .

> Let us remember that the Mormons of a century ago were a persecuted and prosecuted minority, harried from place to place, the victims of violence and occasionally murder, while today, in the short space of 100 years, their faith and works are known and respected the world around, and their voices heard in the highest councils of this country. As the Mormons succeeded, so America can succeed, if we will not give up or turn back.[18]

Robert F. Kennedy would later remark of the Tabernacle address of September 1963 that his brother felt it was "one of the best speeches he had ever given." He said that President Kennedy had even played a tape of his speech for his mother and father.[19]

After President Kennedy spoke in the Tabernacle, the Mormon Tabernacle Choir sang the "Battle Hymn of the Republic." President Gordon B. Hinckley, then an Apostle, recalled the powerful moment of the "magnificent music" of the choir and the "presence in this building of the chief executive of the nation . . . touching the emotions of everyone here assembled." He remembered, "I felt a catch in my throat and a tingle in my spine."[20] On a separate occasion, President Hinckley recalled, "I was seated near him when he spoke in the Salt Lake Tabernacle not long ago. I had come to watch, and I sat and wondered. . . . It was a stirring thing to hear his plea."[21]

The morning following Kennedy's Tabernacle address, President and Sister McKay hosted the President at their Hotel Utah suite for breakfast, along with JFK's Mormon secretary of the interior, Stewart L. Udall; McKay's Democratic counselor Hugh B. Brown; Utah senator Ted Moss; the wives of Udall, Brown, and Moss; and the McKays' daughter, Emma Rae. For this special occasion they had arranged for Chef Gerrard to treat the dignitaries to mountain trout and other specialties.[22] "I asked the blessing on the food. . . . President Kennedy was the only one who had coffee," recorded President McKay. "The conversation at the table was very pleasant," he added, "and in the words of the President, 'It was a refreshing hour.'"[23] Later, when Robert Kennedy came by

*Presidents Kennedy and McKay enjoy breakfast together in President McKay's Hotel Utah suite. "I asked the blessing on the food. . . . President Kennedy was the only one who had coffee," recorded President McKay. "The conversation at the table was very pleasant," he added, "and in the words of the President, 'It was a refreshing hour.'"*

On 22 November 1963, President Kennedy was assassinated in an open air motorcade in Dallas, Texas. Less than two months earlier President Kennedy had traveled the streets of Salt Lake City in a similar manner, and Church leaders and members there joined the nation and world in mourning the slain President. Elder Gordon B. Hinckley remarked at the time, "I did not agree with President Kennedy on many things, but I had a great respect for the sense of dedication with which he pursued his ends and for the tremendous ability he brought to his task."

to visit President McKay he noted, "My brother enjoyed the breakfast with you and Mrs. McKay, and admired all of the fine things you and your Church stand for."[24]

That night, President Kennedy spoke in Tacoma's Cheney Stadium where he related how impressed he was by the previous day's visit to "the Mormon Temple and Tabernacle" built in the most arid part of the country. Utah boasted "a great civilization, a great temple, a great tabernacle," he told the crowd.[25] The President apparently was very pleased with his reception in Utah. Lyndon B. Johnson, then vice president, commented, "President Kennedy returned from Salt Lake City knowing, as he had not known before, that the people of America supported his efforts to make this world safer for all mankind."[26]

## THE MORMON REACTION TO THE KENNEDY ASSASINATION

President McKay's doctor was massaging the prophet's injured leg and arm on 22 November 1963 when the news flashed that John F. Kennedy had been shot. "All are shocked and stunned at the news," recorded President McKay in his diary, "as it was only a few weeks ago that it was our privilege to entertain the President in our apartment; and to now think he is gone is unbelievable!"[27] At the Church offices a number of the Apostles were in a committee meeting when Elder Howard W. Hunter burst into the room agitated and white-faced, carrying the news that President John F. Kennedy had been shot.[28]

The press immediately began calling Church headquarters for a statement, a part of which included President McKay saying, "I am deeply grieved and shocked beyond expression at this tragedy. In behalf of the Church in all the world, I express sincere sympathy to Mrs. Kennedy, their children, and all of the close relatives and friends. . . . Only a few weeks ago it was our privilege to entertain the President, and now to think that he has gone we are stunned as well as shocked."[29]

Hugh B. Brown—President McKay's Democratic first counselor—represented the Church at Kennedy's funeral. That evening he also conducted a memorial service for Kennedy at the Chevy Chase Chapel in the Washington area. "I'm not here to eulogize him but to thank God for his life," said President Brown. "It was our good fortune to live at a time when a world leader was raised up to chart the way and to inspire and fire the youth of our land and of the world. God bless his memory."[30] A few days later while speaking at a memorial service for the slain President at Utah State University, President Brown called John F. Kennedy "the most promising young man of this generation."[31]

On the day of the President's funeral, a memorial service was also held for him in the Salt Lake Tabernacle, where Elder Harold B. Lee said, "We mourn as a national family for the loss of a promising and dynamic young leader, cut down in the prime of his manhood." Then, after speaking of the Savior's Resurrection, he declared, "President John F. Kennedy likewise shall live again."

Elder Lee added, "We have had him frequently in our supplications, as we have sensed somewhat the heavy burdens of responsibility of his great office."[32]

At Brigham Young University another memorial service was being held, this one conducted by Apostle and future Church president Gordon B. Hinckley. Elder Hinckley spoke of "this young and wonderfully able leader," and added, "I did not agree with President Kennedy on many things, but I had a great respect for the sense of dedication with which he pursued his ends and for the tremendous ability he brought to his task."[33]

The many memorial services in Kennedy's name show the great respect the LDS people had for him.

*Hugh B. Brown—President McKay's Democratic first counselor—represented the Church at Kennedy's funeral. President Brown called John F. Kennedy "the most promising young man of this generation" and asked that Church members "thank God for his life."*

# ENDNOTES

1   Benson, *Crossfire*, 530.

2   Hafen, *Neal A. Maxwell: A Disciple's Life*, 207.

3   David O. McKay Diaries, 12 November 1957. See also "President McKay Receives Sen. Kennedy at Church Office," *Church News*, 16 November 1957, 4; Gibbons, *David O. McKay*, 374–75.

4   David O. McKay Diaries, 6 March 1959.

5   Oscar W. McConkie, Jr., interview by Gregory Prince, 24 August 1998.

6   Harold B. Lee, *Ye Are the Light of the World*. See also *Dave Leip's Atlas of U.S. Presidential Elections*.

7   Wilkinson memorandum in David O. McKay Diaries, 7 March 1962.

8   *Church News*, 8 September 1962.

9   David O. McKay Diaries, 13 June 1963. See also Belle S. Spafford, *A Woman's Reach*, 67–68.

10  "Mormon Missionaries Welcome Pres. Kennedy to Germany," *Church News*, 6 July 1963, 13.

11  Gibbons, *David O. McKay*, 374–75.

12  David O. McKay Diaries, 30 January 1960.

13  McConkie, interview, 24 August 1998

14  Gibbons, *David O. McKay*, 375.

15  Ostling and Ostling, *Mormon America*, 135. See also Winder, *Counselors to the Prophets*, 483; Prince and Wright, *David O. McKay and the Rise of Modern Mormonism*, 248.

16  *Salt Lake Tribune*, "Kennedy in Utah," 22 November 2003.

17  Gibbons, *David O. McKay*, 375–76. See also William W. Slaughter, *Life in Zion: An Intimate Look at the Latter-day Saints, 1820–1995*, 168.

18  John F. Kennedy, "Address in Salt Lake City at the Mormon Tabernacle," 26 September 1963, in Woolley and Peters, *The American Presidency Project*, online at http://www.presidency.ucsb.edu/site/docs/sou.php.

19  David O. McKay Diaries, 27 March 1968.

20  Gordon B. Hinckley, "A Challenge from Vietnam," *Improvement Era* (June 1967): 53.

21  "Memorial Services for President John F. Kennedy, George Albert Smith Fieldhouse, Brigham Young University, Monday, 25 November 1963," 10. LDS Church Archives, Salt Lake City.

22  Gibbons, *David O. McKay*, 376.

23  David O. McKay Diaries, 27 September 1963.

24  David O. McKay Diaries, 27 March 1968.

25  John F. Kennedy, "Remarks at the Cheney Stadium in Tacoma," 27 September 1963, in Woolley and Peters, *The American Presidency Project*.

26  Lyndon B. Johnson, "Remarks in Salt Lake City at the Mormon Tabernacle," 29 October 1964, in Woolley and Peters, *The American Presidency Project*.

27  David O. McKay Diaries, 22 November 1963.

28  Kimball and Kimball, *Spencer W. Kimball: Twelfth President*, 345.

29  David O. McKay Diaries, 22 November 1963.

30  "A World Leader Raised Up to Chart the Way; to Inspire and Fire Youth," *Church News,* 7 December 1963, 14.

31  "Memorial Services in Honor of President John Fitzgerald Kennedy, 1917–1963," event program, LDS Church Archives, Salt Lake City.

32  Harold B. Lee, "[Address at] Memorial Service for President John F. Kennedy, Salt Lake Tabernacle, 25 November 1963," 2. LDS Church Archives, Salt Lake City. See also "Services Honoring President Kennedy Held in Tabernacle," *Church News,* 30 November 1963, 4.

33  "Memorial Services for President John F. Kennedy, George Albert Smith Fieldhouse, Brigham Young University, Monday, 25 November 1963," 8, 10. LDS Church Archives, Salt Lake City.

# LYNDON B. JOHNSON

## *1963–1969*

Without question, the friendship between Lyndon B. Johnson and David O. McKay was the strongest bond between a Church president and U.S. President in history. This unique bond forged between a wily politician and a benevolent churchman was as real as it was unlikely. Some might say that Johnson's seeking counsel from the prophet, and to some degree Eisenhower's enlistment of Ezra Taft Benson, was fulfillment of a hundred-year-old prophecy of Brigham Young's first counselor. "The President of the United States," declared Heber C. Kimball, will "come and consult with the authorities of this Church to know what is best to do for his people."[1] This relationship benefited LBJ when Utah reversed its right-wing slant of 1960 to support Johnson in '64, and the relationship benefited the Church when Johnson was able to solve their conundrum with the Defense Department regarding LDS chaplains.

**1931:** Lyndon Baines Johnson, while a young legislative aide in D.C., first learns about the Mormons through his LDS roommate, Truman Young.[2]

**1950s:** Apostle-Secretary Ezra Taft Benson observes, "Lyndon Johnson of Texas quickly stood out as one of the most capable legislators of all in his ability

*(Seated L–R) Lawrence McKay, President N. Eldon Tanner, President David O. McKay, and President Lyndon B. Johnson enjoy a conversation in the White House, along with Johnson's two LDS White House staff secretaries, Nancy Larson and Connie Gerrard (standing).*

to lead men; but it was hard to tell just where he drew the line between politics and principle."[3]

**27 October 1960:** While campaigning as Kennedy's running mate, Johnson makes a courtesy call on LDS Church headquarters. "I thoroughly enjoyed my conference with Senator Johnson," recalls David O. McKay, "and felt that Senator Johnson is a very fine person."[4] Despite this visit, on election day Utah voters prefer Richard Nixon.

**19 October 1962:** LBJ makes his only visit to Utah as vice president. President McKay recalls, "Mr. Johnson expressed admiration for the Church Missionary System, and explained that foreign countries, in which efforts are being made to have the United States Peace Corps serve, announced that the good will and the work of the missionaries encouraged them to hope that the Peace Corps could be successful." Henry D. Moyle then enlists his help in getting visas for missionaries from Australia and Britain who are called to serve in the U.S. but who are being refused long-term entry by the State Department. Johnson thanks them for the visit and says he is "always warmed and inspired by an opportunity to meet the First Presidency."[5]

**January 1964:** Johnson asks President McKay to come counsel with him in the White House, where their unusual friendship continues to develop.

**November 1964:** Johnson wins handily in Utah, with 55 percent to Barry Goldwater's 45 percent. "The people of the country have now made their decision, and have voted for a more liberal form of government!" writes President McKay of election day. "I learned from the nurse that after I had retired this evening, President Johnson called me from his ranch in Texas. As I was sleeping she did not feel to awaken me, and I therefore did not get the opportunity to talk to the President." Johnson does get a hold of McKay on November 29—merely to inquire about the prophet's health.[6]

**18 January 1965:** LBJ enjoys the Mormon Tabernacle Choir at his inauguration.

**3 March 1965:** Elder Boyd K. Packer and Mormon senators meet with Johnson to successfully resolve the Church's chaplain problem.

## THE UNIQUE JOHNSON–MCKAY FRIENDSHIP

On 25 January 1964, just two months after assuming the presidency, the President called President McKay and said, "I wonder if you feel like coming down to Washington and see me some time in the next week or two? I don't have anything emergency, but I just need a little strength I think that would come from visiting with you an hour or so." President McKay, even though he was still recovering from a mild stroke that had occurred the previous November, told the President that he would come.[7]

Five days later, the prophet flew to Washington with his son Lawrence and second counselor, N. Eldon Tanner. The next morning the group called at the White House and enjoyed a personal tour given by the President of the historic mansion. Johnson also introduced the visitors to his two LDS White House staff secretaries, Nancy Larson and Connie Gerrard.[8]

President Tanner reported the subsequent conversations with Johnson as follows:

> Before they went in to have their lunch, President Johnson had
> said to the party that he had some problems. He said that some-

times he felt as he did when he was a little boy when he had more problems than he could handle and would go to his mother and put his head on her breast and get a little sympathy. He mentioned that we have the Panama problem, the matter of the plane that was shot down over East Germany, Viet Nam, etc., and he said he felt the same way now that he did when he was a boy.

After they went into the dining room, President Johnson turned to President McKay and said, "I feel that the spiritual and moral fiber of this country needs strengthening, and we need it badly. I would like to ask you, President McKay if you can tell me how we can get it." He said, "I have been out to see you on two or three occasions before and each time I left you I came away inspired and I feel I would like to have your advice on this."

President McKay answered as though he might have been asked this question a week before and had time to prepare an answer. He said right off, "Mr. President, I have read where you have said you were, first, a free man, second, that you are an American citizen, third, that you are President of the United States, and fourth, a Democrat. I like that. Now you have asked this question. I think you are an honorable man. I think you mean what you are saying, and this condition is something that you want to meet. I would say to you: Let your conscience be your guide, and go forward and let the people see that you are sincere, that this is the problem that you have before you, and one that should be met, and lead out in it and let the people follow."

President Tanner said that President Johnson looked over at him and nodded his head, seemingly pleased with the answer.[9] Following a private interview between the two presidents, they had photographs taken with the LDS members of Congress and Esther Peterson, a Latter-day Saint then serving as assistant secretary of labor. "I think we had better break up before President McKay dismisses us," said President Johnson good naturedly as the gathering was winding down. The President was referring to a humorous incident that had occurred when Eisenhower had invited President McKay to dinner (see chapter 34).[10]

President McKay was the first religious leader invited to the Johnson White House. "The administration didn't really think they would carry Utah, although Johnson and Hubert H. Humphrey did in 1964," commented Edwin B. Firmage, an LDS law professor who served as a White House fellow in the Johnson administration. "They just wanted decent relations with the Mormon people."[11]

*David O. McKay and Lyndon B. Johnson had the closest friendship of any LDS president and American President to date. "Strong friendships seldom depend upon frequency of visits for their strength and meaning," Johnson once wrote to President McKay. "I draw deep strength and inspiration from our bonds with you."*

The White House continued to court the two-million-member Church. Lady Bird Johnson paid a courtesy call to the McKays in their Hotel Utah suite on 15 August while touring the nation advocating her environmental projects.[12] On 17 September, President Johnson made an unscheduled stop in Salt Lake City while en route to Sacramento. "I could not fly over Utah without stopping to see President McKay," he said. "I always feel better after I have been in his presence." He gave President McKay a medallion with the President's likeness on it as a gift and commented how good the ninety-one-year-old prophet looked. "I haven't an ache or a pain," was the reply.[13] Following the brief, spontaneous visit, the President wrote President McKay:

> Strong friendships seldom depend upon frequency of visits for their strength and meaning. While we have had too few occasions to be with you, both Lady Bird and I draw deep strength and inspiration from our bonds with you. I felt that strength especially last week as we flew back to Washington after meeting with you.[14]

Both President and Mrs. Johnson visited the McKays again on 29 October, just days before the general election. They enjoyed breakfast with the McKays in the morning in their apartment, and the President spoke in the Tabernacle.[15] President McKay said on the occasion, "I think a great deal of President Johnson, and he seemed to reciprocate that feeling, and so did Lady Bird, who is very charming."[16]

President McKay's secretaries recalled that Johnson would often phone the prophet. "President Johnson would just want to talk. He would have ideas, and would just talk them out. . . . He liked him. They got along quite well. . . . [Johnson] really liked President McKay. He thought a lot of him. He respected President McKay."[17] One secretary reported that during one of the visits, the two presidents began joking with each other in various accents:

> Johnson could turn that southern accent on like you wouldn't believe. "Why I said to my good friend . . ." you know, with this big Southern accent. Then he'd turn around and say something to his friends, without an accent. I thought, "Oh, wait a minute!" President McKay picked up on it and started speaking with a Scottish accent. It was so cute! He was telling him this joke and he did it with a Scottish accent, and Johnson was having the hardest time understanding. It was so cute, and he laughed his head off after he got through.[18]

*President Johnson visits with Emma Ray McKay and her husband, the Church president, on one of his numerous visits. "I think a great deal of President Johnson," remarked President McKay, "and he seemed to reciprocate that feeling."*

When President McKay was hospitalized in February 1965, the President of the United States sent thirty carnations to his sickroom.[19] The two presidents also exchanged phone calls and telegrams on birthdays.[20]

## JOHNSON'S 1965 INAUGURATION

President Johnson asked the Mormon Tabernacle Choir to sing at his inauguration, which the 363 vocalists did on 18 January 1965. "This is the greatest single honor that has ever come to the Tabernacle Choir," remarked President McKay on the occasion. Just two hours after the inauguration ended, President McKay was surprised to receive a phone call from LBJ. "Dr. McKay, I want you to know I was thinking of you during the inauguration ceremony," the President said. "I think you will be pleased to know that the singing of the Tabernacle Choir was the best thing in connection with the inaugural. . . . You can be mighty proud of your work with them." He then spoke briefly with Sister McKay and told her, "Take care of my good friend President McKay."[21]

In a letter from Johnson that arrived not long after, the President thanked the Mormon prophet again for allowing the Tabernacle Choir to sing at his inauguration. "Our day was marred only by your absence but the personal strength we have taken from you in the past was present— and very real—for both Mrs. Johnson and me." Johnson also sent President McKay one of three flags that flew over the Capitol during the inaugural ceremonies. He kept one and gave the other one to Vice President Hubert Humphrey.[22]

## JOHNSON SOLVES CHURCH CHAPLAIN ISSUE

By the spring of 1965 it had been six years since there were any new LDS chaplains in the U.S. military due to discriminatory Defense Department regulations. When David O. McKay mentioned this trouble in a letter to President Johnson, he immediately said he would meet with Church representatives on the subject.[23] Elder Boyd K. Packer, an assistant to the Twelve and head of the LDS Serviceman's Committee, along with Mormon senators Frank E. Moss (D-UT) and Howard Cannon (D-NV), met with Johnson to discuss the matter on 3 March. During the meeting, the President got Deputy Secretary of Defense Cyrus Vance on the phone to discuss it. Vance evidently protested some, and Johnson bellowed, "I do not care, I want this done. . . .You give these men what they want." After Vance protested a little more Johnson said,

> Listen here, these Mormons, from the minute they are out of
> their mothers' womb, have been praying and teaching and leading
> one another, and then they go out on missions. I would rather

*When Deputy Secretary of Defense Cyrus Vance was protesting allowing new LDS chaplains, President Johnson (right) bellowed, "Listen here, these Mormons, from the minute they are out of their mothers' womb, have been praying and teaching and leading one another, and then they go out on missions. I would rather have one of their boys than one of the preachers you get out of the seminary, so you fix it up so that they can get their chaplains."*

have one of their boys than one of the preachers you get out of the seminary, so you fix it up so that they can get their chaplains. I cannot have Dr. McKay out in Salt Lake City sitting there thinking I am not doing the thing he has asked me to do, so you do it.

Elder Packer reported what happened next:

Later in our conversation he spoke respectfully of the Church indicating that he had never met a poor Mormon. He said "I suppose you have them, but I haven't met them." He indicated his regard for Senators Howard Cannon and Frank Moss.

When I expressed appreciation for the action he had taken, and expressed appreciation from President McKay, he said, as nearly as I can quote, "I don't know just what it is about President McKay. I talk to . . . all of the others [preachers from other faiths] but somehow it seems as though President McKay is something like a father to me. It seems as though every little while I have to write him a letter or something." President Johnson was in all ways courteous to us and certainly in the few minutes we solved a problem that has been insurmountable for the past six years.[24]

Lyndon Baines Johnson was a complex person who had a remarkable relationship with the Mormons and their leaders, especially David O. McKay. He helped them when a need arose, and became the only Democrat since Harry Truman to earn the votes of conservative Utah.

# ENDNOTES

1   Heber C. Kimball, *Journal of Discourses,* 5:93 (26 July 1857).

2   David O. McKay Diaries, 19 October 1962.

3   Benson, *Crossfire,* 106.

4   Gibbons, *David O. McKay,* 375. See also David O. McKay Diaries, 27 October 1960.

5   David O. McKay Diaries, 19 October 1962.

6   *Dave Leip's Atlas of U.S. Presidential Elections.* See also David O. McKay Diaries, 4 November and 29 November 1964.

7   Transcript of telephone conversation between Lyndon B. Johnson and David O. McKay, 25 January 1964. White House Recordings and Telephone Notes, Box 1, Lyndon B. Johnson Library and Museum. See also David O. McKay Diaries, 25 January1964.

8   Gibbons, *David O. McKay,* 376–77. "Pres. McKay Makes Unheralded Visit to Nation's Chief at White House," *Church News,* 8 February 1964, 3.

9   Report of the White House meeting by President Nathan Eldon Tanner, in David O. McKay Diaries, 31 January 1964. See also David Lawrence McKay's memo of the White House visit in David O. McKay Diaries, 31 January 1964; Gibbons, *David O. McKay,* 377–78.

10  Gibbons, *David O. McKay,* 376–78. See also Robert R. King and Kay Atkinson King, "Mormons in Congress, 1851–2000," in *Journal of Mormon History* 26, no. 2 (Fall 2000): 15.

11  Edwin B. Firmage, interview by Gregory A. Prince, 10 October 1996.

12  Gibbons, *David O. McKay,* 379.

13  "Sorrow Expressed at Johnson's Passing," *Church News,* 27 January 1973. See also Gibbons, *McKay,* 379.

14  Lyndon B. Johnson to David O. McKay, 23 September 1964, TR1/ST44, Lyndon B. Johnson Library and Museum.

15  Gibbons, *David O. McKay,* 379.

16  David O. McKay Diaries, 29 October 1964.

17  LaRue Sneff and Lola Timmins, interview by Gregory A. Prince, 3 August 2000.

18  Quoted in Prince and Wright, *David O. McKay and the Rise of Modern Mormonism,* 24.

19  David O. McKay Diaries, 20 February 1965.

20  David O. McKay Diaries, 7 September 1966. See also Lyndon B. Johnson to David O. McKay, 7 September 1966, ME1-2/M, Lyndon B. Johnson Library and Museum.

21  *Church News,* 23 January 1965, 2, 9. See also David O. McKay Diaries, 20 January 1965.

22  Lyndon B. Johnson to David O. McKay, 26 January 1965, PP0-3, PA6-1, Lyndon B. Johnson Library and Museum. See also David O. McKay Diaries, 3 May 1965.

23  David O. McKay Diaries, 26 February 1965.

24  Boyd K. Packer's report to the First Presidency on his White House meeting, in David O. McKay Dairies, 10 March 1965.

# RICHARD M. NIXON

## *1969–1974*

Like the Republican Presidents since his time, Nixon developed a warm relationship with the Church, involved the Mormon Tabernacle Choir in his inaugurations, and enjoyed the counsel and friendship of Latter-day Saints. In fact, as Elder Ralph Hardy Jr. put it, "For a time we had two active high priests in the President's cabinet" with David M. Kennedy as secretary of the treasury, and George Romney as secretary of housing and urban development.[1] Richard Nixon also experienced the Mormon culture in ways other Presidents had not—participating in a youth conference, speaking at a funeral in a stake center, and attending the Days of '47 Rodeo in the Salt Palace. He also had some Mormon cousins.[2]

**26 September 1952:** Thirty-nine-year-old Nixon visits Church headquarters while campaigning as Eisenhower's running mate.[3] Elder Marion G. Romney is not impressed with Nixon's rhetoric. "I listened to some of it, as much as I could swallow. He seems to be a nice boy, but for the life of me I can't discover anything which would qualify him to be Vice President."[4]

**1960:** By the end of their eight years of serving together with Eisenhower, Ezra Taft Benson does not have a positive view of Nixon and even refuses to

*26 September 1952: Senator Richard M. Nixon (R-CA) calls on Church headquarters during his campaign for the vice presidency and meets with President McKay and his two counselors. (L–R) Stephen L Richards, David O. McKay, Richard Nixon, J. Reuben Clark Jr., and an unidentified Utah Republican Party leader.*

campaign for him. "I wish I had more real confidence in the Vice President's ability to provide wise leadership for the nation," he says. "I feel he does not inspire sufficient confidence among the people. How I wish we had another Eisenhower to step into the breach."[5]

**10 October 1960:** Vice President Nixon campaigns at Church headquarters. President McKay says, "I sat by your competitor [Kennedy] in this office a few weeks ago and told him that if he were successful we would support him. In your case I'll say we hope you are successful." This comment is picked up by the media and misinterpreted as a Church endorsement for Nixon. The prophet later clarifies that he is speaking "as a personal voter and as a Republican" to the Republican candidate of his party and that he is not speaking for the Church. Privately, he writes that Nixon "had more experience in world affairs and other fields than any other vice president in the country's history."[6]

*Richard Nixon met with David O. McKay on several occasions, including this visit in 1952. President McKay would later write that he felt Nixon "had more experience in world affairs and other fields than any other vice president in the country's history."*

**November 1960:** Nixon loses by 17/100ths of a percent nationally to John F. Kennedy but defeats Kennedy by ten percentage points in Utah.[7]

**8 May 1962:** Nixon is the featured speaker at an LDS youth conference at the Wilshire Ward in California. The former vice president gave a nonpartisan discussion of the political responsibilities of young people.[8] That November, Nixon loses his race for governor of California, but in the late 1960s he begins his remarkable political comeback.

**1968:** Nixon's successful candidacy for the presidency includes defeating a Mormon candidate for the GOP nomination, making a visit to Utah, and garnering a higher percentage of votes in Utah in than all but two other states.

**January 1969:** Mormon J. Willard Marriott is chair of Nixon's inaugural. Other Latter-day Saints are involved as well, including the Tabernacle Choir.

**24 July 1970:** Nixon visits Salt Lake City for Pioneer Day. The following Halloween he also visits Utah and speaks in the Tabernacle.

**November 1972:** Nixon is reelected handily. In Utah, 68 percent vote for him and only 26 percent for George McGovern. Nixon, whose popularity among the Mormons remains high, wins hands down in every Utah county.[9]

**9 August 1974:** President Nixon resigns. One of the key investigators in the Watergate investigation is Latter-day Saint and future member of the Seventy D. Todd Christofferson, who is a law clerk to Judge John J. Sirica. Christofferson and Sirica are the first to hear the Nixon tapes, which ultimately bring down the President.[10]

**17 August 1985:** Former President Nixon speaks at the funeral of J. W. Marriott in the stake center adjacent to the Washington Temple.

**22 April 1994:** Nixon dies in New York City. Five days later President Thomas S. Monson represents the Church at the funeral in Yorba Linda, California.[11]

## NIXON'S 1968 PRESIDENTIAL VICTORY

As the 1968 race approached, some groups looked to former Eisenhower cabinet member and LDS Apostle Ezra Taft Benson as a right-wing alternative to Richard Nixon, but he was dissuaded by President McKay from running.[12] Another alternative to Nixon that year was the LDS governor of Michigan, George Romney, who lost in the convention. Dick Richards, who seconded Romney's nomination at the Miami convention and later worked for the Nixon campaign, noted, "The Nixon group felt they would easily defeat Romney, and they did not want to offend the Mormons, so they treaded lightly on George Romney during the campaign of '68." Without a viable candidacy in Ezra Taft Benson or George Romney, Republican Latter-day Saints shifted their support to Nixon. Richards was named western coordinator, a role the Mormon filled again for Nixon in 1972.

On 18 September 1968, Nixon stopped in Salt Lake City as part of a campaign swing. "Richard Nixon always liked coming to Utah and speaking in the Tabernacle, because he knew the Mormons would always give him such a great reception," said Dick Richards.[13] However, another Nixon aide, John P. Sears, recalled a visit to Salt Lake City where before they went into the meeting at Church headquarters, Nixon stopped him and said, "John, whatever I say in this meeting, don't you believe a word of it."[14]

In November, Richard Nixon defeated Hubert H. Humphrey with a close popular vote of 43.4 percent to 42.7 percent. All Utah counties went for Nixon, except Tooele and Carbon, with the final state tally showing over 56 percent for Nixon-Agnew and 37 percent for Humphrey-Muskie.[15]

## MORMON INVOLVEMENT IN NIXON'S INAUGURALS

In late October 1968, even before election day, LDS hotel and restaurant magnate J. Willard Marriott was approached by Nixon officials and asked to serve as chairman of the inauguration.[16] His wife, Alice S. Marriott, was put in charge of the inaugural's ladies' reception. Other Latter-day Saints also helped prepare for Nixon's inaugural, including Mark Evans Austad, who coordinated the six inaugural balls; Jesse R. Smith, who served as special coordinator for the concert committee;

and Robert W. Barker, who acted as general counsel for the inaugural committee.[17] As chair of the inaugural, Marriott arranged for Ezra Taft Benson of the Twelve (and Marriott's longtime acquaintance in Washington) to attend the festivities with VIP treatment.[18]

Like his predecessor Lyndon Johnson, Richard Nixon invited the Mormon Tabernacle Choir to sing at his inauguration, which they did on 20 January 1969.[19] "I remember when we came here in the campaign, in the Tabernacle," President Nixon later recalled, "we heard the Mormon Tabernacle Choir, and when it played and sang 'The Battle Hymn of the Republic' I turned to George Romney and said I had

*Michigan governor (and former Detroit Stake President) George W. Romney ran against Nixon for the 1968 Republican nomination. Nixon later appointed Romney to serve in his cabinet as Secretary of Housing and Urban Development. Romney's son, Mitt, would later serve as governor of Massachusetts and run himself for the 2008 Republican presidential nomination.*

David M. Kennedy, a former counselor in the Chicago Stake presidency, was appointed Nixon's Secretary of the Treasury and later served as U.S. ambassador-at-large and ambassador to NATO.

never heard it better. So we had them at the Inauguration."[20] Nixon also invited the choir to perform at the lighting of the nation's Christmas tree in 1970.[21]

For Nixon's second inaugural, Marriott was again head of the inaugural committee, the Tabernacle Choir sang, and BYU's Cougar Band marched in the inaugural parade. About thirty members of the choir sang at the inaugural religious service, which was held in the East Room of the White House. President Harold B. Lee was invited to attend the January 1973 inauguration, but due to a severe case of hoarseness, he was asked by his doctor not to attend. Instead, Elder Boyd K. Packer of the Quorum of the Twelve represented the Church.[22]

## LATTER-DAY SAINTS IN THE NIXON ADMINISTRATION

The incoming President named two Latter-day Saint cabinet members. David M. Kennedy, a former counselor in the Chicago Stake presidency, was appointed Nixon's secretary of the treasury and later served as U.S. ambassador-at-large and ambassador to NATO.[23] George Romney, who had been the first president of the Detroit Michigan Stake, was asked by President Nixon to serve as secretary of housing and urban development, a post he served in until 1972.[24] Another Latter-day Saint, Terrel H. Bell, served as deputy commissioner of education in the Nixon administration.[25] Future Area Seventy Jon M. Huntsman was a special assistant and staff secretary to President Nixon.[26]

At the Presidential Prayer Breakfast in October 1969, President Nixon acknowledged his friendship with the Mormons and noted their rapid growth. He asked his "old friend" from the Senate, Utah's Wallace F. Bennett, to give the scripture at the breakfast, which preceded his remarks. "This is truly an ecumenical meeting," said the President. "There are Catholics and Protestants here; and among the Protestants, all the various groups or most of them are represented: the very large groups like the Baptists, the Presbyterians, the Methodists are in this room, some of the smaller ones like the Mormons, or medium-sized the Mormons grow, I find. I imagine I am the only Quaker in the room."[27]

## NIXON'S PIONEER DAY VISIT

On 24 July 1970, President Nixon called upon the First Presidency and the members of the Twelve. He was in town campaigning for Republicans in the midterm election and had brought along his wife, Pat, daughter Tricia, and his two LDS cabinet members—George Romney and David M. Kennedy.[28] First Presidency secretary Francis Gibbons reported on the meeting that took place in the Church Administration Building:

> This was the first time in the history of the Church that the
> Council of the First Presidency and the Quorum of the Twelve
> had been briefed in private by a president of the United States. . . .

*George W. Romney and Richard Nixon at work in the White House. Romney served as Nixon's Secretary of Housing and Urban Development until the start of Nixon's second term in January 1973. He later served as an LDS patriarch in Michigan until his death in 1995.*

*Prior to meeting with Church General Authorities, President Nixon addresses the public from the steps of the Church Administration Building. Left of Nixon is President Joseph Fielding Smith, and left of him is President Harold B. Lee. To Nixon's right is President N. Eldon Tanner.*

For a half hour, the president of the United States gave the governing hierarchy of the Mormon Church an intimate, off-the-record briefing about the major national and international issues facing the nation. This was preceded by several brief comments when the president made complimentary remarks about George Romney and David Kennedy, saying that he had been criticized for giving undue recognition to such a small group as the Latter-day Saints (who then comprised only about 1 percent of the total population). He defended his selections on the ground that they were the ablest and most experienced men in their particular fields. He also lauded the Church and its members, mentioning especially the favorable impression made by the missionaries at the Mormon exhibit at Expo 70 in Tokyo. He said that according to

*During his Pioneer Day visit in 1970, President Nixon held a private briefing in the Church Administration Building with President Joseph Fielding Smith, his counselors, and members of the Quorum of the Twelve Apostles. They had a thirty-minute off-the-record discussion about pressing national and international issues.*

his daughter Julie and her husband, David Eisenhower, the LDS missionaries were the finest American ambassadors in Japan.[29]

Prior to meeting with the General Authorities, Nixon had made some remarks from the steps of the Church Administration Building. "I want you to know that we always have found our visits to Salt Lake City to be extremely heartwarming," he said. Nixon called the Church "a great institution that has played a part in this administration" and went on to thank the Church publicly for providing the Tabernacle Choir to sing at his inauguration and "for providing for the Cabinet two of the outstanding Americans of our time, two of the most selfless public servants I know—the Secretary of the Treasury, Mr. Kennedy, and the Secretary of Housing and Urban Development, George Romney." The President then gave some crowd-pleasing remarks regarding Pioneer Day, which was being celebrated in Utah that day:

Pioneer Day means something to the people of Utah but it also means something to the people of America, because the pioneers who came here taught other pioneers who went on through the balance of the West. And it is that kind of spirit, the kind of spirit that sees a great problem but the greater the problem puts in great effort, the kind of spirit that doesn't blame adversity on somebody else but tries to do

On 31 October 1970, President Nixon spoke in the Tabernacle on Temple Square. To the far right is Senator Wallace F. Bennett (R-UT), with the Mormon Tabernacle Choir in the background. Left of the podium is First Lady Pat Nixon, and to her left is First Presidency member N. Eldon Tanner. During his remarks, the President said, "I do not know of any group in America . . . who have contributed more to that strong, moral leadership and high moral standards . . . than those who are members of this Church."

something about it himself. That is what built this State; that is what built America. . . . Thank you for giving America such a fine lesson.[30]

During his Pioneer Day visit, President Nixon and his party also attended the Days of '47 Rodeo in the Salt Palace.[31]

Nixon visited Salt Lake City again on 31 October 1970, where he spoke in the Tabernacle on Temple Square. As he entered the Tabernacle, the famous organ bellowed "Hail to the Chief." President Joseph Fielding Smith welcomed him. Nixon was visibly moved by the choir and stood with his eyes closed while they sang "God Be With You." Several times during the performance he leaned over to Isaac M. Stewart, choir president, and said, "This is the world's greatest choir." In his remarks, the President said,

> I do not know of any group in America . . . who have contributed more to that strong, moral leadership and high moral standards—the spirit that has kept America going through bad times as well as good times; no group has done more than those who are members of this Church. I want to thank you for what you've done for the spirit of America. . . . If you can continue those spiritual values, I'm sure America is going to go ahead and do very well.[32]

## NIXON SPEAKS AT MARRIOTT'S FUNERAL

The funeral of J. W. Marriott was held in August 1985 in the LDS meetinghouse in Kensington, Maryland, adjacent to the Washington D.C. Temple. Former President Nixon spoke, along with the Reverend Billy Graham, and Church leaders Ezra Taft Benson, Gordon B. Hinckley, and Boyd K. Packer. "I remember it was quite a sight to see Richard Nixon speaking at the pulpit in the stake center," recalled Ralph W. Hardy Jr., then a member of the Washington Stake presidency. "His remarks were completely memorized and were really terrific." President Hardy was with the former President in the Relief Society room before the service when the family closed the casket and shared a prayer. "It was an interesting situation to be in a typical LDS Relief Society room, not that different from any other in the Church, with Richard Nixon sitting right next to me on those cushy folding chairs that Relief Society rooms always have." For those in attendance, it was historic to see a President of the United States in such a traditional Mormon setting.[33]

Richard Nixon remained a friend to the Mormons until his death, just as he had been during his tumultuous years as President.

# ENDNOTES

1   Ralph W. Hardy, Jr., interview by author, 2 July 2006.

2   "Mormon Girl Valedictorian Interviews Famous 'Cousin,'" *Church News,* 30 June 1956, 6.

3   Gibbons, *David O. McKay,* 311.

4   Howard, *Marion G. Romney: His Life and Faith,* 200.

5   Benson, *Crossfire,* 512. See also Gibbons, *Ezra Taft Benson,* 223–24; Benson, *Crossfire,* 33, 246, 332, 492, 503, 542–43.

6   Memo of Ted Cannon to Clare Middlemiss, 15 September 1960, in David O. McKay Diaries. See also Dexter Ellis, "Nixon Calls on Pres. McKay for Chat," *Deseret News,* 10 October 1960; Gibbons, *David O. McKay,* 375; "President McKay Clarifies Nixon 'Endorsement,'" *California Intermountain News,* 13 October 1960.

7   *Dave Leip's Atlas of U.S. Presidential Elections.*

8   "Former Vice President to Speak at Wilshire," *Church News,* 28 April 1962, 5.

9   *Dave Leip's Atlas of U.S. Presidential Elections.*

10  Holzapfel, et al., *On this Day in the Church,* 156.

11  Holzapfel, et al., *On this Day in the Church,* 83.

12  Gibbons, *Ezra Taft Benson,* 244, 247–48.

13  Richard Richards, interview by author, 26 July 2006.

14  Mark Shields, "The Unnatural Politician," *The Enterprise* (Salt Lake City) 31, no. 53 (24 June 2002): 18.

15  *Dave Leip's Atlas of U.S. Presidential Elections.*

16  O'Brien, *Marriott: The J. Willard Marriott Story,* 293–95.

17  "Mormons in Charge of Inaugural," *Church News,* 11 January 1969, 3.

18  Gibbons, *Ezra Taft Benson,* 261.

19  *Church Almanac,* 562.

20  Richard M. Nixon, "Pioneer Day Remarks in Salt Lake City, Utah," 24 July 1970, in Woolley and Peters, *The American Presidency Project.*

21  Richard M. Nixon, "Remarks at the Lighting of the Nation's Christmas Tree," 16 December 1970, in Woolley and Peters, *The American Presidency Project.*

22  "For at Least 35 Years, LDS Have Participated in Inaugurations," *Church News,* 28 January 1989. See also Gibbons, *Harold B. Lee,* 474.

23  Garr, et al., *Encyclopedia of Latter-day Saint History,* 603. See also "2 Mormons Named to Cabinet," *Church News,* 14 December 1968, 4.

24  Garr, et al., *Encyclopedia of Latter-day Saint History,* 1042.

25  "Renowned Educator Terrel H. Bell Dies," *Church News,* 29 June 1996.

26  Bob Bernick, Jr., and Lucinda Dillon, "Huntsman's Charity Sets Him Apart," *Deseret News,* 15 May 2001.

27  Richard M. Nixon, "Remarks at the Presidential Prayer Breakfast," 22 October 1969, in Woolley and Peters, *The American Presidency Project.*

28  Francis M. Gibbons, *The Expanding Church: Three Decades of Remarkable Growth Among the Latter-day Saints 1970–1999,* 29, 129.

29    Francis M. Gibbons, *Joseph Fielding Smith,* 434.

30    Richard M. Nixon, "Pioneer Day Remarks in Salt Lake City, Utah," 24 July 1970 in Woolley and Peters, *The American Presidency Project.*

31    "Nixon Honors Pioneers," *Church News,* 25 July 1970, 3.

32    "Pres. Nixon Praises Church," *Church News,* 7 November 1970, 3, 5. See also Richard M. Nixon, "Remarks in Salt Lake City, Utah," 31 October 1970, in Woolley and Peters, *The American Presidency Project.*

33    Hardy, interview, 2 July 2006. See also George M. McCune, *Gordon B. Hinckley: Shoulder for the Lord,* 513; "Philanthropist J. Willard Marriott Dies at 84," *Church News,* 18 August 1985, 7.

# GERALD R. FORD

## 1974–1977

Gerald Ford, who grew up listening to Mormon Tabernacle Choir broadcasts over the radio with his mother,[1] came into the presidency with a long background of association with the Mormons and continued to befriend them throughout his administration. He visited Church headquarters on several occasions and had President Spencer W. Kimball as his special guest for the nation's bicentennial. His wife toured the Washington D.C. Temple, and his son attended Utah State University. After leaving the White House, Ford even spent two days on the campus of BYU, culminating with a family home evening with Dallin H. Oaks and his family. This warmth was reciprocated in the form of high popularity among the Saints, and an understanding by the Episcopalian Ford that Mormons not only placed a high value on the importance of the family, but that they also were indeed Christians.

**1949–1973:** As a congressman from Michigan, Ford becomes good friends with numerous Mormons, including Michigan governor George W. Romney, Ezra Taft Benson, and J. Willard Marriott. One of Ford's close friends is James E. Brown, a Latter-day Saint from Tremonton, Utah, who is an FBI agent and Ford's skiing partner. The Fords and the Browns spend many holidays together. Ford says he and his wife feel "a nice closeness to the people of the Mormon faith" because of their "many, many" LDS friends. "As a matter of fact, I think they probably had as big an impact in raising our four children as Mrs. Ford and I did, and it was all to the good, let me assure you," he says.[2]

**June 1974:** Vice President and Mrs. Ford spend three days in Utah and meet with Church leaders.

**October 1975:** Ezra Taft Benson represents the Church at the White House Forum on Domestic Policy. In the thirty-minute meeting the President compliments the Church for placing refugees from Vietnam.[3]

**3 July 1976:** President Ford begins to celebrate the nation's bicentennial with President Kimball and other Latter-day Saints.

**November 1976:** Ford is defeated by Carter but remains popular among the Saints. In Utah he garners his highest percentage of votes in the nation—62 percent to Carter's 34 percent.[4]

**29 November 1977:** Gerald and Betty Ford attend a banquet at Hotel Utah to honor J. Willard and Allie Marriott. Earlier in the day they spend a half hour with the First Presidency, in which the former President is once again given a leather-bound triple combination. Betty Ford is given the book *The Mormon Way*.[5]

**1978:** Ford is given President Kimball's biography, visits BYU, and enjoys a family home evening with the family of Dallin H. Oaks.

## VICE PRESIDENTIAL VISIT

In June 1974, Vice President and Mrs. Ford spent three days in Utah, where he delivered the commencement address at Utah State University. "It was Horace Greeley who said 'Go West, young man,'" said Ford in his speech, "but it was Brigham Young who knew where to stop."[6] They enjoyed a special concert by the Tabernacle Choir, and Mrs. Ford toured the Beehive House while the vice president met privately with President Spencer W. Kimball and his counselors. There they discussed family home evening and the importance of strengthening the family. The visitors had lunch with Church leaders in the newly completed Church Office Building and left with Tabernacle Choir recordings, the booklet "Meet the Mormons," a triple combination of Mormon scriptures, a family home evening manual, and copies of books authored by Presidents Kimball, Tanner, and Romney. Ford said publicly to President Kimball:

*During his June 1974 visit, President Ford met with the LDS First Presidency. (L–R) Presidents Marion G. Romney, N. Eldon Tanner, Gerald R. Ford, and Spencer W. Kimball. During the visit, Ford said to the leaders, "We like people from Utah; we like your country, and we like what you stand for."*

You should be proud of the great work ethic that is such a vital part of the lifestyle of the people of Utah. You should be proud of the high moral principles which in many respects are an example to all of us who live in the other 49 states. Let me say we've appreciated very much the warmth of the welcome we've had here on this visit. It's been a great experience for Mrs. Ford and myself, and we look forward to returning because we like people from Utah; we like your country, and we like what you stand for.[7]

## MORMONS AND THE FORD ADMINISTRATION

Two months after the Utah visit, Nixon resigned the presidency and Ford became President. President Ford utilized the talents of several Latter-day Saints in his administration. He appointed Lieutenant General Brent Scowcroft, a native of Ogden, Utah, as his national security advisor to replace Henry Kissinger, who had been serving in that post in addition to that of secretary of state. He also appointed future BYU president Rex Lee as Assistant Attorney General.[8] Terrel H. Bell served as U.S. commissioner of education in the Ford administration.[9] Ford's White House included four Mormons secretaries: Erlynn Ensign, Jennifer S. Morgan,

*During a June 1974 visit, President Kimball shared with President and Mrs. Ford some LDS publications, including copies of Latter-day Saint scriptures and the booklet "Meet the Mormons." Later in life Ford would remark, "I have visited with Spencer W. Kimball on several occasions and I consider him to be one of the great spiritual leaders of the world. His life has been a sermon that mankind could emulate."*

Christina R. Valentine, and Marla Whyte. Latter-day Saints on Ford's White House staff included Roger B. Porter, executive secretary of the President's economic policy board; Dr. David C. Hoopes, special assistant to the President; and Robert K. Wolthius, deputy assistant to the President for legislative affairs.[10] Stephen M. Studdert, the police chief of Brigham City, Utah, was appointed to Ford's staff as an advance man and press aide.[11]

*Latter-day Saint David C. Hoopes (left) as special assistant to the President helped facilitate the visit of Elder Ezra Taft Benson (center) with President Gerald R. Ford (right) in the Oval Office.*

## BETTY FORD TOURS THE WASHINGTON D.C. TEMPLE

A month after Nixon's resignation, the new First Lady was among the dignitaries who toured the recently completed Washington D.C. Temple. During the open house Betty Ford lingered for some time in front of a mural entitled *The Second Coming* and said she was overwhelmed by the magnificent temple.[12] Local stake president Julian Lowe described a humorous experience he had in the Solemn Assembly Room with the First Lady:

> Having been told that only members in good standing might enter a temple after the building had been dedicated, Betty Ford wanted to know how Temple officials could tell whether or not someone who was worthy to enter. It was then explained that "recommends" are issued and that the person coming to the Temple would show his recommend as he entered. At this point in the conversation, Senator Wallace Bennett, who was in the company, took his recommend out of his pocket to show her. Following that,

each of us in the party took out our recommends. Oddly enough, President Kimball was the last one to find his recommend, and there were a few awkward seconds while he further searched through his wallet. When he found it, with a little bit of mischief in her voice, the First Lady said to President Kimball, "I'm so glad you've got one, too. You had me worried."[13]

As she was leaving the building she said, "This is a truly great experience for me. . . . It's an inspiration to all."[14]

## FORD'S RECOGINITON OF THE CHURCH'S CHRISTIANITY

President Ford appreciated that Mormons were Christians. Utah senator Jake Garn shared how he once spent an entire day alone with Ford at his condo in Aspen, discussing foreign policy and defense. At one point in the day, the President told Senator Garn how much respect he had for the Mormon Church. "Oh, us crazy Mormons, huh?" replied Garn self-deprecatingly. "I know you all put up with a lot," said the President, "and that most people don't understand you. In fact, some say you're not even Christians, but I know that your real name is The Church of Jesus Christ of Latter-day Saints. How can a group with a name like that not be Christian?" Ford also said that he was pleased with the Mormon values and the Mormons he had had a chance to work with.[15]

*(L–R) J. Willard and Alice Sheets Marriott, Gerald and Betty Ford, Camilla and Spencer W. Kimball, and another couple at the Kennedy Center on 3 July 1976 for the Bicentennial Extravaganza.*

# FORD CELEBRATES THE BICENTENNIAL WITH LDS LEADERS

Despite the busy preparations for the nation's bicentennial, President Ford spent some of 3 July 1976 in a personal interview with President Spencer W. Kimball in the Oval Office. President Kimball explained the purposes of the Church, the loyalty Latter-day Saints had for their government, and several of the Church's unique programs. After the meeting, President Ford and President Kimball moved to the south lawn of the White House, where a hundred LDS Primary children sang for the President "I Am a Child of God."[16] While they sang, President Ford walked among the children to shake hands and sign autographs.

*3 July 1976: On the eve of the nation's bicentennial, President Ford (left) and Spencer W. Kimball (right) were greeted by one hundred Primary children on the White House south lawn, who sang "I Am a Child of God." Ford spent some time walking among the children shaking hands and signing autographs.*

That night at the Bicentennial Extravaganza program at the Kennedy Center, the President had the Mormons as his guests in his President's box: Presidents Kimball and Ezra Taft Benson, Elders Gordon B. Hinckley and L. Tom Perry, former LDS cabinet members David M. Kennedy and George W. Romney, program chairman and former Washington D.C. Stake President J. Willard Marriott, and their wives. One of the highlights of the program was a performance by the Mormon Tabernacle Choir. President Kimball was seated on one side of the President, and J. Willard Marriott on the other.[17]

# FORD TALKS ABOUT PRESIDENT KIMBALL AND VISITS BYU

Former Idaho congressman Ralph Harding and Ford's former national security advisor Brent Scowcroft were two Latter-day Saints who participated in the Jerry Ford Invitational Golf Tournament in the summer of 1978. Harding and Scowcroft used the occasion to give the former President an inscribed copy of the biography *Spencer W. Kimball*. Ford said in response:

I have visited with Spencer W. Kimball on several occasions and I consider him to be one of the great spiritual leaders of the world. His life has been a sermon that mankind could emulate. I am grateful to have this biography to learn even more about this great spiritual leader. I have visited Salt Lake City on many occasions and I have several Mormon friends. I really respect the principles, the traditions and the dedication of the Mormon people.[18]

*Gerald R. Ford once remarked, "I have visited Salt Lake City on many occasions and I have several Mormon friends. I really respect the principles, the traditions and the dedication of the Mormon people." When he died, the Church's First Presidency declared, "Gerald R. Ford lived a life of service to others, doing so with kindness, firmness of conviction, and an unwavering sense of right."*

The former President spent a remarkable two days on the Brigham Young University campus in December 1978. He spoke to a political science class at the J. Reuben Clark Law School, toured the campus, visited several classes, and enjoyed the musical group, "The Lamanite Generation," at a luncheon. BYU president and future Apostle Dallin H. Oaks hosted President Ford and his aide, James Shuman, for a family home evening. The evening at the Oaks's home included the showing of two Church films, scripture readings, and a musical number by President Oaks's daughter Cherie Ringger. Lloyd Oaks, a recently returned missionary from the Japan Kobe Mission, answered Ford's questions about missionary work and about Osaka, where the Fords would soon be visiting. The former President shared some personal experiences and feelings about the importance of family. At the conclusion of his visit, he addressed over 9,500 students at the Marriott Center, where he said, "It is an inspiration to be in this atmosphere. Without hesitation or qualification, visiting the BYU family has been an inspiration to me and I thank you. . . . This has been an exceptional visit. I will remember it for years."[19]

On 26 December 2006, Gerald R. Ford passed away. The First Presidency declared, "Gerald R. Ford lived a life of service to others, doing so with kindness, firmness of conviction, and an unwavering sense of right. He will always be remembered as a man of faith and decency."[20]

# ENDNOTES

1   "Vice President Visits in Utah," *Church News,* 15 June 1974, 3–4.

2   Paul B. Skousen, *The Skousen Book of Mormon World Records, Premier Edition,* 43–44. See also "Vice President Visits in Utah," *Church News,* 15 June 1974, 3–4; "President Cherished His Ties to Utah," *Deseret Morning News,* 28 December 2006.

3   Gibbons, *Ezra Taft Benson,* 279. See also "Pres. Ford Praises Church's Refugee Help," *Church News,* 29 November 1975, 3.

4   *Dave Leip's Atlas of U.S. Presidential Elections.*

5   "Marriotts Are Honored," *Church News,* 3 December 1977, 3.

6   "President Cherished His Ties to Utah," *Deseret Morning News,* 28 December 2006.

7   "Vice President Visits in Utah," *Church News,* 15 June 1974, 3–4.

8   Holzapfel, et al., *On this Day in the Church,* 215. See also Ostling and Ostling, *Mormon America,* 135.

9   "Renowned Educator Terrel H. Bell Dies," *Church News,* 29 June 1996.

10  "Pres. Ford Praises Church's Refugee Help," *Church News,* 29 November 1975, 3.

11  "He Learned Priorities at Prophet's Side," *Church News,* 17 December 1988. See also "One of the President's Men," *Church News,* 31 July 1982.

12  "Temple Wows the First Lady," *Church News,* 28 September 1974, 8.

13  Lowe and Thayn, *History of the Mormons in the Greater Washington Area,* 169.

14  Gordon B. Hinckley, *Be Thou an Example,* 23.

15  Jake Garn, interview by author, 2 August 2006.

16  Gibbons, *The Expanding Church,* 130–31.

17  "Prophet Visits Pres. Ford," *Church News,* 10 July 1976, 4.

18  "Church Book Given to Pres. Ford," *Church News,* 5 August 1978, 10.

19  "Pres. Ford Visits BYU," *Church News,* 9 December 1978, 4.

20  "LDS Statement on Ford," *Deseret Morning News,* 28 December 2006.

# JIMMY CARTER

## *1977–1981*

Unlike most modern Republican administrations, Carter's Democrat-dominated White House did not employ many Mormons. However, the thirty-ninth President had a genuine interest in the Latter-day Saints, and his interactions with them underscore the Church's major initiatives of the times. At a time when the Church was expanding missionary work throughout the world, Jimmy Carter learned all he could about the program, and as a former President even helped get LDS missionaries back into Ghana. At a time when the Church announced that all worthy males regardless of race could receive the priesthood, Carter expressed his congratulations. At a time when the Church was emphasizing the good it could do for families, President Carter chose to deliver his address for National Family Week from the Tabernacle on Temple Square. He also became the first President to receive his family history from Church leaders, and his enthusiastic response has made such a gift part of Church-president relations ever since.

**1969:** Charles J. Carter, a Baptist minister in St. Augustine, Florida, joins the LDS Church. After his baptism, he writes his cousin Jimmy, a Georgia politician, about why he had done this and about his newfound religion. "He has never been critical of this action," Charles says of the eventual President.

"He's quite understanding and has a high respect for the Mormon Church and its members. I think he's quite impressed with some of the programs of the Church."[1]

**1976:** Morris "Mo" Udall—an LDS Congressman who has served fifteen terms representing Arizona—is defeated by Carter in the Wisconsin presidential primary by one percentage point, shifting the momentum in the race for the Democratic nomination to Carter.[2]

**November 1976:** Jimmy Carter defeats Gerald Ford in a relatively close race but loses in every Utah county but Carbon and Emery.[3]

**January 1977:** President N. Eldon Tanner of the First Presidency and his wife, Sara, represent the Church at Carter's inauguration. Another Latter-day Saint, Senator Howard W. Cannon (D-NV), is asked by the incoming President to chair the committee on arrangements for the inauguration and to conduct the actual event.[4]

**11 March 1977:** President Spencer W. Kimball meets with Carter in the Oval Office. The President has just returned from South America and requests a meeting with the prophet to discuss Latin American affairs, the Peace Corps, the LDS missionary program, and the family home evening program. During the twenty-minute meeting, Carter compliments the Church on its role in strengthening families.[5]

**June 1977:** Church leaders present Carter with his family history.

**18 April 1978:** Concerned with the LDS view on the Panama Canal treaties, Carter meets with LDS congressmen and has a phone conversation with Gordon B. Hinckley. "I called Salt Lake City to get a report from the Mormon Church," writes Carter. "They told me they don't have any official position on the Panama Canal treaties. Ezra Taft Benson is the only one of the Church's twelve elders who had spoken out against them, and they pointed out that both Mormons and Baptists have people for and against the treaties."[6] The treaties narrowly pass the Senate later that day.

**9 June 1978:** President Kimball announces that the priesthood is now available to all worthy males, regardless of race. As the news spreads, Carter wants to send a telegram to Church headquarters commending President Kimball. However, the President is sensitive to the fact that he probably doesn't understand the entire context of the announcement, so he has Latter-day Saint Jim Jardine, who is working in the White House at the time, draft the telegram. After writing a few thoughts, Jardine calls Neal A. Maxwell, an Apostle and former professor of his, explains the situation, and reviews the proposed telegram with him. The resulting words are the exact telegram that is sent from President Carter to President Kimball commending him "for your compassionate prayerfulness and courage in receiving a new doctrine."[7]

**22 November 1978:** Carter speaks in the Tabernacle during National Family Week.

**November 1980:** Nowhere in the nation is Carter rejected like in the Mormon West, where Utahns give him a mere 21 percent compared to Ronald Reagan's 73 percent.[8]

**July 1990:** The former President and First Lady tour Temple Square.

**November 1990:** Carter helps restore LDS missionaries to Ghana.

## MORMONS IN THE CARTER WHITE HOUSE

LDS Washington observers have called the Carter administration "a desert period for the Church in many ways," since there were no Latter-day Saints in the executive branch at the cabinet level, sub-cabinet level, or sub-subcabinet level for four years.[9] "Besides Bob King who worked in the office of the National Security Advisor, I was the only Mormon in the Carter White House," said Jim Jardine, who was there as a White House fellow.[10] President Carter was not opposed to giving a Mormon a judicial appointment, however, as illustrated in 1977 when he appointed Monroe McKay, a BYU law professor, to the United States Court of Appeals.[11] Also, Wayne Owens, who had served as a congressman from Utah and mission president in Montreal, Canada, was appointed by Carter to serve on the National Advisory Committee on Resource Conservation and Recovery.[12] Carter also became the first President to award a Latter-day Saint the U.S. Presidential Medal of Freedom when he honored Esther Eggertsen Peterson, a national consumer rights advocate.[13]

## JIMMY CARTER AND GENEALOGY

In June 1977 recently released Washington D.C. Stake president W. Donald Ladd and the public relations manager for the Church Genealogical Department, Thomas E. Daniels, visited President Carter. They presented to the President a two-inch-thick volume of Carter family genealogy, as well as a framed 18 x 24-inch, hand-illustrated Carter family tree, showing the names of the President's ancestors as far as could be documented. The President appeared genuinely grateful for the unique and personal gift and remarked, "The research that The Church of Jesus Christ of Latter-day Saints has done is very exciting to me. I look forward to studying the chart. This is an area of knowledge I've never had." The President asked that the two convey his appreciation to the First Presidency and added, "I have a very warm regard and great respect for The Church of Jesus Christ of Latter-day Saints and its leaders."[14]

Later that year, the President's LDS cousin Charles Carter told the *Church News* that he continues to correspond with the President from time to time and that recent letters focused on family history. "Jimmy knows that I'm interested in genealogy and has invited me to go visit the kinfolks to find out all that I can about the family," Charles Carter said. "He's also quite interested in genealogy but has never had a chance to do much about it. I know he was very pleased when the Church presented him all that genealogical information."[15]

## CARTER'S SYMPATHY TO THE CHURCH

Senator Orrin Hatch, who was first elected in 1976, noted that all of the Presidents he has served with, beginning with the Carter administration, went out of their way at cabinet meetings or state dinners that Hatch was attending to make sure he was served something besides coffee, tea, or alcohol. "They were all very aware and sensitive to these beliefs," he recalled.[16] "President Carter was very friendly with members of the Church," noted Ralph Hardy Jr. "He knew the Marriotts and other Latter-day Saints, and was a genuine, Christian man who was helpful to the Church when asked."[17]

On one occasion, Utah senator Jake Garn was traveling with President Carter aboard Air Force One, and the subject of the Mormons came up. "Was it true that they drove your people out of Missouri?" asked the President. "Yes," replied the LDS senator. "In fact the governor of Missouri issued an extermination order to drive us from the state. Being driven from state to state is how we ended up in Utah." Carter shook his head in sincere disgust. "That's unbelievable. That's difficult to believe that it could happen in a country founded on religious freedom," he said. "I will never, ever understand how in the United States of America that could ever happen." Garn said that the President remarked how much he appreciated people who were religious regardless of which faith and that it was good for the country to have religious people.[18] On one occasion when Latter-day Saints were being attacked as not being a Christian religion, former President Carter came to their defense. He declared that Mormons were Christians and any fellow Southern Baptists who thought otherwise were "Pharisees."[19]

## CARTER'S PHONE CALL ABOUT THE MISSIONARY PROGRAM

President Carter had an unquestioned Baptist faith and even served as a deacon in his congregation while governor of Georgia. While in the White House, he occasionally taught a Sunday School class. One Sunday in 1977 he returned home from church with some questions, so he telephoned President Kimball. White House operators tracked down President Kimball presiding at a stake conference in central Utah.

While the prophet was speaking, a stake executive secretary walked up to the front of the chapel where Kimball's secretary, D. Arthur Haycock, was taking notes and relayed to Haycock that there was an important phone call for President Kimball. Haycock stepped down from the stand and left to take the call. "This is President Jimmy Carter," he heard on the other end. "I would like to speak to your president." Haycock explained that President Kimball was at the pulpit in the middle of addressing a congregation of hundreds. "I know he would like to speak with you, Mr. President. His second counselor is here. Would you speak to him?" Carter agreed, and Haycock quickly returned to the chapel to retrieve Marion G. Romney.

The President explained to President Romney that he wanted to talk about creating a more effective missionary program at an upcoming Baptist convention in Mississippi and wanted to better understand what was behind the Mormons' successful program. He learned that there were thirty thousand serving and then asked how much the Church paid them. Carter was stunned to hear the reply, "Nothing. They all pay their own expenses." President Romney told about his own missionary experience of fifty years prior when he had to borrow money to go and then worked hard upon his return to pay it back. Carter then asked how many countries they served in, and

*The LDS First Presidency with the 39th President of the United States. (L–R) Presidents N. Eldon Tanner, Spencer W. Kimball, Jimmy Carter, and Marion G. Romney. President Carter was particularly impressed with the Church's missionary program and later held a significant telephone conversation with President Romney about its details.*

27 November 1978: President Carter speaking in the Tabernacle to celebrate National Family Week. President Kimball at left. The visit marked the first time a President of the United States had traveled to Salt Lake City solely to participate in a Church-sponsored event.

Romney said that the Mormons were following the commission given by Jesus Christ to carry the gospel to every nation, kindred, tongue, and people and were in every country possible. The President replied, "We have this same commission." The President also asked how missionaries were selected and who was eligible to serve and seemed interested to learn of older couples and sister missionaries. President Romney shared how potential missionaries were trained from childhood and that he had a four-year-old grandson who was already singing, "I Hope They Call Me on a Mission." President Carter complimented the Church and said it was an inspired program. He also asked that additional materials on missionary work be sent to him.

A few days later, newspapers reported on President Carter's speech to the Baptists, where he said, "We ought to be more like the Mormon Church. They have thousands of young people out teaching the gospel of Christ."[20] Years later, Carter alluded to his phone call with President Romney in an interview with *Christianity Today*:

> [As President] I was active as a regular church member and felt the need for the Baptist Church to reach out in a broader program of evangelism. . . . I talked to the members of the Mormon church in some depth, and asked them how they went about getting so many volunteer missionaries. We tried to do a similar thing in our Baptist denomination.[21]

## CARTER'S SPEECH IN THE TABERNACLE

In the fall of 1978, President Carter telephoned President Kimball to see if he could speak in the Tabernacle on the family. It was somewhat awkward that the President would skip the traditional protocol of working with the governor or congressional delegation to schedule a visit. "But

Jimmy Carter really liked President Kimball and felt very comfortable going directly to him," noted Jardine.[22] The President had proclaimed the week of Thanksgiving as National Family Week and felt an address in the Tabernacle at the headquarters of the profamily LDS Church was fitting.

The visit, which came on 27 November 1978, was the first time a President of the United States had traveled to Salt Lake City solely to participate in a Church-sponsored event. President Kimball was the first speaker on the program and gave President Carter a bronze statuette of a mother teaching a child to walk to his father. In his twenty-three-minute speech, Carter spoke about his own family and the importance of the family unit. "I know how much less difficult my own duties would be as president if your mammoth crusade for stable and strong families should be successful," he said. "Your great church epitomizes to me what a family ought to be, a church that believes in strong families, in individualism, the right to be different, but the opportunity, and even duty, to grow, as a human being, to prepare oneself for greater service."

During the program on the family President Carter also enjoyed several patriotic musical numbers by the Tabernacle Choir, "I Am a Child of God" sung by 41 ten- and eleven-year-

*As part of the National Family Week celebration in the Tabernacle, President Spencer W. Kimball gave President Carter a bronze statuette of a mother teaching a child to walk to his father. "Your great church epitomizes to me what a family ought to be," remarked Carter after, "a church that believes in strong families, in individualism, the right to be different, but the opportunity, and even duty, to grow, as a human being, to prepare oneself for greater service."*

olds, a Native American song by BYU's Lamanite Generation, and "Love at Home" sung by the Osmonds. The President and the 8,000 in attendance also viewed nine video clips on the family from the Church's award-winning Homefront series on a huge screen in front of the organ pipes.[23]

## THE FORMER PRESIDENT VISITS TEMPLE SQUARE

In the summer of 1990, while Presidents George Bush, Ronald Reagan, Gerald Ford, and Richard Nixon were gathered in Yorba Linda, California, for the dedication of the Nixon Library and Birthplace, Jimmy Carter was conspicuously absent and touring Temple Square. He had been on a whirlwind trip to Ethiopia, Texas, and Montana and had a layover in Salt Lake City. Wanting to return to Temple Square, where he had been only once before—and then just to speak in the Tabernacle—the former President, his wife, and a Secret Service agent found their way to the north gate of the Square. Temple Square supervisor Dene Hinton thought it might be Jimmy Carter but wasn't sure, so he asked the visitors where they were from. "When they said, 'Georgia,' that clinched it," Hinton later said. He turned the guests over to Pam Misbach, a sister missionary from California, who showed them around. "He was very nice, very personable," reported Sister Misbach. "Even though he only had a half hour and he wanted to see the most that he could, he would stop and have his picture taken with people. I thought that was really admirable because who knows when he will get here again." During their tour they were treated to a brief rendition of "Come, Come Ye Saints" by Tabernacle organist Clay Christianson, and only about ten minutes of information from Sister Misbach (due to the many visitors and missionaries who would stop to meet the Carters). During the tour the thirty-ninth President asked about the significance of temple marriage. Rosalynn Carter asked some questions about the Book of Mormon. The former President said he already knew what the Book of Mormon was and had a copy. At the end of their brief tour, the Carters were given a book about Temple Square and a Mormon Tabernacle Choir cassette tape. As they were leaving, Jimmy Carter politely thanked Sister Misbach for the tour and kissed her on the cheek.[24]

## CARTER HELPS RETURN LDS MISSIONARIES TO GHANA

As a former President, Jimmy Carter has been active in humanitarian and diplomatic work and has developed close U.S. ties with leaders of Latin America and Africa. In this capacity he was asked by LDS leaders for help. On 14 June 1989, the government of Ghana expelled Mormon missionaries and forbade Church operations there, including Sunday meetings. After trying in vain to reverse this policy, Church leaders asked Carter to intervene. The former President made a phone call to Ghana's "benevolent dictator," Jerry Rawlings, and convinced him that Latter-day Saints were good and loyal citizens. In very short order the policy was reversed and "The Freeze," as it has since become known, came to an end in November 1990. "I remember having a conversation with President Carter at the 1992 Democratic Convention in New York City," recalled Elder Ralph W. Hardy Jr., chair of the Church's Public Affairs Washington D.C. Advisory Committee, "and thanking him for his assistance in getting our missionaries back into Ghana."[25]

Although not politically popular among most Mormons, Carter's record of respect, tolerance, and friendship toward the Church remains impeccable.

# ENDNOTES

1 "President's Cousin, Ex-cleric Turns LDS," *Church News,* 5 November 1977, 7.

2 Wikipedia article on Morris Udall: wikipedia.com, s.v. "Morris Udall."

3 *Dave Leip's Atlas of U.S. Presidential Elections.*

4 "Church Is Represented at Inaugural," *Church News,* 29 January 1977, 6.

5 "Prophet, President Carter Confer in D.C.," *Church News,* 19 March 1977, 3.

6 Jimmy Carter, *Keeping Faith: Memoirs of a President,* 176. See also Telephone log of President Carter for 18 April 1978, Jimmy Carter Presidential Library.

7 Text of the telegram from "I Knew That the Time Had Come," *Church News,* 4 June 1988. Involvement of Jardine and Maxwell in Hafen, *Neal A. Maxwell: A Disciple's Life.* Details confirmed through author interview with James S. Jardine, 31 July 2006.

8 *Dave Leip's Atlas of U.S. Presidential Elections.*

9 Hardy, interview, 2 July 2006.

10 James S. Jardine, interview by author, 31 July 2006.

11 "New Chief Justice Is Former Member of BYU Law Faculty," *Church News,* 21 September 1991.

12 "Obituaries," *Church News,* 28 December 2002, 15.

13 Holzapfel, et al., *On this Day in the Church,* 12.

14 "Church Gives Carter Roots to President," *Church News,* 11 June 1977, 3.

15 "President's Cousin, Ex-cleric Turns LDS," *Church News,* 5 November 1977, 7.

16 Orrin Hatch, interview by author, 30 May 2006.

17 Hardy, interview, 2 July 2006.

18 Garn, interview, 2 August 2006.

19 "Are LDS Welcome in Top Levels of National GOP?" *Deseret Morning News,* 27 November 2005.

20 Howard, *Marion G. Romney: His Life and Faith,* 236. See also Swinton, *In the Company of Prophets,* 101–2; Jardine, interview, 31 July 2006. Howard lists the stake conference in Fillmore, Swinton has it in Richfield, and Jardine simply recalled "central Utah."

21 "Jimmy Carter: My Personal Faith in God," *Christianity Today,* 4 March 1983, 19. Photocopy available in LDS Church Archives, Salt Lake City.

22 Jardine, interview, 31 July 2006.

23 "Pres. Carter Lauds Family," *Church News,* 2 December 1978, 3, 4, 9.

24 "Jimmy Carter Drops by Temple Square," *Church News,* 28 July 1990.

25 Hardy, interview, 2 July 2006. Story also confirmed in Jardine, interview, 31 July 2006. For background on "The Freeze," see *Church Almanac* article on "Ghana."

# RONALD REAGAN

## *1981–1989*

Although Theodore Roosevelt did the most to bring the Church into mainstream America, Ronald Reagan had the most positive relationship with the Church of any American President to date. "President Reagan knew and loved the Latter-day Saints, and held the Church in highest regard," remarked former LDS Reagan aide Stephen M. Studdert. "From his days as governor of California, the doctrines and the principles of the Church drew his frequent interest. As president he often asked about Church programs." He recognized the Church's moral leadership and social influence, even declaring, "A Mormon contribution to American life is beyond measuring."[1] Historian D. Michael Quinn points out the irony that although the Mormons were being hounded by the federal government in the late nineteenth century, "in a stunning turnabout, a century later the LDS church had become the darling of the Republican White House."[2] Indeed, Reagan's rapport with the Church was historic.

**1930s–60s:** During his acting career, Reagan visits southern Utah numerous times, stars in films opposite Latter-day Saint Rhonda Fleming, and is acquainted with various Mormons in California.[3]

**1968, 1974, 1975, 1976, 1977, and 1980:** Governor Reagan makes several political visits to Salt Lake City, including speaking at the state GOP convention and a Western Republican Conference. He also dines with Church leaders. The results pay off, and in 1976, Utah's delegation to the Republican National Convention gives their votes to former-Governor Reagan over the incumbent, Gerald Ford.[4]

**November 1980:** Reagan defeats Carter handily, including in Utah where he wins 73 to 21 percent. The percentage for Reagan in LDS-dominated Utah is higher than in any other state, and every single Utah county goes for Reagan.[5] One of the chief architects of his victory is pollster Richard B. Wirthlin, a Latter-day Saint and future General Authority as of 1968, who works closely with Reagan. Wirthlin will also serve as director of planning and strategy for the 1984 campaign.[6]

**January 1981:** Reagan has the Mormon Tabernacle Choir sing at his inauguration, and Donny and Marie Osmond perform at various inaugural events. The Church's official guests at the inauguration include President Ezra Taft Benson, then president of the Quorum of the Twelve, and Elder Joseph B. Wirthlin, then of the First Quorum of the Seventy and brother of Richard B. Wirthlin. Latter-day Saint Robert W. Barker, a Washington attorney, serves as chairman of the inaugural's law committee.[7]

**November 1984:** Reagan defeats Mondale in every state except Minnesota and the District of Columbia to win a second term. Reagan wins by a three-to-one margin in Utah, which again is a more pronounced victory than in any other state. Every county of Utah again goes for the Republican incumbent. In 1984, 85 percent of the Latter-day Saints throughout the country vote for Reagan.[8]

**5 June 2004:** In response to Reagan's death, President Gordon B. Hinckley and his counselors release a statement lauding him "as a man of uncommon decency and dignity."[9] In New York City's Radio City Music Hall, President Hinckley shares with members, "This is a very sober time in the history our nation. Buried yesterday (June 11) was President Ronald Reagan. I do not care whether you are a Democrat or a Republican. He was a man who left his mark upon the world. He was a good friend of the Church." After sharing his many experiences with him, President Hinckley says, "I counted him as a friend. I have tonight in my shirt these cuff links which he gave me, which have on their face the seal of the President of the United States of America, and on the reverse side the name of Ronald Reagan."[10]

## REAGAN AND THE BOOK OF MORMON

Ronald Reagan was given his first Book of Mormon in July 1967 by full-time elders serving in the Sacramento area and LDS members of the California legislature. Governor Reagan remarked at the time, "I have always admired the tremendous personal integrity and self-initiative of the Latter-day Saint people, and on a number of occasions I refer to the programs of your Church as outstanding examples of what I feel to be the true American way." The event occurred during the legislative session, and Reagan quipped, "I may not complete reading the book before the end of the session, but I shall place it among my religious books and you can be assured that it shall not be forgotten."[11]

During the primary campaign of 1980, Richard B. Wirthlin was accompanying Reagan at a speech in Peoria, Illinois. During the speech Reagan broke away from his usual cadence and words and said that he wanted to share with them a feeling he had had for a long time—that America was a very special land, bound between two great oceans, attracting to its shores freedom-loving people led by the hand of God. "He was almost quoting Nephi," Wirthlin recalled. "Later in the plane I pulled out my Book of Mormon and read him that scripture (2 Nephi 1:5–7). He said 'I've always believed that very, very strongly my whole life.'"[12]

A similar experience is shared by the Republican National Committee chair at the time, Latter-day Saint Richard Richards. "I was in the President's car, along with Chief of Staff James Baker, traveling to visit the church cannery in Ogden," said Richards, "and I was sharing with them the Book of Mormon teaching that this country is a blessed and chosen land." President Reagan said he agreed with this and also agreed with Richards that Columbus was inspired by the Holy Ghost and that the Founding Fathers were raised up by God to form this nation. "I can't believe that it was mere chance that all of these brilliant men came together when and how they did," said Reagan. "I agree with the Mormons that God had a hand in it."[13]

Reagan was very aware of the Book of Mormon teachings about America's special role and destiny. In thanking the Mormon Tabernacle Choir for singing at his inaugural, he told them that he

President Gordon B. Hinckley reading from the writings of Ether in the Book of Mormon to President Ronald W. Reagan: "Behold this is a choice land, and whatsoever nation shall possess it shall be free from bondage, and from captivity, and from all other nations under heaven, if they will but serve the God of the land, who is Jesus Christ."

and Nancy "want you to know that we share your love for America and your conviction that America is a special land blessed by God with a divine purpose."[14] After leaving the White House, he spoke at Brigham Young University and shared a theme he knew always resonated with the Mormons: "I believe there was a divine plan that placed this great continent here between the two oceans to be found by peoples from every corner of the earth. I believe we were preordained to carry the lamp of freedom for the world."[15]

When asked if he ever discussed the Book of Mormon or other LDS doctrines with President Reagan, Utah senator Orrin Hatch replied, "Yes, and I brought people in to him that did, too. He was very friendly to the Church."[16]

*President Reagan, with his LDS scriptures in hand, converses with President Ezra Taft Benson in the conference room of the Church Administration Building.*

President Reagan once wrote a letter of encouragement and support to Senator Jake Garn's son, who was preparing to leave for a mission in England. He even quoted the Book of Mormon in the letter. It came about as a result of a conversation Garn had had with the President at the end of a routine White House meeting with Senate leadership. They were discussing their sons and the topic of missions came up. "That's a real sacrifice for a young man of nineteen to leave his parents for two years," said the President. "Actually, it's harder on the parents," Garn explained, pointing out how they can only call twice a year and so they eagerly await letters from their missionary, which they are only allowed to write on P-day. "P-day?" replied the puzzled chief executive. "It stands for preparation day," explained the senator. "It is one day a week where they get caught up on laundry, write home, and other non-missionary things." Reagan then asked if there was any limit on the number of letters a missionary could receive, and upon learning "no," he said, "Maybe I should write your missionary son a letter, then." Garn said that that would be wonderful.[17] In the letter, Reagan not only offered words of admiration, respect and encouragement, but also quoted Alma 60:11:

> Behold, could ye suppose that ye could sit upon your thrones,
> and because of the exceeding goodness of God ye could do noth-
> ing and he would deliver you? Behold, if ye have supposed this ye
> have supposed in vain.

President Reagan said, "I have often thought about these words. They came back to me during the campaign, especially when it would be a long day and one that didn't go as well as we had hoped. I thought of them when I was in the hospital, and they have been on my mind since Jake told me that you would soon be leaving on your mission to England."[18]

In the spring of 1984, Ezra Taft Benson, then president of the Quorum of the Twelve Apostles, engaged President Reagan in some correspondence regarding the Book of Mormon. On one occasion he sent the commander in chief lengthy passages from the Book of Mormon about America's divine destiny and concluded with his testimony: "This nation is the Lord's base of operations in these latter days. Here the gospel of Jesus Christ was restored. Here God the Father and His Son, Jesus Christ, appeared to the young man Joseph Smith, which to me is the greatest event that has transpired in this world since the resurrection of the Master." In his reply, Reagan agreed America was a "specially favored land," adding that "as long as Americans have respected spiritual leaders such as yourself, our nation will . . . do wonders in the world."[19] When Ezra Taft Benson became Church president the following year, Reagan sent his congratulations to the stalwart Book of Mormon advocate: "This office is a fitting tribute to your unwavering devotion to your faith and your dedication to the word of God."[20]

The Book of Mormon became a major discussion point when President Reagan visited Church leaders on 4 September 1984, during the height of his reelection campaign. He met for twenty minutes with the First Presidency, the Quorum of the Twelve, and the general presidents of the Primary, Young Women, and Relief Society organizations. As part of the meeting, President Hinckley of the First Presidency joked with Reagan that it was hard to know what to get the man who has everything. He then presented Ronald Reagan with a special leather-bound copy of the LDS scriptures, including the Book of Mormon. He turned to the book of Ether and read to the President chapter two, verse twelve:

> Behold this is a choice land, and whatsoever nation shall possess it shall be free from bondage, and from captivity, and from all other nations under heaven, if they will but serve the God of the land, who is Jesus Christ, who hath been manifested by the things which we have written.

President Hinckley then told President Reagan, "In the Church's view, personal honesty, integrity and a reliance on the Creator form the foundation of the needed strength to confront the overwhelming problems the nation faces." He also affirmed that the Church is nonpartisan and cited a need for men and women of judgment and wisdom from all walks of life to join in efforts to serve the prophetic promise of freedom cited in the Book of Mormon. Reagan shared that he had "the same sense of the destiny of the United States" as expressed in the Book of Mormon and that "those who came to this country for religious freedom were much more successful than those who came for gold."

President Hinckley told the chief executive that the leaders of the Church prayed for him regularly and asked if the visit could conclude with a benediction. Reagan agreed, and President Hinckley invited Elder Dallin H. Oaks of the Twelve to offer the prayer. President Hinckley recorded in his journal:

> Brother Oaks gave a beautiful prayer. I felt that the president was deeply touched in his heart. He was most appreciative as he left us, and I felt that the Lord had answered our prayers, that we had been involved in a most significant occasion when a member of the First Presidency, representing the President of the Church, had read to the president of the United States . . . the word of the Lord concerning this nation and the Constitution which was framed by men whom the God of heaven had raised up unto this very purpose.[21]

While Reagan was in his post-presidency, yet before his Alzheimer's set in, a college-age young woman from Provo was interning at the Reagan Library in California. Once when a member of her Utah home ward was visiting—who happened to be a huge fan of Reagan's—she was able to arrange a brief meeting for them in Reagan's office. As a parting gift, the ward member gave the ex-President a copy of the Book of Mormon, which he politely received. Days later, the intern walked into Reagan's office to deliver a message and found him with his back to the doorway, deeply consumed in reading the Book of Mormon.[22]

## REAGAN'S LOVE OF THE MORMON TABERNACLE CHOIR

"He loved the Tabernacle Choir," said Richard B. Wirthlin of President Reagan, "and had few specific requests for the inaugural, but one of them was to have the Mormon Tabernacle Choir participate."[23] Reagan himself later recalled, "At my first inauguration as President of the United States, I wanted very much to re-ignite the fires of liberty and re-inspire the American Spirit. And no one sings the anthems of America quite like the Mormon Tabernacle Choir."[24] So the choir participated in their third presidential inauguration, and for their first time in the inaugural parade in January 1981.

The Saturday night before Reagan's inaugural, an opening ceremony for the festivities was held at the Lincoln Memorial, where the choir performed for the President-Elect and his guests. As the choir sang, both of the Reagans fought back tears. Reagan later said of the moment, "I've never been filled with such a surge of patriotism. It was so hard not to cry during the whole thing. That choir, the Mormon Tabernacle Choir, singing 'God Bless America.' Well, it was cold, but it was so moving, I was crying frozen tears."[25]

On the day of the President's swearing-in, the choir was the final entry in the inaugural parade and paused in front of the chief executive's review stand to sing. A CBS television commentator said that if it were possible to "bring the house down at an outdoor parade, the Mormon Tabernacle Choir just did it."[26] In Nancy Reagan's account of the festivities, only two entries are mentioned, both of which had her Ron "a little misty-eyed": the band from Ronnie's hometown of Dixon, Illinois, and "the final float in the parade," which "held the entire Mormon Tabernacle Choir, which stopped in front of us to sing 'The Battle Hymn of the Republic,' which Ronnie and I both love."[27] The President himself later noted, "The choir's singing was a highlight of our inauguration, as we knew it would be. . . . There is no more inspirational moment for any American—and that includes Ronald Reagan—than to hear the Mormon Tabernacle Choir sing 'Glory, glory hallelujah, His truth is marching on.'"[28]

Presidents Gordon B. Hinckley, Ronald W. Reagan, and Ezra Taft Benson pose for a photo with the President's new leather-bound scriptures at the conclusion of their visit at Church headquarters.

It was Ronald Reagan that christened the choir "America's Choir"[29] and referred to them as "America's most renowned musical ensemble."[30] Reagan not only appreciated the choir for their musical abilities, but also for the church they represented. "It isn't just your inspirational singing that moves us," he once told them. "It's also the heritage of faith and self-reliance you represent, a heritage handed down from your pioneer forebears who carved homes out of a barren wilderness."

In 1989, when the Mormon Tabernacle Choir celebrated sixty years of weekly broadcasts, a videotaped congratulation was sent by former President Reagan, which was included in their milestone broadcast. In that tribute to the choir he said, "Walt Whitman once wrote: 'I hear America singing.' Well, I do too. And often I hear her in the voices of the Mormon Tabernacle Choir."[31]

## MORMONS IN THE REAGAN WHITE HOUSE

After his 1980 election, Reagan began appointing people to positions in the new administration, and a surprisingly high number were LDS. Stephen M. Studdert, a Latter-day Saint who had been the police chief of Brigham City and later assisted the Reagan campaign as an advance man, listed a number of them:

> Three of us, David Fischer, Gregory Newell and I, served on his personal White House staff. Richard B. Wirthlin was his chief strategist. Ted Bell served as Secretary of Education, Angela Buchanan was Treasurer, Rex Lee was Solicitor General. His White House included Roger Porter [economic policy advisor], Brent Scowcroft [chair of Commission on Strategic Forces], Richard Beal [Special Assistant for National Security], Blake Parish, Jon Huntsman Jr. [advance staff], Dodie Borup [Commissioner for Children, Youth and Families] and Rocky Kuonen [advance staff], and there were many other Latter-day Saints throughout his Administration. President Thomas S. Monson served on a Presidential Commission on Volunteerism. Others were ambassadors. LDS senators and representatives were held in special regard.[32]

*10 September 1982: President Reagan visited the Church's welfare cannery in Ogden, Utah, to see how the Church's welfare system worked firsthand. Afterward he remarked, "What I think is that if more people had this idea back when the Great Depression hit, there wouldn't be any government welfare today, or need for it."*

David C. Fischer, as special assistant to the President, was one of the first to see Reagan each morning, one of the last to see him each night, and accompanied him on all of his travels.[33] Ronald M. Mann served as an assistant to President Reagan from 1981 to 1987 and was appointed by the President to head the National Bicentennial Commission on the Constitution.[34] Prominent Latter-day Saint George Romney, former governor of Michigan and Nixon cabinet member, was appointed by Ronald Reagan to his Private Sector Initiatives Task Force.[35] Reagan also appointed LDS ambassadors, including Keith Foote Nyborg, a returned missionary from Finland, who was named ambassador to Finland.[36] Richard Eyre was appointed by President Reagan as director of the White House Conference on Children and Parents and later as a member of the President's advisory panel on financing elementary and secondary education.[37] Arch L. Madsen, the president of KSL and Bonneville International, was appointed by Reagan to the Board for International Broadcasting, overseeing the operation of Radio Free Europe and Radio Liberty.[38] The list could go on and on of the Mormons who served in the Reagan administration in some capacity or another over his eight-year presidency. "Ronald Reagan truly admired the Latter-day Saints," said Studdert. "His administration included more members of the Church than any other American president, ever."[39]

But why did the Presbyterian chief executive have so many Saints involved in his presidency? "The reason Ronald Reagan had so many Mormons in his administration is because the few Mormon staffers he started with from his days in California tended to bring in fellow Mormons," said Bay Buchanan, "not because Reagan purposely sought after staffers based on religion."[40] Richard B. Wirthlin disagrees and points out that Reagan liked having Mormon staffers because "he felt an affinity with us, he knew our beliefs, he trusted us, he appreciated the Word of Wisdom and that we didn't smoke. I think he had a comfort level with members of the Church philosophically."[41] Senator Orrin Hatch agreed. "Some of Reagan's closest friends were LDS," said Hatch. "Some of his closest advisors were LDS. He had a healthy respect for the Church. Basically, he was one of the most tolerant people I've met in my life, one of the sweetest people I've met in my life."[42]

## REAGAN'S ADMIRATION FOR THE CHURCH WELFARE PROGRAM

As governor of California, Ronald Reagan had an opportunity to tour an LDS welfare facility in Sacramento, a facility which greatly impressed him.[43] During the 1980 transition, the President-Elect had a very thorough briefing on national welfare problems by a number of experts he had brought in. At the end of their presentations, he said, "You know, there is a program that comes very close to being the most ideal way of dealing with those who are poor and unfortunate; and that is the Mormon Welfare Program." Richard B. Wirthlin, who was at the briefing, was then caught by surprise when Reagan began describing very specific details about the program. "At the time I was the counselor in a stake presidency who dealt with welfare issues, but somehow he knew as much as I did and knew very much in detail about the program. He had apparently learned about it long before from some LDS colleague, and with his brilliant memory remembered every detail, because he very much admired the program."[44]

On 24 October 1981, Elder Thomas S. Monson along with community and business leaders met with President Reagan in Salt Lake City, where President Reagan praised the Church welfare program.[45] Elder Monson related the following:

> In 1982 it was my privilege to serve as a member of President Ronald Reagan's Task Force on Private Sector Initiatives. Meeting in the White House with prominent leaders assembled from throughout the nation, President Reagan paid tribute to the welfare program of the Church. He observed: "Elder Monson is here representing The Church of Jesus Christ of Latter-day Saints. If, during the period of the Great Depression, every church had come forth with a welfare program founded on correct principles as his church did, we would not be in the difficulty in which we find ourselves today." President Reagan praised self-sufficiency; lauded our storehouse, production, and distribution system; and emphasized family members assisting one another. He urged that in our need we turn not to government but rather to ourselves.[46]

On 10 September 1982, President Reagan visited Utah to tour the Ogden Area Welfare Service Center and observe the program firsthand. Guided on the tour by President Gordon B. Hinckley and Elder Monson, Reagan said, "[It's] far superior to anything the government has been able to manage."[47] He lamented admiringly, "Oh that our federal welfare worked so perfectly."[48] President Hinckley enjoyed hosting Reagan and noted afterward that he felt the nation's President was a man of integrity.[49]

During the President's tour of the cannery, Sam Donaldson, the ABC News White House correspondent who was there, shoved a microphone toward the President and asked him about some recent legislation. Clearly annoyed, Reagan said tersely, "Sam, why don't you pay attention to what is going on here. The potential to help people with this kind of concept is very important."[50] He went on to say to the press corps, "Here is an entire industry, as you can see [pointing to shelves of

*President Gordon B. Hinckley conducted President Reagan on his tour of the Church's cannery. "[It's] far superior to anything the government has been able to manage," Reagan remarked. "Oh that our federal welfare worked so perfectly."*

*President Ronald Reagan, shown on his tour of a Church welfare facility with President Gordon B. Hinckley. Reagan once remarked to some White House advisors, "You know, there is a program that comes very close to being the most ideal way of dealing with those who are poor and unfortunate; and that is the Mormon Welfare Program."*

food packaged at the cannery]. It is manned by volunteers, people from the Church. The foodstuffs that are here are raised by volunteers, picked by volunteers. . . . And they're used to distribute to those people who have real need here in the state of Utah and all over the country, for that matter." Reagan told the media at the cannery, "What I think is that if more people had this idea back when the Great Depression hit, there wouldn't be any government welfare today, or need for it."

After the half-hour visit to the cannery, the President spoke to 17,000 at a picnic in Hooper. "This is almost as big a crowd as an Osmond family reunion," he said to the crowd. Reagan shared with them how impressed he was with the cannery he had just toured and the spirit of volunteerism there. "It's an idea that once characterized our nation. It's an idea that should be reborn nationwide. It holds the key to the renewal of America in the years ahead."[51] As they drove to the picnic, Congressman Jim Hansen rode with him. "I was in Reagan's limo and someone held up a sign that said, 'Welcome President Hansen.' Reagan said, 'Who is president here?' I explained that I had been the president of an LDS stake, and then explained what that meant," Hansen recalled. "[Afterward] he would always joke about me being the other president."

In 1984, President Reagan made a courtesy call on the General Authorities and officers of the Church. After the meeting, President Hinckley and General Relief Society President Barbara W. Winder took the chief executive on a tour of Welfare Square, where they pointed out once again the concept of self-reliance and helping oneself while helping others.[52]

"I think Reagan's philosophy was similar to most Latter-day Saints," Barbara Winder later observed. "He was especially impressed with the Church's welfare efforts, and how people were able to help themselves."[53]

## THE MX MISSLE CONTROVERSY

In 1981 Ronald Reagan called for a plan to build 200 MX missiles and shuttle them back and forth among 4,600 shelters in the Nevada and Utah desert. In May, the Church's First Presidency issued a strongly worded statement opposing the location of this "mammoth weapons system potentially capable of destroying much of civilization."[54] The LDS opposition was a major obstacle for the MX plan. Reagan biographer Lou Cannon noted, "The Mormon opposition was a psychological blow to MX. It ratified [Secretary of Defense Caspar] Weinberger's belief that the MX/MPS system faced insurmountable obstacles."[55] Weinberger persuaded the President that pushing ahead with the project in light of strong Mormon opposition was "bad Republican politics." After all, Utah had given the President his highest margin of victory, and Church members played increasingly important roles in the GOP.[56]

Senator Hatch noted, "I have no doubt that when the LDS Church came out against the MX proposal that was the end of it. He [Reagan] respected the Church, and he respected the rights of the Church."[57] Others close to the President interviewed by the author confirmed this. It was because of the LDS influence that Reagan was persuaded to back off. The ultimate decision to not place MX missiles in the Great Basin, according to author Lou Cannon, was made as a "political solution, meeting the needs of the western senators and the Mormon Church."[58]

## REAGAN'S RELIGION AND MORMONISM

"Ronald Reagan had a basic spiritual dimension which led to a warm and close bond with the Church, " Richard B. Wirthlin said. "His own beliefs were in many ways very congruent with the Church. He also felt an affinity to the Church concerning our beliefs in agency, and agreed that a future Armageddon was very real and would originate in the Middle East. He definitely believed in the Second Coming of Jesus Christ and also that there would be a great conflict before He came."[59] For example, in 1980 Reagan declared that we were in the last days. "We may be the generation that sees Armageddon," he said.[60]

Ronald Reagan once said to Utah senator Jake Garn, "I think I'd have a little trouble with that anti-coffee thing" if he were a Mormon. He continued, "What do you call that anti-coffee thing?" Garn replied that it was called the Word of Wisdom. "Well there must be some value to it," quipped Reagan, "because all of your leadership are *so* old but in such good health!"[61]

On 30 March 1981, an assassination attempt wounded the President. LDS Secret Service agent (and future Independence Missouri Stake president) C. Kent Wood helped subdue John Hinckley Jr., whose gunshot had missed the President's heart by less than one inch, puncturing his lung instead.[62] In general conference President Kimball requested all members to pray for the chief executive's speedy recovery.[63] A miraculously recovered Reagan later related to Richard B. Wirthlin, RNC chair Dick Richards, and other Latter-day Saints that he felt he was saved by Divine Providence to finish his presidency and to help bring peace and prosperity to America.[64] "Not many people realize how close President Reagan came to not making it," said his LDS personal aide Dave Fischer. "I stayed up with him the entire first night in the recovery room. There are no questions in my mind, and I know there are none in his because he and I have talked about it a great deal, that the Lord saved his life."[65]

In 1984 the Commander in Chief made a historic trip to China, which was largely facilitated by a young Jon M. Huntsman Jr., who did advance work for the White House. While the President was in China, Huntsman heard him tell the Chinese that the reason America was great was because of their faith and trust in God. Future ambassador and governor Huntsman said he thought to himself at the time, "The president is not a Mormon, but he's the best missionary we have here at this moment."[66]

## OTHER REAGAN VISITS WITH CHURCH LEADERS AND PROMINENT SAINTS

Not long after taking office, President Reagan hosted President Spencer W. Kimball and Elder Gordon B. Hinckley.[67] President Kimball related,

> Friday, March 13, in company with Elder Gordon B. Hinckley, we visited with President Ronald Reagan in the Oval Office of the White House. We presented to him his genealogy on his mother's side. We then met with Mrs. Reagan. Both were very warm and gracious and very appreciative of the genealogical record.[68]

President Kimball told the President, "We pray for you to be sustained in every righteous endeavor." Reagan responded that he believed in the value of intercessory prayer. Nancy Reagan

*6 January 1986: Less than two months after being ordained president of the Church, Ezra Taft Benson visited Ronald Reagan in the Oval Office, where he was received with warmth and affection. President Benson presented Reagan with a personalized edition of the new Church hymnbook, and the two discussed world hunger and the recent gift of $10 million from the Church to the world hunger fund, which was raised by special fasts held throughout the Church.*

came out later and said that her husband was delighted with the book, from which the President learned for the first time that one of his ancestors fought in the Civil War.[69]

In 1983 General Relief Society President Barbara B. Smith was invited to a state dinner in honor of the Emir of Bahrain and was seated at the President's table along with the NBA's Moses Malone and astronaut Sally Ride. "I can only think of one reason I was invited," she said. "It was a recognition of Mormon women as a viable force in society."[70]

President Ezra Taft Benson called on Ronald Reagan in the Oval Office on 6 January 1986. "President Benson was warmly greeted by President Reagan," said Church member Steve Studdert, who was there as an aide to Reagan. "It was evident to me that President Reagan greeted him with feelings of fondness and affection." In the ten-minute visit, Reagan commented to the former cabinet member, "This must be like home to you."[71] A main point of conversation was world hunger and the recent gift of $10 million from the Church to the world hunger fund, which was raised by special fasts held throughout the Church. He also presented the chief executive with a personalized edition of the new Church hymnbook.[72]

In 1988, Elder John C. Carmack of the Seventy met with Reagan when the latter presented the Church with a President's Historic Preservation Award for renovating the Newel K. Whitney store in Kirtland, Ohio.[73] According to one aide close to Reagan, "Virtually every contact he had with the leaders of the Church during his administration he felt were positive meetings."[74]

In addition to Church leaders, Ronald Reagan also met with a large number of prominent Mormons. Sharlene Wells visited Reagan during her reign as Miss America. He sang with Donny and Marie Osmond, and he visited with Atlanta Braves all-star Dale Murphy after the outfielder was named Sportsman of the Year by *Sports Illustrated*.[75] BYU football coach LaVell Edwards visited Reagan in the White House, where he presented him with a football signed by all the players of the championship team of 1984. Reagan prominently displayed the ball on a shelf in his personal study, adjoining the Oval Office. Leaders of the Mormon Youth Symphony and Chorus also met with Reagan to present all seven of their albums and a bronze replica of the Nauvoo Monument to Women for Reagan to give to his wife.[76]

Even after leaving the White House, Reagan was a friend to the Mormons. At the request of Rex Lee, his former solicitor general who was then president of Brigham Young University, the former President spoke at BYU in 1991. "I have great admiration for your school here. I know how great it is and know how successful you are in so many ways," he told the students. "BYU is strong, a birthplace of many talented leaders and athletes." Reagan was presented with a plaque commemorating his visit; a video copy *of A More Perfect Union, America Becomes A Nation,* produced by the BYU Motion Picture Studio; and a BYU Cougars sweatshirt. Also during that visit he paid a courtesy call at Church headquarters, where he was greeted by President Gordon B. Hinckley, President Thomas S. Monson, and members of the Quorum of the Twelve. After the forty-five-minute visit, President Hinckley presented Reagan with a statue of a white seagull.[77]

Today, Ronald Reagan has a permanent place in the heart of many Mormons due to his remarkable interest in the programs of the Church and for his admiration of the values the Saints espouse. Richard B. Wirthlin commented, "I've been associated with six presidents, and Reagan was so far ahead of the others in how he knew, understood, and appreciated the Church."[78]

# ENDNOTES

1   "President Reagan Praises Church's Accomplishments," *Church News,* 1 August 1987, 5. See also *Church News,* "President Reagan Respected Church," 12 June 2004, 7.

2   Quinn, *The Mormon Hierarchy: Origins of Power,* ix.

3   See listing for "Rhonda Fleming," online at http://www.ldsfilm.com/bioActress.html.

4   "Leader's Many Visits to Utah Left a Deep Imprint on Residents," *Deseret Morning News,* 6 June 2004.

5   *Dave Leip's Atlas of U.S. Presidential Elections.*

6   Richard B. Wirthlin, interview by author, 14 June 2006.

7   "For at Least 35 Years, LDS Have Participated in Inaugurations," *Church News,* 28 January 1989. See also *Church News,* "Choir a smash hit at inaugural," 24 January 1981, 3.

8   *Dave Leip's Atlas of U.S. Presidential Elections.* See also, Donald Q. Cannon, ed., *Encyclopedia of Latter-Day Saint History,* s.v. "Republican Party."

9   "President Reagan Respected Church," *Church News,* 12 June 2004, 7.

10  "'It Is Our Job to Make a Difference,'" *Church News,* 19 June 2004, 4.

11  "Scriptures Given Gov. Reagan," *Church News,* 22 July 1967, 6.

12  Wirthlin, interview, 14 June 2006.

13  Richards, interview, 26 July 2006.

14  "Reagan Thanks Choir for 'Gift of Love for America,'" *Church News,* 21 March 1981, 6.

15  "Reagan Visits BYU, Church Leaders," *Church News,* 23 February 1991.

16  Hatch, interview, 30 May 2006.

17  Garn, interview, 2 August 2006.

18  *Church News,* June 1982.

19  Ezra Taft Benson to Ronald Reagan, 29 May 1984, and Ronald Reagan to Ezra Taft Benson, 17 July 1984, quoted in Dew, *Ezra Taft Benson,* 470.

20  Ronald Reagan to Ezra Taft Benson, 13 November 1985, quoted in Dew, *Ezra Taft Benson,* 485.

21  Gordon B. Hinckley Journal, 4 September 1984, quoted in Dew, *Go Forward with Faith,* 407. See also "Campaign Trail Leads to Utah," *Church News,* 9 September 1984, 3, 10; McCune, *Gordon B. Hinckley: Shoulder for the Lord,* 500–502.

22  As related to the author. Source wishes to remain anonymous.

23  Wirthlin, interview, 14 June 2006.

24  "Choir Looks Back on 60 Years of Broadcasting 'Voice of Peace,'" *Church News,* 22 July 1989.

25  Lou Cannon, *Reagan,* 18.

26  "For at Least 35 Years, LDS Have Participated in Inaugurations," *Church News,* 28 January 1989.

27  Nancy Reagan, *My Turn: The Memoirs of Nancy Reagan,* 198.

28  "For at Least 35 Years, LDS Have Participated in Inaugurations," *Church News,* 28 January 1989.

29  "President Reagan Respected Church," *Church News,* 12 June 2004, 7.

30   "Choir Touches Lives in 25,000-Mile South Pacific Tour," *Church News,* 9 July 1988.

31   "Choir Looks Back on 60 Years of Broadcasting 'Voice of Peace,'" *Church News,* 22 July 1989.

32   "President Reagan Respected Church," *Church News,* 12 June 2004, 7.

33   "That's Not Just a Friend; That's the President," *Church News,* 11 September 1983, 5.

34   "President Reagan Respected Church," *Church News,* 12 June 2004, 7.

35   "BYU Names Institute of Public Management after George Romney," *Church News,* 25 April 1998, 5.

36   *Ensign,* 3 May 1986.

37   Eyre, "About the author."

38   "Renowned Broadcaster Eulogized," *Church News,* 19 April 1997, 10.

39   "President Reagan Respected Church," *Church News,* 12 June 2004, 7.

40   Angela "Bay" Buchanan, interview by author, 13 May 2006.

41   Wirthlin, interview, 14 June 2006.

42   Hatch, interview, 30 May 2006.

43   "Pres. Reagan Sees How LDS Care for Own," *Church News,* 18 September 1982, 3, 8.

44   Wirthlin, interview, 14 June 2006.

45   Holzapfel, et al., *On this Day in the Church,* 207.

46   Thomas S. Monson, "A Provident Plan—A Precious Promise," *Ensign,* May 1986, 62.

47   Wirthlin, interview, 14 June 2006.

48   "President Reagan Respected Church," *Church News,* 12 June 2004, 7.

49   Dew, *Go Forward with Faith,* 393.

50   Richards, interview, 26 July 2006.

51   "Pres. Reagan Sees How LDS Care for Own," *Church News,* 18 September 1982, 3, 8.

52   McCune, *Gordon B. Hinckley: Shoulder for the Lord,* 500–502. See also "Leader's Many Visits to Utah Left a Deep Imprint on Residents," *Deseret Morning News,* 6 June 2004.

53   Author's conversation with Barbara W. Winder, 13 May 2006.

54   "Statement of the First Presidency on Basing of the MX Missile," *Church News,* 9 May 1981, 2.

55   Lou Cannon, *Reagan,* 389.

56   Lou Cannon, *President Reagan: The Role of a Lifetime,* 164–65.

57   Hatch, interview, 30 May 2006.

58   Lou Cannon, *Reagan,* 392. This conclusion is affirmed in Allen and Leonard, *The Story of the Latter-day Saints,* 660.

59   Wirthlin, interview, 14 June 2006. See also "Opinion Researcher Knows Gospel Values Are Strong Motivators," *Church News,* 15 June 1996.

60   Jon Meacham, *American Gospel: God, the Founding Fathers, and the Making of a Nation,* 223.

61   Garn, interview, 2 August 2006.

62   *Church News,* "Flag Day—July 4: A Period of Patriotism," 3 July 2004, 6.

63   Spencer W. Kimball, "We Are on the Lord's Errand," *Ensign,* May 1981, 78.

64  Wirthlin, interview, 14 June 2006. See also Richards, interview, 26 July 2006.

65  "That's Not Just a Friend; That's the President," *Church News,* 11 September 1983, 14.

66  "China: Presidential Trip a Highlight of His Life," *Church News,* 13 May 1984, 5–6.

67  Holzapfel, et al., *On this Day in the Church,* 50.

68  Spencer W. Kimball, "A Report of My Stewardship," *Ensign,* May 1981, 5.

69  "Pres. Kimball Visits with Pres. Reagan," *Church News,* 21 March 1981, 3.

70  "'Like Cinderella,' in White House," *Church News,* 7 August 1983.

71  "Prophet Is 'At Home' in Capital," *Church News,* 12 January 1986, 3.

72  Gibbons, *The Expanding Church,* 131. See also Dew, *Ezra Taft Benson,* 490.

73  "Whitney Store Receives Presidential Award," *Church News,* 26 November 1988.

74  Wirthlin, interview, 14 June 2006.

75  "LDS Athlete Dale Murphy Receives Honor from Magazine," *Church News,* 16 January 1988.

76  "Chorus Presents Music, Statue to Pres. Reagan," *Church News,* 1 January 1983.

77  "Reagan Visits BYU, Church Leaders," *Church News,* 23 February 1991. See also "Year in Review: 1991," *Church News,* 28 December 1991.

78  Wirthlin, interview, 14 June 2006.

# GEORGE BUSH

## *1989–1993*

George Herbert Walker Bush maintained the warm relationship with the Mormons that his predecessor built. Bush utilized LDS talent in his administration; his National Security Advisor, Brent Scowcroft, became a close associate of the President and coauthor of his memoirs. He loved the Tabernacle Choir, having them sing at his inauguration. He even made a spontaneous visit to one of their concerts. The forty-first President met with Church leaders on numerous occasions, both in Washington and in Salt Lake City, where the General Authorities appreciated his decency, piety, and openness. He also became the first sitting President to speak at BYU, and he campaigned for his LDS friends even after leaving the White House. Senator Orrin Hatch summarized the relationship well: "The first President Bush was a very tolerant man who recognized and appreciated the contribution of the Latter-day Saints."[1]

**1944:** Lieutenant George Bush's aircraft is shot down at the Bonin Islands, and he is rescued by the submarine USS *Finback*. Aboard the Finback with him for a month is Latter-day Saint Calvin McPhie. "On a submarine, you get to know everyone quite well," says McPhie, and the two friends exchange Christmas cards each year thereafter.[2]

**29 January 1982:** Vice President Bush makes his first official visit to Utah and meets with Church leaders. He is presented a replica of the Monument to Women statue by President N. Eldon Tanner of the First Presidency. Another visit to Church headquarters occurs on 2 September 1982.[3]

**January 1986:** While in Washington D.C. new LDS Church President Ezra Taft Benson meets with Bush in the vice president's office and gives him a leather-bound copy of the new LDS hymnbook. "I hope I'm not expected to sing," he quips. President Benson briefed Bush on the LDS aid that's been raised to help with famine relief in Africa. Bush replies that he has already heard good things about the Mormon Church's efforts toward famine relief. "I am not a member of your Church but I have great respect for the Mormon people," he says. He expounds on his friendship with former cabinet member George Romney and hotelier J. Willard Marriott.[4]

**February 1986:** Vice President and Mrs. Bush visit with Presidents Benson and Hinckley, several Apostles, and general Church officers in the Church Administration Building. They talk about the growth of the Church throughout the world, and Barbara Bush is given a ceramic sculpture of a seagull by President Benson, who explains to them the account of the seagulls saving the pioneer crop from crickets.[5]

**November 1988:** Bush wins the presidency. In Utah, Bush beats Dukakis 66 percent to 32 percent, winning all counties but Carbon. Mormons support Bush nationally more than any other religious group. One 1988 study showed that 46 percent of the Latter-day Saints in the United States are Republican, compared with 27 percent of Protestants, 18 percent of Catholics, and 11 percent of Jews.[6]

*29 January 1982: Vice President Bush makes his first official visit to Utah and meets with Church leaders. He is presented a replica of the Monument to Women statue by President N. Eldon Tanner of the First Presidency, since President Spencer W. Kimball's health at the time prohibited him from participating in the meeting. (L–R) N. Eldon Tanner, Barbara Bush, Vice President Bush, Marion G. Romney, and Gordon B. Hinckley.*

*Bush visits again with Church leaders in a February 1986 trip to Utah. (L–R) Vice President Bush, Ezra Taft Benson, Gordon B. Hinckley, and Barbara Bush. Bush once said to President Benson, "I am not a member of your Church but I have great respect for the Mormon people."*

**January 1989:** Bush invites the Tabernacle Choir to perform at his inauguration.

**August 1989:** President Bush honors Ezra Taft Benson with the Presidential Citizens Medal. "Your service has been the very model of selfless devotion and compassion," Bush says when announcing the award via video during the prophet's ninetieth birthday celebration. "No matter how difficult the task, no matter how distant the problem, you've always been willing to extend a helping hand to those in trouble." He sends Brent Scowcroft to Utah to bestow the medal—second in significance only to the Presidential Medal of Freedom.[7]

**18 September 1991:** Bush enjoys a half-hour meeting in the Church Administration Building with General Authorities and auxiliary officers. In the meeting they discuss the Church's global expansion, humanitarian projects, and their concern about the deterioration of America's families. President Elaine Jack speaks of the Relief Society's efforts to promote literacy, which has also been an initiative of Barbara Bush's.[8]

# BUSH AND THE TABERNACLE CHOIR

Presidents Ezra Taft Benson and Thomas S. Monson represented the Church at Bush's inauguration on 19 January 1989, in which the Mormon Tabernacle Choir participated. The choir was one of the few "national" entries in the parade, because Bush felt they represented members of the Church worldwide and not just a single state. The choir had the honor of being the final entry in the parade and paused in front of the presidential reviewing stand to sing "The Battle Hymn of the Republic." "He [Bush] sang along with us," said choir member Dee Hemeyer. "He kind of waved, and wiped away a tear." The new President referred to them on this occasion as the "nation's choir."[9]

President Bush would later pay tribute to the choir on the anniversary of their sixtieth year of broadcasting, calling them "one of America's greatest treasures."[10] "He sincerely loved the choir," noted Senator Hatch.[11] This love was evidenced once when he broke away from his busy travel schedule once to enjoy one of their concerts.

While in Salt Lake City in July 1992, the President decided to make a spontaneous visit to the Tabernacle Choir's pretour concert on Temple Square. Choir president Wendell M. Smoot received word at six thirty that the President would like to attend the seven-thirty concert. Smoot said he did not know how President Bush learned of the concert or what prompted him to attend.

> He came unobtrusively and unannounced to be in our audience. When the crowd realized he was in the Tabernacle, they all arose to their feet and gave thunderous applause. He shook hands with people and waved as he walked across the front part of the Tabernacle.
>
> I greeted him, and thanked him for coming. I reminded him of the marvelous experience the choir had in singing at his inauguration in 1989. President Bush said he was delighted to attend. He added that he just wanted to enjoy the concert.

The President sat on the twelfth row on the Tabernacle's main floor and promptly took off his jacket amid the heat of the Tabernacle. As President Smoot welcomed the audience to the concert, he said, "If there are any of you that would care to take your coats off, please follow the example of the president of the United States." President Bush stayed for the first half of the concert, leaving at intermission. "We were greatly honored to have President Bush attend the concert," said Smoot. "His presence was a great send-off for our tour, which is to commemorate the 500th anniversary of Columbus coming to America."[12]

*George Bush made a couple of trips to Utah as President, including the first-ever visit to Church-owned Brigham Young University by a sitting President. These tickets and snapshots by the author remain his mementos from the historic visits.*

## MORMONS IN THE BUSH ADMINISTRATION

After his election, President Bush announced that LDS member Lieutenant General Brent Scowcroft, who had also been national security advisor for President Ford, would serve as his national security advisor. Regarding Scowcroft, Senator Hatch remarked, "Although I don't believe he was very active in the Church, he was certainly friendly toward the Church and derived many of his values and morals from his faith, which he used to advise George Bush."[13] Scowcroft and Bush became so close that after Bush's presidency, they chose to write their memoirs together in the book *A World Transformed*.

In addition to Scowcroft, there were many Mormons serving in the Bush administration, including some who had served in the Reagan administration who continued on in various capacities. Stephen Studdert was a senior campaign adviser for Bush and served as executive director of Bush's inauguration.[14] Roger Porter was President Bush's economic and domestic policy adviser.[15] Jeffrey R. Holmstead worked in the Bush White House as an associate counsel, focusing on environmental policy.[16] Jay S. Bybee, future federal judge, was also an associate counsel to President Bush.[17] Jon Huntsman Jr., the future Utah governor, was appointed by Bush first as deputy assistant secretary of commerce in the International Trade Administration, and later as deputy assistant secretary of commerce for East Asian and Pacific Affairs. At age thirty-two, Huntsman Jr. was appointed by Bush as ambassador to Singapore, making him the youngest U.S. ambassador in a century.[18]

Dr. James O. Mason, who later served as a General Authority, served as head of the Centers for Disease Control (CDC) and was appointed by President Bush to serve as assistant secretary for

*President Gordon B. Hinckley (right) shares a laugh with former President Bush at the centennial commencement ceremonies for Southern Utah University in 1997.*

health and head of the U.S. Public Health Service in the Department of Health and Human Services.[19] Michael K. Young, future president of the University of Utah, served in the Bush administration as ambassador for trade and environmental affairs, deputy undersecretary for economic and agricultural affairs, and deputy legal advisor to the U.S. Department of State.[20] D. Michael Stewart, a former Salt Lake County commissioner, was appointed to the National Advisory Commission on International Relations.[21] L. Ralph Mecham, director of the Administrative Office of the United States Courts, was appointed by Bush to the National Advisory Council on Public Service.[22]

Following the Church's donation to the construction of a new interfaith chapel at Camp David, Elder M. Russell Ballard of the Quorum of the Twelve was invited to the building's dedication in May

1991. Elder Ballard told President Bush at the time that the members of the Church appreciate his leadership, especially in announcing a National Day of Prayer and National Day of Thanksgiving, and that the President and his family would be remembered in "our prayers." Bush thanked Elder Ballard for coming and talked about his respect for members of the Church, including "my good friend," Brent Scowcroft. "What a blessing it is to have as President and First Lady a couple with such deep-rooted feelings for the Savior," Elder Ballard said after attending the spiritual dedicatory service.[23]

## BUSH'S 1992 VISIT TO CHURCH HEADQUARTERS

During his campaign for reelection, the President stopped again in Utah, this time for a twenty-two-hour visit to the state on 17 July 1992. He met again with Presidents Hinckley and Monson and most of the Twelve in the Church Administration Building, where they discussed family values, religious freedom, the Church's humanitarian aid programs, the value of the Scouting program, and the Church's missionary program, especially its activities in the former Soviet Bloc. "President Bush congratulated the Church for the work it is doing with families and for the family values it holds," reported Bruce L. Olsen, managing director of Public Affairs for the Church. "President Hinckley and President Monson told him some of the things the Church does to foster family values, such as holding family home evenings and family prayer, studying the scriptures, and discussing plans for missions and college, and family budgeting." During the meeting, the General Authorities presented the chief executive with a statue entitled "The First Step," which depicts a child learning to walk, between her father and mother.

When asked afterward in the Administration Building's lobby what was discussed, Bush replied, "It was a total tour of the whole world. I learned a great deal from them." When the media asked a political question, the President said he was not going to answer the question "in this hallowed setting. It would be most inappropriate."[24] Regarding the incident, President Hinckley recorded in his journal, "I felt it was a classic answer, and the expression of a gentleman who carries respect for that which is good and sacred."[25] President Hinckley also recorded Bush's genuine interest in the LDS missionary program:

> We talked about our missionary work in various parts of the world. He asked how we go about opening a new country. He seemed sincerely curious. We told him the procedures we follow. We talked about our program to strengthen families. He was deeply interested. We were free to ask anything and he did not hesitate to respond. He talked openly and freely and in a very friendly way.

President Bush later wrote President Hinckley, "The fact that your church has an active mission program around the world is a wonderful thing. Not only does the program project commitment by the individual missionaries, but it also shows the church's concern for this wonderful but troubled world in which we live. You do care and that comes through loud and clear."[26]

That night he made his surprise appearance at the Tabernacle Choir's pretour concert, and the following morning the President addressed 15,000 people in BYU's Marriott Center. It was the first time in the university's 117-year history that a serving President had spoken there. During his address he had the largely LDS crowd on their feet wildly applauding when he quoted former Church President David O. McKay: "Americans need to understand something that you all know very, very well—no other success can compensate for failure in the home."[27]

## LDS INTERACTIONS IN BUSH'S POST-PRESIDENCY

While Bush was defeated in 1992 by Arkansas governor Bill Clinton, he retained support in Mormon Utah, where every county but one had a majority of voters supporting the incumbent.[28] Eighteen months later, upon learning of President Ezra Taft Benson's death, former President Bush sent a letter of condolence.[29] In March 1995 when Gordon B. Hinckley became the new Church president, George Bush wrote to him, "As you assume your important responsibilities, I just want to check in to wish you well and to pay my respects. I have great admiration for the work of the Church. I know your challenge will be great; but I also know you, and I am sure things will go well."[30]

When Elder Neal A. Maxwell was hospitalized for leukemia in 1997, he, too, received a letter from former President Bush, who had lost a daughter to the same disease. "Leukemia is a tough disease. We learned that the hard way years ago. But . . . medicine is making dramatic strides in treating [it]," wrote the forty-first President. "Barbara and I just wanted to wish you the speediest possible recovery." In his reply, Elder Maxwell informed the Bushes that the leukemia survival rate for children had moved from 17 to 70 percent since the death of their child.[31]

President Bush still goes out of his way to help LDS friends, like kicking off Senator Bob Bennett's 1998 reelection campaign (they had been friends since their fathers served in the U.S. Senate together). That year, the only candidate-stumping the forty-first President did was for his sons in Texas and Florida and for Bob Bennett. He also openly endorsed Jon Huntsman Jr. in 2004 in his bid for Utah's governorship even before the GOP primaries, reflecting the longtime friendship Bush has had with the Huntsmans, including Area Seventy and industrialist Jon M. Huntsman Sr. As a senior statesman, George Herbert Walker Bush continues to be a friend of the Mormons.

# ENDNOTES

1     Hatch, interview, 30 May 2006.

2     "Visit Offers Brief Reunion of World War II Buddies," *Church News,* 21 September 1991.

3     Holzapfel, et al., *On this Day in the Church,* 22. See also Gibbons, *Ezra Taft Benson,* 303.

4     "Prophet Is 'At Home' in Capital," *Church News,* 12 January 1986, 3, 12.

5     "Vice President Calls on Church Leaders," *Church News,* 2 March 1986, 7.

6     *Dave Leip's Atlas of U.S. Presidential Elections.* See also Donald Q. Cannon, *Encyclopedia of Latter-day Saint History,* s.v. "Republican Party."

7     "U.S. President 'Marvels at Achievements' of Idaho Farm Boy," *Church News,* 5 August 1989. See also "Prophet Receives U.S. Presidential Medal," *Church News,* 2 September 1989.

8     "Bush Visits with Church Leaders," *Church News,* 21 September 1991.

9     "'Nation's Choir' Performs at Inaugural Events," *Church News,* 4 February 1989. See also Holzapfel, et al., *On this Day in the Church,* 15; "A Chronological Reflection: The 1980s in Retrospect," *Church News,* 30 December 1989.

10     *Encyclopedia of Mormonism,* 951.

11     Hatch, interview, 30 May 2006.

12     "President Bush Lauds Church's Efforts To Bolster Family Values," *Church News,* 25 July 1992.

13     Hatch, interview, 30 May 2006. See also Skousen, *The Skousen Book of Mormon World Records,* 132–33.

14     "He Learned Priorities at Prophet's Side," *Church News,* 17 December 1988.

15     "Teen Addresses Congressional Committee," *Church News,* 2 April 1994. See also "LDS Leave Their Mark in Washington, D.C.," *Church News,* 2 December 1989.

16     "EPA Administrator Draws on Mission Experience," *Church News,* 15 March 2003.

17     "LDS Federal Judges Raising the Bar," *Church News,* 6 November 2004, 10.

18     "Ambassador's Term Brief, Yet Notable," *Church News,* 12 June 1993.

19     "'Vision': Watchword That Has Guided Life of General Authority," *Church News,* 14 May 1994.

20     Michael K. Young biography at http://www.admin.utah.edu/president/pres_bio.html

21     "New Mission Presidents," *Church News,* 17 January 1998.

22     "President Bush Appoints Church Leader To National Council on Public Safety," *Church News,* 5 September 1992.

23     "Elder Ballard Attends Dedication of Chapel at Presidential Retreat," *Church News,* 4 May 1991.

24     National Archives and Records Administration, "Appendix A—Digest of Other White House Announcements," online at http://bushlibrary.tamu.edu/papers/1992/app_a.html. See also "President Bush Lauds Church's Efforts To Bolster Family Values," *Church News,* 25 July 1992.

25     Gordon B. Hinckley Journal, 17 July 1992, quoted in Dew, *Go Forward with Faith,* 487.

26     George Bush to Gordon B. Hinckley, 21 July 1992, quoted in Dew, *Go Forward with Faith,* 487.

27     "Enthusiastic Crowd at BYU Hails the Chief," *Deseret News,* 19 July 1992, A1.

28     *Dave Leip's Atlas of U.S. Presidential Elections.*

29     "President Benson Eulogized," *Church News,* 11 June 1994.

30     George Bush to Gordon B. Hinckley, 13 March 1995, quoted in Dew, *Go Forward with Faith,* 510.

31     Hafen, *Neal A. Maxwell: A Disciple's Life.*

# BILL
# CLINTON

## *1993–2001*

Although he didn't have many Latter-day Saints in his administration, especially compared to his Republican predecessors, the forty-second President was remarkably respectful toward the Church. Clinton also helped the Church with his support for the Religious Freedom Restoration Act and another measure prohibiting zoning discrimination against new churches and temples. Church leaders and Washington Mormons noted how Clinton's staff went out of their way to include the Church, yet politically Utah was clearly the most anti-Clinton state in the Union. He met with First Presidency members and Apostles both in Salt Lake City and at the White House.

**15 September 1992:** Presidential candidate Bill Clinton calls on Church headquarters for a twenty-minute visit, where he is presented with a porcelain seagull and told the story of how the gulls saved the pioneer crop from the scourge of crickets. Clinton thanks the Church for helping victims of Hurricane Andrew, which has just clobbered Florida the month prior, and President Hinckley uses that opportunity to explain the LDS practice of fasting for two meals each month and offering at least the value of the two meals for relief of the poor. "The Church," President Hinckley states, "uses that money to assist the needy of the Church as well as to help those in serious distress in various parts

*16 November 1993: Following the Rose Garden ceremony at the White House, where President Clinton signed into law the Religious Freedom Restoration Act, Elder M. Russell Ballard of the Twelve (left), Senator Orrin Hatch (R-UT), and President Bill Clinton (right) converse and celebrate the legislation.*

of the world." "Bill Clinton is very impressed with the First Presidency," Senator Orrin Hatch later recalls of the visit. "He showed tremendous respect toward the leadership of the LDS Church."[1]

**November 1992:** Clinton wins the presidency, but in heavily Mormon Utah he loses decisively—43 percent goes for Bush, 27 percent for Perot, and less than 25 percent for Clinton, making Utah the only state in the Union to relegate the incoming President to third place. Elder James E. Faust of the Quorum of the Twelve, and a former Democratic legislator, represents the Church at the inauguration in January and also attends the inauguration's morning prayer service.[2]

**16 November 1993:** Clinton signs into law the Religious Freedom Restoration Act, which overturns a 1990 Supreme Court ruling that says government no longer needs a "compelling interest" to intervene with religion. Apostle Dallin H. Oaks testifies for its passage. (It is only the third time in the history of the Church that an official representative was sent to testify before Congress.) Another member of the Twelve, M. Russell Ballard, accompanies Senator Hatch to the White House Rose Garden to meet the President and see it signed into law. Hatch says it is a good visit and that Clinton likes Elder Ballard. "Bill Clinton was overjoyed to be part of this," notes Senator Hatch. "He wanted this bill and was thrilled to sign it. Bill Clinton believed strongly in the freedom of religion, and was not as far left on this issue as many in his party."[3]

**13 November 1995:** President Gordon B. Hinckley and Elder Neal A. Maxwell meet with President Clinton in the Oval Office.

**November 1996:** Clinton wins reelection, but in Utah the Senate Majority Leader garners 54 percent of the vote compared to 33 percent for Clinton, giving the President a smaller percentage of the vote than in any state but Alaska.[4]

**September 2000:** President Clinton helps the Latter-day Saints by signing into law a bill sponsored by Orrin Hatch that bans discriminatory land zoning against new churches and temples.[5]

## DID CLINTON HOLD A GRUDGE TOWARDS UTAH?

In 1992, Utah was the only state to give Clinton third place, and in 1996 they gave him a lower percentage than anywhere but Alaska. "I don't think he held a grudge against the Mormons about this, however," said Senator Hatch. "He was not the type to hold a grudge against a religious institution; and even if he did, he would get over it pretty quickly. He's the type of person that if it is to his advantage, he can like anyone."[6] Elder Ralph W. Hardy Jr., an Area Seventy and chair of the Church's Public Affairs Washington D.C. Advisory Committee agreed. "I met Bill Clinton as a representative of the Church on several occasions, and he was always very respectful to the Church, and never reflected a grudge for how Utah voted."[7] Mike Leavitt, an active Latter-day Saint who served as Utah's governor throughout the Clinton administration, noted, "President Clinton understands politics and knew with certainty that members of the Church of Jesus Christ of Latter Day Saints were not a natural constituency." However, he added, "I don't think he spent a lot of time thinking about it."[8]

## CLINTON'S RECOGNITION OF THE CHURCH

The Clinton White House was "very open, helpful, and inclusive," remarked Elder Ralph W. Hardy Jr. "They went out of their way to make sure the Church was included in various roundtable discussions and events, and in their dealings with the Church they were as good as it gets. I can't say enough good things about President Clinton's staff."[9] Examples of this include an invite to the Church to lend their expertise on volunteerism with the President's Summit for America's Future in 1997. Elder Jeffrey R. Holland of the Quorum of the Twelve served as a cochair of the Communities of Faith section of the summit.[10] President Clinton also sent condolences upon the deaths of Ezra Taft Benson and Howard W. Hunter.[11] "I would characterize Clinton's relationship with the Church as cordial," remarked former Governor Leavitt. "Likewise, I think the institution of the Church was careful to maintain its traditional respectful relationship with the government."[12]

On 1 February 1996, President Clinton, along with the First Lady and Vice President Al Gore and his wife, attended the annual National Prayer Breakfast. Chaired by LDS member Senator Bob Bennett of Utah, both Bennett and the President spoke about the importance of the family. The guests were treated to "Come, Come, Ye Saints" and a couple of musical numbers from LDS member Ariel Bybee of the Metropolitan Opera, including "How Great Thou Art" and "Amazing Grace." Elder Vaughn J. Featherstone of the Seventy and president of the North America Northeast Area joined the presidential party at the event.[13]

On the occasion of the Mormon pioneer sesquicentennial, President Clinton sent greetings to those celebrating in Salt Lake City. "The story of the Mormon pioneers is in many ways the story of America," said the President. "Today, we marvel at what they accomplished. With faith, courage, and determination, they built a life for their families and made the desert bloom. . . . It is the story of a people who know that, with hard work and faith in God, they can accomplish anything."[14]

## PRESIDENT HINCKLEY'S VISIT TO THE WHITE HOUSE

At the September 1995 general Relief Society meeting, President Hinckley announced and read the "Proclamation to the World" on the family. There was much attention given to this landmark Mormon document, and after hearing about it, President Clinton invited President Hinckley to come to the White House to discuss it. On 13 November President Hinckley, along with Elder Neal A. Maxwell of the Twelve (who attended in his capacity as chairman of the Church's Executive Committee on Public Affairs), met with the President in the Oval Office for thirty minutes. President Hinckley presented President Clinton with a copy of the "The Family: A Proclamation to the World," which urges government officials to "promote those measures designed to maintain and strengthen the family as the fundamental unit of society."

The "Proclamation" led to a discussion on the importance of families. "President Clinton has spoken a good deal about family values recently and we discussed that and expressed our appreciation for what he has said," said President Hinckley. He told the chief executive, "It is our feeling that if you're going to fix the nation, you need to start by fixing families. That's the place to begin."

He also noted President Clinton was very respectful and appreciative of what Church leaders had to say on the subject.

The President was also presented a volume prepared by the Church containing six generations of his family history and another containing that of First Lady Hillary Rodham Clinton. A copy of each family history was also provided for their daughter Chelsea. President Hinckley described the President "as most appreciative and very grateful" to have the history and twice thanked the LDS leaders for the unique gift. "He leafed through the book and we talked about his forebears," President Hinckley said. A few items of interest were pointed out, such as Hillary Clinton's English ancestry tying into a family line of Vice President Al Gore's.

President Hinckley then said to the President:

> We advocate in the Church a program we call family home evening, reserving one night a week where father, mother and children sit down together and talk—talk about the family and about one another and study some together. You might get Hillary and Chelsea and sit down with those books and have a family home evening.

*President Clinton and President Hinckley. According to Elder Ralph W. Hardy Jr., the Clinton White House was "very open, helpful, and inclusive" toward the Church. "They went out of their way to make sure the Church was included in various roundtable discussions and events, and in their dealings with the Church they were as good as it gets. I can't say enough good things about President Clinton's staff."*

President Clinton said that he would take the family history books with him to Camp David for Thanksgiving and have an evening with his family to "discuss our heritage."[15] When Elders Maxwell and Ballard later gave similar family histories to Vice President Gore, Elder Ballard noted the vice president's excitement about the gift. "I think part of his enthusiasm was generated by President Clinton's enthusiasm for what he got. They must have talked about it because he was very pleased to receive it."[16]

During the half-hour visit, President Clinton and President Hinckley did not discuss any political matters, but in addition to conversations on the family the leaders also talked about welfare, education, and the need for parents to be actively involved in their children's lives.

*13 November 1995: President Gordon B. Hinckley and Elder Neal A. Maxwell of the Twelve (who attended in his capacity as chairman of the Church's Executive Committee on Public Affairs), meet with President Bill Clinton and Vice President Al Gore in the Oval Office to discuss the Church's proclamation on the family, and to give President Clinton his family history. (L–R) Elder Maxwell, Vice President Gore, President Clinton, President Hinckley, and a staff member.*

President Hinckley said, "We had a very delightful visit." Vice President Al Gore was also present for a short time during the visit.

As they were concluding the visit, Elder Maxwell mentioned to President Clinton that the First Presidency and the Twelve had recently prayed for him and for the country in the Salt Lake Temple, following a longstanding custom regarding the occupants of the Oval Office. As the men rose to say their good-byes, one of the senior White House aides suggested it might be appropriate to invite President Hinckley to offer a word of prayer. Clinton agreed, and the group gathered in a loose circle. "I had my arm around the back of the President and his arm was around my back, and I offered a prayer," President Hinckley recorded of the experience. "I thought it was a rather wonderful thing, to pray for the President of the United States in his office. When we left he expressed his gratitude for our coming. I thought he was sincere." When asked if there would be any follow-up visit, President Hinckley said, "I expect when he campaigns in '96 that he will come by and see us again. Our doors are always open."[17]

Coincidentally, the visit of the prophet to the President of the United States to discuss the importance of chastity and the family was uncanny in its timeliness. Earlier in the day before President Hinckley arrived at the White House, a young intern named Monica Lewinsky began her first day on the job as a paid staffer in the White House office of legislative affairs. Just two days later, her controversial relationship with Bill Clinton would begin.[18]

## MORMONS AND BILL CLINTON'S IMPEACHMENT

On 8 September 1998, President Hinckley was interviewed by Larry King for his television news program on CNN. The interview occurred the week independent counsel Kenneth Starr delivered his report to Congress regarding the Monica Lewinsky scandal, so King asked the Mormon prophet repeatedly about President Clinton. King asked President Hinckley if he would join other religious leaders who were calling for Clinton's resignation. "President Clinton must make his own decision, and the Congress must make its decision," said the prophet. "I feel very sorry for him, in the first place," President Hinckley said. "Here is a man of great talent and capacity, who has evidently just hurt himself so seriously that it must be a terrible thing for him. Personally, I forgive him. . . . But he still has accountability. He's accountable to the Congress. He's accountable to the people of the United States who elected him. He's accountable to God. . . . That's what he must face."

As his interviewer asked other questions about the President and his conduct, President Hinckley remarked again:

> Right is right, and wrong is wrong. Thou shalt not commit adultery. Thou shalt not steal. Thou shalt not bear false witness. These aren't suggestions. These are commandments, given by Jehovah on Sinai. The Ten Commandments are as applicable today as when they were first given. I am not trying to hold any malice against him or anybody else. I think that it is my responsibility to extend the hand of forgiveness and helpfulness, but at the same time, the position of President of the United States carries with it a tremendous trust. In my judgment, an inescapable trust. You can't divorce private behavior from public leadership. I don't think it is asking too much of any public officer to stand tall, be a model before the people, not only in ordinary aspects of leadership, but in the manner in which he conducts himself.

"Is it asking too much of our public servants to not only make of this nation the greatest nation on earth politically, militarily, but also to give moral leadership to the world?" President Hinckley said in the interview. Responding to a call about what counsel he had for Church members in regard to President Clinton, President Hinckley replied, "Let the established procedures run their course."[19]

In January, the Senate began the trial of the President, and Utah's Mormon congressional delegation helped lead the charge against him. "All these acts obstruct justice. All these acts are federal felony crimes. All these acts were committed by William Jefferson Clinton," declared Representative Chris Cannon (R-UT), one of the House managers who prosecuted Clinton before the Senate. "We cannot trust his word, whatever the issue," exclaimed Senator Bob Bennett (R-UT). "We will always be fearful of where that trait of his could take us, and we should be." All LDS Republican congressmen voted for all counts against Clinton.[20] Even the Senate's lawyer for the impeachment trial, Thomas B. Griffith, was an LDS stake president.[21] However, Senator Harry Reid (D-NV), also a Latter-day Saint, presented a different point of view—that immoral as the President's acts were, they did not meet the constitutional test for removing the President from office:

> Bill Clinton fell from grace. Driven by the private sin of lust, he violated his marriage vows and when his sins were uncovered by his enemies, he tried to conceal them by lying to his wife, his friends, and ultimately to all of us. . . . I have no doubt that he has strayed from the path of goodness. . . . But I have no doubt whatsoever that, under the circumstances of this case, the crimes alleged do not rise to the level of an impeachable offense.[22]

The majority of the Senate would agree with him, and in February they voted to keep Bill Clinton in office. Later that month, Clinton escaped the pressures of the recent impeachment trial with a family vacation in Park City, Utah. His three nights there are a record for the longest continuous time any U.S. President has spent in Utah. Someone on Main Street asked him why of all places he came to Utah. The President simply answered, "It's a great place to be."[23]

# ENDNOTES

1    "Clinton Meets with LDS Leaders," *Church News,* 19 September 1992. See also McCune, *Gordon B. Hinckley: Shoulder for the Lord,* 554; Hatch, interview, 30 May 2006.

2    *Dave Leip's Atlas of U.S. Presidential Elections.* See also "Elder Faust Attends Events," *Church News,* 23 January 1993

3    Hatch, interview, 30 May 2006. See also "Religious Freedom Restoration Act: 'Historic Legislation' Signed," *Church News,* 20 November 1993; Lee Roderick, *Leading the Charge: Orrin Hatch and 20 Years of America,* 397–98.

4    *Dave Leip's Atlas of U.S. Presidential Elections.*

5    "New Law Prohibits Unfair Zoning Decisions," *Church News,* 30 September 2000, 13.

6    Hatch, interview, 30 May 2006.

7    Hardy, interview, 2 July 2006.

8    Michael O. Leavitt, interview by author, 28 August 2006.

9    Hardy, interview, 2 July 2006.

10   "Church Lends Expertise with Voluntarism," *Church News,* 3 May 1997.

11   "Pres. Benson Dies at Age 94; Life Marked by Constancy," *Church News,* 4 June 1994. See also "Civic, Religious Leaders Send Condolences," *Church News,* 11 March 1995.

12   Leavitt, interview, 28 August 2006.

13   "'All Walks of Life Gather,' Espouse Family Values at National Prayer," *Church News,* 10 February 1996.

14   Bill Clinton, 26 July 1997, letter to The Church of Jesus Christ of Latter-day Saints, reprinted in "Pres. Clinton Sends Greetings," *Church News,* 26 July 1997.

15   "White House Visit: Pres. Clinton Meets with Pres. Hinckley," *Church News,* 18 November 1995. See also Dew, *Go Forward with Faith,* 528; Hafen, *Neal A. Maxwell: A Disciple's Life,* "The Fellowship of Christ's Suffering, I Should Have Seen It Coming"; McCune, *Gordon B. Hinckley: Shoulder for the Lord,* 570–71.

16   "Church Officials Visit U.S. Vice President," *Church News,* 9 March 1996, 6.

17   "White House Visit: Pres. Clinton Meets with Pres. Hinckley," *Church News,* 18 November 1995. See also Dew, *Go Forward with Faith,* 528; Hafen, *Neal A. Maxwell: A Disciple's Life,* "The Fellowship of Christ's Suffering, I Should Have Seen It Coming"; McCune, *Gordon B. Hinckley: Shoulder for the Lord,* 570–71.

18   "Time Line," *Washington Post,* 13 September 1998, A32.

19   "Pres. Hinckley Speaks Out on Live TV Show," *Church News,* 12 September 1998, 3.

20   Ostling and Ostling, *Mormon America,* 132–33.

21   "BYU Counsel Mentioned for D.C. Court," *Salt Lake Tribune,* 4 November 2003.

22   *Congressional Record,* 12 February 1999.

23   "Clinton—Cool, Calm, Rejected," *Deseret News,* 3 March 1999, B1. See also "Presidential Visits," *Deseret Morning News,* 29 August 2006, A6.

# GEORGE W. BUSH

## 2001—

Among the Mormons, George W. Bush will be remembered for bestowing the Presidential Medal of Freedom on President Gordon B. Hinckley and for inviting the prophet to the White House after 9/11. The second President Bush did not have as many LDS staffers as did his father or Ronald Reagan, but he did appoint more Mormons to judgeships than any previous President and utilized Latter-day Saint Mike Leavitt in his cabinet. Bush also participated with Church members and the Tabernacle Choir during the 2002 Olympic Winter Games in Salt Lake City. Also, like many recent Presidents, Bush had the choir sing at his inaugural.

For his part, the President will likely remember Utah as the state that consistently gave him the highest percentage of support, both in elections and in approval ratings. "Something like 90 percent of Mormons vote Republican in presidential races," noted then chair of the Utah Republican Party, Joe Cannon. "Mormons are the African-Americans of the Republican Party—something like 90 percent of black Americans vote Democratic."[1] Consequently, just as Bill Clinton was sometimes referred to as "America's first black President" because he was attuned to the substance, style, and issues of black Americans, one journalist has likewise referred to George W. Bush as "America's first Mormon President"—pointing to the fact that in 2006 the three states with the highest Bush approval ratings (Utah, Idaho, and Wyoming) were also the three states with the highest percentage of Latter-day Saints.[2]

**November 1997:** Bush, then governor of Texas, hosts a delegation of prominent Texas Mormons as he signs a proclamation setting aside the last week in November as National Family Week. Elders Larry W. Gibbons and James S. Olson, Area Authority Seventies, lead the delegation and present Governor Bush with a copy of "The Family: A Proclamation to the World." Governor Bush praises his own LDS friends as "happy, content, successful people."[3]

**November 1998:** Governor Bush and Utah Governor Mike Leavitt travel together to Israel, sharing spiritual insights together.

**July 1999:** Governor Bush, early in his presidential campaign, stops by Salt Lake City for a fundraiser and to meet with the First Presidency for an hour. "These are great leaders. I can learn from them," he says upon arrival. "We talked about the need for good strong values," Bush reports afterward, adding that he fully supports the values of the LDS Church.[4] Governor Leavitt comments on the meeting with George W. Bush and the First Presidency: "We had a delightful visit and he commented to me after, as most people do, about how pleasant and thoughtful the conversation was."[5]

**November 2000:** Bush wins the presidency with a narrow electoral vote of 271 to 266, thanks in part to Utah's five electoral votes. Bush beats Gore in the predominantly LDS state 67 percent to 26 percent—one of the strongest showings for Bush in the country. Nationally a higher percentage of Mormons voted for George W. Bush than any other bloc (88 percent compared to 84 percent among white Christian evangelicals).[6]

**20 January 2001:** The Mormon Tabernacle Choir sings at Bush's inauguration. He later honors the choir on a couple of occasions.

**September 2001:** President Hinckley is invited to the White House to join other key religious leaders in meeting with President Bush. The prophet and the President meet again during the 2002 Olympics, during the presentation of the Presidential Medal of Freedom, and during visits to Salt Lake City.

**November 2004:** Bush defeats John F. Kerry, and Utah is the most pro-Bush state in the Union, where his victory is 72 percent to Kerry's 26 percent. As in 2000, every Utah county goes for Bush (Rich County even gave the President an amazing 89 percent of their votes). One study shows that nationally, Mormon support for Bush is even higher in 2004 than in 2000 (95 percent are for Bush in 2004, up from 88 percent in 2000).[7]

**16 October 2006:** Clyde Larsen, a dentist from Price, Utah, presents an elaborate handmade horse riding saddle to President Bush in the Oval Office. While there, Larsen also gives the President a Book of Mormon and invites him to read and pray about it. "The President said thank you and graciously accepted the gift," he reports.[8]

## GOVERNORS BUSH AND LEAVITT IN ISRAEL

*President Bush and Utah Governor Michael O. Leavitt prepare their remarks before speaking at a function during the 2002 Winter Olympic Games. The friendship the two began when both were serving as governors continued once Bush was in the White House, and Leavitt was appointed first to head the Environmental Protection Agency and later as Secretary of Health and Human Services.*

While governor of Texas, George W. Bush developed a friendship with Utah governor Mike Leavitt, a Mormon he had first met in 1994. The two sat side by side for years at the alphabetically arranged table at the National Governors Association meetings, and shared a memorable trip to Israel together in November 1998. "The trip to Israel was my first, as it was for then Governor Bush," said Leavitt. "It was a time of reflection for both of us and we have talked many times since about the trip's importance to us personally. On several occasions during the trip, particularly as we visited sites of religious significance, the subject of our spiritual lives was discussed." While visiting the spot where Jesus gave the Sermon on the Mount near the Sea of Galilee, for example, the two were awestruck by a sense of history and spirituality. "Just to commemorate that moment, we each rendered something that was important to us, about that time, about that place," Leavitt recalled. "I recounted the teachings of Jesus on that occasion. Governor Bush recited the Lord's prayer." The small group then walked down to the Sea of Galilee. "The comment was made, that among us there was Protestant, Catholic, Mormon and Jew; each bathing our hands in the Sea of Galilee together." Leavitt continued with, "You can't go through the Holy Land without getting to know a person's spiritual side, if you will. We did some things there that you just don't experience in other places . . . sharing our spiritual side. We talked about things that are important to us personally."

As governors, Bush spoke highly of his prominent LDS fellow governor, whom he affectionately called "Mikey." "He's a thoughtful guy. I'm impressed," Bush said. "I watched him very carefully while we were in Israel, and he asks great questions."[9]

## POLITICAL SUPPORT OF BUSH BY LDS MEMBERS

"The Mormons have been crucial to George W. Bush's political campaigns," notes writer Suzan Mazur. She points to strong support for Bush by businessman Bill Marriott, Utah governor

The Mormon Tabernacle Choir sang for President Bush in Utah's capitol rotunda during the 2002 Winter Olympic Games. The President "loves the choir, and so does his wife," according to Senator Hatch. President Bush had the choir sing at his inauguration, and awarded them the National Medal of Arts. "You have brought music and inspiration to generations of Americans," he remarked in honor of the choir's 4,000th broadcast, "and I wish you continued success in the future."

Mike Leavitt, and other prominent Latter-day Saints.[10] Another example of support by Saints for Bush was when prominent Mormon attorney Lew Cramer helped the Republican National Committee recruit 1,000 Utah students, mostly LDS, for President Bush's reelection campaign in "battlefront states."[11] During Bush's reelection contest, the Republican National Committee included the Latter-day Saints when they launched various campaign websites aimed at specific groups. At www.kerry-wrongformormons.com, the RNC pointed out Kerry's support for abortion rights, civil unions, and his vote against increasing the child tax credit—all hot issues with LDS voters.[12]

When Bush's popularity plummeted nationally, the forty-third President remained more popular in Utah than anywhere else. In October 2005, Bush's approval rating was only 38 percent, but in Utah his approval rating was the highest in the nation at over 60 percent.[13] In July 2006 surveys, Utah again led the nation in its support for President Bush, this time over 66 percent. "Bush is a deeply moral man," pointed out Joe Cannon, then chair of the Utah Republican Party. "The President takes on the tough issues that resonate with Utahns."[14]

Yet, despite the slanted political demographics of its members, the Church itself remains politically neutral and does not endorse any party or candidate. Though statistically small, there are still anti-Bush Mormons among even the most active Latter-day Saints. Senate Majority Leader Harry Reid (D-NV) is one of them, who disagreed with the President on numerous issues, even maintaining that "President Bush is a liar."[15] Most Latter-day Saints agreed with Elder John H. Groberg, however, when he declared at the American Freedom Festival, "How grateful we should be to have a God-fearing man in the White House today."[16]

## BUSH AND THE MORMON TABERNACLE CHOIR

For the sixth time, the Mormon Tabernacle Choir was invited to participate in a presidential inaugural, an invitation that was secured by LDS senator Orrin Hatch.[17] On a rainy 20 January 2001, with twenty-degree temperatures, "America's Choir" rode on a 150-foot float, the largest entry in the parade. The 319 choir members sang "Battle Hymn of the Republic," "America the Beautiful," and "God Bless America" to the cheers and applause of parade goers and to the thumbs-up of President Bush from the reviewing stand.[18] "That one moment," said Director Craig Jessop of the President's acknowledgment, "made worthwhile all the challenges and hardships the choir endured."[19] The President "loves the choir, and so does his wife," according to Senator Hatch. "He not only had them sing at his first inaugural, but he would have had them sing at his second inaugural if they desired, but the choir was not able to justify the large expense to do it twice."[20]

In November 2003, President and Mrs. Bush awarded the Tabernacle Choir with the nation's highest award for artistic achievement, the National Medal of Arts, at a presentation in the Oval Office. Choir President Mac Christensen, along with the choir's music director, Craig Jessop; associate director Mack Wilberg; organist John Longhurst; assistant to the choir president Stan Parrish, and the announcer for choir broadcasts Lloyd Newell accepted the award on behalf of the choir. "It's a long-overdue recognition of the contribution the choir has made," said the President, "not only to the cultural life of the nation, but to its spiritual life as well."[21]

On 30 April 2006 the choir celebrated its 4,000th broadcast. A recorded message from President Bush was shown during the landmark broadcast. "The Mormon Tabernacle Choir has many distinguished accomplishments throughout its history," he said in his message. "You performed for Presidents going back to William Howard Taft. You performed at six presidential inaugurals, including my own. . . . You have brought music and inspiration to generations of Americans, and I wish you continued success in the future."[22]

## LDS APPOINTMENTS IN THE BUSH ADMINISTRATION

"He's very favorable to the Church," said Senator Orrin Hatch of the President. "He has appointed a whole raft full of Mormons to various positions within the administration, and to key positions in the judiciary."[23] Bush's most notable Mormon appointment was naming his friend Mike Leavitt as administrator of the Environmental Protection Agency in August 2003, and promoting him to be Secretary of Health and Human Services in December 2004. Bush described the former Utah governor as "a trusted friend, a capable executive." For the first time since Terrell Bell served as Reagan's Secretary of Education, a Latter-day Saint was in the President's cabinet, overseeing one of the largest departments at that ($548 billion budget with nearly 67,000 employees).[24]

LDS appointments by Bush in the White House itself included Timothy Flanigan as deputy White House counsel and later as deputy attorney general; and Kyle Sampson as associate White House counsel.[25] Flanigan noted that for as pronounced as LDS support was for George W. Bush, there was a relatively small number of Mormons in the White House itself. For example, during his service, Flanigan was the only Latter-day Saint in the West Wing, and yet there were fifteen or so Jews despite these two religious groups being of equal size in the United States and despite the overwhelming LDS support for Bush.[26]

Bush did name Mormons to other positions in the executive branch, however, including Randal Quarles as assistant secretary of the Treasury for International Affairs;[27] Jeffrey R. Holmstead as assistant administrator for Air and Radiation in the EPA;[28] and Bruce Thompson as a regional administrator for the U.S. Small Business Administration.[29] In addition, Bush has appointed Latter-days Saints to key positions in the Peace Corps, the Bureau of Land Management, and the State Department.[30] Steve Young, former quarterback of the San Francisco 49ers and Church member, was named by Bush to a new national committee aimed at promoting voluntarism and mentoring across the country.[31] In July 2007, Bush appointed Rodney J. Brown, dean of Brigham Young University's College of Life Sciences, to the Presidential Committee on the National Medal of Science.[32]

"This administration has appointed more Latter-day Saint judges than any presidency," pointed out Senator Hatch, "including Ronald Reagan's."[33] Bush set a new record when he appointed six LDS judges in a single presidential term during 2002 and 2003: David G. Campbell, U.S. District Court for Arizona; Kent A. Jordan, U.S. District Court for Delaware; Robert Clive Jones, U.S. District Court for Nevada; Michael W. Mosman, U.S. District Court for Oregon; Jay S. Bybee, Ninth Circuit Court of Appeals; and Lawrence J. Block, U.S. Court of Federal Claims.[34] In his second term, the President appointed Thomas B. Griffith to the United States Court of Appeals for the DC Circuit and was "very much aware of his Latter-day Saint faith while making the decision," said Hatch, who serves as the highest-ranking member of the Senate Judiciary Committee. He also appointed Milan D. Smith and N. Randy Smith to the Ninth Circuit Court of Appeals,[35] and David Grant Campbell to the U.S. District Court for the District of Arizona.[36]

Yet, despite George W. Bush's friendship with a few Latter-day Saints, he was still relatively unfamiliar with the Church upon first moving into the White House. "He does not know Mormons well at all," said Tim Flanigan. "He does not know what to make of them." As evidence, Flanigan points toward a conversation Bush had with Flanigan's boss at the time, Alberto Gonzales, the future attorney general. The President asked, "Tim has a big family of fourteen children, is he Catholic?" Gonzales replied, "No. He's a Mormon." Bush then asked, "Will that create any problems?" Gonzales replied that it wouldn't.[37] "I don't think he had a deep understanding of the Church before he was elected," admitted Health and Human Services Secretary Mike Leavitt of the President. He noted, however, that this understanding has steadily increased. "We have referenced the Church many times in our conversations," noted the Mormon cabinet member in 2006, who also pointed out that Bush has since been given a copy of the Book of Mormon. "I have no idea if he has read any of it," Leavitt said.[38]

*(Right) 23 June 2004: President George W. Bush presents President Gordon B. Hinckley with the Presidential Medal of Freedom. President Bush remarked at the time, "Today this wise and patriotic man receives his country's highest civil honor." No better moment could have symbolized how far the Church has come since Joseph Smith was rejected by Martin Van Buren.*

## MORMONS AND BUSH AFTER SEPTEMBER 11TH

Like most American churches, The Church of Jesus Christ of Latter-day Saints heeded the President's call to observe a National Day of Prayer and Remembrance following the terrorist attacks of 11 September 2002. In the Tabernacle on 14 September, Church leaders prayed for America and President Bush specifically. "May Thine infinite power which rules this world lead our President, George W. Bush," prayed First Presidency counselor President James E. Faust, "and his councils, to do their best for our nation, to secure again peace, hope, security, and prosperity for our nation and its people."[39]

After the terrorist attacks, President Gordon B. Hinckley was one of twenty-six religious leaders who were invited to the White House to meet with the President. The leaders, who met on 20 September, endorsed and signed a statement that they released through the White House regarding the tragic events that had occurred. The group sat in a circle with the President in the Roosevelt Room and spent time listening to the President's concerns and offering advice. After some brief remarks to the religious leaders, President Bush then asked for responses. President Hinckley quickly spoke up and said, "I just want you to know, Mr. President, that we are behind you. We pray for you. We love this 'nation under God.'" President Bush responded, "Thank you, President Hinckley. I'm glad that you could come." At the end of the forty-five-minute meeting they concluded by all holding hands in prayer, offered by a Greek Orthodox archbishop, and spontaneously singing "God Bless America."[40]

To ensure that the Church maintained positive relations with the Bush White House, Elder Dallin H. Oaks of the Twelve met with Karl Rove in early 2002. "I was very impressed with how Elder Oaks handled that meeting," remarked Tim Flanigan, who also attended. "Rove was a former Olympus High graduate and Salt Lake City resident and already knew numerous Mormons whom he respected and admired." Elder Oaks assured Rove that the LDS Church could be a strong ally if treated well. Given the Church's nonpartisan nature, such visits are routine regardless of the party in power.[41]

When asked if being an evangelical Christian has tainted Bush's view of the Mormons, Hatch replied, "Not one bit." Senator Hatch acknowledged that Karl Rove has been influential in the Bush presidency in giving Mormons a fair shake. This administration "has been very favorably disposed toward the LDS Church as a result," Hatch said.[42]

A year after 9/11 a similar gathering of religious leaders was held again in the White House's Roosevelt Room, and President Bush once again invited the Church to participate. President Hinckley sent Elder Ralph W. Hardy Jr. to participate.[43]

## MEDAL OF FREEDOM AND OTHER BUSH INTERACTIONS
## WITH LDS LEADERS

On 8 February 2002, President Bush and his wife, Laura, who were in Salt Lake City to formally open the 2002 Winter Games, visited with President Hinckley and his counselors, Presidents Thomas S. Monson and James E. Faust, in the Church Administration Building. The First Presidency presented the President and First Lady with a copy of their family histories, which they then took some time to go through. President Bush and the First Presidency also discussed current international challenges, and the First Family remarked that they were looking forward to hearing the Tabernacle Choir at the Utah capitol later that day and at the Winter Games opening ceremonies that evening.[44]

A highlight in the story of the Mormons and the White House occurred on 23 June 2004, when President Hinckley was awarded the nation's highest civilian honor, the Presidential Medal of Freedom. In presenting the medal to the Church leader in the East Room of the White House, President Bush said,

Millions of Americans reserve a special respect for Gordon B. Hinckley, who still works every day as President of the Mormon Church, and who, on this very day, turns 94 years old. Mr. Hinckley is the grandson of Mormon pioneers and has given devoted service to his church since 1935. He's always shown the heart of a servant, and the gifts of a leader. Through his discipline and faithfulness, he has proven a worthy successor to the many fine leaders before him. His church has given him its highest position of trust, and today this wise and patriotic man receives his country's highest civil honor.

The official written citation with the award states,

As the president of The Church of Jesus Christ of Latter-day Saints, and throughout his nearly 70 years in church leadership, Gordon B. Hinckley has inspired millions and has led efforts to improve humanitarian aid, disaster relief and education funding across the globe. His tireless efforts to spread the word of God and to promote good will has strengthened his faith, his community and our nation. The United States honors Gordon B. Hinckley for his devoted service to his church and to his fellow-man.

A smiling President Hinckley joked with Bush as the gold medal was placed around his neck. When President Hinckley was asked later what the two said, he responded, "I was so awestruck that I can't remember what he said."[45]

It was truly "a marvelous Mormon moment," as LDS senator Gordon Smith (R-OR), who was in attendance, described the occasion. But how did it come about? "President Bush is fully aware of the LDS faith," answered Senator Hatch. "He knows President Hinckley. He has visited with the First Presidency and has visited with President Hinckley several times. The Medal of Freedom was given fully on the basis of President Bush knowing President Hinckley and recognizing what a great leader he is. The President is aware that despite being elderly, President Hinckley has been the most active Church president in traveling throughout the world as part of his ministry."[46]

Elder Hardy, who attended the medal ceremony, said it was "a stunning occasion" and a real milestone in the relationship between the White House and the Saints. "The limousine that was sent by the White House to pick up President Hinckley for the event was running late, and so President Hinckley, in typical fashion, decided to walk to the White House from his hotel to make sure he was there on time." Elder Hardy continued, "I remember standing at the east gates of the

White House and looking down F Street as President Hinckley walked up, on the arm of his son for support. I could not help but think of Joseph Smith and Elias Higbee, who also walked to the White House, to call on Martin Van Buren."[47]

LDS leaders continued to interact with President Bush throughout his second term. In June 2006, Elder Russell M. Nelson of the Quorum of the Twelve Apostles met with President Bush at the White House to express support for a proposed federal constitutional amendment banning gay marriage. Along with other religious leaders, Elder Nelson stood with President Bush as he called on Congress to pass the ban.[48]

Bush visited Salt Lake City on 30–31 August 2006 to speak to an American Legion convention. It was his first overnight stay in Utah, and with his approval ratings so low everywhere else, he especially appreciated the warm welcome in the city of the Saints. "I can't thank you enough for this fantastic Utah welcome. I am delighted to be here in Salt Lake City," he said to the thousands of supporters who cheered him as he exited Air Force One.[49] "I've heard from a number of

*In August 2006, President Bush and advisor (and one-time-Utahn) Karl Rove met privately with President Hinckley, his counselors, and executive secretary F. Michael Watson in the Council Room of the Church Administration Building. The contents of this meeting were not made public, but it marked the fifth time President Hinckley and President Bush have met, and represents the ever-improving progress in the relationship between the White House and the Mormons.*

people very close to President Bush that he was truly buoyed and heartened by his trip to Utah," reported political observer LaVarr Webb. "The Utah visit provided a big boost for the president. He appreciated the crowds, the support, and felt some genuine affection here."[50] Part of his friendly reception was from the First Presidency, to whom the President and Deputy Chief of Staff Karl Rove made a forty-minute courtesy call in the Council Room of the Church Administration Building.[51] The contents of this meeting were not made public, but it marked the fifth time President Hinckley and President Bush have met, and represents the ever-improving progress in the relationship between the White House and the Mormons.

# ENDNOTES

1 "Utah No. 1 in Approval of Bush," *Deseret Morning News,* 28 July 2006.

2 Bob Fertik on 19 April 2006, online at http://www.democrats.com/first-mormon-president.

3 "From Around the World," *Church News,* 20 December 1997, 10.

4 "Bush Musters Some Spirited Utah Support," *Deseret News,* 7 July 1999.

5 Leavitt, interview, 28 August 2006.

6 *Dave Leip's Atlas of U.S. Presidential Elections.* See also "Onward, Mormon Soldiers: How the Latter-day Saints Could Make Mitt Romney President," *The Boston Phoenix,* online at http://www.bostonphoenix.com/boston/news_features/other_stories/multi-page/documents/04538494.asp.

7 *Dave Leip's Atlas of U.S. Presidential Elections.* See also Terry Eastland, "In 2008, Will It Be Mormon in America?" *The Weekly Standard* 10, no. 36 (6 June 2005).

8 Clyde Larsen, interview by author, 13 November 2006. See also "Saddle Up, Utahn Tells Bush: Price Dentist Presents Elaborate Handmade Gear in D.C. Visit," *Deseret Morning News,* 13 November 2006.

9 Leavitt, interview, 28 August 2006. See also "Bush, Leavitt: GOP buddies," *Deseret Morning News,* 28 December 1998, A1.

10 Suzan Mazur, "Bush and the Mormons," *Scoop Independent News,* 26 October 2004.

11 "Mormons in D.C.—Members Increasingly Influential in Washington Scene," *Salt Lake Tribune,* 10 April 2005.

12 "Preaching to the Choir?" *Salt Lake Tribune,* 28 September 2004.

13 "Bush Is Most Popular in Utah," *Salt Lake Tribune,* 19 October 2005.

14 "Utah No. 1 in Approval of Bush," *Deseret Morning News,* 28 July 2006.

15 *Las Vegas Sun,* 5 March 2002.

16 "Spirit of America Is 'Liberty and Justice for All,'" *Church News,* 13 July 2002, 3.

17 Abanes, *One Nation Under Gods,* 403.

18 *Deseret News 2003 Church Almanac,* 579–80.

19 "Mormon Tabernacle Choir on Parade," *Church News,* 27 January 2001, 3.

20 Hatch, interview, 30 May 2006.

21 "National Medal of Arts Honors Tabernacle Choir," *Salt Lake Tribune,* 13 November 2003. See also "Tabernacle Choir Honored in D.C.," *Church News,* 15 November 2003, 6.

22 "4,000th Broadcast for 'America's Choir,'" *Church News,* 6 May 2006, 3.

23 Hatch, interview, 30 May 2006.

24 "LDS Utahn Tapped for Environmental Post," *Church News,* 16 August 2003, 4. See also "Michael Leavitt Tapped for HHS Cabinet Post," *Church News,* 18 December 2004, 7.

25 Hatch, interview, 30 May 2006. See also Mark W. Cannon, "New LDS Federal Judges Share Common Values," *Meridian Magazine,* online at http://www.ldsmag.com/ideas/041028judges.html.

26 Timothy E. Flanigan, interview by author, 24 July 2006.

27 "Mormons in D.C.," *Salt Lake Tribune,* 10 April 2005.

28 "EPA Administrator Draws on Mission Experience," *Church News,* 15 March 2003, 7.

29 "Appointed to Business Post," *Church News,* 10 November 2001, 14.

30 "Mormons in D.C.," *Salt Lake Tribune,* 10 April 2005.

31 "National Volunteer Commission," *Church News,* 8 February 2003.

32 8 July 2007, *Deseret Morning News.*

33 Hatch, interview, 30 May 2006.

34 "LDS Judges Raising the Bar," *Church News,* 6 November 2004, 10.

35 Hatch, interview, 30 May 2006. See also Mark W. Cannon, "New LDS Federal Judges Share Common Values," *Meridian Magazine,* online at http://www.ldsmag.com/ideas/041028judges.html.

36 "Attorney Appointed to US District Court," *Church News,* 1 November 2003, 15.

37 Flanigan, interview, 24 July 2006.

38 Leavitt, interview, 28 August 2006.

39 "President James E. Faust: Special Prayer," *Church News,* 22 September 2001, 4.

40 Jean Bethke Elshtain, "An Extraordinary Discussion," *Sightings,* online at http://www.americanrhetoric.com/speeches/prayer-withthepresident.htm. See also "Religious Leaders at White House," *Church News,* 29 September 2001, 4.

41 Flanigan, interview, 24 July 2006. See also "Mormons in D.C.," *Salt Lake Tribune,* 10 April 2005; Tony Carnes, "Bush's Defining Moment: How a Nation Discovered the Soul of Its Leader," *Today's Christian,* March/April 2002, online at http://www.christianitytoday.com/tc/2002/002/2.28.html.

42 Hatch, interview, 30 May 2006.

43 Hardy, interview, 2 July 2006.

44 "First Presidency Greets World Leaders," *Church News,* 16 February 2002, 7.

45 "Medal of Freedom," *Church News,* 26 June 2004, 3.

46 Hatch, interview, 30 May 2006.

47 Hardy, interview, 2 July 2006.

48 "Elder Nelson Touts Marriage Amendment," *Deseret Morning News,* 6 June 2006. See also "Bush, LDS Church Unite on Marriages," *Salt Lake Tribune,* 6 June 2006.

49 Author's personal recollection of Bush's remarks, 30 August 2006.

50 LaVarr Webb, "Bush Enjoys Utah Lovefest," *Utah Policy Daily,* 1 September 2006, online at http://www.utahpolicy.com.

51 "U.S. President Visits First Presidency," *Church News,* 2 September 2006, 3. See also Peggy Fletcher Stack, "Bush and Hinckley Meet for a Fourth Time," *Salt Lake Tribune,* 1 September 2006.

# AFTERWORD

The story of America's Presidents and the Latter-day Saints continues to be written as The Church of Jesus Christ of Latter-day Saints seeks respect from and a working relationship with each new President and as each new chief executive seeks support and a working relationship with America's fastest-growing religion. Someday the United States may elect an LDS vice president, and someday we may see a Mormon in the Oval Office. Such developments would clearly add exciting new chapters to this story, one that becomes increasingly relevant as a growing number of Americans are either LDS, have interactions with Latter-day Saints, or are influenced in some way by the Mormons.

Since the preface to this study incorporates my experience in church with a Republican President, it only seems balanced and appropriate to conclude with my experience in church with a Democratic President. Please forgive my indulgence as I share a journal entry once again:

22 April 2007, Atlanta, Georgia

Last month I was in the Governor's office
visiting with my friend Mike Mower, when

Mike revealed to me a fact that would make any armchair presidential historian smile and scheme: Our 39th President was not only alive and well in Plains, Georgia, but he still taught Sunday School most weeks and posted his schedule on that Baptist church's website. So six weeks and some Sky Miles later, I was with my dad and a rent-a-car tooling our way out of Atlanta on State Road 19, heading deeper and deeper into the Deep South, towards Jimmy Carter's Plains and a possible presidential encounter.

Dad and I had fun exploring various places in Georgia, including some Civil War sites, the city of Winder, and of course Plains. The Maranatha Baptist Church is not far from the petite historic business district of Plains. In fact, it is just around the corner and up the road from Billy Carter's service station and the old railroad depot that served as his brother's 1976 campaign headquarters. The town boasts a population of 640, and on a warm April afternoon buzzed with the excitement of a Saturday wedding at the church (where the former President had given away the bride), the antique car show (where Carter awarded the winning trophy), and the dozens of visitors like ourselves who had descended on the peanut-farming community for the weekend to attend the famed Sunday School class. In every aspect of small town life, this was still very much Carter's town.

If you arrive at the church ninety minutes before the doors to the building open on Sunday, you just might beat the couple tour buses in town, and this morning we did. Soon the Secret Service and their bomb sniffing dog were perusing the queue. Later, we were wanded and searched by them before being led into the white building and to our seats in the chapel by "Miz Jan"—a cheerful, but firm, ex–school teacher that "Mista Jimma" had appointed years ago to help manage the waves of visitors to their Sunday services. Our early arrival paid off, and Dad and I found ourselves in the center section of the front row.

As the pastor prayed before the class, the former President and First Lady slipped into the room. President Carter greeted the group with his famous toothy smile, and his blue eyes were full of life as he asked the visitors where they were from. When we said

*The view from the front row of Jimmy Carter's Sunday School class. Photographs are only allowed while the former President is learning where his visitors are from and must cease once the lesson begins.*

"Utah" he mentioned that he has a cousin that lives in Salt Lake City. He then asked the class if there were any current or former pastors or missionaries in the group, and to state where they had served. Several Baptist ones spoke up, and then Dad raised his hand and said that he was a former Mormon bishop from Salt Lake, and I relayed that I had served a two-year LDS mission in Taiwan. He bade us special welcome, and began his class.

Carter wasted no time in beginning his lesson about the fifth chapter of Revelations. He was clearly well versed in the scriptures, and we were able to participate as he asked what we knew about the Apostle John who wrote Revelations. Carter's vitality at age 82 was impressive, and his love for Jesus Christ unquestionable. Doctrinally we didn't disagree a thing with this particular lesson. "Trouble don't last forever," he preached, "Jesus will fix it after a while."

Only two other U.S. presidents besides Jimmy Carter have been awarded the Nobel Peace Prize (Teddy Roosevelt and Woodrow Wilson), and it was an amazing thing to sit literally inches in front of Carter as he taught us from the pages of the New Testament (we literally could not sit with our legs crossed, or we would have kicked him as he paced back and forth along the front row). Whether you agree or disagree politically with Jimmy Carter, he is a man that values his family, his hometown, his relationship with Jesus Christ, and serving others. "The activities in our own lives measure the power of Christ today," he reminded us.

After his lesson, but before the main service, I was able to talk to President Carter by the drinking fountain in the hall. I mentioned that Mom and Dad had met his son Jack recently in Las Vegas, and also told him about my book on the White House and the Mormons. I gave him the chapter on himself and told him to let me know if there was anything I needed to correct or add. He was gracious and friendly, and he and Rosalynn remembered who we were and talked with us as we posed for a photo after the service.

*The author, Jimmy Carter, Rosalynn Carter, and the author's father Kent Winder pose for a photo after Sunday School at the Maranatha Baptist Church in Plains, Georgia.*

As I stood and sang "Christ the Lord Is Risen Today" with the Carters and the rest of the congregation this morning, I felt that although there would be disagreements about authority and ordinances, spiritually there was more that united than divided the beliefs of this American President and the Mormons. As we recited the Lord's Prayer together, I recalled George W. Bush, whom I recited this same prayer with thirteen months ago in an Episcopalian church in Washington D.C. He, too, was worshipping God according to the dictates of his own conscience. And so it has been with all of our country's Presidents. They have grappled with their own spiritual lives, their own relationships with God, and their own political realities of their times, and viewed The Church of Jesus Christ of Latter-day Saints accordingly through those lenses. And in the end there was harmony and friendship between the White House and the Mormons; but it had been quite a journey to get there.

# SOURCES CITED

**Primary Sources**

Adams, Charles Francis, ed., *Memoirs of John Quincy Adams: His Diary from 1795 to 1848,* 12 vols. (Philadelphia: J.B. Lippincott, 1877).

Adams, John Quincy, *Diary of John Quincy Adams* (Library of Congress, Washington, DC).

Angle, Paul M., comp., *New Letters and Papers of Lincoln* (Boston: Houghton Mifflin, 1930).

Basler, Roy P., ed., *The Collected Works of Abraham Lincoln* (New Brunswick, NJ: Rutgers University Press, 1953).

Brimhall, George H., Papers, Brigham Young University Library.

Buchanan, Angela "Bay" (former U.S. Treasurer), interview by author, 13 May 2006.

Buchanan, James, *The Works of James Buchanan,* ed. John Bassett Moore (New York: Antiquarian Press, 1960).

Cannon, Sylvester Q., Diary, LDS Church Archives, Salt Lake City.

Carter, Jimmy, *Keeping Faith: Memoirs of a President* (Toronto: Bantam Books, 1982).

Clark, J. Reuben Jr., Papers, Department of Archives and Special Collections, Harold B. Lee Library, Brigham Young University, Provo, Utah.

Clark, James R., comp., *Messages of the First Presidency of The Church of Jesus Christ of Latter-day Saints,* 6 vols. (Salt Lake City: Bookcraft, 1965–75).

Cleveland, Grover, *The Writings and Speeches of Grover Cleveland,* ed. George F. Parker (New York: Cassell Publishing, 1970).

Conference Reports of the General Conferences of The Church of Jesus Christ of Latter-day Saints (Salt Lake City: Hawkes Pub., 1880–2003).

Congressional Record, United States Congress, Washington, DC.

Correspondences of President Hayes, Hayes Presidential Center, Spiegel Grove, Ohio.

Cutler, Wayne, ed. *Correspondence of James K. Polk* (Nashville: Vanderbilt University Press, 1989).

Faulring, Scott, ed., *An American Prophet's Record: The Diaries and Journals of Joseph Smith* (Salt Lake City: Signature Books, 1989).

Firmage, Edwin B., interview by Gregory A. Prince, 10 October 1996.

Flanigan, Timothy E. (former Bush White House staffer), interview by author, 24 July 2006.

Garn, Jake (former U.S. Senator, R-UT), interview by author, 2 August 2006.

Garfield, James A., *The Diary of James A. Garfield: Volume II 1872–1874,* ed. Harry James Brown & Frederick D. Williams ([East Lansing, MI]: Michigan State University Press, 1967).

Grant, Heber J., journal sheets, LDS Church Archives, Salt Lake City.

Grant, Ulysses S., *Personal Memoirs of U. S. Grant* (New York: C. L. Webster & Co., 1885–1886).

Grant, Ulysses S., Presidential Papers, Library of Congress, Washington, DC.

Hardy, Ralph W., Jr. (Area Authority Seventy and chair of The Church of Jesus Christ of Latter-day

Saints' Washington D.C. Public Relations Advisory Committee), interview by author, 2 July 2006.

Harrison, Benjamin, *Speeches of Benjamin Harrison,* ed. Charles Hedges (New York: United States Book Company, 1892).

Hatch, Orrin (U.S. Senator, R-UT), interview by author, 30 May 2006.

Hayes, Rutherford B., *Diary and Letters of Rutherford Birchard Hayes,* ed. Charles Richard Williams (Columbus, OH: The Ohio State Archaeological and Historical Society, 1924).

Heath, Harvard S., ed., *In the World: The Diaries of Reed Smoot* (Salt Lake City: Signature Books, 1997).

Jardine, James S. (attorney and White House Fellow in Carter Administration), interview by author, 31 July 2006.

Johnson, Clark V., ed. *The Mormon Redress Petitions: Documents of the 1833–1838 Missouri Conflict,* Provo, Utah: Religious Studies Center, 1992).

*Journal of Discourses,* 26 vols. (London: Latter-day Saints' Book Depot, 1854–86).

Kane, Thomas L., correspondence to President Franklin Pierce from Philadelphia, 3 Sept 1854, LDS Church Archives, Salt Lake City.

Kenney, Scott G., ed., *Wilford Woodruff's Journal, 1833–1898,* 9 vols. (Midvale, Utah: Signature Books, 1983–85).

Larsen, Clyde (man who gave a Book of Mormon to George W. Bush and invited him to be baptized), interview by author, 13 November 2003.

Larson, Stan, ed., *A Ministry of Meetings: The Apostolic Diaries of Rudger Clawson* (Salt Lake City: Signature Books, 1993).

Leavitt, Michael O. (U.S. Secretary of Health and Human Services, former Utah governor), interview by author, 28 August 2006.

Letters and Correspondence, Lyndon B. Johnson Library and Museum.

Letters and Correspondence, Truman Presidential Museum and Library.

Mackay, Lachlan E. (historic sites coordinator, Community of Christ), interview by author, 19 June 2006.

*Manuscript History of Brigham Young,* LDS Church Archives, Salt Lake City.

McKay, David O., Diaries, Special Collections, Marriott Library, University of Utah, Salt Lake City.

McKay, David O., Scrapbooks, Special Collections, Marriott Library, University of Utah, Salt Lake City.

Memorandum on the Monroe Doctrine, Dept. of State Publication #37, 17 December 1928.

Middleton, Charles F., "Notes from a Priesthood Meeting Held in 1892," LDS Church Archives, Salt Lake City.

Mulder, William, & A. Russell Mortensen, eds., *Among the Mormons: Historical Accounts by Contemporary Observers* (New York: Alfred A. Knopf, 1958).

Murdock, Franklin J., oral history, 1973, typescript, LDS Church Archives, Salt Lake City.

Nauvoo Baptismal Record Index, Family History Library, Salt Lake City.

Polk, James K., *Diary of James K. Polk,* ed. Milo Milton Quaife (London: A.C. McClurg & Co., 1910).

———, *Polk: the Diary of a President, 1845–1849, Covering the Mexican War, the Acquisition of Oregon, and the Conquest of California and the Southwest,* ed. Allan Nevins (London: Longmans Green, 1929).

———, Papers, Library of Congress Manuscripts Division, Washington, DC.

Post-Presidential Individual File, Hoover Presidential Library, West Branch, Iowa.

Quincy, Josiah, *Figures of the Past from the Leaves of Old Journals* (Boston: Roberts Brothers, 1883).

Reagan, Nancy, *My Turn: The Memoirs of Nancy Reagan* (Random House: New York, 1989).

Richards, Richard (former chair of the Republican National Committee), interview by author, 26 July 2006.

Richardson, James D., comp., *A Compilation of the Messages and Papers of the Presidents, 1789–1902* (Washington, DC: Bureau of National Literature 1897).

Roosevelt, Theodore, *The Letters of Theodore Roosevelt,* ed. Elting E. Morison (Cambridge: Harvard University Press, 1951).

Sessions, Gene A., ed., *Mormon Democrat: The Religious and Political Memoirs of James Henry Moyle* (Salt Lake City: Signature Books/Smith Research Associates, 1975; 2nd ed., 1988).

Simon, John Y., ed., *The Papers of Ulysses S. Grant,* 26 vols. (Carbondale, IL: Southern Illinois University Press, 1988).

Smith, John Henry, *Church, State, and Politics: The Diaries of John Henry Smith,* ed. Jean Bickmore White (Salt Lake City: Signature Books/Smith Research Associates, 1990).

Smith, John Henry, Letters, Special Collections, Marriott Library, University of Utah, Salt Lake City.

Smith, Joseph, *The Memoirs of President Joseph Smith: 1832–1914,* ed. Mary Audentia Smith Anderson (Independence, MO: Herald Publishing House, 1934–1937).

Smith, Joseph, *The Words of Joseph Smith: The Contemporary Accounts of the Nauvoo Discourses of the Prophet Joseph,* comp. Andrew F. Ehat & Lyndon W. Cook (Provo, Utah: Religious Studies Center, 1980).

Smith, Joseph F., *From Prophet to Son: Advice of Joseph F. Smith to His Missionary Sons,* comp. Hyrum M. Smith III & Scott G. Kenney.

Sneff, LaRue, & Lola Timmins, interview by Gregory A. Prince, 3 August 2000.

Staker, Susan, ed., *Waiting for World's End: The Diaries of Wilford Woodruff* (Salt Lake City: Signature Books, 1993).

Telephone logs of President Carter, Jimmy Carter Presidential Library, Atlanta, GA.

Truman, Harry S, *Miracle of '48: Harry Truman's Major Campaign Speeches & Selected Whistle-Stops,* ed. Steve Neal (Carbondale, IL: Southern Illinois University Press, 2003).

Van Buren, Martin Papers, Manuscript Division of the Library of Congress, Washington, DC.

White House Recordings and Telephone Notes, Box 1, Lyndon B. Johnson Library and Museum.

Williams, T. Harry, ed., *The Diary of a President [Rutherford B. Hayes], 1875–1881* (New York:

David McKay Co., 1964).

Winder, Barbara W. (former Relief Society general president), 13 May 2006.

Wirthlin, Richard B. (General Authority Emeritus and former Reagan strategist), interview by author, 14 June 2006.

Young, Brigham, *Discourses of Brigham Young,* comp. John A. Widtsoe (Salt Lake City: Deseret Book, 1925).

Young, Brigham, *Letters of Brigham Young to His Sons,* ed. Dean C. Jessee (Salt Lake City: Deseret Book, 1974).

Young, Brigham, Manuscript History of Brigham Young and Brigham Young Correspondence, LDS Church Archives, Salt Lake City.

## Newspapers

*Alton Telegraph,* Alton, IL

*Church News,* Salt Lake City, Utah

*Columbus Enquirer,* Columbus, GA

*Deseret News,* Salt Lake City, Utah

*Enterprise,* Salt Lake City, Utah

*Erie Observer,* Erie, PA

*Evening and Morning Star,* Independence, MO

*Las Vegas Sun,* Las Vegas, NV

*Michigan Christian Advocate,* Adrian, MI

*New York Daily Tribune,* New York, NY

*New York Times,* New York, NY

*Painesville Telegraph,* Painesville, Ohio

*Paysonian,* Payson, Utah

*Prophet of the Jubilee* (Welsh church periodical)

*Quincy Whig,* Quincy, IL

*Salt Lake Herald,* Salt Lake City, Utah

*Salt Lake Tribune,* Salt Lake City, Utah

*Sangamo Journal,* Springfield, IL

*Times and Seasons,* Nauvoo, IL

*Weekly Sun,* New York, NY

*Western Courier,* Ravenna, Ohio

*Wilmington News,* Wilmington, DE

## Periodicals

*Atlantic Monthly*

*BYU Studies*

*Christianity Today*

*Ensign of The Church of Jesus Christ of Latter-day Saints*
*Hayes Historical Journal*
*Improvement Era of The Church of Jesus Christ of Latter-day Saints*
*Journal of Mormon History*
*Kansas City Times*
*Lincoln Lore: Bulletin of The Lincoln National Life Foundation* (A publication of the Lincoln
National Life Insurance Company, Ft. Wayne, IN)
*Meridian Magazine*
*Pioneer* (publication of the Sons of the Utah Pioneers)
*Scribner's Magazine*
*Ulysses S. Grant Association Newsletter*
*Utah Historical Quarterly*
*Western Humanities Review*
*Western Political Quarterly*

## Unpublished Documents

Adams, Henry, *Charles Francis Adams Visits the Mormons in 1844* (Boston, MA: n.p., 1952).

Andreason, Byron, "Latter-day Saint Connections to Abraham Lincoln-era Springfield" (address
to the Sangamon County Historical Society), 26 April 2005.

Baird, Mark J., & Rhea A. Baird, *Reminiscences of John W. Woolley and Lorin C. Woolley*, 4 vols.
(Draper, Utah: n.p., n.d.).

Barrett, Gwynn, "John M. Bernhisel, Mormon Elder in Congress" (Ph.D. diss., Brigham Young
University, 1968).

Call, Michel L., "The ancestry of King Edward I of England for 6-generation chart," LDS Church
Archives, Salt Lake City.

*Journal History,* LDS Church Archives, Salt Lake City.

Nibley, Preston, "Lincoln and the Latter-day Saints," manuscript, LDS Church Archives, Salt
Lake City.

## Pamphlets and Booklets

*The Great Prologue: A Prophetic History and Destiny of America* (Salt Lake City: First Presidency of
The Church of Jesus Christ of Latter-day Saints, 1976).

Lee, Harold B., "[Address at] memorial service for President Dwight D. Eisenhower, March 31,
1969," LDS Church Archives, Salt Lake City.

Lee, Harold B., "[Address at] memorial service for President John F. Kennedy, Salt Lake
Tabernacle, November 25, 1963," LDS Church Archives, Salt Lake City.

*Lincoln Lore: Bulletin of The Lincoln National Life Foundation* (a publication of the Lincoln
National Life Insurance Company, Ft. Wayne, IN), February 1975.

"Memorial services for President John F. Kennedy, George Albert Smith Fieldhouse, Brigham

Young University, Monday, November 25, 1963," LDS Church Archives, Salt Lake City.

"Memorial services in honor of President John Fitzgerald Kennedy, 1917–1963," event program, LDS Church Archives, Salt Lake City.

"Special organ recital tendered to President and Mrs. Warren G. Harding on the occasion of their visit to Salt Lake City," event program, LDS Church Archives, Salt Lake City.

"Theodore Roosevelt Refutes Anti-Mormon Falsehoods: His Testimony as to Mormon Character; Advice Concerning Polygamy," pamphlet reprinting, 15 April 1911, *Collier's* article (Eborn Books, 1995).

## Online Resources

Carnes, Tony, "Bush's Defining Moment: How a nation discovered the soul of its leader," *Today's Christian,* March/April 2002; online at http://www.christianitytoday.com/tc/2002/002/2.28.html

Cleveland's first inaugural address, http://www.bartleby.com/124/pres37.html.

Elshtain, Jean Bethke, "An Extraordinary Discussion," *Sightings;* online at http://www.americanrhetoric.com/speeches/prayerwiththepresident.htm

"Evangelicals Outraged Over Bush's 'Same God' Remark," *World Net Daily*, 24 November 2003. Online at http://www.worldnetdaily.com/news/article.asp?ARTICLE_ID=35787

Garfield's inaugural address, http://www.bartleby.com/124/pres36.html

International Genealogical Index (IGI) accessible at www.familysearch.org

Jefferson-Hemings Scholar Commission's report, www.people.virginia.edu/~rjh9u/tomsally.html

Laura Bush Foundation for America's Libraries, Press Release of 4 June 2002; online at http://www.laurabushfoundation.org/release_060402.html

*Leip's Atlas of U.S. Presidential Elections*, http://www.uselectionatlas.org/

National Archives and Records Administration, "Appendix A—Digest of Other White House Announcements," at http://bushlibrary.tamu.edu/papers/1992/app_a.html

Norton, C. Michael, "Theodore Roosevelt's 1907 Nashville Visit," http://pages.prodigy.net/nhn.slate/nh00050.html

"Onward, Mormon Soldiers: How the Latter-day Saints Could Make Mitt Romney President," *The Boston Phoenix*, online at http://www.bostonphoenix.com/boston/news_features/other_stories/multi-page/documents/04538494.asp

Roosevelt City, Utah, History on the Roosevelt City website, http://www.rooseveltcity.com/history.html

Roosevelt, Franklin D., Presidential Library and Museum, online database at http://www.fdrlibrary.marist.edu

Rutledge, Ann and Abraham Lincoln's romance outlined in http://members.aol.com/RVSNorton/Lincoln34.html

Scott, Richard G., "Learning to Succeed in Life," speech at BYU found online at http://speeches.byu.edu/reader/reader.php?id=3640

"Spirituality and President Bush," PBS Religion and Ethics Newsweekly, episode 421, posted online on 19 January 2001 at http://www.pbs.org/wnet/religionandethics/week421/news.html.

Webb, LaVarr, "Bush Enjoys Utah Lovefest," *Utah Policy Daily*, 1 September 2006, online at http://www.utahpolicy.com

Woolley, John, & Gerhard Peters, University of California-Santa Barbara, *The American Presidency Project* available at http://www.presidency.ucsb.edu/site/docs/sou.php

## Books

Abanes, Richard, *One Nation Under Gods: A History of the Mormon Church* (New York: Four Walls Eight Windows, 2002).

Alexander, Thomas G., *Things in Heaven and Earth: The Life and Times of Wilford Woodruff, a Mormon Prophet* (Salt Lake City: Signature Books, 1991).

Allen, James B., & Glen M. Leonard, *The Story of the Latter-day Saints*, 2nd ed. (Salt Lake City: Deseret Book, 1992).

Anderson, Dawn Hall, & Susette Fletcher Green, eds., *Women in the Covenant of Grace: Talks Selected from the 1993 Women's Conference* (Salt Lake City: Deseret Book, 1994).

Anderson, Joseph, *Prophets I Have Known* (Salt Lake City: Deseret Book, 1973).

Anderson, Nels, *Desert Saints: The Mormon Frontier in Utah* (Chicago: University of Chicago, 1966).

Andrus, Hyrum L., *Doctrines of the Kingdom* (Salt Lake City: Bookcraft, 1973).

———, *Joseph Smith and World Government* (Salt Lake City: Deseret Book, 1958).

Angle, Paul, *Here I Have Lived* (New Brunswick, NJ: Rutgers University Press, 1935).

Arrington, Leonard J., & Davis Bitton, *The Mormon Experience: A History of the Latter-day Saints*, 2nd ed. (Urbana, IL: University of Illinois, 1992).

Arrington, Leonard J., Feramorz Y. Fox, & Dean L. May, *Building the City of God: Community and Cooperation among the Mormons*, 2nd ed. (Urbana, IL: University of Illinois Press, 1992).

Auchampaugh, Philip Gerald, *Robert Tyler, Southern Rights Champion 1847–1866: A Documentary Study Chiefly of Antebellum Politics* (Duluth, MN: Himan Stein, 1934).

Backman, Milton V., Jr., *American Religions and the Rise of Mormonism* (Salt Lake City: Deseret Book, 1965).

———, *Heavens Resound: A History of the Latter-day Saints in Ohio 1830–1838* (Salt Lake City: Deseret Book, 2002).

Baker, LeGrand L., *Murder of the Mormon Prophet: The Political Prelude to the Death of Joseph Smith* (Salt Lake City: Eborn Books, 2006).

Bauer, K. Jack, *Zachary Taylor: Soldier, Planter, Statesman of the Old Southwest* (Baton Rouge: Louisiana State University Press, 1985).

Bennett, Richard E., *We'll Find the Place: The Mormon Exodus 1846–1848* (Salt Lake City: Deseret Book, 1997).

Benson, Ezra Taft, *Crossfire: The Eight Years with Eisenhower* (Garden City, NY: Doubleday, 1962).

————, *Teachings of Ezra Taft Benson* (Salt Lake City: Deseret Book, 1988).

Berrett, William E., *The Restored Church: Brief History of the Growth and Doctrines of The Church of Jesus Christ of Latter-day Saints* (Salt Lake City: Deseret Book, 1969).

Berrett, William E., & Alma P. Burton, *Readings in L.D.S. Church History,* 3 vols. (Salt Lake City: Deseret Book, 1955).

Bitton, Davis, *George Q. Cannon: A Biography* (Salt Lake City: Deseret Book, 1999).

Bitton, Davis, & Maureen Ursenbach Beecher, eds., *New Views of Mormon History: Essays in Honor of Leonard J. Arrington* (Salt Lake City: University of Utah Press, 1987).

Black, Susan Easton, & Larry C. Porter, eds., *Lion of the Lord: Essays on the Life and Service of Brigham Young* (Salt Lake City: Deseret Book, 1995).

Boller, Paul F., Jr., *George Washington and Religion* (Dallas: Southern Methodist University Press, 1963).

Britsch, R. Lanier, *Unto the Islands of the Sea: A History of the Latter-day Saints in the Pacific* (Salt Lake City: Deseret Book, 1986).

Brodie, Fawn M., *No Man Knows My History* (New York: Vintage Books, 1995; original edition by Alfred A. Knopf, 1945).

————, *Thomas Jefferson: An Intimate History* (New York: W.W. Norton, 1974).

Bushman, Richard Lyman, *Joseph Smith: Rough Stone Rolling* (New York: Alfred A. Knopf, 2005).

Byrnes, Mark E., *James K. Polk: A Biographical Companion* (Santa Barbara, CA: ABC-CLIO, 2001).

Cannon, Lou, *Reagan* (New York: G. P. Putnam's Sons, 1982).

————, *President Reagan: The Role of a Lifetime* (Simon & Schuster: New York, 1991).

Carmack, John K., *Tolerance* (Salt Lake City: Bookcraft, 1993).

Church Education System, *Church History in the Fulness of Times: The History of The Church of Jesus Christ of Latter-day Saints* (Salt Lake City: The Church of Jesus Christ of Latter-day Saints, 2000).

Conkling, J. Christopher, *A Joseph Smith Chronology* (Salt Lake City: Deseret Book, 1979).

Cowan, Richard O., *The Church in the Twentieth Century* (Salt Lake City: Deseret Book, 2000).

Day, Robert B., *They Made Mormon History* (Salt Lake City: Deseret Book, 1968).

*Deseret News 2003 Church Almanac* (Salt Lake City: Deseret News, 2002).

Dew, Sheri L., *Ezra Taft Benson: A Biography* (Salt Lake City: Deseret Book, 1987).

————, *Go Forward With Faith: The Biography of Gordon B. Hinckley* (Salt Lake City, Deseret Book, 1996).

*Doctrine and Covenants* (Salt Lake City: The Church of Jesus Christ of Latter-day Saints, 1981).

Doenecke, Justus D., *The Presidencies of James A. Garfield and Chester A. Arthur* (Lawrence, KS: The Regents Press of Kansas, 1981).

Donald, David Herbert, *Lincoln* (New York: Simon and Schuster, 1995).

Dyer, Alvin R., *Who Am I?* (Salt Lake City: Deseret Book, 1973).

Eisenhower, Dwight D., *The White House Years* (Garden City, NY: Doubleday, 1963).

Ellis, Joseph J., *American Sphinx: The Character of Thomas Jefferson* (New York: Vintage Books, 1996).

———, *His Excellency: George Washington* (New York: Vintage Books, 2004).

*Encyclopedia of Mormonism,* 6 vols. (New York: Macmillan, 1992).

Evans, Beatrice Cannon, & Janath Russell Cannon, eds., *Cannon Family Historical Treasury* (Salt Lake City: Publisher's Press, 1967).

Evans, John Henry, *Joseph Smith, an American Prophet* (New York: Macmillan, 1933).

Eyre, Linda, & Richard Eyre, *Teaching Children Responsibility* (New York: Fireside, 1994).

Fox, Frank W., *J. Reuben Clark: The Public Years* (Provo, Utah: Brigham Young University Press, 1980).

Freidel, Frank, *Our Country's Presidents* (Washington, DC: National Geographic Society, 1981).

Garr, Arnold K., et. al., eds., *Encyclopedia of Latter-day Saint History* (Salt Lake City: Deseret Book, 2000).

Garr, Arnold K., & Clark V. Johnson, eds., *Regional Studies in Latter-day Saint History: Missouri* (Provo, Utah: Department of Church History and Doctrine, Brigham Young University, 1994).

Garrett, H. Dean, ed., *Regional Studies in Latter-day Saint History: Illinois* (Provo, Utah: Department of Church History and Doctrine, Brigham Young University, 1995).

Gibbons, Francis M., *Brigham Young: Modern Moses, Prophet of God* (Salt Lake City: Deseret Book, 1981).

———, *David O. McKay: Apostle to the World, Prophet of God* (Salt Lake City: Deseret Book, 1986).

———, *Ezra Taft Benson: Statesman, Patriot, Prophet of God* (Salt Lake City: Deseret Book, 1996).

———, *George Albert Smith: Kind and Caring Christian, Prophet of God* (Salt Lake City: Deseret Book, 1990).

———, *Harold B. Lee: Man of Vision, Prophet of God* (Salt Lake City: Deseret Book, 1993).

———, *Heber J. Grant: Man of Steel, Prophet of God* (Salt Lake City: Deseret Book, 1979).

———, *John Taylor: Mormon Philosopher, Prophet of God* (Salt Lake City: Deseret Book, 1985).

———, *The Expanding Church: Three Decades of Remarkable Growth Among the Latter-day Saints 1970–1999* (Bountiful, Utah: Horizon Publishers, 1999).

———, *Wilford Woodruff: Wondrous Worker, Prophet of God* (Salt Lake City: Deseret Book, 1988).

Gottlieb, Robert, & Peter Wiley, *America's Saints: The Rise of Mormon Power* (New York: G. P. Putnam's Sons, 1984).

Grant, Heber J., *Gospel Standards: Selections from the Sermons and Writings of Heber J. Grant*, comp. G. Homer Durham (Salt Lake City: Improvement Era, 1941).

Hafen, Bruce C., *Neal A. Maxwell: A Disciple's Life* (Deseret Book, Salt Lake City: 2002).

Hansen, Klaus J., *Quest for Empire* (Lansing, MI: Michigan State University Press, 1967).

Hartshorn, Leon R., comp., *Classic Stories from the Lives of Our Prophets* (Salt Lake City: Deseret Book, 1971).

Hinckley, Bryant S., *Sermons and Missionary Services of Melvin J. Ballard* (Salt Lake City: Deseret Book, 1949).

———, *Heber J. Grant: Highlights in the Life of a Great Leader* (Salt Lake City: Deseret Book, 1951).

Hinckley, Gordon B., *Teachings of Gordon B. Hinckley* (Salt Lake City: Deseret Book, 1997).

Hirshon, Stanley P., *The Lion of the Lord: A Biography of the Mormon Leader, Brigham Young* (New York: Alfred A. Knopf, 1969).

Holzapfel, Richard Neitzel, et. al., *On this Day in the Church: An Illustrated Almanac of the Latter-day Saints* (Salt Lake City: Eagle Gate, 2000).

Holzapfel, Richard Neitzel, and R. Q. Shupe, *My Servant Brigham: Portrait of a Prophet* (Salt Lake City: Bookcraft, 1997).

Howard, F. Burton, *Marion G. Romney: His Life and Faith* (Salt Lake City: Bookcraft, 1988).

Jenson, Andrew, *Encyclopedic History of the Church* (Salt Lake City: Deseret News, 1941).

Kengor, Paul, *God and Ronald Reagan: A Spiritual Life* (New York: Regan Books, 2004).

Kennedy, James H., *The Early Days of Mormonism* (New York: C. Scribner's Sons, 1888).

Kimball, Edward L., & Andrew E. Kimball, Jr., *Spencer W. Kimball: Twelfth President of The Church of Jesus Christ of Latter-day Saints* (Salt Lake City: Bookcraft, 1977).

Kimball, Stanley B., *Heber C. Kimball: Mormon Patriarch and Pioneer* (Urbana, IL: University of Illinois Press, 1981).

Klein, Philip Shriver, *President James Buchanan: A Biography* (University Park, PA: Pennsylvania State University Press, 1962).

Knowles, Eleanor, *Howard W. Hunter* (Salt Lake City: Deseret Book, 1994).

Kunhardt, Phillip B., Jr., Phillip B. Kunhardt III, & Peter W. Kunhardt, *The American President* (New York: Riverhead Books, 1999).

Lee, Harold B., *Ye Are the Light of the World* (Salt Lake City: Deseret Book, 1974).

Leonard, Glen M., *Nauvoo* (Salt Lake City: Deseret Book, 2002).

Linn, William Alexander, *The Story of the Mormons: From the Date of their Origin to the Year 1901* (New York: Macmillan, 1902).

Long, E. B., *The Saints and the Union* (Urbana and Chicago: Univ. of Illinois Press, 1981).

Lowe, Julian C., & Florian H. Thayn, eds., *History of the Mormons in the Greater Washington Area: Members of The Church of Jesus Christ of Latter-day Saints in the Washington, D.C. Area 1839-1991* (Washington, DC: Community Printing Service, 1991).

Lundwall, N. B., *Temples of the Most High* (Salt Lake City: Bookcraft, 1949)

Mangum, Garth, & Bruce Blumell, *The Mormons' War on Poverty: A History of LDS Welfare, 1830–1990* (Salt Lake City: University of Utah Press, 1993).

Mansfield, Stephen, *The Faith of George W. Bush* (Tarcher, 2003).

McCloud, Susan Evans, *Brigham Young: An Inspiring Personal Biography* (American Fork, Utah: Covenant Communications, 1996).

McCollister, John C., *God and the Oval Office: The Religious Faith of Our 43 Presidents* (Nashville:

W Publishing Group, 2005).

McCoy, Donald R., *Landon of Kansas* (Lincoln: University of Nebraska Press, 1966).

McCune, George M., *Gordon B. Hinckley: Shoulder for the Lord* (Salt Lake City: Hawkes Publishing, 1996).

McKay, David Lawrence, *My Father, David O. McKay* (Salt Lake City: Deseret Book, 1989).

Meacham, Jon, *American Gospel: God, the Founding Fathers, and the Making of a Nation* (New York: Random House, 2006).

Merrill, Milton R., *Reed Smoot: Apostle in Politics* (Logan, Utah: Utah State University Press, 1990).

Miner, Caroline Eyring, & Edward L. Kimball, *Camilla: A Biography of Camilla Eyring Kimball* (Salt Lake City: Deseret Book, 1980).

Morrell, Jeanette McKay, *Highlights in the Life of President David O. McKay* (Salt Lake City: Deseret Book, 1966).

Morris, Edmund, *Dutch: A Memoir of Ronald Reagan* (New York: Random House, 1999).

———, *Theodore Rex*, (New York: The Modern Library, 2002).

Mulder, William, & A. Russell Mortensen, eds., *Among the Mormons: Historical Accounts by Contemporary Observers* (New York: Alfred A. Knopf, 1958).

Newell, Linda King, & Vivian Linford Talbot, *A History of Garfield County* (Salt Lake City: Utah State Historical Society and Garfield County Commission, 1998).

Nibley, Preston, *Brigham Young: The Man and His Work* (Salt Lake City: Deseret Book, 1970).

Nichols, Roy Franklin, *Franklin Pierce: Young Hickory of the Granite Hills,* 2nd ed. (Philadelphia: University of Pennsylvania Press, 1958).

Nyman, Monte S., & Charles D. Tate, Jr., eds., *Second Nephi: The Doctrinal Structure* (Provo, Utah: Religious Studies Center, Brigham Young University: 1989).

Oaks, Dallin, & Marvin Hill, *The Carthage Conspiracy* (Urbana, IL: University of Illinois Press, 1975).

O'Brien, Robert, *Marriott: The J. Willard Marriott Story* (Salt Lake City: Deseret Book, 1977).

Ostling, Richard N., & Joan K. Ostling, *Mormon America: The Power and the Promise* (New York: HarperCollins Publishers, 1999).

Otten, L. G., and C. M. Caldwell, *Sacred Truths of the Doctrine and Covenants* (Salt Lake City: Deseret Book, 1993).

Peskin, Allan, *Garfield* (Kent State University Press: 1978).

Petersen, Mark E., *Adam: Who Is He?* (Salt Lake City: Deseret Book, 1976).

Prince, Gregory A., & Wm. Robert Wright, *David O. McKay and the Rise of Modern Mormonism* (Salt Lake City: University of Utah Press, 2005).

Quinn, D. Michael, *Elder Statesman: A Biography of J. Reuben Clark* (Salt Lake City: Signature Books, 2002).

———, *The Mormon Hierarchy: Extensions of Power* (Salt Lake City: Signature Books, 1997).

———, *The Mormon Hierarchy: Origins of Power* (Salt Lake City: Signature Books, 1994).

Ricketts, Norma Baldwin, *The Mormon Battalion: U.S. Army of the West, 1846–1848* (Logan, Utah: Utah State University Press, 1996).

Roberts, B. H., *A Comprehensive History of The Church of Jesus Christ of Latter-day Saints, Century I* (Salt Lake City: Deseret News Press, 1930).

———, *Life of John Taylor* (Salt Lake City: George Q. Cannon & Sons, 1892).

Roderick, Lee, *Leading the Charge: Orrin Hatch and 20 Years of America* (Carson City, Nevada: Gold Leaf Press, 1994).

Sessions, Gene A., ed., *Mormon Democrat: The Religious and Political Memoirs of James Henry Moyle* (Salt Lake City: Signature Books/Smith Research Associates, 1998).

Simon, Paul, *Lincoln's Preparation for Greatness: The Illinois Legislative Years* (Norman, OK: University of Oklahoma Press, 1965).

Skousen, Paul B., *The Skousen Book of Mormon World Records, Premier Edition* (Springville, Utah: Cedar Fort, 2004).

Slaughter, William W., *Life in Zion: An Intimate Look at the Latter-day Saints, 1820–1995* (Salt Lake City: Deseret Book, 1995).

Smith, Elbert B., *The Presidencies of Zachary Taylor and Millard Fillmore* (Lawrence: University Press of Kansas, 1988).

Smith, Joseph, *History of The Church of Jesus Christ of Latter-day Saints,* ed. B. H. Roberts, 2nd ed. rev., 7 vols. (Salt Lake City: The Church of Jesus Christ of Latter-day Saints, 1902–1932).

Smith, Joseph Fielding, *Church History and Modern Revelation,* 4 vols. (Salt Lake City: The Quorum of the Twelve Apostles, 1946).

———, *Essentials in Church History,* 8th ed. (Salt Lake City: Deseret Book, 1941).

———, *The Progress Of Man* (Salt Lake City: Genealogical Society of Utah, 1936).

Smith, Joseph Fielding, Jr., & John J. Stewart, *The Life of Joseph Fielding Smith* (Salt Lake City: Deseret Book, 1972).

Smith, Lucy Mack, *History of Joseph Smith by His Mother* (Salt Lake City: Bookcraft, 1979).

Snow, Lorenzo, *The Teachings of Lorenzo Snow,* ed. Clyde J. Williams (Salt Lake City: Bookcraft, 1984).

Spafford, Belle S., *A Woman's Reach* (Salt Lake City: Deseret Book, 1974).

Stewart, John J., *George Washington and the Mormons* (Salt Lake City: Deseret Book, 1967).

———, *Thomas Jefferson and the Restoration of the Gospel of Jesus Christ* (Salt Lake City: Mercury Publishing, 1959).

———, *Thomas Jefferson: Forerunner to the Restoration* (Bountiful, Utah: Horizon Publishers, 1997).

Stout, Wayne, *The Mighty John Taylor* (Salt Lake City: Stout, 1977).

Swinton, Heidi S., *In the Company of Prophets* (Salt Lake City: Deseret Book, 1993).

Talmage, James E., *Story and Philosophy of Mormonism* (Liverpool: Millennial Star, 1910).

Tastmona, Thotnu, *It Is As If: Solution of the President Kennedy Death Mystery* (New York: Thothmona Book, 1966).

Thayer, William M., *From Log Cabin to White House* (New York: Hurst & Company, 1882).

Tullidge, Edward W., *History of Salt Lake City and Its Founders* (Salt Lake City, 1886).

Van Wagoner, Richard S., *Sidney Rigdon: A Portrait of Religious Excess* (Salt Lake City: Signature Books, 1994).

Winder, Michael K., comp., *Counselors to the Prophets* (Salt Lake City: Eborn Books, 2001).

Yorgason, Blaine M., *Courageous Defender of Truth: The Story of John Taylor* (Ogden, Utah: The Living Scriptures, 2002).

# INDEX

220–222, **220**, **221**, **222**, 225, 226, **227**, 228, 233, 234, 235, 239, 245, 246, **247**, 248, 249, 251, **251**, 253, 257, 258, **259**, 260, **261**, 262–267, **263**, **267–267**, 268–269, 270, 273, 274, 277, 286, **287**, **288**, 289–290, 291–296, **293**, **294–295**, 296, 301, 302, 303, 304, 305, 308, 311, **312**, 313, 314, 315, 316, 317–321, **320**, 325, 336–328, **327**, 330, 331–332, **332**, 335, 336, 337, 338 **340**, 341–342, 345, 346, 347, 348, 350, **352**, 354, 356, 337, 358, 365, 366, **366**, 367, **367**, 368, 369, **369**, 370, **370**, 371–372, 375, 376, 377, 378, 380, 382, 383, 385, 386, 387, **387**, **388–389**, 389, 390, 392, 393, 395, 401
Utah County, Utah, 172
Utah State University, 296, 325

Valentine, Christina R., 328
Van Buren, Martin, **x–1**, 1, 2, 35, **46**, 47–52, **49**, **50**, **52**, 55, **57**, 59, **125**, 199, **392–393**, 395
Vance, Cyrus, 307, **308**
Van Der Kemp, F. A., 22
Vermont, 21, 27, 151, 202, 251
Vietnam, 304, 326
Vincent, Steve, 3
Vinson, Frederick M., 275
Virginia, 21, 27, 28, 31, 32, 62, 77, 237, 62, **62**

Waddoups, William M., 246
Washington D.C., 2, 8, **28**, 35, 48, 50, 61, 66, **66**, 69, **78**, 81, 90, 91, 97, 99, 99, 110, 116, 122, 131, 143, 152, 175, 176, 185, 188, 189, **189**, **203**, 218, 228, 235, 237, **238–239**, 239, 246, 250, 258, 261, 267, 277, 278, 279, 280, 296, 301, 303, 305, 315, 321, 331, 337, 342, 346, 365, 366, 375, 377, 403
Washington D.C. Temple, 314, 321, 325, 329–330
Washington, George, 1, **6**, 7–12, **9**, **10**, **12**, 15, 28
Washington State, 296
Watkins, Arthur, **276**, **278**
Webb, LaVarr, 395
Webster, Daniel, 85
Webster, Noah, 22
Weinberger, Caspar, 357
Welch, Robert, 279
welfare, *see* Church Welfare Program
Wells, Daniel H., 85, **132**, 136, **185**
Wells, Emmeline B., 132, **132**, 211, **211**
Wells, Heber M., **185**
Wells, Sharlene, 360
West Valley City, Utah, 2
Whitman, Walt, 351
Whitney, Newel K., 360
Whyte, Marla, 328
Widtsoe, John A., 261
Wilberg, Mack, 390
Wilcox, Anthony, 184
Wilhelm, Friedrich, II, 184
Wilkinson, Ernest, **269**, 279, 286
Williams, Henry, 37
Williams, Zina Young, 132, **132**

Wilson, John, 78, 79
Wilson, Woodrow, 5, 187, 190, 202, **206**, 207–214, **210**, **211**, **212**, **213**, **214**, 249, 402
Winder, Barbara W., 357
Winder, John R., 2, 192
Wirthlin, Joseph L., 24, **24**, 346
Wirthlin, Richard B., 346, 347, 350, 352, 353, 357, 358, 360
Wisconsin, 336
Wolthius, Robert K., 328
Wood, C. Kent, 358
Woodruff, Wilford, 1, 8, 11, 12, **12**, 17, **18**, 52, 72, 96, 100, 107, 120, 124, 168, **168**, 171
world hunger fund, **359**, 360
Wyoming, 96, 99, 160, 176, 190, 386

Yorba Linda, California, 314, 341
Young, Alfales, 126
Young, Brigham, 43, 44, **44**, 47, 51, 59, 62, 66, 68, 69, 72, **72**, 73, 78, **78**, 79, 81, 82–83, **83**, 84, **84**, 85, 89, **90**, 92, **92**, 95, 96, 98, **98**, 99, 100, **100**, 101, 107, 108, **108**, 109, 110, 111, **111**, 115, 116, **116**, 120, **121**, **123**, 124, **125**, 126, **127**, 131, 132, 142, 220, 257, 258, **259**, 260, 261, 265, 267, 301, 326
Young, Brigham, Jr., 152, 156
Young, John W., 115, 120, 116, **116**, 157
Young, Michael K., 370
Young, Richard W., 126, **127**
Young, Steve, 391
Young, Truman, 301

Zane, Charles S., 152
Zion National Park, 222, **222**

# PHOTO CREDITS

The following abbreviations are used throughout the photo credits:

**IRI:** © by Intellectual Reserve, Inc., the nonprofit corporation that holds copyright title for works owned by The Church of Jesus Christ of Latter-day Saints. Used by permission.
**LDS:** Courtesy of LDS Church Archives, Salt Lake City, Utah.
**LOC:** Courtesy of Library of Congress Prints and Photographic Division, Washington, DC.
**UofU:** Special Collections Department, J. Willard Marriott Library, University of Utah. Used by permission.
**USHS:** Used by permission, Utah State Historical Society, all rights reserved.

x Gordon B. Hinckley receives Medal of Freedom, by Susan Walsh, Associated Press. Used by permission.
3 St. John's Episcopal Church. Courtesy of the author.
5 Business card. Courtesy of the author.
6 George Washington, by Gilbert Stuart. LOC.
9 Lt. Gen. Smith. LDS.
10 The Prayer at Valley Forge, by H. Brueckner. LOC.
12 St. George Temple, 1877. LDS.
14 John Adams, by Gilbert Stuart. LOC.
16 Abigail Adams, by Gilbert Stuart. LOC.
17 Eliza R. Snow. LOC.
17 John Adams, by John Singleton Copley. LOC.
18 Declaration of Independence, by John Trumbull. LOC.
18 John Adams, by Charles Willson Peale. LOC.
20 Thomas Jefferson, by Gilbert Stuart. LOC.
22 Thomas Jefferson, by Rembrandt Peale. LOC.
23 Writing the Declaration of Independence, by Jean Leon Gerome Ferris. LOC.
24 Jefferson Standing, by Rembrandt Peale. LOC.
26 James Madison, by Gilbert Stuart. LOC.
28 Dolley Madison, by Gilbert Stuart. LOC.
29 James Madison, by Thomas Sully. LOC.
30 James Monroe, by Gilbert Stuart. LOC.
32 First Vision Stained Glass Window, Los Angeles Meetinghouse, 1913. LDS.
32 Monroe Doctrine political cartoon, 1912. LOC.
33 James Monroe, by William James Hubbard. LOC.
34 John Quincy Adams, by George Peter Alexander Healy. LOC.
36 Orson Pratt. LDS.
36 John E. Page. LDS.
38 John Quincy Adams, by Thomas Sully. LOC.
40 Andrew Jackson, by James Barton Longacre. LOC.
42 Trail of Tears, by Robert Lindneux. LOC.
42 Mobbers Raiding Printing Property, by Charles Brent Hancock. LDS.
44 Major General Andrew Jackson, by Thomas Sully. LOC.
46 Martin Van Buren. LOC.
49 White House 1840s. LOC.
50 John Reynolds, courtesy of McClure's Magazine, January 1896.
50 Joseph Smith and President Van Buren, by Robert T. Barrett. IRI.
52 Martin Van Buren. LOC.
54 William Henry Harrison, by James Henry Beard. LOC.
56 Death of Harrison, by Currier and Ives. LOC.

57 Harrison campaign ribbon. LOC.
58 John Tyler. LOC.
60 Scene at Carthage, by Charles Brent Hancock. LDS.
62 Karl G. Maeser. LDS.
64 James K. Polk, by Mathew Brady. LOC.
66 Sarah Polk, by Levin C. Handy. LOC.
67 The Prophet, June 22, 1844. LDS.
67 Lt. Gen. Joseph Smith. LDS.
69 James K. Polk. LOC.
71 Thomas Kane and Jesse Little with President Polk, by Michael Malm. IRI.
72 Scene of Battalion Boys in California, by Charles Brent Hancock. LDS.
76 Zachary Taylor, by Mathew Brady. LOC.
78 Major General Zachary Taylor, by John Sartain. LOC.
78 Dr. John M. Bernhisel. LDS.
80 Millard Fillmore, by Mathew Brady. LOC.
82 Territorial Statehouse in Fillmore. LDS.
83 Brigham Young. LDS.
84 Thomas L. Kane. LDS.
85 Millard Fillmore, by John Sartain. LOC.
88 Franklin Pierce, by Mathew Brady. LOC.
90 Edward J. Steptoe, courtesy of Yakima Valley Regional Library.
92 White House 1850s. LOC.
92 John Taylor. LDS.
94 James Buchanan. LOC.
96 Johnston's Army. LOC.
97 Albert Sidney Johnston. LDS.
98 James Buchanan. LOC.
100 Alfred Cumming. LDS.
101 James Buchanan, by Mathew Brady. LOC.
104 Abraham Lincoln, by Alexander Gardner. LOC.
106 Abraham Lincoln, by Edward Mendel. LOC.
107 Library of Congress ledgers, courtesy of Paul B. Skousen.
108 Pinkerton, Lincoln, and McClernand at Antietam, by Alexander Gardner. LOC.
109 Abraham Lincoln, by Nicholas H. Shepherd. LOC.
110 White House 1860s. LOC.
111 Abraham Lincoln, by Anthony Berger. LOC.
112 Abraham Lincoln, by Alexander Gardner. LOC.
114 Andrew Johnson, by Mathew Brady. LOC.
116 William H. Hooper. LDS.
116 John W. Young. LDS.
118 Ulysses S. Grant. LOC.
121 George Q. Cannon. LDS.
122 Ulysses S. Grant, by Mathew Brady. LOC.
123 "The Mormon Problem Solved," by Frank Leslie. LOC.
125 Brigham Young. LDS.
127 Grant's funeral procession, by J.I. Lloyd. LOC.
130 Rutherford B. Hayes, by Mathew Brady. LOC.
132 Emmeline B. Wells. LDS.
132 Zina Presendia Young Williams. LDS.
135 Eli H. Murray, by Fox & Symons. LDS.
136 Rutherford B. Hayes. LOC.
138 Rutherford B. Hayes. LDS.
140 James A. Garfield. LOC.
142 Kirtland Temple. LDS.
143 White House in Mourning. LOC.
145 Garfield Inaugural, by Frank Leslie. LOC.
146 Panguitch, Utah. USHS.
150 Chester A. Arthur, by Chalres Milton Bell. LOC.
152 Chester A. Arthur. LOC.

153 Capitol Snowball Fight. LOC.
154 Grover Cleveland. LOC.
156 Cleveland's Inaugural, by George Grantham Bain. LOC.
158 George Q. Cannon and others at Sugarhouse Penitentiary. USHS.
159 Grover Cleveland. LOC.
160 Statehood celebration on Main Street. USHS.
160–61 Tabernacle at Statehood. LDS.
162 Statehood in Deseret News. LDS.
162–63 ZCMI at Statehood. LDS.
164 Flag on Temple. UofU.
166 Benjamin Harrison. LOC.
169 First Presidency. LDS.
170 Harrison's Amnesty in Deseret News. LDS.
171 Flag on Temple. UofU.
172 Benjamin Harrison. LOC.
174 William McKinley. LOC.
176 William McKinley, by Frances Benjamin Johnston. LOC.
177 George Albert Smith. LDS.
178 John Henry Smith. LDS.
179 Lorenzo Snow. LDS.
182 Theodore Roosevelt, by Pach Brothers. LOC.
185 Roosevelt at Saltair. UofU.
186 Ben E. Rich. LDS.
189 Reed Smoot. LDS.
190 Teddy delighted with Smoot Hearings, by Alan L. Lovey, UofU.
191 Roosevelt in Salt Lake City. IRI.
193 Roosevelt on Deseret Evening News. LDS.
194 Roosevelt speaking in Tabernacle. LDS.
195 Grant and Smoot. LDS.
198 William Howard Taft. LDS.
200 Taft on Deseret Evening News. LDS.
201 Taft speaking at Fairpark. USHS.
203 William Howard Taft. LOC.
204 Taft in Provo Tabernacle, by Anderson and Larson. LDS.
205 Taft in Tribune. LDS.
206 Taft in Provo. L. Tom Perry Special Collections, Harold B. Lee Library, Brigham Young University.
206 Taft standing. LOC.
208 Woodrow Wilson. LOC.
210 James Henry Moyle. LDS.
211 Emmeline B. Wells. LDS.
212 Woodrow Wilson, by J. A. Randel. LDS.
213 President & Mrs. Wilson in car. USHS.
214 Wilson at Utah Capitol. USHS.
216 Warren G. Harding. LOC.
219 Florence Harding. LOC.
220 Harding in Car. USHS.
221 Harding at Salt Lake Country Club. USHS.
222 Harding and party. UofU.
224 Calvin Coolidge. LOC.
226 J. Reuben Clark. LDS.
227 Reed Smoot, by Ecker. LDS.
228 Coolidge and White House. LOC.
230 Calvin Coolidge. LOC.
232 Herbert Hoover, by Underwood and Underwood. LOC.
236 George Albert Smith and Herbert Hoover. IRI.
237 South porch of the White House. LOC.
238 Reed and Alice Smoot. LDS.
241 Ezra Taft Benson. LDS.
244 Franklin D. Roosevelt, by Elias Goldensky. LOC.
247 Roosevelts arrive in Salt Lake City. USHS.

249 First Presidency. LDS.
251 Franklin D. Roosevelt. LOC.
252 Roosevelt and Churchill. Courtesy of Franklin D. Roosevelt Presidential Library and Museum.
256 Harry S Truman, by Edmonston Studio. LOC.
259 Truman in Salt Lake City. USHS.
261 George Albert Smith and Harry S Truman. LDS.
263 Trumans and George Albert Smith leaving train. USHS.
264 Truman, Smith, and Maw. LDS.
266–67 Truman at Hotel Utah. USHS.
269 Truman at BYU. LDS.
272 Dwight D. Eisenhower. LDS.
274 Ivy Baker Priest. USHS.
275 Benson's swearing in. LDS.
276 Louise Lake and dignitaries. USHS.
278 Eisenhower, et. al. LDS.
280 Eisenhower and Benson Family. LDS.
282 Eisenhower and McKay. UofU.
284 John F. Kennedy, by Cecil Stoughton. Courtesy of John F. Kennedy Presidential Library and Museum.
287 JFK speaking in Tabernacle. USHS.
288 Kennedy in Tabernacle. USHS.
290 Stewart Udall. Courtesy the National Trust for Historic Preservation.
291 Kennedy and McKay. LDS.
293 Kennedy at breakfast with McKay. LDS.
294–95 Kennedy motorcade. USHS.
297 Hugh B. Brown. LDS.
300 Lyndon B. Johnson. LOC.
302 McKay's White House Visit. LDS.
305 McKay and LBJ. LDS.
306 Pres. & Sis. McKay and Johnson. LDS.
308 Lyndon B. Johnson. LOC.
310 Richard M. Nixon. By Hartmann. Courtesy National Archives and Records Administration.
312 First Presidency and Nixon. LDS.
313 Nixon and McKay. LDS.
315 George W. Romney. LDS.
316 David M. Kennedy. LOC.
317 Romney and Nixon. UofU.
318 Nixon at LDS Admin Bldg. LDS.
319 Nixon in LDS conference room. LDS.
320 Nixon in Tabernacle. LDS.
324 Gerald R. Ford. LOC.
327 Ford and First Pres. LDS.
328 Fords and Pres. Kimball. LDS.
329 Hoopes, Benson and Ford. LDS.
330 Fords and Mormons. LDS.
331 Ford, Kimball, and Primary kids. LDS.
332 Gerald R. Ford. LOC.
334 Jimmy Carter. LOC.
339 Carter and First Pres. LDS.
340 Carter at Tabernacle pulpit. LDS.
341 Carter and Kimball in Tabernacle. LDS.
344 Ronald Reagan. LOC.
347 Reagan and Hinckley. LDS.
348 Reagan and Benson. LDS.
351 Hinckley, Reagan and Benson. LDS.
352 Reagan at Cannery. LDS.
355 Reagan and Hinckley at Cannery. LDS.
356 Reagan and Hinckley inspecting can. LDS.
359 Reagan and Benson. By Pete Souza, White House photographer.

# ABOUT THE AUTHOR

*The author and George W. Bush's vice president, Dick Cheney, after both
spoke at the Utah Republican Party's 1994 State Convention.*

**Michael K. Winder** is a lifelong student of the American presidency and Mormon history. He has an MBA and Honors BA in History from the University of Utah, where he graduated *magna cum laude* and was awarded the Hans Morrow Award for the most outstanding history student. He has also completed an executive leadership program at Harvard's John F. Kennedy School of Government. An author of six published books, Mike has been named by *Utah Business* magazine as one of "40 Rising Stars Under 40" and is a member of the West Valley City Council, a vice president of Winder Farms (formerly Winder Dairy), and a former instructor in the Church Education System. In 2005, Mike was appointed by Governor Jon M. Huntsman Jr. to a four-year term on the Utah Board of State History. He is also a member of the Center for the Study of the Presidency, the Mormon History Association, and a contributor to the White House Historical Association. He lives in West Valley City, Utah, with his wife, Karyn, and their three children.